GREEK AND ROMAN
GOLD AND
SILVER PLATE

GREEK AND ROMAN GOLD AND SILVER PLATE

D. E. STRONG

METHUEN
LONDON AND NEW YORK

First published 1966

This edition reprinted 1979
by Methuen & Co. Ltd
11 New Fetter Lane, London EC4P 4EE
Published in the USA by
Methuen & Co.
in association with Methuen, Inc.
733 Third Avenue, New York, NY 10017

Printed in Great Britain by
Whitstable Litho Ltd, Whitstable, Kent

ISBN *0 416 72510 4*

British Library Cataloguing in Publication Data

Strong, Donald Emrys
Greek and Roman gold and silver plate.
– (Methuen library reprints).
1. Goldwork, Greek 2. Silverware, Greek
3. Goldwork, Roman 4. Silverware, Roman
I. Title
739.2'0938 NK7107.3 79–40753
ISBN *0–416–72510–4*

Contents

Contents

Acknowledgements

My colleagues at the British Museum have been my chief source of help and information in writing this book, especially D. E. L. Haynes, R. A. Higgins and D. M. Bailey of my own Department, P. E. Lasko and K. S. Painter of the Department of British and Mediaeval Antiquities, T. G. H. James and A. F. Shore of the Department of Egyptian Antiquities and R. D. Barnett of the Department of Western Asiatic Antiquities.

The Authorities of many museums and collections have generously supplied me with photographs of objects and permission to publish them. A list of the sources of the photographs is given on pp. 221–3. I am also grateful for the kindness of many people in helping me to study the objects themselves and for providing information. I should like to thank particularly D. von Bothmer, H. W. Catling, J. Charbonneaux, B. F. Cook, N. Cook, Mlle. C. Devès, Chr. Djambov, N. Firatlı, A. de Franciscis, A. Greifenhagen, Miss D. K. Hill, M. S. F. Hood, Mrs. C. Karouzou, E. Kofler-Truniger, R. Laur-Belart, K. Majewski, M. Moretti, R. V. Nicholls, R. Noll, A. Oliver, Jr, Miss A. Peredolskaya, H. Sichtermann, Miss H. Speier, R. B. K. Stevenson, S. Stucchi, J. Gy. Szilagyi, C. C. Vermeule, Miss H. Waugh.

The text-figures are the work of Clive Metcalfe, and I am most grateful to him for the trouble he has taken over them. Fig. 3*b* was kindly drawn by Ian McIntyre. My wife has devoted an immense amount of her time to the preparation of the text and I cannot thank her adequately for what she has done.

Plates

BETWEEN PAGES 220 AND 221

Text Figures

Abbreviations

AA: *Archäologischer Anzeiger* (Suppl. to *JdAI*).
ABC: *Antiquités du Bosphore Cimmérien,* Imperial Archaeological Commission, St Petersburg, 1845.
ActaA: *Acta Archaeologica.*
AD: *Antike Denkmäler.*
AdI: *Annali dell'Istituto di Corrispondenza Archeologica.*
A Delt: *'Αρχαιολογικὸν Δελτίον.*
Adriani, *Coppa Paesistica*: Adriani, A., *Divagazioni intorno ad una coppa paesistica del Museo di Alessandria,* Rome, 1959.
Adriani, *Gobelet*: Adriani, A., *Le Gobelet en Argent* (*Société Royale d'Archéologie d'Alexandrie, Cahier no. 1*), 1939.
AE: *'Αρχαιολογικὴ 'Εφημερίς.*
AEArq: *Archivo Español de Arqueologia.*
AJA: *American Journal of Archaeology.*
AK: *Antike Kunst.*
Alvarez-Ossorio, *Tesoros Españoles Antiguos*: Alvarez-Ossorio y Farfan de los Godos, F., *Tesoros Españoles Antiguos en el Museo Arqueologico Nacional,* Madrid, 1954.
AM: *Mitteilungen des deutschen archäologischen Instituts: Athenische Abteilung.*
Annuario: *Annuario di R. Scuola Archaeologica di Atene.*
AntJ: *Antiquaries Journal.*
Arch Camb.: *Archaeologia Cambrensis.*
Arch Ért.: *Archaeologiai Értesitö.*
Arch Rep.: *Archaeological Reports* (Suppl. to *JHS*).
Arneth, *Gold- and Silber-Monumente*: Arneth, J., *Gold- und Silber-Monumente in Wien,* Vienna, 1850.
Ashmolean, *Summary Guide*: Ashmolean Museum, *A Summary Guide to the Collection,* 1951.
AZ: *Archäologische Zeitung.*
Babelon, *Berthouville*: Babelon, E., *Le Trésor de Berthouville,* 1920.
BABesch.: *Bulletin van de Vereeniging tot Bevordering der Kennis van de antieke Beschaving.*
BCom.: *Bullettino della Commissione Archeologica Comunale.*
BCH.: *Bulletin de Correspondance Hellénique.*
BdA: *Bollettino d'Arte.*
Bendinelli, *Marengo*: Bendinelli, G., *Il Tesoro di Argenteria di Marengo,* Turin, 1937.
BJ: *Bonner Jahrbücher.*
Blegen, *Troy*: Blegen, C. W., *Troy*, vols. 1–4, Princeton, 1950–8.

Abbreviations

Blümner, *Technologie*: Blümner, H., *Technologie und Terminologie der Gewerbe und Künste bei Griechen un Römern*, 4 vols., 1875–86.

BMCJ: Marshall, F. H., *Catalogue of the Jewellery, Greek, Etruscan and Roman, in the British Museum, London, 1912.*

BMCP: Walters, H. B., *Catalogue of the Silver Plate, Greek, Etruscan and Roman, in the British Museum*, 1921.

BMECA: Dalton, O. M., *Catalogue of the Early Christian Antiquities in the British Museum*, 1927.

BMFA: *Bulletin of the Museum of Fine Arts, Boston.*

BMMA: *Bulletin of the Metropolitan Museum of Art, New York.*

BMQ: *British Museum Quarterly.*

v. Bothmer, *Private Collections*: von Bothmer, D., *Ancient Art from New York Private Collections*, 1961.

Brailsford, *Mildenhall*: Brailsford, J. W., *The Mildenhall Treasure*, 1947.

Brooklyn Museum, *Five Years*: Brooklyn Museum, *Five Years of Collecting Egyptian Art, 1951–1956*, New York, 1956.

Brunn, *Geschichte*: Brunn, H., *Geschichte der griechischen Künstler*, 2 vols. Braunschweig, 1853.

Bruns, *Schatzkammer*: Bruns, G., *Schatzkammer der Antike*, Berlin, 1946.

BSA: *Annual of the British School at Athens.*

BSAAl.: *Bulletin de la Société d'Archéologie d'Alexandrie.*

BSOAS: *Bulletin of the School of Oriental and African Studies.*

BSR: *Annual of the British School at Rome.*

Bull. Inst. Bulg.: *Bulletin de l'Institut Archéologique Bulgare.*

Cabrol, *Dictionnaire*: F. Cabrol & H. Leclerq, *Dictionnaire d'Archéologie Chrétienne et de Liturgie*, Paris, 1914.

CAH: *Cambridge Ancient History.*

Catling, *Cypriot Bronzework*: Catling, H. W., *Cypriot Bronzework in the Mycenaean World*, Oxford, 1964.

Cesnola, *Atlas*: de Cesnola, L. P., *Atlas of the Cesnola Collection*, 3 vols., Boston & New York, 1885–1901.

CIL: *Corpus Inscriptionum Latinarum.*

Clara Rhodos: *Clara Rhodos, Studi e Materiali pubblicati a cura dell'Istituto Storico—Archeologico di Rodi.*

CR: *Comptes Rendus de la Commission Impériale Archéologique.*

Curle, *Traprain*: Curle, A. O., *The Treasure of Traprain*, Glasgow, 1923.

Dalton, *Oxus*: Dalton, O. M., *The Treasure of the Oxus*, London, 1926.

Daremberg & Saglio: C. Daremberg & E. Saglio, *Dictionnaire des Antiquités Grecques et Romaines.*

Delbrueck, *Consulardiptychen*: Delbrueck R., *Die Consulardiptychen und verwandte Denkmäler*, Berlin & Leipzig, 1929.

Dodd, *Stamps*: Dodd, E. K., *Byzantine Silver Stamps*, Princeton, 1961.

Dohrn, *Spätantikes Silber*: Dohrn T., 'Spätantikes Silber aus Britannien' in *Mitteilungen des deutschen archäologischen Instituts*, II, 1949, p. 67 ff.

Ebert, *Reallexikon*: Ebert, M. (ed.), *Reallexikon der Vorgeschichte*, Berlin, 1924–32.

Economic Survey: Tenney, Frank (ed.), *An Economic Survey of Ancient Rome,* 5 vols., 1933–40.
Eggers: Eggers, H. J., *Der römische Import im freien Germanien,* Hamburg, 1951.
Evans, *P of M*: Evans, Sir Arthur, *The Palace of Minos at Knossos,* 4 vols., London, 1921–35.
Evans, *PTK*: Evans, A. J., 'Prehistoric Tombs of Knossos', in *Archaeologia,* lix, 1906.
Evans, *SG*: Evans, Sir A., *The Shaft Graves and Bee-hive Tombs of Mycenae,* London, 1929.
Evans *TDA*: Evans, A. J., 'The Tomb of the Double Axes, etc.', in *Archaeologia,* lxv, 1914.
Falchi, *Vetulonia*: Falchi, I., *Vetulonia e la sua necropoli antichissima,* Florence, 1891.
FA: *Fasti Archaeologici.*
Filow, *Duvanlij*: Filow, B., *Die Grabhügelnekropole bei Duvanlij,* Sofia, 1934.
Filow, *Trebenischte*: Filow, B., *Die archaische Nekropole von Trebenischte,* Berlin, 1927.
Fogg Private Collections: Fogg Art Museum, *Ancient Art in American Private Collections,* 1954.
Forbes, *Metallurgy*: Forbes, R. J., *Metallurgy in Antiquity,* Leiden, 1950.
Friedländer, *Sittengeschichte*: Friedländer, L., *Darstellungen aus der Sittengeschichte Roms* (9th Edition), 4 vols., Leipzig, 1919–21.
Furumark, *Analysis*: Furumark, A., *The Mycenaean Pottery; Analysis and Classification,* Stockholm, 1941.
GA: *Gazette Archéologique.*
García y Bellido, *Esculturas Romanas*: García y Bellido, A., *Esculturas Romanas de España y Portugal,* Madrid, 1949.
GBA: *Gazette des Beaux Arts.*
Grünhagen, *Gross Bodungen*: *Der Schatzfund von Gross Bodungen* (Röm-Germ Forschungen 21, 1954).
Gusman, *L'Art Decoratif*: Gusman, P., *L'Art Decoratif de Rome,* 3 vols., Paris, 1912–1914.
Higgins, *Jewellery*: Higgins, R. A., *Greek and Roman Jewellery,* London, 1961.
IG: *Inscriptiones Graecae.*
ILN: *Illustrated London News.*
Ippel, *Guss- und Treibarbeit*: Ippel, A., *Guss- und Treibarbeit in Silber* (97 Winckelmannsprogramm, 1937.)
JdAI: *Jahrbuch des deutschen archäologischen Instituts.*
JRGZM: *Jahrbuch des Römisch-Germanischen Zentralmuseums Mainz.*
JHS: *Journal of Hellenic Studies.*
JRS: *Journal of Roman Studies.*
Kantor, *Aegean & Orient*: Kantor, H. J., *The Aegean and the Orient in the Second Millennium B.C.* (The Archaeological Institute of America, 1947).
Karo, *Schachtgräber*: *Die Schachtgräber von Mykenai,* Munich, 1930–3.
Kluge, *Grossbronzen*: Kluge, K., & Lehmann-Hartleben, K., *Die antiken Grossbronzen,* Berlin & Leipzig, 1927.
Köster, *Antikes Tafelsilber*: Köster, A., *Meisterwerke in Berlin, Antikes Tafelsilber,* Berlin, 1923.

Küthmann, *Toreutik*: Küthmann, H., *Untersuchungen zur Toreutik des zweiten un ersten Jahrhunderts vor Christus*, Basel, 1959.
La Baume, *Kunstgewerbe*: La Baume, P., *Römisches Kunstgewerbe*, Braunschweig, 1964.
Laur-Belart, *Kaiseraugst*: Laur-Belart, R., *Der spätrömische Silberschatz von Kaiseraugst (Aargau)*, 2nd ed., 1963.
Levi, *Parabiago*: Levi, A., *La Patera di Parabiago* (Opera d'Arte, fasc. 5), 1935.
Lucas, *Materials*: Lucas, A., *Ancient Egyptian Materials and Industries*, London, 3rd ed., 1948.
Luschey: Luschey, H., *Die Phiale*, Bleicherode, 1939.
MA: *Monumenti Antichi pubblicati per cura della Reale Accademia dei Lincei.*
MAAR: *Memoirs of the American Academy in Rome.*
MAGZ: *Mitteilungen der antiquarischen Gesellschaft in Zürich.*
Maiuri, *Casa del Menandro*: Maiuri, A., *La Casa del Menandro*, Rome, 1936.
Majewski, *Importy*: Majewski, K., *Importy Rzymskie w Polsce*, Warsaw, 1960.
Mariemont: *Les Antiquités du Musée de Mariemont*, Brussels, 1952.
Marinatos & Hirmer: Marinatos, S., & Hirmer, M., *Crete and Mycenae*, London, 1960.
Marquardt, *Privatleben*: Marquardt, J., *Das Privatleben der Römer*, Leipzig, 1886.
Maryon, *Metalwork*: Maryon, H., *Metalwork and Enamelling*, 1954.
Maspero, *Le Musée Egyptien*: Maspero, M. G., *Le Musée Egyptien*, vols. I–III, Cairo, 1907.
Materials: *Materials for the Archaeology of Russia published by the Imperial Archaeological Commission* (in Russian).
Matzulewitsch, *Byzantinische Antike*: L. Matzulewitsch, *Byzantinische Antike: Studien auf Grund der Silbergefässe der Hermitage*, Berlin and Leipzig, 1929.
Mélanges: *Mélanges d'Archéologie et d'Histoire.*
Milani, *Firenze*: Milani, L. A., *Il R. Museo Archeologico di Firenze*, Florence, 1912.
Minns, *S & G*: Minns, E. H., *Scythians and Greeks*, Cambridge, 1913.
Minto, *Marsiliana*: Minto, A., *Marsiliana d'Albegna*, Florence, 1921.
Minto, *Populonia*: Minto, A., *Populonia*, Florence, 1943.
Mon Piot: *Fondation Piot, Monuments et Mémoires.*
Mühlestein, *Die Ursprünge*: Mühlestein, H., *Die Kunst der Etrusker. Die Ursprünge*, 1929.
Mylonas, *Ancient Mycenae*: Mylonas, G. E., *Ancient Mycenae*, Princeton, 1957.
Myres, *Cesnola*: Myres, J. L., *Handbook of the Cesnola Collection of Antiquities from Cyprus*, New York, 1914.
Mzkhetha I: Apakidze, A. M. and others, *Mzkhetha I, Archaeological Excavations at Armazis-khevi near Mzkhetha in 1939–1946*, Tiflis, 1958.
Neugebauer *Privatbesitz*: Neugebauer, K. A., *Antiken im deutschen Privatbesitz*, Berlin, 1938.
NS: *Notizie degli Scavi di antichità communicate alla Reale Accademia dei Lincei.*
L'Art dans L'occident romain: *L'Art dans l'occident romain* (Exhibition Paris, July–October, 1963).
Odobesco, *Petrossa*: Odobesco, A., *Le Trésor de Petrossa*, Paris, 1889–1900.
OGIS: *Orientis Graecae Inscriptiones Selectae.*
ÖJh: *Österreichische Jahreshefte.*

Ori e Argenti: *Ori e Argenti dell'Italia Antica* (Exhibition in Turin, 1961).
dall'Osso, *Guida*: dall'Osso, *Guida Illustrata del Museo Nazionale di Ancona.*
Oud Meded: *Oudheidkundige Mededelingen uit het Rijksmuseum van Oudheden te Leiden.*
PAE: *Πρακτικὰ τῆς 'Αρχαιολογικῆς 'Εταιρείας, 'Αθήνησι.*
Pallottino, *Etruscan Painting*: Pallottino, M., *Etruscan Painting*, Geneva, 1952.
Pareti, *Regolini-Galassi*: Pareti, L., *La Tomba Regolini-Galassi*, Vatican, 1947.
Payne, *Necrocorinthia*: Payne, H., *Necrocorinthia, A Study of Corinthian Art in the Archaic Period*, Oxford, 1931.
Pennsylvania Transactions: *University of Pennsylvania, Transactions of the Department of Archaeology.*
Perachora, i & ii: Payne, H. G. G., *Perachora*, i, Oxford, 1940, & T. J. Dunbabin, *Perachora*, ii, Oxford, 1962.
Pernice & Winter, *Hildesheim*: Pernice, F., & Winter, F., *Der Hildesheimer Silberfund*, Berlin, 1901.
Persson, *New Tombs*: Persson, A. W., *New Tombs at Dendra*, Lund, 1942.
Persson, *Royal Tombs*: Persson, A. W., *The Royal Tombs at Dendra*, Lund, 1934.
Pesce, *Oreficeria*: Pesce, G., *Il Museo Nazionale di Napoli; Oreficeria, Toreutica etc.*,
Plenderleith, *Conservation*: Plenderleith, H. J., *The Conservation of Antiquities and Works of Art*, London, 1956.
Poulsen, *Der Orient*: Poulsen, F., *Der Orient und die frühgriechische Kunst*, Leipzig-Berlin, 1912.
PW: Pauly-Wissowa, *Real-Encyclopädie der classischen Altertumswissenschaft.*
RA: *Revue Archéologique.*
Radnóti, *Bronzegefässe*: Radnóti, A., *Die römischen Bronzegefässe von Pannonien*, Leipzig, 1938.
Randall-MacIver, *Villanovans*: Randall-MacIver, D., *Villanovans and Early Etruscans*, Oxford, 1924.
REA: *Revue des Études Anciennes.*
Richter, *Dumbarton Oaks*: Richter, G. M. A., *Catalogue of the Greek and Roman Antiquities at Dumbarton Oaks*, 1956.
Richter, *Etruscan Collection*: Richter, G. M. A., *The Metropolitan Museum of Art. Handbook of the Etruscan Collection*, New York, 1940.
Richter, *Greek Collection*: Richter, G. M. A., *Metropolitan Museum of Art. Handbook of the Greek Collection*, Harvard, 1953.
de Ridder, *Bijoux*: de Ridder, A., *Musée National du Louvre, Catalogue Sommaire des Bijoux Antiques*, 1924.
RM: *Mitteilungen des deutschen archäologischen Instituts, Römische Abteilung.*
Rosenberg, *Niello*: Rosenberg, M., *Geschichte der Goldschmiedekunst: Niello*, 1924.
Rostovtzeff, *I & G*: Rostovtzeff, M. I., *Iranians and Greeks in South Russia*, Oxford, 1922.
Rostovtzeff, *SEHRE*: Rostovtzeff, M., *A Social and Economic History of the Roman Empire*, 2nd ed., 2 vols., Oxford, 1957.
Rostovtzeff, *SEHHW*: Rostovtzeff, M., *A Social and Economic History of the Hellenistic World*, 3 vols., Oxford, 1941.
Rubensohn, *Silbergerät*: Rubensohn, O., *Hellenistisches Silbergerät in antiken Gipsabgüssen*, 1911.

SA: *Sovetskaya Archeologiya.*
SCE: *The Swedish Cyprus Expedition.*
Schaeffer, *Ugaritica*: Schaeffer, C. F. A., *Mission de Ras Shamra III, Ugaritica,* vols. 1–4, Paris, 1939–62.
Schaeffer, *Enkomi-Alasia*: Schaeffer, C. F. A., *Enkomi-Alasia,* Paris, 1952.
von Schaewen, *Opfergeräte*: von Schaewen, R., *Römische Opfergeräte, ihre Verwendung im Kultus und in der Kunst,* Berlin, 1940.
Schliemann, *Mycenae*: Schliemann, H., *Mycenae and Tiryns,* London, 1878.
Schliemann, *Ilios*: Schliemann, H., *Ilios, City & Country of the Trojans,* London, 1886.
Schlunk, *Spätantike*: Schlunk, H., *Kunst der Spätantike im Mittelmeerraum,* Berlin, 1939.
Schmidt, *Schliemanns Sammlung*: Schmidt, H., *H. Schliemanns Sammlung Trojanischer Altertümer,* 1902.
Schreiber, *Toreutik*: Schreiber, T., *Die Alexandrinische Toreutik,* Leipzig, 1894.
SE: *Studi Etruschi.*
Seager, *Mochlos*: Seager, R. B., *Explorations in the Island of Mochlos,* Boston, 1912.
Segall, *Benaki*: Segall, B., *Museum Benaki, Katalog der Goldschmiede-Arbeiten,* Athens, 1938.
SHA: *Scriptores Historiae Augustae.*
Sieveking, *Antike Metallgeräte*: Sieveking, J., *Antike Metallgeräte,* Munich, 1928.
Smirnov, *Argenterie Orientale*: Smirnov, V., *L'Argenterie Orientale,* St Petersburg, 1909.
Spinazzola: Spinazzola, V., *Le Arti Decorative in Pompeii,* Milan, 1928.
Stais, *Musée Nationale*: Stais, V., *Guide Illustré du Musée Nationale,* vol. II, Athens.
Stathatos Collection: *Collection Hélène Stathatos iii, Objets Antiques et Byzantines,* Strasburg, 1963.
Survey of Persian Art: Pope, A. U., *A Survey of Persian Art,* 6 vols., Oxford, 1938–9.
Svoboda & Končev, *Neue Denkmäler*: Svoboda, B., & Končev, D., *Neue Denkmäler antiker Toreutik,* Prague, 1956.
Toynbee, *Art in Britain*: Toynbee, J. M. C., *Art in Britain under the Romans,* Oxford, 1964.
Tuchelt, *Tiergefässe*: Tuchelt, K., *Tiergefässe in Kopf- und Protomengestalt,* Berlin, 1962.
Tylecote, *Metallurgy*: Tylecote, R. F., *Metallurgy in Archaeology,* London, 1962.
de Villefosse, *Boscoreale*: de Villefosse, H., 'Le Trésor de Boscoreale' in *Monuments Piot,* v, 1899–1902.
Volbach, *Early Christian Art*: Volbach, W. F., *Early Christian Art,* London, 1961.
Volbach, *Metallarbeiten*: Volbach, W. F., *Metallarbeiten des christlichen Kultus,* Mainz, 1921.
WAG Exhibition: *Walters Art Gallery Exhibition of Early Christian and Byzantine Art,* 1947.
Willers, *Neue Untersuchungen*: Willers, H., *Neue Untersuchungen über die römische Bronzeindustrie von Capua und von Niedergermanien,* Hannover-Leipzig, 1907.
Wuilleumier, *Tarente*: Wuilleumier, P., *Tarente des origines à la conquète romain,* Paris, 1939.
Wuilleumier, *Trésor*: Wuilleumier, P., *Le Trésor de Tarente,* Paris, 1930.
ZfN: *Zeitschrift für Numismatik.*
ZSAK: *Zeitschrift für schweizerische Archäologie und Kunstgeschichte.*

Introduction

Long before they appeared as media of exchange, gold and silver were used for making objects of luxury, the possession of which made a man the envy of his fellows and was a symbol of his power and authority among them. From excavations in the Bronze Age cities of Crete and Greece we know that their overlords and wealthy nobles drank at their tables and performed the ritual of worship from vessels of precious metal which they also took with them to their graves. These discoveries have amply confirmed the half-remembered descriptions that we get from Homer of the wealth in gold and silver of the Greek heroic age – as when Odysseus wins a silver krater as an athletic prize,[1] when gifts of plate are exchanged between guest and host,[2] or kingly Nestor drinks from his richly decorated cup.[3]

After the fall of the Mycenaean palaces, gold and silver plate became the survivals of a bygone age. Some pieces were, no doubt, treasured for generations and survived above ground until the time of Homer who, perhaps, had some direct knowledge of Mycenaean objects, but so far as we know no new plate was made from raw materials and the arts of the goldsmith and silversmith died out. It seems to have been the Phoenicians who, during the eighth century B.C., re-introduced such objects of luxury to the Greek world; typical products are the series of silver bowls with engraved scenes of Egyptian and Syrian derivation which have been found in the eastern Mediterranean and in Etruria, and which may have been a direct source of inspiration for descriptions of precious objects in Homer.[4] With developing prosperity in seventh-century Greece we hear of vessels made of precious metal dedicated at Greek sanctuaries, and the earliest finds of precious metal plate in Greece belong to this period. The well-known gold bowl found at Olympia (pl. 8A) bears an inscription declaring it to be the thank-offering of the sons of Kypselos, tyrant of Corinth, from the spoils of

[1] *Iliad*, xxiii, 741. [2] *Odyssey*, iv, 615. [3] *Iliad*, xi, 632.
[4] cf. J. L. Myres in *JHS*, liii, 1933, 29.

war. In the sixth century such dedications became increasingly common; many were made by non-Greeks, like Alyattes and Croesus of Lydia whose domestic wealth was legendary. Croesus, who especially cultivated the oracle at Delphi, is said to have dedicated there two immense mixing-bowls, one of gold and one of silver, which were placed in prominent positions in the Temple.[1] Despite the increasing wealth of the Greek city-states, gold and silver were still confined to ritual vessels and to dedications at the temples of the gods and had no place at the tables of the wealthy. In marked contrast with archaic Greece is the aristocratic society of early Etruria where the wealthy local lords were buried with rich private possessions of plate and jewellery comparable to that of Mycenaean Greece.

The booty of gold and silver from the Persian wars, the discovery of a rich vein of ore in the silver mines of Laurion, the Athenian control of the gold mines of Thrace were some of the factors that lead to a great increase in the production of plate in fifth-century Greece. The temple treasures of classical times, as we know from surviving inventories and other sources, contained vast accumulations of gold and silver plate.[2] The inventory of the Treasury of Athena in 418–417 mentions 163 *phialai* (sacrificial dishes) weighing 16,653 drachmas. There were 1600 *phialai* alone in the Temple of Apollo at Delos in the second century[3] and the little Treasury of Metapontum in Olympia housed 132 silver dishes and two vessels for holding wine.[4] Domestic silver, however, was still very rare and it is not until towards the end of the fifth century that we find references to its presence at the tables of the wealthy.[5] A suggestion of this new development is the fact that in 416 B.C. the Syracusan expedition celebrated its departure from Athens with gold and silver vessels, though this was presumably brought from the public treasury for the occasion.[6]

In the early fourth century, domestic plate, to judge from references in the comic poets,[7] was coming into much more general use and Alexander's conquests in the east led to a vast influx of precious metals into the Greek world. If Philip II, Alexander's father, kept his only gold

[1] Herodotus, i, 50–2.
[2] *IG*, i, 138–9, 142, 150–1; *IG*, ii, i, 699–701, 768 ff.
[3] *BCH*, vi, 1882, 105/53.
[4] Athenaeus, xi, 479 f.
[5] Plutarch, *Alcibiades*, iv; it was becoming much more common in the early 4th century cf. Aristophanes, *Plutus*, 813.
[6] Thucydides, vi, 32; cf vi, 46
[7] Athenaeus, vi, 231.

saucer under his pillow for safety, his son would certainly have had no cause to take such precautions. Athenaeus' account of the gold and silver in the festival procession of Ptolemy II Philadelphus is almost unbelievable.[1] Typical of his time was Antiochus IV Epiphanes of Syria, who used to haunt the workshops of the craftsmen discussing the latest fashions and tastes and amassed a huge collection of expensive plate.[2] Nor were possessions of gold and silver plate confined to kings and princes. Wealthy businessmen of the Hellenistic World looked upon hoarded silver plate as a fine means of investment, and the craft of the goldsmith and silversmith flourished as never before.

Rome was the heir of the Hellenistic World. Throughout her early life she had been poor in precious metals and she did not strike a silver coinage until 269 B.C.; for some time after this silver plate was rare in the city. But the Second Punic War gave her control of the Spanish silver mines and very soon her conquests in Italy and in the East brought her the loot in gold and silver of the cities of the Hellenistic World. Whereas in the third century B.C. only a few pieces of sacrificial plate in each household would have been of silver, by the first century B.C. there were enormous private collections of plate for show and for use (see chapter 7). At this time the love of collecting plate aroused a covetousness which is caricatured by the activities of the notorious C. Verres during his governorship of Sicily.[3]

Legislation introduced in the early years of the Empire to curb private luxury seems to have had little effect, though gold vessels were used only by the Imperial house between Tiberius and Aurelian.[4] The accounts of private wealth in silver plate under the Empire are even more remarkable than those of the late Republic. Slaves, it seems, often had large private collections[5] and in some households even the cooking utensils were made of silver;[6] perhaps even Martial's chamber-pot of silver set with precious stones was not entirely mythical. Almost every household would have acquired some pieces of silver plate and to have been brought up in a household that possessed none was the sign of the most abject poverty.[7] The temples of the gods continued to have large collections of *ex voto* plate; the rich Treasure of Berthouville in the Bibliothèque Nationale, Paris represents the contents of a comparatively

[1] *ibid.* v, 196A. [2] *ibid.* v, 194C; Polybius, xxvi, 10. [3] Cicero, *Verr.* ii, 4, 46–7.
[4] Tacitus, *Annals*, ii, 33; SHA, *Aurelian*, 16. [5] cf. *CIL*, vi, 5197.
[6] *Digest*, 34, 2, 19, 12; Pliny, *NH*, xxxiii, 139 ff. [7] Suetonius, *Domitian*, i.

small and unimportant Gaulish shrine. Roman plate played a significant role in foreign trade and diplomacy.[1] In the later years of the Empire the taste for silver continued unabated and new types of vessels for use in Christian worship were now added to the repertory of the silversmith. The hoards of the last years of the Roman Empire in the west are among the richest that have come down to us not only in quantity but in the skills of the silversmith.

This book is concerned with the history of ancient plate in the period outlined above – from the Bronze Age to the fifth century A.D. Before describing in detail the development of gold and silver plate throughout this long period, it is proposed to give as introduction brief accounts of the sources of precious metals in the ancient world; of the ancient craftsmen and his techniques; and of the organisation of the trade of the goldsmith and silversmith. The first chapter also contains a section on inscriptions on ancient plate, the rediscovery of ancient plate in modern times, and on museums and collections.

[1] cf. Tacitus, *Germania*, 5.

CHAPTER ONE

General Background

1. PRECIOUS METALS IN THE ANCIENT WORLD

All the plate discussed in this book is made of *gold, silver,* or *electrum* which is a natural or artificial alloy of the two.

GOLD

A] *Metallurgy*

Gold became known in the Aegean during the early Bronze Age. As in modern times, gold supplies were obtained either from the alluvial detritus of gold-bearing rocks (known as *placer gold*) or from the mining of auriferous rock (known as *reef gold*).[1] The methods of obtaining gold from placers are simple; the earth has to be sifted and washed away until only the gold is left. Reef gold must first be broken up and then sifted to free the gold. Native gold is not pure, but it is usually an alloy of gold and silver with some copper and iron; the proportions of the alloy vary considerably. Davies[2] gives 75–90 per cent gold for deposits in the Aegean islands and Lucas[3] 76–90 per cent for Nubian gold.[4] If the native gold contains a high proportion of silver it is generally known as *electrum*; the placers of the Pactolus river,[5] the 'white gold' of the Lydians, are the classic example of this natural alloy with a high silver content. In the natural alloy the silver hardly ever exceeds 35 per cent; in the artificial alloys widely differing proportions are found. Pliny[6] says that if there is 20 per cent silver present, the alloy is called *electrum*.

Several methods of refining native gold were known to the ancients but the history of their use is not clearly established. *Cupellation* was used to get rid of the base metals by oxidation processes and improved

[1] e.g. at Dolaucothy in Wales, *Arch Camb* 91, 1936, 51–7.
[2] 'Bronze Age Mining round the Aegean', in *Nature*, December 31st, 1932.
[3] Lucas, *Materials*, 262.
[4] There are some modern statistics in Tylecote, *Metallurgy*, 4–5.
[5] *Class. Journ.* xvii, 1924, 186–8.
[6] Pliny, *NH*, xxxiii, 80.

methods, known as *liquation* and *amalgamation* (which requires the use of mercury) were introduced in Roman times. The next step – the separation of the gold and silver – was carried out by two processes: (i) the *salt process* and (ii) the *sulphur process;* in both these processes the sulphur or salts are used to compound the silver leaving refined gold.[1] After refining, the alloy could be tested by the use of the touchstone (βασάνος)[2] and other methods, such as assay by cupellation, may also have been practised.[3] Until a far larger number of analyses of ancient plate have been carried out we shall know very little about the early history of refining gold in the ancient world. Analyses of Trojan gold yielded 65·10, 67·91 and 75·8 per cent;[4] Schliemann also refers to 'very pure gold' but does not give analyses. A miniature gold double-axe from Crete was analysed and stated to be made from unrefined native gold;[5] a piece of gold foil and some sheet gold from Mycenae gave widely differing results, suggesting an artificial alloy with 73·11 per cent gold in the case of the former and a native gold of 89·36 per cent[6] in the case of the latter. The gold bowl from Olympia (see pp. 57–8) has a low silver content (9 per cent) and may have been refined. By classical Greek times certainly, the refining of gold had been brought to a high pitch of skill.[7]

B] *Sources*

In the Bronze Age local sources of gold in Greece (Arcadia?) and the Aegean islands (Siphnos?) were probably being tapped, but gold from Egypt, where the main deposits are on the Red Sea Coast and in the Nubian desert, was almost certainly imported. In archaic and classical times, a few of the Aegean islands, especially Siphnos and Thasos, and the coastal regions of Thrace and Macedonia were the principal local sources of gold for the Greek World and these sources were much coveted by rival powers. The mines of Pangaion[8] in Thrace

[1] The salt process is described in Diodorus, iii, 14.

[2] Theophrastus, *De lapidibus*, 46; *Class. Journ.* xxxii, 1936–7, 428–31.

[3] Blümner, *Technologie*, iv, 136; Cicero, *ad. fam.* ix, 16, 2.

[4] Schliemann, *Ilios*, 496–7.

[5] *BMFA*, lvii, 1959, 19; the analysis was 82 per cent gold, 12 per cent silver, 3 per cent copper, 3 per cent iron.

[6] Schliemann, *Mycenae and Tiryns*, 368.

[7] See J. Hammer, 'Der Feingehalt der griech. und röm. Münzen', in *ZfN*, 26, 1908, 1 ff.

[8] PW sv. Pangaion; S. Casson, *Macedonia, Thrace and Illyria*, Oxford, 1926, 59–71.

came into the possession of Athens in 462 and were an important part of her revenue in the fifth century; in 356 B.C. they passed to Philip II of Macedon and played an equally important part in the development of Macedonian power. The classical Greeks also seem to have obtained some gold from Asia Minor and gold from the Altai mines probably came to them indirectly via the S. Russian colonies. In Hellenistic times the widening of Greek horizons brought with it direct knowledge of the gold of Afghanistan, Turkestan and India.[1] Nubian gold became the monopoly of the Ptolemies[2] and the riches of the Seleucids depended largely on eastern sources of gold and silver. The Romans were able to tap most of the same sources while developing new mines in Spain, the Danube provinces and even in Britain. The gold of Dacian mines which flowed into Rome at all times came briefly under Roman control as a result of Trajan's campaigns.[3] The Nubian mines were worked under a state monopoly; some late Roman ingots with assay stamps in the British Museum include two of the late third century from Aboukir.[4]

SILVER

A] *Metallurgy*

Silver from the early Bronze Age throughout ancient times was obtained almost entirely by smelting lead ores and then separating the silver they contain. The commonest of these lead ores is *galena* (lead sulphide, PbS) which occurs in surface deposits in many parts of the classical world and could also be mined from deeper strata. The most famous of the deeper deposits of *galena* were the mines of Laurion in Attica which are said to have had more than 2,000 shafts, some reaching to a depth of 250 ft.[5] After mining the ore, crude lead was obtained by smelting and then purified. The lead will contain something between 20 and 200 ounces of silver per ton, the latter being the highest figure estimated for the Laurion mines and was desilvered by a process which involves repeatedly melting and cooling to achieve a greater concentration of silver; finally the silver is separated from the lead by cupellation which involves the oxidation of the lead and other base metals. It

[1] On Alexander's prospectors see especially Rostovtzeff, *SEHHW*, 1170–3.

[2] For the mines in the period, Diodorus, iii, 12.

[3] *Dacia*, i, 1924, 28 ff.; cf. *JRS*, 20, 1930, 55 ff.

[4] *BMCJ*, nos. 3148–9.

[5] For these mines see E. Ardaillon, *Les Mines du Laurion*, 1897.

is thought that the Greeks could desilver lead to 0·002 per cent and that the Romans got this down to 0·001 per cent.[1] Silver in the Bronze Age varies a good deal in purity; part of a silver vase from one of the Shaft Graves at Mycenae yielded 95·59 per cent silver and only 0·44 per cent lead while other examples have yielded up to 30 per cent lead.

Silver was usually artificially alloyed in the manufacture of plate, since pure silver is generally considered too soft for making vessels. The Enkomi cup (pl. 7B) was shown to contain 87·6 silver, 3·4 gold and 9 copper which may be compared with the 92·5 silver to 7·5 copper of the sterling standard. In Roman times the silver used for plate was surprisingly pure, corresponding perhaps with the alloy of the contemporary coinage; under the early Emperors this was very fine (95–99 per cent), though Nero alloyed it with 10 per cent copper; in later times it dropped much lower, coming down to as low as 80 per cent at certain times.[2] In the analyses so far carried out it is impossible to trace any consistent pattern. One of the Augustan or late Republican silver cups in the British Museum (see p. 115) was made from an alloy 98–99 per cent fine; a pair of *saucepan paterae* of the first century A.D. in the Gideon Stieff collection (p. 147) contained 90 per cent silver and a little gold. The silver mirror of the third century A.D. from Wroxeter (p. 179) contained 86·6 per cent silver and 12·2 per cent copper. A high standard of purity is found in the silver of the late Roman hoards. Three analyses carried out on the Traprain Law hoard gave 94·08, 96·2, and 95·3 per cent. The Mildenhall silver has been shown to have been made of a good alloy of 95·3 per cent.[3] The consistently high silver content in manufactured plate is explained by the fact that the Romans of the Empire collected plate as a means of hoarding their wealth; in the late Empire, as the hoards of 'Hacksilber' (see p. 182) show, a great deal of plate was reconverted into bullion and it is in this period, the fourth century A.D., that we get what appear to be assay marks on manufactured plate (see pp. 183–4) which, like the mint marks on gold and silver ingots, were a guarantee of the quality of the alloy in the piece. Appendix III is a list of the analyses of ancient plate known to the author.

[1] A method used in the fourth century B.C. is referred to in *Arch Rep* 1961–2, 5; for the methods of Roman times, Strabo, ix, C 399.

[2] Hammer, *art. cit.* (note 7 on p. 2).

[3] For these analyses see appendix 3.

B] *Sources*

There are very widespread surface deposits of *galena* in Asia Minor which is generally thought of as the home of silver production and which was certainly exporting large quantities of silver from the third millennium onwards.[1] In Bronze Age Greece local sources of silver must have been in use; some of the Cyclades – Melos, Paros and Thera – were probably producing silver and some early silver objects from Amorgos which contain a high proportion of gold and copper may have been made from a local source of silver. It is uncertain whether the mines of Laurion were in use at the time; if so, they went out of use again until the sixth century B.C., and the richest seam was not revealed until 483 B.C. The mines of Cyprus were not apparently used in Mycenaean times but were certainly exploited later.[2] It has been argued that silver from Spanish mines reached Crete as early as 2,000 B.C. but we have no definite evidence about them before they were worked by the Phoenicians and the first record of Spanish silver being acquired by Greeks belongs to about 650 B.C.[3] After the collapse of the Mycenaean world the supplies of precious raw materials in the Greek world had evidently been interrupted but the spread of silver coinage in the eighth and seventh centuries shows that these metals were becoming common again. The prosperity of sixth-century Siphnos derived from silver mines which were later flooded by the sea.[4] Silver working on the island of Lesbos is associated with seventh-century pottery.[5] The Spanish mines produced not only for the Greeks but also for the Etruscans who, with the aid of the Phoenicians and Carthaginians, were able to supplement their more slender local resources.

As in the case of gold, the conquests of Alexander and the activities of prospectors in his retinue opened up rich new sources of silver and in Roman times, as Pliny notes, almost every province was producing the metal.[6] Spain was certainly the principal source; the rich mines started by Hannibal were acquired by the Romans after the Second Punic War[7] and remained very productive. Augustus opened up new mines which

[1] Alybe, east of the Paphlagonians, is the birthplace of silver in Homer (cf. Strabo, XII, 549–52).

[2] Strabo, xiv, 684.

[3] A. Schulten, *Tartessos*, Hamburg, 1922, 14.

[4] *JHS*, vi, 1885, 231 ff.

[5] Davies, *art. cit.* (note 2 on p. 1).

[6] Pliny, *NH*, xxxiii, 96.

[7] *Economic Survey*, iii, 111–12.

were either let to contractors or directly run under Imperial control.[1] Of the other provinces, Britain produced a good deal of silver.[2] Lead pigs found in the province bear inscriptions stating that they were cast from the residue of the desilverisation process and a number of silver ingots of fourth-century date give the names of the factories.[3] The Danube provinces, Asia Minor and Macedonia continued to be principal sources for the Roman world.

It may be noted here that the relative value of gold and silver in the classical Greek period was approximately 13½ to 1. Under Alexander it dropped to 12 to 1 and with the full influx of the hoarded treasure of the Persians it came down as low as 10 to 1. This remained the ratio in the late Republic but it rose to about 12¼ to 1 under Augustus and remained approximately so throughout the Empire.

BIBLIOGRAPHY

E. Ardaillon, *Les Mines du Laurion dans l'Antiquité*, Paris, 1897.
K. C. Bailey, *The Elder Pliny's Chapters on Chemical Subjects*, London, 2 vols. i, 1929; ii, 1932, esp. vol. i.
F. von Bissing, 'Zur Geschichte des Silbers und des Electrons', in *Acta Orientalia*, iv, 1925, pp. 138–41.
Blümner, *Technologie*, vol. iv.
M. Cary in *Mélanges Glotz*, ii, 1932, pp. 133–44.
O. Davies, *Roman Mines in Europe*, Oxford, 1933.
R. J. Forbes, 'Silver & Lead in Antiquity', in *Jaarbericht ex Oriente Lux*, viii, 1942, pp. 747–51.
R. J. Forbes, *Studies in Ancient Technology*, viii, 1964.
W. Gowland, 'Silver in Roman & Early Times', in *Archaeologia*, lxix, 1918, 121–60.
Lucas, *Materials*, 257–68, 278–85.
A. Lucas, 'Silver in Antiquity', in *JEA*, xiv, 1928.
PW sv. Gold and Silber.
C. Singer, E. J. Holmyard, A. R. Hall, T. I. Williams, *A History of Technology*, ii, 1956.
C. H. V. Sutherland, *Gold*, London, 1960.

[1] For the organisation of the Spanish mines see the *Lex Metallis Dicta* of Hadrian (*Fontes Iuris Romani Antejustiniani*, I, no. 104, p. 498) and the *Lex Metalli Vipascensis* of the second century A.D. (ibid. no. 105).

[2] Strabo, iv, 199; but see Tylecote, *Metallurgy*, 89 f.

[3] e.g. *BMCP*, no. 118.

2. THE ANCIENT CRAFTSMAN AND HIS TECHNIQUES

NAMES

The Greek word for goldsmith is *χρυσουργός* or *χρυσοποιός*; for silversmith *ἀργυροποιός*[1] is most normal. The art of working in metals, especially precious metals, is *τορευτική*; basically this word seems to mean the art of chasing metal with a *τορεύς* (Lat: *caelum*) but it is used to cover all the processes of decoration, i.e. repoussé, chasing, engraving, etc.[2] The equivalent word in Latin is *caelatura* which is defined by Quintilian[3] very generally as work in gold, silver, bronze and iron, though it applies especially to the two former. The Roman silversmith is *argentarius,* but the word when it stands alone, may also mean a banker. It, therefore, appears very commonly with an explanatory word, as *faber argentarius* (*CIL,* iii, 1652), *argentarius caelator* (*CIL,* vi, 917) and *argentarius vascularius* (*CIL,* ii, 3749). There were also a large number of names for specialised crafts connected with the manufacture of plate and some of these are mentioned below.

TECHNIQUES

There is no contemporary treatise on the techniques used by ancient silversmiths in the manufacture of plate; we draw our evidence, therefore, from the objects they produced, from contemporary literary sources, of whom the most important is Pliny the Elder, and by analogy with later techniques. An important later source is the book of the mediaeval monk Theophilus[4] of the twelfth century which describes the work of a practical craftsman of the day and probably makes use of ancient technical treatises as well. Much of what he says may be taken to apply to classical times. Unfortunately only very few examples of ancient plate have been examined by a skilled silversmith in conjunction with an experienced archaeologist and most of what has been written about technique lacks authority and conviction. This section aims only at a very general account of ancient techniques but some technical details are discussed more fully in the following chapters.

[1] *ἀργυροκόπος* is also found. [2] *AJA*, xlv, 1941, 390. [3] *Inst. Or.*, ii, 21, 8.

[4] Theophilus, *De Diversis Artibus* (Edition and Translation by C. R. Dodwell), London 1961.

A] *Basic techniques*

The basic techniques in ancient times for manufacturing gold and silver vessels are the same as those employed by craftsmen today. The most important is the process of *raising* which consists of hammering a flat disc of metal supported on a stake into the shape of a vessel by means of a series of concentric hammer blows from the outside. During the process the metal must be frequently *annealed* (i.e. heated and cooled by quenching in water) since it becomes hard when submitted to repeated blows and will eventually crack. A simple foot may also be hammered out and a rim produced by bending and hammering the metal. The smoothing of the surface of the vessel is known as *planishing*, which is done with a special kind of hammer; various fine abrasives are used to give the final polish. From the Bronze Age onwards ancient craftsmen were able to *raise* complicated and deep shapes from flat sheets of metal; very deep shapes were generally made from a number of pieces which were soldered or riveted together; feet and handles were usually made separately and soldered or riveted to the body.

The *casting* of feet and handles to be attached to hammered vessels seems to have been introduced in the archaic Greek period; Payne[1] puts the invention of cast-bases, rims and handles around 600 B.C. From about the fifth century B.C. onwards the bodies of metal vessels were sometimes cast. The heavy metal *kylikes* and other drinking cups which occur both in bronze and silver from the fourth century B.C. onwards were cast. The method demands the use of a lathe for cleaning up the casting and this seems to have been known as early as the fifth century B.C.[2] In Roman times casting seems to have been commonly used, not only for decorated vessels but also for plain dishes and bowls. The Corbridge lanx and the Oceanus dish from Mildenhall (see p. 197) were first cast plain, the thickness of the metal in the case of the former being 0·083 – 0·15 inches.

A fast revolving lathe could also be used for *spinning*, a process which is in common use among manufacturing silversmiths today; in this process sheet metal is burnished into the shape of a prepared form set up on a lathe. There is evidence that this method was introduced in Hellenistic times and it would have been especially suitable for the

[1] Payne, *Necrocorinthia*, 213.
[2] *ÖJh*, viii, 1905, 51–60.

mass-production of little perfume pots and the like. It could also be used for making stems and handles of vessels.

The various parts of vessels were attached to one another either by means of rivets, which were in common use from the Bronze Age onwards, or by the use of solder. The two types of solder used are known as *hard solder* and *soft solder*. Hard silver solder is made by alloying the metal with copper (Theophilus recommends two parts silver to one of copper) and gold solder with copper or copper and silver. Soft solder, which is composed of lead and tin, does not seem to have been used until Hellenistic and Roman times. Little is known about the composition of and use of hard solder in ancient times; the soft solder used on the silverware from Traprain Law is said to have contained 85 per cent tin and 15 per cent lead.[1] The solders, especially soft solder, require the use of a flux to prevent the formation of an oxide film when heating; tallow or resin are suitable for this purpose. Two pieces of sheet silver can also be joined together by hammering if they are heated to approximately 500° C.

B] *Decorative techniques*

Surface decoration on gold an silver vessels is carried out by means of *flat chasing* which is done with the aid of hammer and punches. In this process no metal is removed from the vessel, a line being composed of a series of oblique indentations of the punch. The term may be used to cover a variety of different effects, from the simple linear patterns made by means of a blunt tool on Bronze Age bowls (fig. 3) to the punched ornament on Roman bowls and the elaborate geometric and floral designs on late Roman dishes (e.g. pl. 65). Flat chasing can also achieve low-relief designs on the surface of the metal and according to Maryon the application of this technique to heavy metal vessels was used to produce the relief on the Oceanus dish from Mildenhall and other late Roman silver.[2] The design was first drawn out on the front, the background was then driven down leaving the figures in relief to a maximum height of one-sixteenth inch and the final details were modelled with chasing tools.

Engraving with various fine pointed tools was used to draw designs on

[1] Curle, *Traprain*, 78.

[2] H. Maryon, 'The Mildenhall Treasure, some Technical Problems', in *Man*, 1948, 25 and 43.

metal and appears on the Attic drinking vessels of the fifth century B.C. and in all later periods. In the process of engraving the metal is actually removed by cutting the line. For this reason it may be grouped together with the process of *cold tooling* which involves carving and chasing relief designs in solid metal. This technique was probably used from the first century A.D. onwards[1] and was especially popular in the workshops of Roman Gaul during the third century A.D. A special technique, which Pliny seems to be referring to as fashionable in his day,[2] is the cutting of openwork designs in thin metal perhaps to serve as a casing for glass or some other material. There is one early Imperial example of this technique and more elaborate ones of the later Empire (see below p. 188).

The commonest form of decoration on ancient plate is *repoussé* relief, the term being used to describe embossed work which is carried out by hammering from the back.[3] The vessel to be decorated in this way is set face downwards on a bed of soft pitch and the work carried out with hammered punches; a tool called a snarling iron is used to boss up the inside of a narrow vessel at points that are outside the reach of normal tools. If the relief is to be high, the work will have to be annealed and weak parts of the relief may have to be supported with lead filling.[4] The final details are done by chasing from the front by means of punches to define the outlines of the relief and put in detail. Repoussé work was done on gold and silver plate from Mycenaean times onwards. Two methods related to the process of free repoussé are relief work done with the aid of carved or moulded punches or by hammering the metal into a negative die. These different techniques have been found among the relief-decorated *phialai* of classical times (see pp. 81–2).

Relief decoration may also be carried out by *casting*. The technique of solid cast appliqué figures seems to have been introduced in Corinthian metalwork at the same time as cast handles and bases.[5] By the fourth century, if not before, relief decoration on silver vessels was commonly

[1] See below, p 180.

[2] *NH*, xxxiii, 140.

[3] The Greek word is *προσελαύνειν*; a vase with repoussé reliefs is *ἔκτυπος*, cf. *IG*, xi, 2, 161, B 76. In Quintilian, ii, 4, 7, *caelatura* is used especially for relief work.

[4] i.e. *plumbatura*, referred to in Digest, vi, 123; xxxiv, 2, 32, 1; a good example occurs on the Cybele dish in the Hildesheim Treasure (Pernice and Winter, 19 and text to pls. IV and V).

[5] Payne, *Necrocorinthia*, 213.

carried out by casting and in late Hellenistic and Roman times the methods of thin hollow casting by 'cire perdue' had been brought to a high pitch of skill.[1] The series of plaster casts from ancient metalwork (see pp. 84, 139) seem to have been distributed with a view to preparing moulds for casting cups and other vessels. The relief decoration on handles of Roman saucepan-*paterae* is usually cast; a number of steatite moulds have survived which must be connected in some way with the mass-production of these handles.[2] Cups, bowls, dishes and other vessels were commonly cast in Roman times.

Various forms of *inlaying* and *overlaying* were used to decorate silver in ancient times. In Mycenaean times, the overlaying of fairly thick foil on silver and gold was common.[3] On the Etruscan bowls discussed on pp. 66–7 a very fine leaf seems to have been used to gild some examples and a thicker foil occurs on others. In the classical Greek period gilding was carried out with metal foil which is described as being about the thickness of strong paper; on the engraved silver cups from the tumuli of the Seven Brothers group in the Kuban (e.g. pl. 15A) the leaf was laid over the engraved design and then beaten on to it without the use of adhesive.[4] The thickness of the best Roman gold leaf has been calculated as ten times that of modern gold leaf which can, apparently, be beaten to 1/9000 mm.[5] It is not known when gilding with the use of mercury was first employed; it has been reported on vessels of the fourth century B.C.[6] and was probably common in Hellenistic times. In this process the gold and the mercury form an amalgam which is painted on to the surface of the silver. When the mercury is evaporated a thin film of gold remains fused to the silver. In Roman times when mercury was available on a commercial scale this was the normal, but not universal, method of gilding silver; the gilding on vessels in the Hildesheim Treasure is stated to have been carried out by this means.[7] It is interesting that Pliny refers to the use of

[1] For this see especially Ippel, *Guss- und Treibarbeit.*

[2] *ÖJh*, vii, 1904, 180 ff.; they were probably used for making wax models rather than for direct casting of metal.

[3] cf. *Odyssey*, vi, 232.

[4] CR, 1881, 6; *Athenian Studies presented to W. S. Ferguson*, Harvard, 1940, 191.

[5] Kluge, *Grossbronzen*, 31–4.

[6] A silver relief of the 7th century B.C. in New York (Richter, *Greek Collection*, 32) is said to be mercury gilded.

[7] Pernice and Winter, 18.

mercury in gilding but associates it with leaf; he may simply have misunderstood the process or, in fact, the practice of his day may have differed from normal mercury gilding.[1] *Silvering* of bronze could be done by the same process to produce cheap imitations of silver plate and plated bronze vessels of this kind were common in Roman times but are not included in this handbook.[2] The overlaying of gold with patterns of gold granules is a remarkable refinement of soldering technique which has a very important place in the history of gold jewellery;[3] it was also used to decorate gold vessels by the Etruscans (e.g. pl. 12A) in the seventh century B.C.

Inlaying of silver plate with other metals was also practised from Mycenaean times onwards. The recesses for the inlay were prepared either by stamping or cutting and the edges of the recesses were usually bevelled to hold the gold or copper inlay in position. A common form of inlay on silver in the Roman period is a black compound of silver and copper sulphide known as niello which is inlaid in the form of a powder; it becomes plastic when heated, sets hard on cooling, and is burnished to a final surface. The earliest examples of its use in Roman times occur on vessels in the Hildesheim Treasure which were made in the first century A.D.;[4] it became increasingly popular in the third century when floral patterns were cut in the silver and filled with niello, and in the silver of the fourth and fifth centuries elaborate figured scenes were carried out in a combination of niello, gilding and engraving.[5] There has been some controversy about the nature and chemical composition of a similar black inlay which is used on Mycenaean vessels in conjunction with gold and copper inlays (e.g. pl. 6A).[6] In Hellenistic and Roman times, silver and gold plate were also inlaid with precious stones and a number of examples of the technique have survived. A curious late Roman lead vase[7] in the British Museum

[1] Pliny, *NH*, xxxiii, 65 and 125.

[2] Imitations of silver plate were also produced in pewter, especially in the late Empire, and in an alloy of copper, tin and lead (cf. *ÖJh*, xv, 1912, Beibl. 108 ff.; examples in the Varna Museum).

[3] Higgins, *Jewellery*, 18 ff.

[4] Pliny, *NH*, xxxiii, 131, refers to the intentional staining of silver plate and gives a recipe which would, in fact, produce a satisfactory niello, but he is not speaking of inlays.

[5] Rosenberg, *Niello*, discusses the technique in detail; for the composition of niello see *Studies in Conservation*, 2, 1953, 49 ff.

[6] Schaeffer, *Enkomi-Alasia*, I, 379 ff.; *Nature*, 187, 1960, 1051–2.

[7] Registration, 67, 5–8, 813.

studded with glass-pastes was probably made in imitation of silver vessels, and a small silver pot with a series of openwork ovals[1] and a lining of blue glass produces much the same effect as a silver vessel studded with blue stones (pl. 50c). Glass vessels with fittings of precious metal also originated in Hellenistic times. The little glass cups of the second or first century B.C. from Severskaya in Moscow have gold fittings and handles on the upper part of the vessel inlaid with semi-precious stones.[2]

BIBLIOGRAPHY

C. Alexander, 'A Roman silver relief', in *BMMA*, xiv, 1955-6, 64.
P. E. Arias, 'La patera di Cesena', in *Annuario*, xxiv–xxvi, 1946–8, 309–344 (gilt and niello technique).
Blümner, *Technologie*, vol. iv.
BMCP, introduction.
W. Campbell, *Greek and Roman Plated Coins*, New York, 1933.
B. Cuzner, *A Silversmith's Manual* (2nd edition), 1949.
Daremberg and Saglio sv. 'caelatura'.
Ebert, *Reallexicon.*
D. K. Hill, 'Ancient Metal Reliefs', in *Hesperia*, xii, 1943, 97.
A. Ippel, *Der Bronzefund von Galjub*, Berlin 1922.
A. Ippel, *Guss- und Treibarbeit* (repoussé and casting).
Kluge, *Grossbronzen*, i, 177 ff. (gilding).
Maryon, *Metalwork and Enamelling.*
H. Maryon, 'Metalworking in the Ancient World', in *AJA*, liii, 1949, 93.
H. Maryon, 'The Mildenhall Treasure, some technical problems', in *Man*, 1948, 25 & 43.
A. A. Moss, 'Niello', in *Studies in Conservation*, 2, 1953, p. 49 ff.
PW sv. Toreutik (by G. Lippold).
E. Pernice, 'Untersuchungen zur antiken Toreutik', articles in *ÖJh*, vii, 1904; viii, 1905; xi, 1908.
H. J. Plenderleith in *Enkomi-Alasia*, I, 379 ff. (Mycenean 'niello').
G. M. A. Richter, articles in *AJA*, xlv, liv, lxii (on classical relief vessels).
G. Rodenwaldt, 'Ein toreutisches Meisterwerk' in *JdAI*, 41, 1926, 191.
Rosenberg, *Niello.*
D. B. Thompson in *Hesperia*, viii, 1939, 285.
ibid., suppl. 8, 1949, 365 ff.
H. A. Thompson in *Athenian Studies Presented to W. S. Ferguson*, Harvard, 1940, 191 ff. (gilding).
H. Wilson, *Silverwork and Jewellery*, London 1903.
W. Züchner, 'Von Toreuten und Töpfern' in *JdAI*, 65-6, 1950–1, 175.

[1] Registration, 70, 9–12, 1; Plenderleith, *Conservation*, pl. 29.
[2] Rostovtzeff, *I & G*, 127, fig. 16.

c] *Cleaning and Repairs*

Fine silver derives much of its attraction from the brilliant polish that the craftsman gives to it and this has always required constant attention to maintain, since sulphur in the atmosphere quickly dulls and blackens it. In antiquity silver may not always have been given a high polish but a fine finish was expected in the best pieces.[1] Chalk was very commonly used to clean silver and vinegar is also mentioned for the same purpose.[2] Sodium carbonate (*nitrum*) was also used.[3] Theophilus (lxxx) recommends charcoal to remove the tarnish and chalk for polishing. It may be imagined that in wealthy Roman families that had amassed large collections of plate, the slaves (*servi ab argento* or *ad argentum*) were heavily occupied in this duty; in a passage of Juvenal[4] we read that one slave cleans the plain silver and a second works on the figured pieces. In the Imperial house these duties were performed by slaves under a *praepositus* (*praepositus auri escari, praepositus argenti escari*).

Plate which had been kept in the possession of a family for several generations often became worn and damaged. Pliny refers to pieces so old that the detail on them could no longer be made out. A number of examples of plate with ancient repairs have survived from Roman times; patched dishes were found in the Hildesheim Treasure and in the Casa del Menandro.[5] Ancient pieces of plate that have lain for a long time in sulphurous conditions have a uniform shiny skin of black deposit (e.g. a vase from Vicarello in the British Museum). Pieces which have lain in salty soil have a badly incrusted surface with a thick deposit of grey silver chloride, generally known as 'horn-silver' (cerargyrite – AgCl).[6]

3. THE TRADE OF THE SILVERSMITH IN ANTIQUITY

In Minoan and Mycenaean times the royal craftsman worked for his master in the palace. The king would control the source of raw materials and the products of the silversmith's skill and it is unlikely that any

[1] For *creta argentaria*, used for polishing, Pliny, *NH*, xxxv, 199.
[2] Pliny, *NH*, xxxiii, 131. [3] Lucas, *Materials*, 303–4. [4] Juvenal, XIV, 60–2.
[5] Pernice and Winter, 60, fig. 29; Maiuri, *Menandro*, 259, n. 36.
[6] For the cleaning and treatment of old silver, Plenderleith, *Conservation*, 212 ff.

silversmith worked freely for the whole community.[1] In Homer's world the craftsman is a journeyman moving from place to place to work with materials supplied by his patrons; the same man would be capable of working different metals.[2] In archaic times, the Greek silversmith was just as free in his activities; he might travel to work for foreign kings like Alyattes of Lydia and at home might move from place to place wherever his services were in most demand. Some of the city-states soon became especially famous for their silverwork and silversmiths. In the temple inventories we read of Corinthian, Rhodian, Chiote gold and silver vessels and often the names of the silversmiths who made them. In the fifth century famous artists like Pheidias and Polykleitos seem to have been skilled metalworkers who may have made some of the costly plate dedicated at Greek sanctuaries (see below p. 74). In the Hellenistic world when the demand for expensive plate had increased enormously, the shops of the silversmiths in the various cities would have been gathered together in the silversmiths' quarter where the customers could admire the work of rival firms. This was also the era of the court artist and we find that silversmiths were permanently in the service of Hellenistic kings; Stratonikos of Cyzicus, for example, seems to have worked for the kings of Pergamon.[3] Cleopatra VII of Egypt went to Rhosus in Syria for her gold and silver plate and the workshops there were very famous in the last two centuries B.C.

The real development of mass production belongs to Roman times. The great demand for silver plate was met by the creation of big firms employing a very big staff,[4] and inscriptional evidence from Rome suggests a high degree of specialisation in the factories. We hear of a *tritor argentarius* (*CIL*, iv, 9950 = polisher), a *flaturarius* (*CIL*, vi, 9418 = caster?) and an *inaurator* (gilder). A *crustarius* specialised in relief-work and the *vasa crustata* gave their name to the *tabernae crustariae*, shops specialising in this kind of plate.[5] Certain firms, like those of Clodius, Furnius, and Gratius were famous for their work which seems to have been imitated by the smaller men.[6] The firm of Septicius is the butt of

[1] For Bronze Age craftsmen see A. J. B. Wace and F. H. Stubbings, *A Companion to Homer*, London, 1962, 534 ff.

[2] cf. *Odyssey*, iii, 425.

[3] Athenaeus, xi, 782B; Brunn, *Geschichte*, I, 442–3.

[4] cf. *CIL*, vi, 9391; a certain Junius has five freedmen who are silversmiths and they were presumably at one time his slaves.

[5] On this in general, *Economic Survey*, 212 ff. and *Klio*, xiv, 134 ff.

[6] Pliny, *NH*, xxxiii, 139; cf. *CIL*, vi, 9222.

Martial for the inferior quality of its plate.[1] The inscriptions of Roman craftsmen with premises on the Sacra Via suggest that there were also many silversmiths in a small way of business who would make vases from silver provided by their customers[2] and their importance and number are shown by the fact that Nero, when he was reconstructing this area of the city gave the silversmiths an elaborate system of between 150 and 200 new shops. A third category of silversmiths would be those in private employ. Verres in the late Republic had *caelatores* and *vascularii* among his private slaves.[3] We hear of a wealthy patron who equipped the shop of a silversmith and the imperial house employed large staffs to prepare silver both for palace use and for distribution as presents on the occasion of imperial anniversaries (cf. the *palatini artifices* of the Byzantine period). As to the status of the silversmiths and goldsmiths, a few free men are found but the vast majority are *liberti* (freedmen) or slaves.[4] Guilds of silversmiths existed in Rome and in many cities of the provinces;[5] there were also guilds of craftsmen employed in specialised roles connected with the craft (e.g. *brattiarii inauratores* = leaf gilders).[6] The dealers in silverware were called '*negotiatores argentarii vascularii*' and we hear of a *basilica argentaria* where silver plate was bought and sold. The *clivus argentarius* below the Capitol takes its name for the shops selling silver plate; Martial describes shops that specialised in antique pieces and for these, especially signed original works (*archetypa*), high prices were paid.[7] The export of silver plate, as we know from many finds outside the confines of the Empire, formed an important part of foreign trade;[8] the demand was met not only by the workshops of Italy in such places as Capua and Aquileia but by those of most of the large provincial cities, especially the industrial cities of Gaul and the main centres of the eastern parts of the Empire. Much of the silver plate found at Pompeii must have been made in local shops like those of Laelius Erastus who owned a large house in town[9] or that of Pinarius Cerialis.[10]

[1] Martial, iv, 88, 3; viii, 71, 6.
[2] A common practice cf. Gaius, iii, 147; Digest, xix, 2, 31; xxxiv, 2, 34.
[3] Cicero, *Verr.*, iv, 24, 54.
[4] *Klio*, xiv, 134 ff.; J. M. C. Toynbee, *Notes on Artists in the Roman World*, 51 ff.
[5] *Economic Survey*, 251. [6] *CIL*, vi, 95. [7] Martial, viii, 6 and 34.
[8] Roman craftsmen must also have worked outside the frontiers, cf. Cassius Dio, lxvii, 7.
[9] *CIL*, x, 8071, 10/11.
[10] *Rivista Indo-Greco-Italica*, 8, 1924, 121; *Pompeiana*, 1950, pp. 206–9.

BIBLIOGRAPHY

Friedländer, *Sittengeschichte*, iv, 301 ff.
D. H. F. Gray, 'Metalworking in Homer', in *JHS*, lxxiv, 1954, 1 ff.
H. Gummerus, 'Die römische Industrie', in *Klio*, 15, 1918, pp. 256 ff.
Marquardt, *Privatleben*, 695.
Economic Survey, especially vol. V (Rome and Italy of the Empire), 210 ff.
I. Calabi Limentani, *Studi sulla società romana: il lavoro artistico*, Milan-Varese, 1958.
Rostovtzeff, *SEHHW*, pp. 374-6, 1212 ff.
J. M. C. Toynbee, 'Some Notes on Artists in the Roman World', *Latomus*, 1951.

4. THE DISCOVERY OF GREEK AND ROMAN PLATE

Only a small fraction of ancient gold and silver plate has survived to the present day. Looting by invaders, melting down of gold and silver in times of emergency, replacement of old and worn pieces by newer ones have combined to make ancient plate, especially Greek plate, comparatively rare. Almost every piece of metal plate that must once have adorned the palaces of Cretan kings has gone, looted and in time assigned to the melting-pot when the palaces were destroyed. Fortunately the burial customs of Mycenaean lords have preserved many of their treasured possessions which have been recovered by the excavations of Schliemann and others. The vast riches of religious shrines in the classical world are almost entirely lost; only a few chance survivals have come down to us. The Greeks of the homeland in the Classical period were not buried with rich possessions, but the wealthy barbarians in the Balkans and S. Russia were accompanied to their graves with a large show of private wealth which included many choice pieces of plate acquired from Greek sources. The Thracian tombs of the Balkans and Scythian tombs, in the Dniepr valley and the Kuban especially, constitute our principal source of knowledge for the styles of Greek plate during the fifth and fourth century B.C.

The great increase in the quantity of domestic plate during the Hellenistic period has resulted in a proportionately larger number of discoveries but still we have only a very partial picture of the plate of the period. It is not, in fact, until Roman times that the finds are adequate to give a good cross-section of the production of gold and silver plate.

By the extraordinary chance of the sudden, catastrophic burial (in A.D. 79) of the towns of Campania beneath the lava and ash of Vesuvius, we have preserved to us complete services of Roman domestic silver in excellent state of preservation. The earlier discoveries at Pompeii[1] and Herculaneum were overshadowed by the discovery in 1895 of the famous Treasure of Boscoreale consisting of over 100 pieces of silver plate that had been placed for safe-keeping in a wine vat below the house and lost beneath the lava and ash that suffocated its guardian. In 1930 the silver treasure of 118 pieces came to light in the Casa del Menandro at Pompeii, stowed away in the cellar of the house in a bronze-bound wooden chest and wrapped in cloth.

No other period in the history of ancient plate is so well-documented as the first century A.D. The later hoards we owe in general to the troubled times of Imperial history when men were persuaded to bury their possessions to prevent them falling into the hands of barbarians. In this way we have preserved to us considerable collections of ancient temple plate like the Treasure of Berthouville, of domestic silver like the Treasure of Chaourse in the British Museum, both of which were buried in the late third century and re-discovered by chance. The Berthouville Treasure, found in a field by a farmer in 1830, was shown by later excavation to have belonged to the treasury of a temple destroyed about the end of the third century. Less certain are the circumstances and date of burial of the famous Hildesheim Treasure which may even have been the loot of barbarians plundered from the Roman province. Unfortunately not all the hoards of Roman silver discovered in recent times have survived to the present. A treasure, apparently of late Hellenistic silver weighing a total of over 41 lb., which was found at Cività Castellana in 1810, was quickly dispersed and mostly melted down.[2] Another found at Wettingen (Switzerland) in 1663 was apportioned among the Cantons and disappeared, while the Treasure of Trier[3] turned up by the hand of providence on the property of the Jesuits who yielded, in the words of the contemporary account 'praesenti necessitati quae optimi non semper consilii est capax' and used it to relieve their financial difficulties. A collection of plate,

[1] e.g. those of 1836 (*BdI*, 1836, 161) and 1887 (*NS*, 1887, 416).

[2] *Atti. Accad. Rom. Arch.*, 1, 2, 303 ff.; see below pp. 109–10

[3] See appendix I. The same fate befell the smaller treasures of Limoges and Beaumesnil (*GA*, 1884, 344).

30 pieces in all, rumoured to have been found in Tivoli[1] was once in the hands of a M. Warneck who bought it in Rome; several of the pieces are now in the Metropolitan Museum, New York, and the rest found its way to the Field Museum, Chicago.

The latest Roman hoards that fall within the scope of this book are those of the late fourth and early fifth centuries – the period when the Roman Empire in the West was finally collapsing. One of the most recently discovered, the Treasure of Kaiseraugst in Switzerland, was the chance find of a mechanical excavator working within the walls of a Roman fort; the famous Mildenhall Treasure, buried for safety at the time when Britain was being finally evacuated by the Romans, was turned up by a plough in a field near Mildenhall, Suffolk. Other hoards of the same period, like the Treasure of Traprain Law, are more likely to have been the loot of barbarian plunderers, just saved from the melting pot by a sudden reversal of fortune. A good many pieces, presumably, survived the catastrophies; some remained in private hands or were incorporated in the coffers of churches and cathedrals. The fourth-century Risley lanx apparently survived a long history above ground only to be lost again after its rediscovery in 1779 (see below p. 185). No ancient plate, so far as is known, has had a continuous survival above ground to the present day.

5. INSCRIPTIONS ON PLATE

Inscriptions of various kinds that have been found on ancient gold and silver plate throw much light on the social history of plate and on the work of the silversmith. The earliest inscriptions on Greek plate occur on a few surviving pieces from Greek sanctuaries which give the name of the donor and the circumstances of his gift, or, simply, the name of the shrine to which they belonged.[2] When, as in the case of archaic Etruscan silver, the pieces were privately owned, the name of the owner is inscribed, sometimes prominently, upon them. In the fifth century B.C. the Thracian chief who was buried with classical silver in a tumulus near Duvanli in S. Bulgaria proudly inscribes his outlandish name in Greek letters upon it. No artist's signature on silver of the classical

[1] *Mem. Soc. Ant. de France*, 58, 1897, 365 f.; *BMMA* 1964–5, 177–85.

[2] As on the *phiale mesomphalos* from Kozani (*AE*, 1948/9, 96–7); see below p. 57.

period has, in fact, survived but from the Temple inventories of the fourth century and by analogy with painted vases we may conclude that pieces were sometimes signed. In the fourth century, if not earlier, the custom of giving details of weight on objects of precious metal seems to have begun;[1] this information simplified the work of the stewards responsible for drawing up temple inventories and enabled private owners to estimate their hoarded wealth, and thereafter weight inscriptions became one of the commonest kinds of inscription. The maker would generally record this information for his patron and in Roman times he usually did this in careful pointillé on the underside of the vessel, sometimes giving considerable detail;[2] the owner or a less careful craftsman would scratch the information in graffito. In the case of sets of vessels – pairs of cups or services of plate – an inscription on one gives the total weight of the set; a good example of this occurs on a little monogrammed dish in the Esquiline Treasure, one of a set of four, which bears the inscription SCVT(ELLAE) IIII PV (i.e. the set of four weighs 5 lb.). The maker might also add the name of the person for whom the order was executed; on a decorated cup from Boscoreale, the name of the original owner is in neat pointillé and the names of two apparently subsequent owners in graffito. Trimalchio in Petronius' *Satyricon* preferred to have his name together with the weight prominently engraved on the rim of his vessels.[3] Artists' or craftsmen's inscriptions were never very common; only work of the highest quality made by skilled individuals seems to have been signed while the workshops, unlike those that produced the cheaper bronze vessels, did not generally stamp or mark their products. A pyxis from Taranto is signed by the artist Mikon; the freedman M. Domitius Polygnos signs in pointillé a mirror from Boscoreale. The two famous cups from Hoby in Denmark are both signed by the artist Cheirisophos; on one, the Priam and Achilles cup, he gives his name in Greek, on the Odysseus and Philoctetes cup he writes the Latin version.[4] On one of the recently discovered pieces from Kaiseraugst is the signature of Pausylypos of Thessalonica, on another, the mark of EVTICIVS NAISI (of Niş). The

[1] The earliest weight measurement occurs in the Panagyurishte Treasure (see below p. 102).

[2] e.g. the inscription on the Africa dish from Boscoreale (*Mon. Piot*, v, 42). For Roman weight inscriptions in general see Friedländer, *Sittengeschichte*, iv, 301 ff.

[3] Petronius, 31.

[4] *Nordiske Fortidsminder*, ii (1911–35), 128–9.

inscription on a fine saucepan-*patera* from Vindonissa (see below p. 168) seems to give both the name of the artist-craftsman and the firm for which he worked; it reads ANTEI SALONINI O(fficina) CALVI MELCATORIS. Many of the more carelessly written inscriptions on late Roman silver are difficult to interpret. Most of the vessels in the Treasure of Caubiac in the British Museum have names written in *graffito* on the undersides but it is impossible to tell whether the owner or maker is meant, and the word *Eutherios* on two of the silver plates from Mildenhall raises an intriguing question of identity.[1]

Silver plate from Roman shrines, of which a typical group is the plate from Berthouville in the Cabinet des Médailles, often has the name of the god to whom the piece was dedicated and the name of the donor prominently inscribed or inlaid upon it. At Berthouville, the principal benefactor had his silver marked with pointillé; a typical formula is MERCVRIO AVGVSTO Q. DOMITIVS TVTVS EX VOTO. On a phiale dedicated by a certain Julia Sibylla the letters are inlaid in gold; on another they are neatly engraved round a central medallion. In Roman times a great variety of interesting inscriptions have been found on plate. A group of vessels dedicated to the deities of the curative springs at Aquae Apollinares (Bagni di Vicarello) includes a number with inscriptions giving all the names of the principal towns en route from Spain to Rome; it is thought that they were used on the journey and then dedicated at the sanctuary. Vessels given as wedding presents often had the names of the recipients, and in later Roman times an inlaid monogram often formed the main decorative motif; they might also bear a good luck message to bride and groom. Late Roman spoons, given as presents, often bear inscriptions of this kind; a spoon found at Vermand in France has the words PONE CVRIOSE on it, apparently an injunction to place it carefully on the table. Presents given on the occasion of an imperial anniversary had the details of the event commemorated prominently inscribed upon them.[2] Good luck messages and Christian inscriptions or symbols, especially the chi-rho monogram, become common in the plate of the later Empire. Finally in the fifth century A.D. the practice of stamping silver ingots to guarantee the quality of the metal was extended to plate and a number

[1] *JRS*, 38, 1948, 102.

[2] On these see below pp. 199–201.

of stamped vessels of the period have survived; they are discussed below in chapter ten.

A NOTE ON THE ROMAN WEIGHT INSCRIPTIONS

The Roman pound (*libra*), equivalent to 0·72 of an English pound or 327·45 grammes, was divided into 12 ounces (*unciae*). The ounce was divided into 24 scruples (*scripula*). The following list shows the marks most commonly used on Roman silver for the pound and its fractions:

Libra		=	1
Deunx	(11/12)	=	S = = −
Dextans	(10/12)	=	S = =
Dodrans	(9/12)	=	S = −
Bes	(8/12)	=	S =
Septunx	(7/12)	=	S −
Semis	(6/12)	=	S
Quincunx	(5/12)	=	= = −
Triens	(4/12)	=	= =
Quadrans	(3/12)	=	= −
Sextans	(2/12)	=	=
Sescuncia	(3/24)	=	Σ −
Uncia	(1/12)	=	−
Semuncia	(1/2 uncia)	=	Σ
Binae sextulae (2/3 uncia)		=	S S
Dimidia sextula (1/12 uncia)		=	Ꞩ
Scripulum (1/24 uncia)		=	∋

A Roman weight inscription is usually preceded by the letter P= *Pondo*. A typical example is provided by the inscription on the Africa dish from Boscoreale (pl. 36B) which gives the weight of the dish and emblema together and then the two separately. It reads:

PHI(ALA) ET EMB(LEMA) P(ENDENTIA)
P(ONDO) II (=2 librae) S = = (=dextans) 〉∨ | (=6 scripula)
PHI(ALA) P(ENDENS) P(ONDO) II (=2 librae) = (=sextans) Σ (=$\frac{1}{2}$ uncia)
EMB(LEMA) P(ENDENS) P(ONDO) S — (=septunx) Σ (=$\frac{1}{2}$ uncia).

A number of variant notations occur. For example a *quadrans* may be marked :. :· ≂~ ⊃⌣. On silver of eastern origin notation in

Greek signs and letters occurs (e.g. on a little dish from the Caubiac hoard) and sometimes a different system of weight from the Roman libral system.

Roman weights and measures are fully discussed by F. Hultsch, *Griechische und Römische Metrologie*, Berlin 1882.

6. COLLECTIONS

Most of the major discoveries of ancient plate have remained in the public collections of the countries where they were found. The contents of the Shaft Graves and the tombs at Dendra constitute the main part of the magnificent collection of Mycenaean gold and silver in the National Museum at Athens. The Etruscan finds in Italy are largely divided between the Villa Giulia Museum in Rome and the Archaeological Museum in Florence. The silver of all periods that has been found in S. Russia makes the collection of the Hermitage Museum in Leningrad the most important in the world for the general study of ancient silver. Bulgaria, Rumania and Yugoslavia have important finds from the northern periphery of the classical world; the finds from Duvanli and the Panagyurishte hoard are in Plovdiv. Most of the silver found in the Campanian sites has passed into the collection of the National Museum at Naples; the French hoards have gone to the Musée du Louvre or the Cabinet des Médailles; English finds under the law of Treasure Trove to the British Museum or the National Museum of Antiquities of Scotland; Danish finds, such as the Hoby cups, to the National Museum in Copenhagen.

In the eighteenth and nineteenth centuries, however, some very important hoards left the country of their origin and passed to other European and American collections. The Louvre acquired the major part of the Boscoreale Treasure in 1895; the British Museum got the Esquiline Treasure and several hoards from France, notably those of Chaourse and Caubiac. Occasionally groups were split up between Museums as in the case of the late Roman Carthage Treasure which is divided between the Louvre and the British Museum; one piece from the Esquiline Treasure is in the Petit Palais in Paris. Even today important finds defeat the Antiquities' Laws of the countries where they are found and arrive in other parts of Europe or America, usually without definite information as to their discovery; groups of objects become dispersed and records of their original discovery lost.

There is very little ancient plate in private hands. The two historical cups from the Boscoreale Treasure are owned by the family of Baron Edmond de Rothschild who was instrumental in getting most of the Treasure for the Louvre.[1] The same owner has some of the silver from the Treasure of Tarentum. Private Collections in America and Switzerland contain notable pieces, but, in the main, plate is too rarely on the market to be collected by private persons.

[1] Another silver vessel said to have belonged to this Treasure is in the Museo Lazaro Galdiano, Madrid (J. C. Aznar, *Guia Abreviada del Museo Lazaro Galdiano*, 5th edition, 1962).

CHAPTER TWO

The Bronze Age

1. ANATOLIA

About the middle of the third millennium B.C. the wealth of silver from the surface deposits of *galena* that stretch across Asia Minor, and the gold from local mines and other sources became available for objects of luxury. The absence of gold and silver ores in Mesopotamia meant that the metals had to be imported, and the trade which supplied Sumerian craftsmen with their raw materials also served to break down the isolation of the inhabitants of Anatolia and introduced the techniques of metalworking invented in Mesopotamia.[1] There is considerable evidence for the lively trade between the plateau and the river valleys during the Copper Age and at a somewhat later period (*c.* nineteenth century B.C.) we have direct records of the commerce from the Assyrian trading post of Kültepe in Cappadocia where the standard of prices was set by silver.

The Royal burials at Alaca Hüyük in Cappadocia (2400–2200 B.C.) represent the richest manifestation of the Anatolian Copper Age.[2] The wealth of Alaca seems to have its origin in Sumerian trade and the skill of the craftsmen who made the vessels of gold, silver and electrum rivals that of the metal workers at Ur. At Alaca the goldsmiths were highly proficient in 'raising' sheet metal and used solders for joining the parts of vessels; they executed ornament in repoussé and inlaid one metal into another. The commonest shapes among the vessels of precious metal found at Alaca are long-spouted jugs and cups or bowls, usually with repoussé decoration of lines in chevrons or hatching or curvilinear patterns, and these were not confined to Alaca as we know from

[1] H. Frankfort, *The Art and Architecture of the Ancient Orient*, London 1954, 113; *Anatolian Studies*, 4, 1954, 212.

[2] R. O. Arik, *Alaca Höyük Hafriyati*, Ankara, 1937; H. Z. Koşay *Ausgrabungen von Alaca Hüyük*, *Ankara*, 1944; *Les Fouilles de Alaca Hüyük* 1937–9, 1951.

recent finds at other places in central Anatolia, for example, at Amasya.[1]

In Western Anatolia the city of Troy II grew rich on trade with east and west. In the 'Treasures' associated with the late phase of this city (*c.* 2200 B.C.),[2] Schliemann found many pieces of expensive plate – cups, including the characteristic Anatolian two-handled beaker (e.g. fig. 2), bowls, and bottles with cup-shaped covers and tubular lugs on the shoulders pierced for suspension. Schliemann's 'Great Treasure' had three gold vessels, including the famous 'sauceboat', one goblet of electrum, four tankards, two saucers, a shallow bowl, a goblet, two bottle-shaped vessels, and a small lid, all of silver. Some of these vessels which are 'raised' from sheet metal are attractive shapes decorated with vertical and spiral fluting, but the outstanding piece was a gold spouted goblet with two tubular handles of a form generally known as a

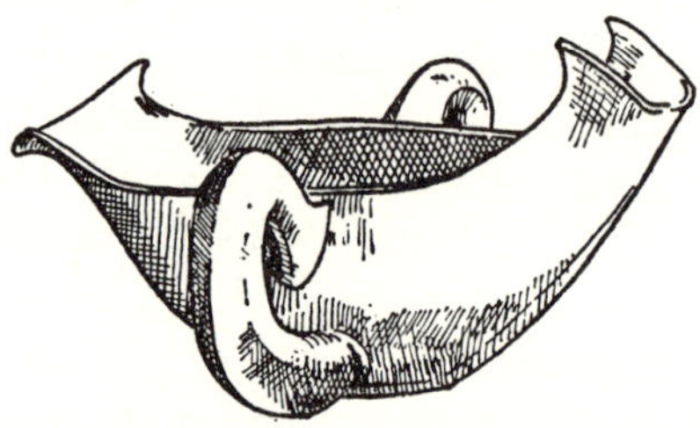

FIG. 1: Gold 'sauceboat' from Troy. Scale 1:3

'sauceboat' (fig. 1). This 'sauceboat' was beaten from a single sheet of gold and the handles were attached with solder; Schliemann offers a charming explanation for its use: 'The person who filled the cup' he writes 'may have first drunk from the small mouth as a mark of respect, to let the guest drink from the larger or . . . a person holding the cup before him by two handles may have poured a libation from the further spout and have drunk out of the nearer.' Blegen prefers a ritual use for the vessel. The exquisite gold and silver vases of about the same period from graves at Dorak near the Sea of Marmara, not far east of Troy, are known only from drawings made at the time they were

[1] H. F. Seton Lloyd, *Early Anatolia*, London, 1956, 100; cf. the gold jug in a sale at Luzern (*Ars Antiqua A. G. Luzern, Antike Kunstwerke Auktion*, II, 1960).

[2] Schliemann, *Ilios*, 464 ff.; Schmidt, *Schliemanns Sammlung*, 229 ff.; for the date of the 'treasures', Blegen, *Troy*, I, 207; and for the metalwork of the period in general, *JdAI*, 74, 1959, 1 ff.

discovered.[1] One grave, identified as that of a Queen, contained a spouted vase in fluted silver, a gold jug with cut-away spout and a high-handled bowl; a second tomb had a tall two-handled drinking cup in fluted gold, the finest example of its kind yet found. A less

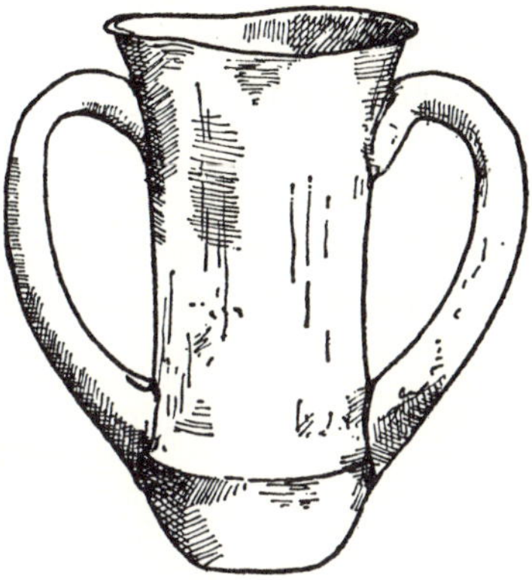

FIG. 2: Silver two-handled beaker ('depas amphikypellon') from Asia Minor; British Museum. Scale 1:3

graceful version of the shape in silver said to have been found somewhere near Troy is now in the British Museum (fig. 2).[2] Schliemann christened this type of cup found at Troy with the Homeric name of 'depas amphikypellon' by which it is still known.

2. EARLY CYCLADIC AND EARLY HELLADIC

The city of Troy II owed some of its prosperity to its favoured position for trade and the spread of characteristically Troadic products across the Aegean was the outcome. The 'sauceboat', for example, became a characteristic shape among the clay vessels of the Early Helladic II period in Greece (2200–2000 B.C.) and one or two examples in precious metal have been found. The Helladic version, illustrated by the example in gold said to have been found near Heraea in Arcadia (pl. IA), differs from the Troadic; it has a single horizontal strap handle

[1] *ILN*, Nov. 28, 1957; Stuart Piggott (ed.), *The Dawn of Civilisation*, London, 1961, 168–9.

[2] Department of Western Asiatic Antiquities, no. 132150; *BMQ*, 27, 1963, pl. XXIXb.

attached to the vase by rivets instead of the soldered tubular handles of the Trojan example and there is only one spout.[1] Another similar sauceboat which also seems to have come from the Peloponnese was once on the Berlin antique market but has now disappeared.[2] The two-handled goblet also spread to Greece. Forsdyke[3] has traced the development of this shape which spread from Anatolia across the Greek islands to the mainland; but no gold or silver example has so far been found in Greece.

The islands of the Cyclades provided the trading links between Anatolia and Greece, and it is not surprising that a number of finds of precious metal vessels bearing strong Anatolian affinities have come to

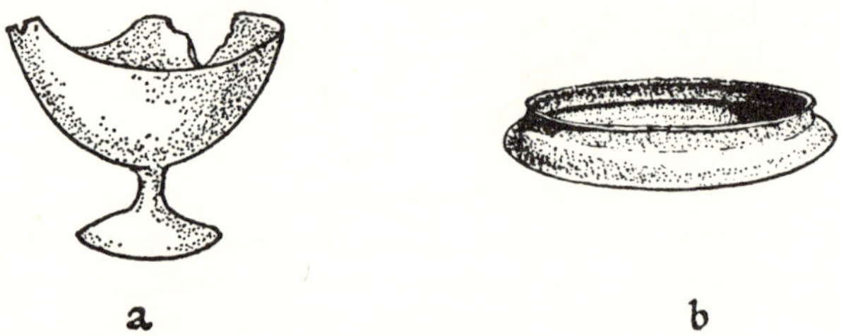

FIG. 3: (*a*) Silver goblet and (*b*) Silver bowl from Amorgos (*a*, after *AM* 1886; *b*, from the object). Scale 1:3

light. A stemmed goblet of Early Cycladic date from Amorgos (fig. 3*a*)[4] is related to a vase from Alaca Hüyük; the same find contained a silver bowl with offset rim (fig. 3*b*) of a type which was also found in a treasure of gold and silver vessels discovered on the island of Euboea. The contents of this treasure have now become dispersed; three of the vessels in the find, two gold (fig. 4) and one silver bowl, are now in the Benaki Museum at Athens,[5] another silver bowl is in the Metropolitan Museum (pl. 1B)[6] and yet another, in a New York Private Collection,[7] seems to be from the same source. The gold bowl or cup in fig. 4*a* was 'raised' from sheet metal; on the bottom there is a shallow omphalos

[1] *JHS*, xliv, 1924, 163.

[2] Segall, *Benaki*, 13.

[3] *JHS*, xxxiv, 1914, 127 ff.; see also *AJA*, 62, 1953, 95 ff.

[4] *AM*, 1886, Beilage I, D 3; the bowl (fig. 3*b*), but not the goblet, is in the Ashmolean Museum, Oxford.

[5] Segall, *Benaki*, 11 ff., 211–12, pls. 1–3, 67–8, 69; see also F. Schachermeyr, *Die ältesten Kulturen Greichenlands*, Stuttgart, 1955, 159 ff.

[6] Richter, *Greek Collection*, 16, pl. 11 i.

[7] von Bothmer, *Private Collections*, no. 96; Walter C. Baker Collection.

and on the body ornament of parallel lines chased with a blunt tool. The second gold bowl, which also has a little omphalos (fig. 4*b*), is decorated with zig-zag lines carried out in the same technique. On the silver vessel in New York the decoration consists of a more complicated

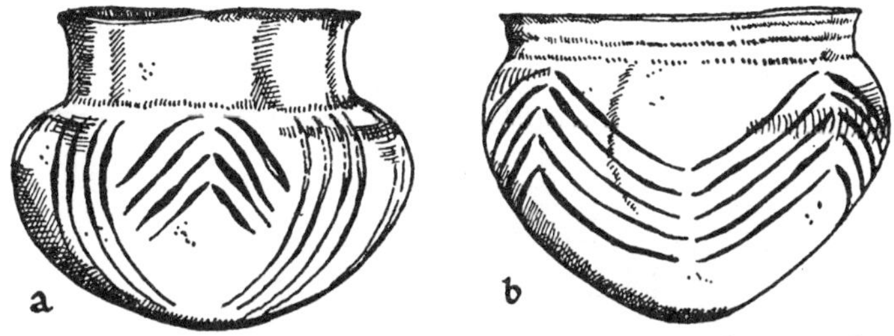

FIG. 4: Gold bowls from Euboea; Benaki Museum, Athens. Scale 1:3

pattern of hatching on the body (pl. 1B). Miss Segall, publishing the Benaki bowls, draws comparisons from pottery at Ahlatlibel near Ankara and compares the chased lines with ornament on gold jugs from Alaca Hüyük. Comparison may also be made with hatched ornament on Early Cycladic pottery vessels from Antiparos, Naxos and Paros.[1] It seems likely, therefore, that the metal vessels are local products but obviously under strong influence from Anatolian metalwork. It is possible that sources of precious metals in the Cyclades were already being tapped and that these vessels were made from local raw materials.

3. CRETE, EARLY AND MIDDLE MINOAN

The contacts between early Bronze Age Crete and Anatolia were less direct than those of the islands and Greek mainland. Anatolia, however, was almost certainly the source of any silver that got to Crete and it is interesting that the earliest vessels of precious metal show some unquestionable Anatolian influence. Although considerable private wealth may be inferred from the contents of some Early Minoan[2] tombs, no vases of precious metal have survived before the very end of the E.M. period, and indeed, the influences of metal on ceramic shapes before this seems to have been confined to the imitation of Egyptian

[1] *BMC Vases*, vol. 1, part 1, 54 ff. cf. *BSA*, ii, 1896–7, 35 ff.

[2] Hereafter Early Minoan is E.M., Middle Minoan M.M., Late Minoan L.M.

copper vessels. From an E.M. III context at Mochlos comes a small silver cup or bowl[1] decorated with rows of beading round the lower part; in shape and decoration it seems to be the obvious prototype of E.M. III clay cups found at Vasiliki and elsewhere.[2] E.M. silver plate was, no doubt, very rare but at the beginning of the M.M. period, as wealth was concentrated more and more into the hands of royal rulers and as precious metals, which were not available locally, could be imported more freely from abroad, it began to be increasingly common.

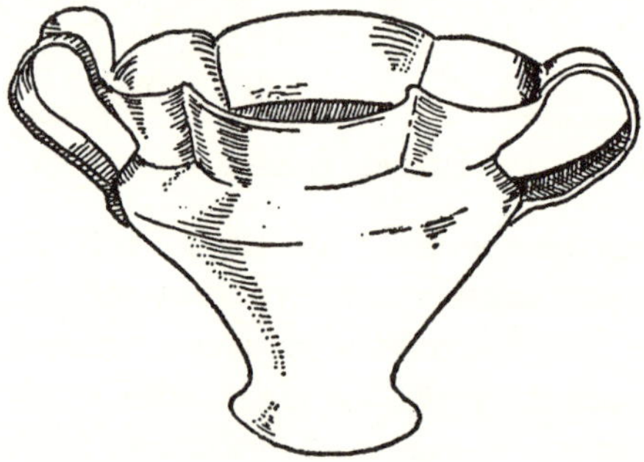

FIG. 5: Silver cup from Gournia, Crete. Scale 1:3

The only surviving example of Middle Minoan plate from Crete was found in M.M.I. 'house-tomb' at Gournia. It is a two-handled cup (fig. 5) with a fluted rim, a sharply angled shoulder and a tapering stem;[3] the handles were fixed to the rim by pairs of bronze rivets and to the body of the vase by a silver rivet. A remarkable instance of the copying of metal forms in pottery is provided by a grey-ware vase from Pseira[4] which, although it is larger and differs somewhat in the detail of base and handles, is very close to the Gournia silver cup; its complete dependence on a metallic original is shown by the clay rivet-head on the handle. This type of goblet is closely related to Hittite vessels from the fourth city of Boğazköy and from Alişar in Cappadocia. Although the Gournia vessel is unique, other delicately shaped vessels in clay, of metallic form and often with a metallic sheen, presuppose highly skilled craftsmanship in metal.

[1] Seager, *Mochlos*, 52, fig. 22.
[2] *Pennsylvania Transactions*, ii (part 2), 121, fig. 4.
[3] *Pennsylvania Transactions*, i (part 3), 1905, 187, fig. 6 (p. 189); H. B. Hawes, *Gournia*, Philadelphia, 1908, Colour Plate C.
[4] *Pennsylvania Transactions*, iii (part 1), 20, fig. 5.

In the M.M. II period pottery imitations of metalwork were very frequent and as Evans pointed out 'It is to the existence of these ceramic copies that we owe the best evidence of the wealth of Minoan lords in precious metals in the palmy days of the Middle Minoan age'.[1] The Kamares and eggshell wares from Phaestos[2] and Knossos include beakers related to the later Vaphio shape and there are pottery examples of a kind of jug with a high spout and a heavy roll at the base of the neck which exists in the metal original (c.f. pl. 4) to conceal the junction of the two pieces of metal from which it is made. Relief decoration on some black wares suggests the repoussé of metal technique and the lustrous surface seems to be imitating silver plate. The painted decoration also implies metal origins – on one M.M. II cup the delicate fluting on the original is reproduced in orange-red on a dark ground, and on another a design of arcading so clearly recalls the repoussé ornament on two gold cups from the Shaft Graves of Mycenae that Evans was encouraged to think that the latter 'may well have found an earlier resting place in the Cnossian Treasury'.[3] But despite the clear evidence for the existence of metal counterparts to the clay vases, the actual finds of M.M. vases in precious metal are extremely rare. Apart from the Gournia vase, all that survives in Crete are a few gold fragments of M.M. I/II from the Mesara which may have belonged to gold vases.[4]

Although they were not found in Crete, two other metal vessels, one of gold and one of silver, were perhaps made there during the Middle Minoan period. The first is a fragmentary silver bowl or cup from the tomb of Abi Chemou at Byblos which is obviously an Aegean import (fig. 6);[5] the tomb is contemporary with the M.M. II period in Crete. The vessel has an angular offset rim and the body is decorated with a design of linked spirals in repoussé. The tomb in which it was found contained other vessels of gold and silver including a silver 'teapot' with angular spout and fluted body which has also been thought of as Cretan.[6] Another larger version of the 'teapot' was found in the nearby

[1] Evans, *P of M*, I, 241 ff.

[2] L. Pernier, *Il Palazzo Minoico di Festos*, Rome, 1935, pls. XXVI, XXVII, XXX.

[3] See below p. 35.

[4] S. Xanthoudides, *The Vaulted Tombs of the Mesará*, Liverpool, 1924, 111.

[5] P. Montet, *Byblos et L'Egypte*, Paris, 1928, pls. CXI–CXII.

[6] F. Matz (*CAH* (Rev. Ed.), *Minoan Civilisation*, p. 23) thinks that the 'teapots' are Minoan and the bowl made 'at least under strong Minoan influence'.

tomb of Ip Chemou Abi. The contents of these tombs are in the Museum at Beirut. The second vessel is a small one-handled gold cup (pl. 2A) from the so-called Aegina Treasure in the British Museum;[1] its shape – a shallow bowl with a low foot and a concave offset rim – is

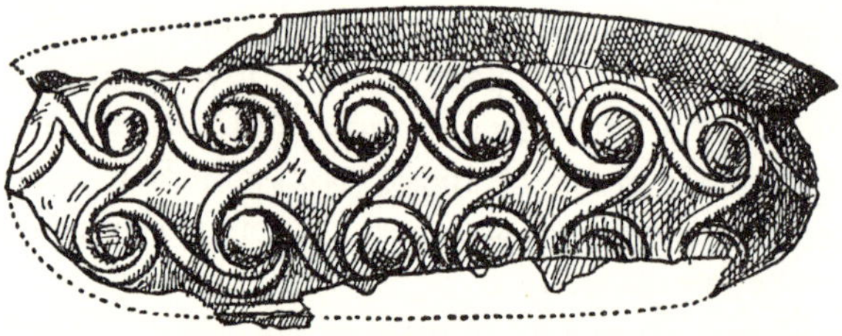

FIG. 6: Fragment of silver bowl from the Tomb of Abi Chemou, Byblos; Beirut Museum. Scale 1:2

difficult to parallel exactly but the decoration of spirals on the body and a rosette on the base, especially the latter, should be compared with M.M. II/III polychrome cups from Knossos and elsewhere.[2] The only metal vessel at all comparable is a cup with spiral ornament from the L.M. I find of silver in the South House at Knossos.[3] Higgins[4] has given reasons for thinking that all the objects in the Aegina Treasure were originally found in Crete and that they date from the M.M. III/L.M. I periods.

The Egyptian Treasure of Tod which is dated by the cartouche of Ammenemes II to *c.* 1929–1895 B.C. adds some problematic evidence to our knowledge of Aegean metalwork in the middle Bronze Age.[5] It contains at least two silver vases and the fragment of another which are closely related to Aegean examples (figs. 7*a–d*). A deep cup of globular body with an everted rim and a single strap handle is almost exactly paralleled by M.M. clay vessels from Phaestos (fig. 7*b*); another cup is somewhat like a *kantharos* of 'Minyan' shape (see below) with the same characteristic high handles but much less clear-cut profiles (fig. 7*a*). The Treasure also contained a cup with a handle of the so-called Vaphio type (fig. 7*d*). Kamares ware from Abydos provides a firm synchronism between the Egyptian Twelfth Dynasty and Middle Minoan II and it

[1] *BMCJ*, no. 768.
[2] cf. Evans, *P of M*, i, 241, pl. IIa.
[3] *ibid.* ii, 387.
[4] *BSA*, 52, 1957, p. 54.
[5] F. Chapouthier, *Le Trésor de Tod*, Cairo, 1953; F. Schachermeyr, *Die Minoische Kultur des alten Kreta*, Stuttgart, 1964.

has been suggested that the vessels found at Tod were made in Crete at that time. On the other hand the *kantharos* is generally thought of as a mainland rather than a Cretan form (see below p. 38) and all the vessels seem to lack the purity and precise detail of Cretan work.

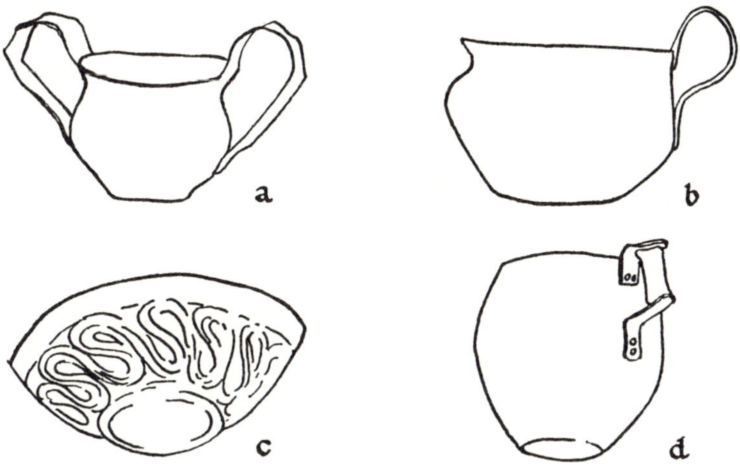

FIG. 7: (*a–d*) Silver cups from the Tod Treasure; Cairo Museum

Perhaps a more likely hypothesis is that the Tod vessels were made somewhere in the E. Mediterranean in imitation of imported Aegean vessels. Schachermeyr thinks they are of Anatolian origin.

4. THE GREEK MAINLAND: THE SHAFT GRAVES OF MYCENAE

With the rise of the Minoan palaces and Cretan control of maritime trade, the Cycladic culture which had flourished in the early Bronze Age went into decline. On the mainland, too, there was no wealth comparable with that of Middle Minoan Crete; instead, the stage was being set, though slowly, for the flowering of Mycenaean culture at the end of Middle Helladic and the beginning of the Late Helladic period. An event recognised to be of great significance in the development of prehistoric Greece is the appearance, at a date still uncertain, of the pottery known as Minyan, generally a grey ware of the Bucchero type. Whatever its place of origin and that of the people who used it, there is little doubt that many of the Minyan shapes imitate metal forms. The most characteristic in this respect are the two-handled cups and the tall, stemmed goblets; it has even been argued that the influence of the metal originals is carried to the colours and texture of Minyan. The clay is greasy to the touch with a fine natural lustre and it occurs in three colours – grey, red and yellow – which are said to suggest silver, copper and gold. This Minyan ware occurs over most of mainland Greece with its centre perhaps in Boeotia; the Argolid, Laconia and other areas had their own, to some extent, distinctive varieties. It is a curious fact that although Minyan is so clearly metal-inspired, no metal vessels contemporary with the earliest Minyan in Greece have, in fact, survived nor is there anything to suggest that Greece in Middle Helladic I and II was prosperous enough to possess them. Forsdyke[1] in tracing the development of the Minyan two-handled cup from Troy (see above p. 28) was inspired to argue that the 'Minyans' who may be identified as the ancestors of the Greeks entered Greece from Anatolia.[2] However this may be, the influence of Middle Helladic shapes is still very apparent in what is now considered to be the first flowering of a Greek civilisation, the age represented by the Royal Burials at Mycenae which belong to the late Middle Helladic and the beginning of Late Helladic.

The finds from the six Shaft Graves excavated by Schliemann (Grave Circle A)[3] and those more recently discovered (Grave Circle B)[4] form a most impressive collection of expensive plate testifying to the very considerable wealth of their owners. The chronology of the graves and the various burials in them is not established in detail, but of those which contain gold and silver vessels the earliest are Grave Nu and Iota of Circle B (Late M.H.) and Grave VI of Circle A belongs to the transition M.H./L.H. I; Graves II, III and V are all L.H. I and the latest, probably, is Grave I of Grave Circle A (L.H. I/II). Of these Graves IV, with 22 complete vases and fragments of many others, and V are incomparably the richest in gold and silver vessels but all the people buried in the other graves of Circle A possessed at least one vase of precious metal; the three women buried in Grave I each had two silver cups and in the wealthy Grave III, which contained five burials of women and children, the women had three or more vessels of precious metal while their

[1] *JHS*, xxxiv, 1914, 127 ff.

[2] On this see also *AJA*, 62, 1953, 95 ff.

[3] Schliemann, *Mycenae*; Karo, *Schachtgräber*.

[4] Mylonas, *Ancient Mycenae*.

children were buried with charming little miniature vases of gold. The contents of all the tombs are now in the National Museum at Athens.[1]

The commonest type of vessel found in the Shaft Graves is the drinking cup (fig. 8), but the finds also include ritual vessels of various

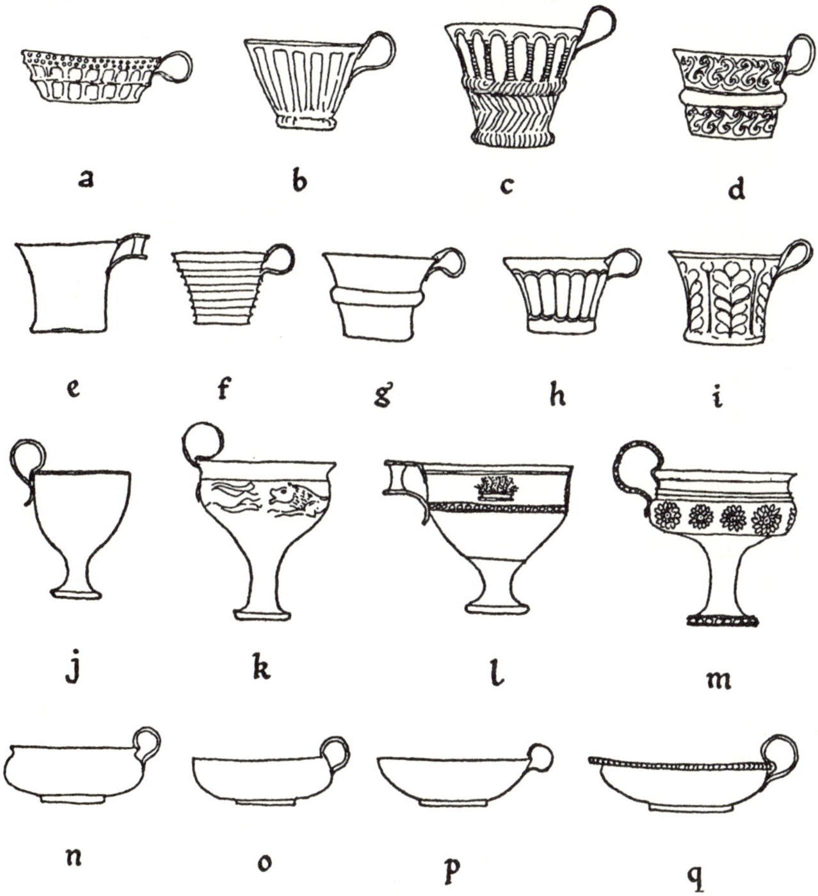

FIG. 8: Shapes of gold and silver drinking vessels from Shaft Graves, Mycenae

kinds, toilet vessels, jugs and a number of unusual and exotic shapes. The gold vessels are usually worked very thin (so thin indeed, that a purely funerary purpose has been argued for some of them); the silver vases are usually much more robust. While the gold is well-preserved,

[1] The numbers given in the text are National Museum numbers.

much of the Shaft Grave silver is in poor condition; one of the few well-preserved examples is the goblet (no. 390) with inlaid decoration from Grave IV (pl. 3B) made of an alloy containing a higher proportion of gold which has prevented the deterioration suffered by the pure silver pieces. The goldsmiths and silversmiths were masters of many techniques of manufacturing and decorating plate – inlaying, repoussé, overlaying, appliqué – which are discussed below in the description of the vessels that have been found.

CUPS

The oldest of the Shaft Graves, Grave Nu of Grave Circle B contains the earliest example of one of the three main types of drinking cup found at Mycenae (fig. 8). The little gold cup (fig. 8*a*)[1] is an unusually shallow and wide version of the flat-bottomed beaker which commonly occurs in gold and silver in the Shaft Graves. The decoration consists of two bands of fluting concave on the outside, separated by a horizontal ridge; there is a double row of punched dots just below the rim and punched ornament of lines and dots on the bottom. This kind of cup can be traced back to the E.M. III period in Crete and is popular in the M.M. periods. The shallow form of the example from Grave Nu and the division of the decoration into two zones is closely paralleled by a bronze cup of M.M. III date from Mochlos.[2] The handle of the Shaft Grave cup is of loop type, made of sheet metal bent under at the edges to form a rim; this type of handle is more common at Mycenae than the Vaphio[3] type which consists of a tubular upright between two horizontal plates riveted to the body of the vessel, though the latter does occur both on these cups (e.g. fig. 8*e*) and on other vessels. No. 8621 (fig. 8*b*) is a more normal form of this kind of cup in silver, found in another early grave, grave Iota, of Grave Circle B.[4] The body is decorated with vertical ribbing with a narrow roll moulding at the bottom; the proportions are much nearer those of the standard Vaphio form. The handle is of the loop type and the rim is overlaid with gold leaf. Grave Gamma contained a similar vessel in gold with broader concave fluting on the body and one with two zones of fluting separated

[1] Mylonas, *Ancient Mycenae*, fig. 69.
[2] Seager, *Mochlos*, 62, pl. XIIf.
[3] This handle takes its name from the examples found in the Tholos at Vaphio (see p. 46).
[4] Mylonas, *Ancient Mycenae*, fig. 71.

by a horizontal roll moulding and with another roll moulding at the bottom.

The L.H. I graves in Grave Circle A all contained examples of this type of cup, the most popular form having a roll moulding which divides the body into two zones; the moulding is generally decorated with cable ornament and the two zones with repoussé. A design of arcading appears on several cups, for example no. 628 from Shaft Grave V (fig. 8*c*). A gold cup (no. 73) from Grave III has dolphins engraved above and below the central moulding; one from Grave V (no. 629) has repoussé linked spirals as ornament (fig. 8*d* and pl. 3A). Plain silver cups of orthodox form with the Vaphio handles (e.g. fig. 8*e*) occurred in a number of graves (e.g. nos. 755, 630 and 866 in Grave V). A pair of exquisite gold cups with loop handles, decorated with close-set horizontal fluting (no. 392 and 393) were found in Grave IV (fig. 8*f*).

The second type of drinking vessel is the stemmed and footed goblet (fig. 8*j*–*m*) of which a number of variants were found in Graves IV and V. The simplest version is the cup of rather heavy gold from Grave IV with a thick stem, wide foot and hemispherical bowl (no. 427); it was raised from a single sheet of metal and fitted with a disc of metal to close the stem. Among the more elaborate variants on the form are the gold cup from Grave V with a narrow concave section below the rim and repoussé decoration showing hunting scenes on the body (no. 656); the electrum cup (no. 390) from Grave IV (pl. 3B) with a rather wider concave zone decorated with inlaid ornament of gold and niello (see below) and a Vaphio-type handle (fig. 8*e*); and a gold cup from the same tomb with a series of angular mouldings dividing the concave from the convex section of the bowl, and decorated with repoussé rosettes on the convex section (no. 351) (fig. 8*m*).

The third type of drinking cup is a shallow bowl-shaped vessel standing on a low base ring (fig. 8*n*–*q*) and equipped with a single loop-handle which may either be made in one piece with the cup or made separately and riveted on. This, too, has a number of variants; an example (no. 509) from Grave IV has an everted rim and a high loop handle (fig. 8*n*); another from Grave I (no. 213), which is probably one of the latest vessels, has convex sides in a continuous curve (fig. 8*p*). A third variant (no. 212, fragments only), also from Grave I, has a broad horizontal rim overlaid with repoussé gold (fig. 8*q*). This last example belongs to a type which continued to be popular, especially in metal, during later Mycenaean times.

A fourth type of drinking vessel which must also have been popular during the period is represented by only one example from the Shaft Graves; this is the so-called Minyan *kantharos* of gold (no. 440) from Grave IV (fig. 9). The cup is a two-handled vessel with a double profile,

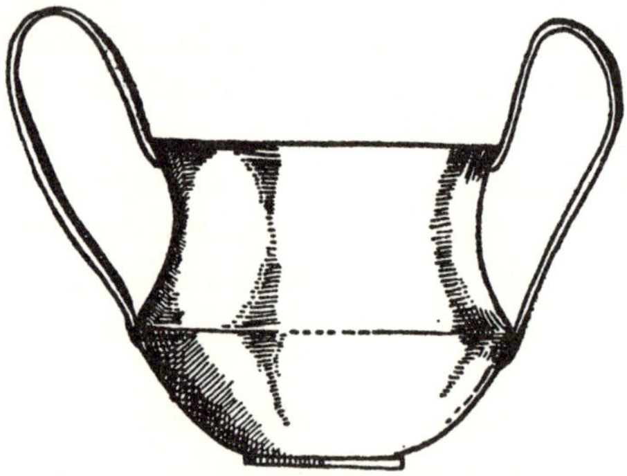

FIG. 9: Gold *kantharos* from Shaft Grave IV, Mycenae; Athens, National Museum. Scale 1:3

concave above and convex below, narrowing to a broad and slightly offset base ring. Although only one of these vessels was found at Mycenae other examples are known and the shape is M.H. in origin, occurring as early as M.H. I/II. Another fine example in gold, now in the National Museum at Athens (no. 2381) was found at Kalamai in the Peloponnese together with gold ingots and two very battered smaller vessels probably of the same form.[1] An interesting detail of the large cup is the presence of double spirals forming terminals to the handles where they are riveted to the body. There is another, much smaller, example of the same type of cup in the Metropolitan Museum which has the handles decorated with repoussé leaf patterns (pl. 2B).[2]

The golden stemmed goblet (no. 412) from the Grave IV (fig. 10) does not fall into any of the main types of drinking vessel in the Shaft Graves; Schliemann christened it Nestor's Cup from its similarity to the vessel described by Homer.[3] It consists of a straight-sided cup on a tall tubular stem with a pair of handles of the Vaphio type joined to the foot

[1] *BSA*, 52, 1957, 239–40; *AJA*, xlii, 1938, 308.

[2] Richter, *Greek Collection*, 16, pl. 11h.

[3] Schliemann, *Mycenae and Tiryns*, 235–7.

by openwork supports of sheet metal; on the flat top of each handle a little bird is perched. In Homer's account of Nestor's cup the birds on the handles were doves; these have been identified as falcons. The goblet is made of thin gold and was perhaps, like other vessels at Mycenae, intended only for libations; it is argued that the cup was originally taller and handle-less, but was subsequently cut down and

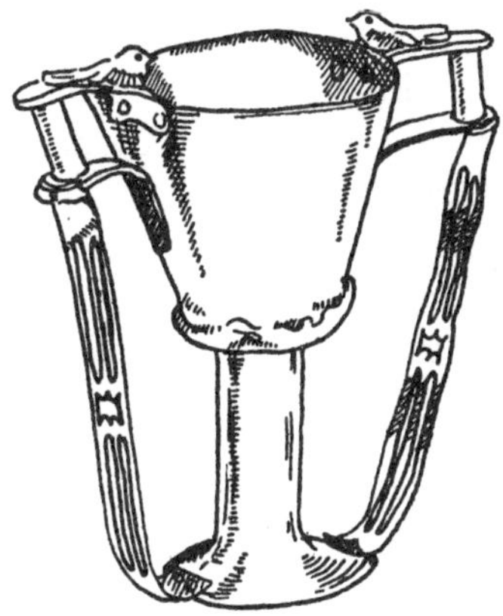

FIG. 10: Gold goblet ('Nestor's cup') from Mycenae; Athens National Museum. Scale 1:3

given two handles with the curious openwork supports. In its original form it would have looked like a kind of goblet that seems to have been of Cretan origin.[1] There is a related vessel in the Musée du Cinquantenaire, Brussels[2] which consists of a hemispherical bowl decorated with repoussé relief showing lions attacking a stag and standing on a tall columnar stem very similar to that of 'Nestor's cup'.

LARGER VESSELS

A number of large vessels of silver found in the Shaft Graves are connected with the service of liquids. The best preserved is the jug from Grave V (no. 855) (pl. 4) which is 34·5 cms. high; the body narrows downwards to the foot ring, the shoulder curves sharply to a narrow neck with rounded mouth. The handle tapers downwards and is riveted to the neck and shoulder. The body of the jug was raised from a single

[1] *AM*, 40, 1915, 45; *Festschrift Schweitzer*, 11–18.

[2] H. T. Bossert, *Geschichte des Kunstgewerbes*, Berlin, 1928, pl. XXI, 5.

sheet, the neck was made separately and riveted to the body with a roll moulding serving to conceal the joint between the two. The vessel is richly decorated with repoussé ornament; on the shoulder is a spiral pattern and immediately below it a design of arcading. The rest of the body is decorated with close-set horizontal fluting. The handle, of heavy silver, is grooved along its length and edged with beading. Another interesting piece is the silver bucket, 75 cm. high, which has been restored from fragments (no. 909a). In form it is not unlike a stemmed goblet and the bucket handle of thick wire is attached to loops riveted on either side of the rim. There are many fragments of other large vases including a group from a large, probably amphora-like, vessel with a diameter at the neck of 40·5 cm.; it was richly decorated with repoussé reliefs showing battle scenes. A large silver lid (no. 608) comes from a vessel similar in form to the little 'toilet vessel' no. 391.

RITUAL VESSELS

The vessels which served purely ritual purposes included two outstanding pieces: a gold rhyton in the form of a lion's head and a silver rhyton in the form of a bull's head (no. 384 from Grave IV). The latter (pl. 6B) was apparently worked from a single sheet of silver, the horns are of gold sheet and the ears of bronze plated with gold and silver. The liquid was poured in through a hole between the horns and ran out through a hole in the mouth. A plate, now missing, closed the back of the head. The lion's head rhyton is similar in form but much more stylised in the rendering of the animal head. In Grave IV were found fragments of another ritual vase of a typical Minoan form. The vessel (no. 481) was a conical rhyton decorated with repoussé reliefs showing soldiers attacking a fortified place by the sea.[1] Another remarkable vessel is a little vase in the form of a stag also from Grave IV (no. 388) with a necked opening on its back. The vase, which is reported to be made from an alloy of two-thirds silver and one-third lead, is generally believed to be an import from Anatolia and may be compared with clay vessels from Kültepe and other places in Cappadocia.[2] It, too, probably served a ritual use.

[1] *AE*, 1891, 11; *A Delt*, 1926, 78 ff. Fragments of a big vase with battle scenes were found in the same grave (nos. 605–7).

[2] *AA*, 1923–4, 106; Tuchelt, *Tiergefässe*, 17 ff.

'TOILET VESSELS'

In the Shaft Graves, especially in Graves III and IV, were found a number of miniature vessels, mostly of gold, which are too small to have served as table vessels. They have been thought of as the possessions of children but served more probably as containers for ointments, scents, oil etc.; they come generically under the head of 'toilet vessels'. These miniature vessels include a high-spouted jug with repoussé spirals on the body (no. 74 from Grave III), a cylindrical pyxis with a flat lid (Grave III, no. 72) and various kinds of little globular pots with lids (e.g. nos. 83, 84 of Grave III). The little gold spouted jug is related to a larger one of silver from Grave IV (no. 511) and another from Grave Alpha of Grave Circle B. Among the 'toilet vessels' may also be included the reconstructed six-sided wooden box overlaid with repoussé and chased reliefs with ornamental and figured designs (nos. 808-811) from Grave V (fig. 11).

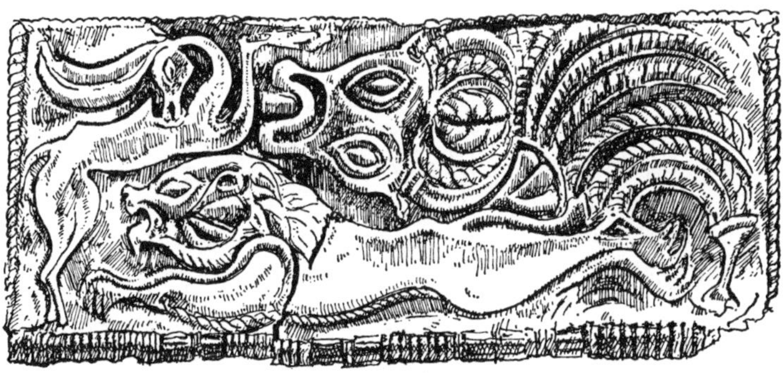

a

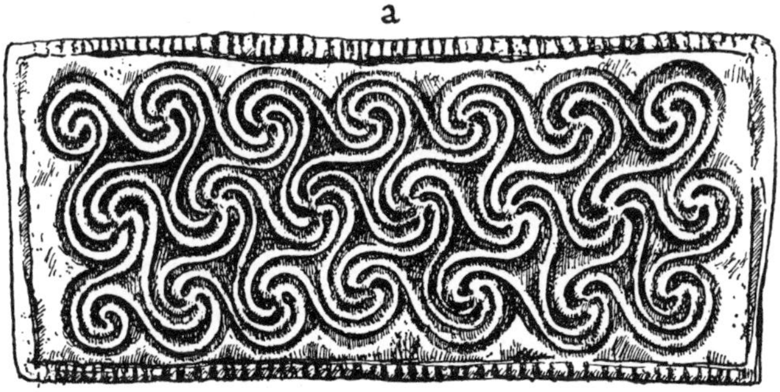

b

FIG. 11: Gold repoussé overlays from a wooden box; Shaft Grave V, Mycenae

TECHNIQUES

The craftsmen who made the gold and silver vessels found in the Shaft Graves were extremely skilled in the art of 'raising' metal. The deep goblets were generally hammered up from single sheets of metal making use of wooden cores to form the feet and stems. The gold goblet no. 351 from Shaft Grave IV was made in this way and the foot also contains a copper plate to give it solidity. If a shape had to be made of more than one piece of metal, as in the case of the electrum goblet (no. 390), the separate parts were generally riveted together and the joint skilfully masked in some way. Solder was known but seems to have been distrusted for vessels. The metal is generally folded over or hammered down to form the rims and the handles are fixed on by rivets; occasionally the handle is made of a tongue of metal in one piece with the cup, bent over to form a loop and sometimes riveted to the body, as on cup no. 519 from Grave IV. The relief decoration was carried out by repoussé and chasing; repetitive patterns like the rosettes on the gold vase no. 351 may have been made with the aid of stamps, or by hammering and chasing over a die. The decorated gold overlays on the handles and rims of silver vessels were probably made on the fairly thick foil in the same way. The foil was often laid over bronze sheet or wire and not directly on the silver and Schliemann in discussing the technique of the overlay on the silver bull-rhyton thought that 'the Mycenaean goldsmith evidently did not understand the art of plating silver with gold for whenever he had to do it he first plated the silver with copper and then plated the copper with gold'.[1] This same technique is believed to have been found on a large number of other Mycenaean vessels.[2] In the case of the electrum vase from the Grave IV, Schliemann thought that the whole vessel had been plated with copper and then with gold but, in fact any copper incrustation must have been derived from associated objects or from the copper content in the alloy. When cleaned there was no trace of bronze overlay. The use of bronze plate and wire as intermediaries was probably intended to give a greater appearance of solidity (cf. below p. 51).

Inlaying of one metal into another, as is evidenced by the magnificent scenes inlaid on bronze daggers from the Shaft Graves, was very

[1] Schliemann, *Mycenae and Tiryns*, 218.

[2] Persson, *New Tombs*, 49.

skilfully carried out. The only vessel decorated in this technique is the electrum goblet from the Grave IV (pl. 3B), where the inlay seems to be a combination of gold and a black substance which has been generally identified as niello. If we accept this identification and the technique of inlaying as established by Plenderleith for the cup from Enkomi described below (p. 51) strips were cut out of the silver at the top and bottom of the concave part of the bowl, the niello was put in the recesses in powder form, and the gold bands and discs set into it. When the niello was gently heated it became plastic and acted as an adhesive for the gold. Flower pots with dittany plants growing in them were cut out of gold sheet and similarly inlaid into prepared recesses. This technique of inlaying, of which the Shaft Graves provide the earliest examples continued to be popular in later Mycenaean times.

ORIGINS AND STYLE

It is now generally believed that in the sixteenth century, to which most of the Shaft Graves belong, Mainland Greece and Crete were both rich and independent. The close artistic affinities of the Shaft Grave gold and silver with the art of Crete, although it is no longer used as an argument for the dependence of the one place upon the other, still demands clarification and explanation. Although there are no finds of comparable richness from M.M. III/L.M. I tombs in Crete, the influence of Crete on the shapes, techniques and decoration of the Shaft Grave vessels is certain. Some pieces, such as the conical rhyton, are pure Minoan luxury or ritual vases; in Cretan paintings these rhytons are shown being offered to a female person, probably a goddess, and carried in a ritual procession. The two animal head rhytons from Shaft Grave IV, are also Minoan ritual vessels and may well have been imported from Crete or, at least, made by Cretan craftsmen. The Vaphio cup form and the details of the decoration on several Shaft Grave examples may be traced back to the M.M. IIA period in Crete.

On the other hand, some of the shapes of vessel found in the Shaft Graves seem to be uninfluenced by Cretan metalwork; the so-called Minyan *kantharos* is the best example of this. But while the stemmed cup is basically a Helladic, not a Minoan shape some of the Shaft Grave goblets seem to be strongly influenced by unstemmed Minoan forms,[1]

[1] On this Furumark, *Analysis*, 56–7.

and a little later both the stemmed goblets and the shallow one-handled cups are found in Crete in forms indistinguishable from those of the mainland. Moreover, of the stemmed vessels the most unusual, Nestor's cup, may be confidently claimed as Minoan; it is closely related to the type of stemmed chalice of which examples in alabaster and other materials have been found in Crete. A similar vessel is shown in the hand of a figure on the so-called Camp Stool fresco at Knossos.[1] As with the shapes, so with the decoration the influence of Crete is paramount. The arcading, horizontal fluting and other ornamental motifs on the Vaphio-type cups seem certainly of Cretan derivation; so are the spirals and arcading on the big jug (no. 855) (pl. 4) or the dolphin friezes on the cup (no. 73) from Grave III.

Although it is rash to speculate too far, it is possible that some of the gold and silver vessels from the Shaft Graves are Cretan of a date as early as M.M. II/III and the lords of Mycenae may have obtained them as the spoils of war or, more probably, as a result of legitimate trade with the island. Other pieces which have mainland elements in their form and decoration could be the work of artists trained in Cretan workshops and some of the techniques, such as inlaying with niello and metals which originated in the east and have not so far been found in Crete, may have been developed by artists on the mainland. Many problems of this kind are raised and left unanswered by the contents of the Shaft Graves largely because of the great poverty of actual finds made in Crete.

5. CRETE, LATE MINOAN

Although no wealthy tombs of L.M. date have so far been discovered a few chance finds made on the island tend to confirm the conclusion that the vases of precious metal found in the Shaft Graves of Mycenae also represent the metalwork of contemporary Crete. Evans who compared a silver jug from Shaft Grave V (pl. 4) with a bronze example found in the N.W. Treasure House at Knossos supposed that both were made in the same atelier at Knossos of M.M. IIIB or L.M. IA[2] and it is particularly interesting that a similar scheme of decoration – a band of double running spirals above an arcade – occurs on a shallow cup of

[1] Evans, *P of M*, iv, Colour Plate XXXI.

[2] Evans, *SG*, 26 ff., for these jugs see now Catling, *Cypriot Bronzework*.

pale gold found in a grave of L.M. I A or B date at Ayios Ioannis near Knossos (Heraklion Mus. no. 758).[1] This cup has a single handle in the form of a tail of gold bent over from the rim and not apparently fixed to the body below.[2] A fragmentary one-handled silver cup, badly squashed out of shape, was found recently in an L.M. IB context at Zakro. The cup was made of fairly heavy silver and decorated with strips of gold overlay with punched dots; the base ring was overlaid with plain gold sheet. A find of silver vessels of L.M. I date from the South House at Knossos (Heraklion Mus. nos. 401–5)[3] includes a jug, a bowl decorated with repoussé spirals, and three plain cups or bowls. Stemmed goblets have also been found in Crete; a fragmentary example of silver was found in the Royal Tomb at Isopata (L.M. II)[4] and, recently, fragments of a more elaborately decorated cup of silver and gold were discovered in a tomb at Knossos (L.M. II/III).[5] In the latter most of the bowl was missing; the rim was overlaid with milled gold and the strap handle had a gold rib of cable pattern with a band of gold at the base. A few other Minoan silver vessels (L.M. I?) were found in tombs near the Harbour Town of Knossos and are referred to but not described by Evans.[6]

Two indirect sources of information widen our knowledge of late Bronze Age metalwork in Greece and Crete: the representations of Aegean vessels that appear on paintings of the New Kingdom in Egypt and the ideograms and descriptions of plate on Linear B tablets from Knossos, Pylos and elsewhere. Emissaries of the land of Keftiu are shown on a series of Theban tombs ranging in date from the late sixteenth to the middle of the fifteenth century B.C. The earliest is the tomb of Senmut, vizier of Hatshepsut; later in the series are the tombs of Useramon, Rekhmire and Menkeperrasoneb.[7] In all these paintings the bearers carry some vases, obviously made of precious metals, which may be recognised as deriving from the Aegean world; Senmut has Vaphio-type cups apparently with inlaid ornament, a jug and a pithos with shield and rosette ornament; Useramon has two animal

[1] *BSA*, 51, 1956, 81 ff.

[2] cf. the cup on a tablet from Pylos (M. Ventris and J. Chadwick, *Documents in Mycenaean Greek*, 338, no. 238).

[3] Evans, *P of M*, ii, 387.

[4] Evans, *PTK*, 155, fig. 139.

[5] *BSA*, 51, 1956, 73, fig. 3, pl. 8a.

[6] Evans, *P of M*, ii, 235; cf. *BSA*, 51, 1956, 81 ff.

[7] Evans, *P of M*, i, 667; ii (vol. ii), 655–8; Kantor, *Aegean and Orient*, 41 ff.

rhytons; Rekhmire rhytons, including the conical variety, and an ingot in the form of a hide; Menkeperrasoneb has a bull's head rhyton and a Vaphio cup. The tomb of Senmut gives the most accurate versions of Aegean offerings; all the other paintings seem to show some non-Aegean offerings in the hands of the Keftiu. The Keftiu must come from the Aegean area,[1] though whether from Crete or Greece cannot be determined[2] with certainty.

The evidence of the tablets from Knossos and Pylos also throws some interesting light on contemporary metal-work. The word for gold is *kuoro-so* and silver is *a-ku-ro*. Knossos 229, a fragmentary tablet, seems to refer to a ladle and jug with raised rim round the neck; another refers to bull's head rhytons gilded (?) on the horns and three silver cups of Vaphio-type with the rim of gold. In the Cretan and mainland tablets the same kind of vessels, most of which are represented in actual finds from the mainland and Crete, occur as ideograms. The inventories of metalware do not normally record where the pieces were made but in Pylos 236 the words 'ke-re-si-jo we-ke' applied to a tripod cauldron have been interpreted as meaning 'of Cretan workmanship'.[3]

6. LATER MYCENAEAN

Two of the most famous of surviving Mycenaean vessels of precious metal were found in a tholos tomb at Vaphio in Laconia dating to the L.H. II period (1500–1450 B.C.).[4] The two gold cups (N.M. nos 1758 and 1759) which give the name to the so-called Vaphio form are decorated with repoussé scenes of bull-hunting depicted in vigorous and life-like detail. Each cup consists of a decorated outer case and a plain lining; the lining was bent over at the top to form the rim and, at the same time, an edge to the figure scene. The decoration of the straight walls of this type of cup with figured scenes seems to be a development that took place later than the Shaft Graves. The scenes are combined into a single composition on each cup. On the first we see a bull attacking the hunters, then a bull caught in a net and again a bull in flight (pl. 5A); on the second cup a bull is shown being tethered by one

[1] A different view is taken by G. A. Wainwright, *JHS*, 51, 1931, 1–38.

[2] Kantor, *Aegean and Orient*, 48.

[3] Ventris and Chadwick, 323 ff.

[4] *AE*, 1889, 153; good illustrations in Marinatos and Hirmer, pls. 178–85.

of the hunters while a second bull appears in the company of a decoy-cow. Another bull, head down, is coming cautiously upon the scene. The poses and actions of the figures are conveyed with remarkable realism.

The Vaphio tholos also contained a number of other interesting objects of precious metal including a shallow silver cup (N.M. no. 1875) with single loop handle and a horizontal rim overworked with decorated gold sheet and a gold-plated handle; the overlay on the handle and rim are both decorated with 'whorl-shell' motif. This type of cup (see fig. 8*q*) occurs in Grave I of Grave Circle A at Mycenae which is the latest of all the Shaft Graves, and it seems to have been particularly popular in the later Mycenaean contexts. There were also two cups (N.M. nos. 1887–8) of the standard Vaphio form (i.e. with slightly concave sides narrowing to a flat base and tubular handle between horizontal plates) made of heavy silver and decorated with three zones of close-set parallel lines, a silver ladle (N.M. no. 1876), and a little spatula or flat spoon (N.M. no. 1877). The end of the spatula is leaf-shaped and decorated; presumably it is not an eating implement, but it may be compared in some ways with the spoon with a flat 'bowl', also decorated with repoussé from Chamber Tomb no. 10 at Dendra (see below p. 49). Both are probably 'toilet' implements of some kind. These two examples seem to be the only surviving 'spoons' of Mycenaean times since the examples from Cyprus referred to by Persson[1] are presumably Phoenician, archaic Greek or later. A series of little 'ear-spoons' which are apparently toilet implements has been found in Late Helladic contexts; there is a little scoop at one end and the opposite end is formed into a little coil. There are four silver examples from Prosymna and one of gold from Mycenae.[2] The little silver ladle from the Vaphio tholos has a round bowl and the end of the stem bent over to form a hook. It seems to be unique in Mycenaean times but the type of ladle of which this is the earliest example in the classical world has a long later history with hardly any change in its basic form down to Roman times.

The finds from tombs at Dendra not far from the citadel of Mideia in the Argolid belong in the main to the period around 1400 B.C. and they include some of the finest examples of Mycenaean gold and silver

[1] Persson, *New Tombs*, 90.

[2] C. W. Blegen, *Prosymna*, Cambridge, 1937, 272, figs 146, 487, 543; C. Tsountas and J. I. Manatt, *The Mycenean Age*, London, 1897, 187.

plate that have been found so far.[1] In the Tholos Tomb (dated L.H. IIB/IIIA) there were two main burials identified as those of a Lord of Mideia and his wife. The outstanding piece among the burial gifts of the king was the gold 'octopus cup' (N.M. no. 7341); the shape of this vessel is a developed form of a type found in the Shaft Graves and in Crete – a shallow cup with a single handle, convex body and concave flaring rim (pl. 5B). The Dendra example was beaten up from a single sheet of gold and decorated in repoussé. The rim was formed by overlaying gold sheet with ribbed decoration and the handle, which is of rather thicker sheet gold, was riveted on from the inside by means of gold studs. The reliefs on the cup depict the bottom of the sea peopled by octopus and other marine creatures. Persson, the excavator, was convinced – as others have been convinced in the case of the Vaphio cups – that this octopus cup must be Minoan work of about 1500, in this case obtained as loot by the Lord of Mideia around 1400 (in the supposed sack of the Cretan palaces) but others have preferred to think of it as a mainland product made about the period it was buried.[2] Persson speaks of it as being of pure gold with a reddish patina and he thinks that the reliefs were 'chased over an embossed model'. The handle was fixed below with a plate in the form of a lotus and this he compared with a similar handle in silver found in the Royal Tomb at Isopata and on the gold cup from Tomb 10 at Dendra, mentioned below. The king's burial also contained a cup, very fragmentary, of Vaphio type (M.N. no. 7340) with figures of bulls in repoussé relief on the outside. The cup consists of a case of heavy silver with an inner lining of sheet gold. A silver stemmed goblet with hunting scenes in relief (N.M. 7339) which is most closely related in form to Nestor's Cup, but lacks the incidental details, has been compared with alabaster vases from the fourth and fifth Shaft Graves and the shape seems to be Cretan. The burial gifts of the Queen included a magnificent silver cup decorated with bulls' heads inlaid with gold and 'niello' (N.M. no. 7336), one of a number of fine examples of this technique on silver plate in later Mycenaean times. The cup has an inner lining of sheet gold and a single handle of the 'wishbone' form that was popular among silversmiths in the Argolid and Cyprus during the period 1450–1350 B.C. (see also below p. 51).

[1] Persson, *Royal Tombs* and *New Tombs*.

[2] Kantor, *Aegean and Orient*, 94.

In a second series of Chamber tombs found later at Dendra a number of vessels in precious metal were found. Tomb no. 10 of L.H. II/III date contained, in Shaft I, a shallow one-handled gold cup of exquisite workmanship which has the same basic shape as the octopus cup but the rim is worked in a series of eight lobes or scallops and overlaid with ribbed gold sheet. The cup was beaten up from pure gold sheet and the base ring was probably worked over a wooden disc. The concave upper part of the cup is plain; on the convex part is a continuous pattern of sacral ivy in repoussé relief between convex bands with vertical ribbing. The loop handle of the cup, made of rather thicker metal tapers downwards and ends with a riveting plate in the form of a papyrus capital; a central rib runs down the handle and its edges are also ribbed. A cup of basically similar shape and decoration, but without the scalloped rim, was found in another of the Chamber Tombs, no. 2, which is dated L.H. III B.

In Shaft II of Chamber Tomb no. 10 there were six silver vessels; the largest was a silver crater or goblet with two loop handles, a spreading foot and a flaring rim; its handles were attached by rivets and the foot had a bronze plate to steady it. There was also a pair of one-handled stemmed goblets very similar in shape to the first piece but squatter. The most remarkable piece was a stemmed goblet with high loop handle and the body decorated with repoussé reliefs; the handle is inlaid with 'niello' and the decorated zone on the body consists of a series of curious leaf-shaped medallions each containing a flying waterfowl against a background of waves. There was also a shallow cup with a broad flat rim decorated with repoussé gold overlay with 'whorl-shell' motif, very like the example from the Vaphio tholos; it has been compared to a fragmentary piece from Berbati (unpublished). The silver spoon from this tomb has already been mentioned; the bowl is rather flat and decorated with repoussé 'whorl-shell', a very attractive piece. In the same shaft as these silver objects there was also found a set of clay vases which are direct counterparts of the silver ones. 'One might simply speak of one set for festive occasions,' says Persson, 'one for everyday use." They illustrate very clearly the close connections between clay and metal drinking vessels in later Mycenaean times; generally the clay copy the silver but, as Furumark has shown, the inventions of the potter are not always secondary to those of the metalworker.

From Mycenae itself there have been a number of important finds of metal plate later than the Shaft Graves. A set of four gold stemmed goblets was discovered by Schliemann's engineer in a deposit against the south retaining wall of the Grave Circle (N.M. nos. 957–60).[1] Three of them were very fragmentary but all seem to have been identical in form; the stem and foot is made separately from the body and the two parts were riveted together. The handles are hollow tubes ending in dog's heads biting on the rim of the cup (pl. 7A). According to Furumark who thinks that the shape is influenced by clay forms of L.H. IIIA I they date around 1400 B.C. One of the finest examples of the Mycenaean technique of inlaying in silver is a shallow cup (N.M. no. 2489) found in 1886–7 in a chamber tomb on the citadel with a frieze of bearded heads in gold and niello between two bands of leaf ornament (pl. 6A); the handle is also decorated with inlaid leaf ornament and is riveted to the body by means of three rivets passing through a broad plate above it.[2] Some detached bearded heads presumably from a similar cup were found recently at Pylos in the western Peloponnese[3] and a number of other fragments of inlay from vessels of this kind have been found at Mycenae, including one from the House of Lead with the wing of a griffin or sphinx of gold sheet inlaid in silver, apparently without any accompanying niello,[4] and a Vaphio handle with inlaid rosettes (N.M. no. 7639).

Another fine piece of silver from Mycenae is a bowl or cup found in another Chamber tomb, no. 78, of the citadel area in 1892–9. The bowl was 'raised' from a single sheet and has a flaring rim; the body is decorated with a design of arched network, a popular motif throughout the late Helladic period. A curious feature of the profile is the triple step moulding which is very closely paralleled on the gold stemmed goblet (N.M. no. 351) from Shaft Grave IV. Another chance find from Mycenae is a shallow cup of rather angular profile with a single handle and the horizontal rim characteristic of later Mycenaean contexts.

Later Mycenaean finds of metal plate in other parts of Greece are very rare. A shallow one-handled gold cup from Salamis in the National Museum at Athens (N.M. no. 6441) is made of thick metal with the handle made in one piece with the cup bent over to form a loop and

[1] Schliemann, *Mycenae and Tiryns*, 350 ff.; *BSA*, 39, 1938–9, 65–87.

[2] *AE*, 1888, 159; Becatti, *Oreficerie*, pl. IX, 16a and b.

[3] Marinatos and Hirmer, pl. 204.

[4] *BSA*, 51, 1956, 121, pl. 28.

apparently not fixed to the body of the vessel below. The shape of the cup differs hardly at all from that of a cup found in Shaft Grave I at Mycenae though the context in this case is late Mycenaean. A similar plain gold cup from a Tholos Tomb at Marathon dates to L.H. IIIA.[1] A gold stemmed one-handled goblet in the British Museum[2] is very close in shape to the vessels from Shaft II of Grave 10 at Dendra. The foot is weighted down with a copper or bronze disc and the handle which is riveted on to the body is decorated with a milled edge and grooves made by a burnishing tool down its length. A silver cup decorated with repoussé figure-of-eight shields was found recently at Pharai in Achaea in an L.H. IIIB context.[3]

7. CYPRUS

The Mycenaean settlement of Enkomi-Alasia in Cyprus has produced one of the finest examples of inlaid silver plate of this period – a shallow footless bowl decorated with a series of frontal bull's heads on the body and a flower design round the base, all carried out in gold and niello inlaid into the silver (pl. 7B).[4] The context in which the cup was found is dated to the early fourteenth century B.C., not much later than the date of the Queen's cup from Dendra to which in many respects it is similar. When found the decoration was completely concealed under a green corrosion which had leached out from the copper alloyed to the silver. The vessel was cleaned and submitted to a technical examination by the Research Laboratory of the British Museum. The silversmith's procedure seems to have been as follows: shallow beds were chiselled out of the metal to receive the inlay, these were then filled with a black powder of niello type and 'cut-outs' of gold foil were laid on them. When heated the 'niello' melted and acted as an adhesive for the gold: the surplus niello was then rubbed away. Of the facts revealed in this examination, the form and composition of the substance called niello remains uncertain and even its original colour has been questioned. The Enkomi cup argues the presence of highly skilled Mycenaean silversmiths on the island; the shape of the vessel – a shallow footless bowl (the so-called 'Milk Bowl') – seems to be Cypriot though the wishbone

[1] *PAE*, 1933, 35 f. and 1934, 29 f.
[2] *BMCJ*, no. 820.
[3] *PAE*, 1956, pl. 8.
[4] Schaeffer, *Enkomi-Alasia*, i, 379 ff.

handle is also found on mainland vessels, for example the Dendra cup mentioned above (p. 48). Another example of the same shape in silver comes from earlier excavations at Enkomi and is now in the British Museum;[1] it was raised from sheet metal, the marks of the hammer being very clearly seen on the inside, and the rim, which was thickened up by hammering, is decorated with punched circles. Another silver vessel from tomb 66 at Enkomi in the British Museum may or may not be a local product; it is a Vaphio cup of plain form with horizontal bands of engraved lines round the body.[2] Its shape and decoration are identical with a cup found in the Vaphio tholos itself.[3]

CONCLUSIONS

The history of the art of the silversmith during the Aegean Bronze Age shows a mastery of almost all the basic skills used in the production of gold and silver plate. In the early Bronze Age, vessels of precious metal were already being raised from sheet metal and decorated with repoussé or chasing. Riveting was used for attaching various parts of the vessels. During Middle Minoan times in Crete, repoussé ornament of elaborate kind, the overlaying of one metal on another and perhaps inlaying were practised and it seems fairly certain that the achievements of Cretan craftsmen are represented by the finds from the Shaft Graves at Mycenae. Only casting and spinning among the principal techniques generally used in making plate were still unknown, and soldering, though it occurs in jewellery[4] was obviously distrusted by the makers of metal vessels.

Throughout the Bronze Age nearly all gold and silver vessels were connected with the service of liquids, especially cups, jugs, bowls; the only other large class of vessels in use at the time of the Shaft Graves are the toilet vessels and there were also a few small implements for various purposes. Gold and silver were the possession of the very wealthy or of the shrines of the gods, and as tokens of great luxury they played an important role in the diplomacy and trade of the Bronze Age Mediter-

[1] Registration 1897, 4–1,300. [2] *BMCJ*, no. 821.

[3] Catling (*Cypriot Bronzework*, 46) believes that all three of these silver vessels from Cyprus are imports.

[4] Higgins, *Jewellery*, chap. 9.

ranean. The rarity of precious metal vessels, no doubt, explains the slow development of metal forms and the long survival of certain traditional shapes like the 'Vaphio cup'. Only very few craftsmen, in the employ of the lords of the cities, can have been engaged in making plate and, indeed, after about 1400 B.C. gold and silver vessels were probably very rare. Although there are references in the Linear B tablets to luxury plate stored in the palaces and to rich dedications to the gods, as for example in Pylos *Tn* 316, the finds of precious metalwork of the period after 1400 B.C. have been very few.

POST-MYCENAEAN

In the final collapse of the Mycenaean world, a few examples of Bronze Age plate must have survived above ground and four hundred years later Homer writes as though he had knowledge of some of the technical achievements of the Mycenaean Age. Slender threads of continuity between Mycenaean and archaic Greece may also have survived in areas outside the Aegean world. The export of Aegean products to the eastern Mediterranean had played an important part in the spread of Mycenaean and Minoan decoration and techniques. Two pieces of plate found at Ras Shamra (Ugarit)[1] on the Syrian coast – a gold bowl and a patera from the vicinity of the Temple of Baal, both dated by Schaeffer to the period 1450–1365 – show strong Mycenaean influence in the figure-style and may be claimed as ancestors of the series of 'Phoenician' bowls of the ninth–seventh centuries B.C. which were among the main agents by which oriental motifs and ideas reached the Greek world in its 'orientalising' period.

[1] Schaeffer, *Ugaritica*, ii, 1 ff.

CHAPTER THREE

Archaic Greece and Etruria

In the eighth century B.C. began the expansion of Greek colonisation and trade which led to a great increase in the wealth and population of the Greek cities. The influx of ideas and techniques from the older civilisations of the Mediterranean world inspired a renaissance of Greek art and put an end to the 'Dark Ages' that had followed the destruction of the Mycenaean world. By the seventh century dedications of gold and silver plate were being made at Greek sanctuaries, metalwork was imported from the eastern Mediterranean, and, when local and foreign supplies of precious metals again became available, gold and silver plate began to be made in the richer Greek city-states. But the development of private luxury was cut short by the downfall of the Greek tyrants and of the gifts made to temples and shrines almost nothing has survived. The result is that we have very little direct evidence for the history of gold and silver plate in archaic Greece. The slender evidence is, however, supplemented by finds from Etruria. In Etruria the possessions of a wealthy aristocracy have been found among the rich contents of the tombs in which they were buried and these include many vessels of precious metal. Moreover these are often purely Greek in form, either copied from imported Greek examples or actually made by Greek craftsmen; vessels imported into Etruria from farther afield are often expensive versions, in gold and silver, of types which in Greece are represented only by bronze examples.

ARCHAIC GREEK

According to one ancient writer[1] the dedications of Gyges, King of Lydia (*c.* 687-652), were the first of gold and silver to be made at

[1] Theopompus, fragment 219.

Delphi. Gyges thereby set a fashion which was quickly followed by other rich rulers who came into contact with Greeks, and then by the Greeks themselves. In the second half of the seventh century the Cypselid tyrants of Corinth built a treasury to house not only the Gygian treasure but also many remarkable objects that they themselves had dedicated.[1] About 580 B.C. the Greek Glaukos of Chios made a silver crater for Alyattes of Lydia which, according to Herodotus, was the most notable of all the offerings at Delphi.[2] Croesus, Alyattes' son, presented, among other gifts, two vast craters one of gold and one of silver, made probably by some Greek craftsman such as Theodorus of Samos who is mentioned as having worked for the Lydian King.[3]

The earliest expensive metalwork in archaic Greece was of oriental type, either acquired as the dedication of some foreign ruler or through foreign trade. No silver examples of the large series of so-called Phoenician bowls have so far been found on Greek soil although there is one silver oriental bowl, rather outside the main series, from Rhodes in the British Museum;[4] bronze examples are known from Olympia[5] and elsewhere. There must also have been many silver ones in seventh-century Greece and there are references to silver vessels made by Phoenicians in Homer.[6] These bowls were an important source of inspiration for Greek artists during the 'orientalising' phase in the eighth and seventh centuries B.C. The sources and places of manufacture are discussed below (pp. 66–7) in the section on Etruscan silver since many examples of precious metal have been found in Etruscan tombs of the period.

THE PHIALE MESOMPHALOS

Another vessel of oriental origin became known to the Greeks in the early archaic period and was quickly adopted as their own. This is the so-called *phiale mesomphalos,* a handle-less cup or bowl which was soon produced in a variety of different forms and became the Greek libation vessel 'par excellence' with an immensely long history.[7] In its simplest form the vessel is a shallow flat-bottomed bowl with curving sides and a central boss (*omphalos*) punched up on the inside, which was used as a finger-grip when drinking or pouring libations. It was already in

[1] Herodotus, i, 14.
[2] *ibid. i,* 25.
[3] *ibid.* i, 51.
[4] *BMCP,* no. 1.
[5] *Olympia,* iv, pl. LII; *JdAI,* xxii, 1907, 165.
[6] *Iliad,* xxiii, 743; *Odyssey,* iv, 615 ff.
[7] Discussed in detail by Luschey, *Phiale.*

common use as a sacrificial vessel in Greece during the seventh century B.C. The rarity of silver vessels in this period may be judged from the fact that only one plain silver *phiale mesomphalos* was found in the sanctuary of Hera Limenia at Perachora, a site which produced over 200 bronze examples of various kinds.[1] It is described as being 'badly broken, quite plain, hammered with a hammered rim; the sides of the boss rise vertically and there is a slight rim round it'. The only other plain silver *phiale mesomphalos* of the archaic period is one found in the rich late Hallstatt tomb at Vix; the *omphalos* is covered with gold foil and the vessel dates from the later sixth century B.C.[2]

Several decorated forms of the *phiale mesomphalos* were also adopted in the archaic period. One of these is the *phiale* decorated with a pattern of leaves and palmettes, based upon the forms of the Egyptian lotus, radiating from the omphalos. The earliest silver example was found in a cremation burial at Ialysos on Rhodes, which may be dated around

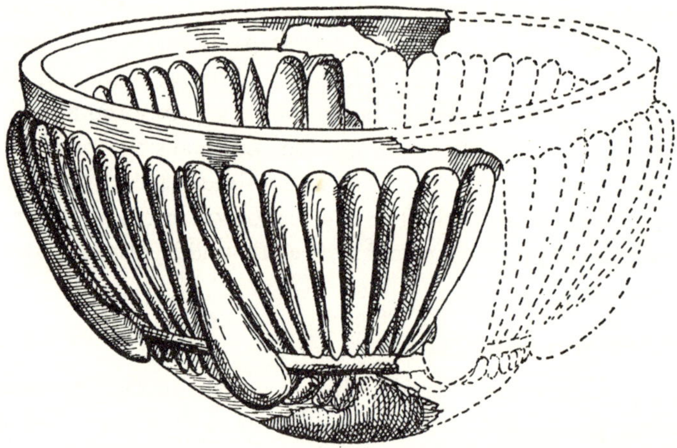

FIG. 12: Silver *phiale* with lotus ornament from Ialysos, Rhodes

650 B.C. The *phiale* (fig. 12) is an unusually deep vessel of a shape which seems to be confined to the archaic period.[3] The shallow (and orthodox) version of this type occurs in silver in the sixth century. Two examples, both with radiating friezes of leaves and palmettes (pl. 9A), now in the

[1] *Perachora*, i, 150. [2] *Mon. Piot*, 48, 1954, 30–1, pl. XXV.
[3] *Clara Rhodos*, iii, 110, fig. 103; Luschey, *Phiale*, 101.

Staatliche Museen, Berlin, are said to come from Asia Minor; they have been dated to the second half of the sixth century B.C.[1] Another more developed one comes from Kozani[2] and bears an inscription which has been dated to around 500 B.C. The inscription records that the *phiale* was dedicated to the Megarian Athena from whose sanctuary it eventually found its way into a tomb of much later date in Macedonia. Yet another, heavily restored, example in the National Museum at Naples (Inv. no. 25314) may be of this period; it has no certain provenance.[3] Another type of *phiale* in which the whole bowl was decorated like the open flower of a lotus plant was known in the seventh and sixth centuries; the type is illustrated by a bronze example from Perachora[4] and two silver versions, one nearly complete, the other fragmentary, were found in a sixth-century tomb at Kameiros.[5] *Phialai* with radial fluting on the body also occur. At Rhitsona in Boeotia there was found a fragmentary silver bowl, with a plain rim and fluting on the body, which was probably a *phiale mesomphalos* and there were fragments of what might have been another similar piece.[6]

The most remarkable survival of archaic Greek plate is a gold *phiale mesomphalos* of rather unusual form which may be one of the earliest surviving precious vessels of the post-Mycenaean period, though its date cannot be closely established. A gold bowl of deep shape (pl. 8A) with a series of wide radial flutings and a central omphalos was found in 1917 at Olympia to the east of the Altis between the Stadium and the river Alpheios and is now in the Museum of Fine Arts, Boston (Inv. no. 21.1843).[7] The central omphalos has a simple ornamental frame punched round it and on the outside near the rim there is an inscription recording that the bowl was dedicated by the sons of Kypselos of Corinth from the spoils of Herakleia.[8] According to Miss Jeffery the Kypselids who defeated Herakleia may have been those sent to colonise the route to the west at the time of Kypselos or those of the next generation, contemporaries of Psammetichos Kypselos; the bowl, therefore, may

[1] Luschey, *Phiale*, 103.

[2] *AE*, 1948–9, 92 ff., figs. 8–9; L. H. Jeffery, *The Local Scripts of Archaic Greece*, Oxford, 1961, 137.

[3] *Klio*, 30, 1937, 114.

[4] *Perachora*, i, 151.

[5] *Clara Rhodos*, iv, 43.

[6] P. N. Ure, *Aryballoi and Figurines from Rhitsona in Boeotia*, Cambridge, 1934, 78; *BSA*, 14, 1907–8, 256.

[7] *BMFA*, xx, 1922, 65 ff.; Payne, *Necrocorinthia*, 161, 211–12.

[8] Jeffery, *op. cit.* (note 2), 127–8.

be as early as 625 and as late as 550 B.C. She thinks that the offering was made and lettered in Corinth, and a closely comparable clay bowl of smaller size has actually been found there.[1] There are also parallels from Samos and Sparta.[2] The general form of the vessel may be compared with that of the lotus *phiale* from Ialysos on Rhodes. Dedications of this kind at Greek sanctuaries usually took the form of a definite amount of gold and silver and it has been noted that this particular piece weighs the equivalent of two Babylonian *minas*.

OTHER VESSELS

The existence of gold and silver counterparts for many characteristic bronze and pottery shapes of Greek vessels from the seventh to the end of the sixth century may be inferred, despite the lack of direct evidence. At Corinth where the manufacture of bronze vases was an important industry the same shapes were probably also made in precious metals and it is not impossible that some of the examples of these shapes from Etruria which are discussed below (p. 64) are of Corinthian manufacture. A silver *kantharos* from Rhodes in the Louvre,[3] (pl. 8B and C) dated by Jacobsthal to the first quarter of the sixth century B.C., is one of the very rare examples of plate from the Greek world of this period; the vessel was raised from sheet with the base made separately and soldered on and the handles riveted to the body. The decoration consists of a repoussé medallion of thin gold on the inside and the handles are overlaid with gold foil engraved with geometric patterns. The shape of this *kantharos* is not paralleled in Greek pottery vessels but is very closely related to *kantharoi* of 'bucchero sottile' of the late seventh and early sixth centuries in Etruria. A comparable vessel is a little cup made of very thin silver found at Olympia;[4] the two strap handles have very simple punched ornament with the dots arranged in lines and triangles.

A little silver *aryballos* with a hinged lid found at Leontini dates from the early sixth century B.C.;[5] the repoussé decoration is very similar to that found on the *phiale mesomphalos* – a radiating pattern of pointed leaves with smaller palmettes filling the spaces between them (p. 56). The aryballos must be Corinthian, related to pottery examples of the

[1] *AJA*, 67, 1963, 346.
[2] *Perachora*, i, 151, note 10.
[3] A. Salzmann, *Nécropole de Camiros, Fouilles*, i-iv, Paris, 1875, pl. 2; *JdAI*, 44, 1928, 214.
[4] *Olympia*, iv, 94 (no. 650), pl. XXXV.
[5] 59 *Berlin Winckelmannsprogram*, 1899, 30–1.

early sixth century. A stemmed *kantharos* in the Walters Art Gallery, Baltimore (pl. 9B) has been dated around 500 B.C., its form being compared with black-glaze examples from Rhitsona.[1] It was raised from sheet, the handles were made in one piece with the lip and soldered on to the ridge between the body and the bowl; the base was separately hammered and soldered to the bowl. It is doubtful whether such an early date can be accepted for this piece; in form it seems to differ very little from examples found in contexts dating around 450 B.C. (see below p. 79).

OVERLAYS

Silver and gold repoussé sheet was also used in this period for overlaying wooden or metal objects. A thin silver relief with two

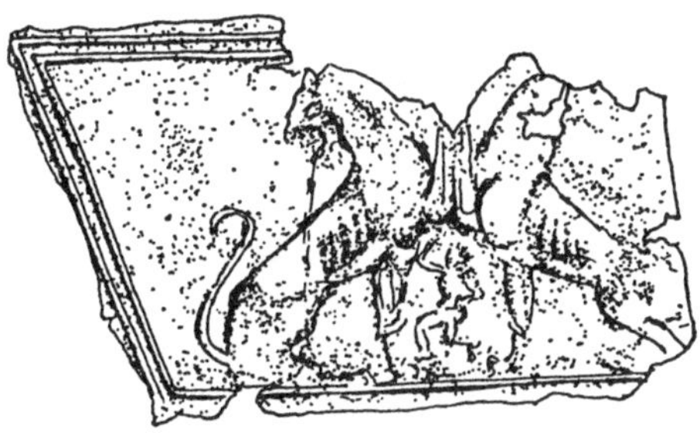

FIG. 13: Silver plaque with repoussé relief, from Delphi. Scale 1:2

heraldic lions flanking the tiny figure of a man (fig. 13) was found at Delphi, and seems from its trapezoidal shape to have been used to overlay the lid of a wooden box.[2] It belongs to the class of repoussé reliefs known as 'Argive-Corinthian', of which it is a late example made towards the end of the sixth century B.C. The Delphi fragment is the only one of the class made of silver. The reliefs were made in Corinth apparently by hammering the metal over matrices; in some examples matrices of different kinds and dates were combined.[3] It may be remembered that the famous chest (*larnax*) of the Cypselids was partly of wood with gold overlay.[4] Although there are no other examples in

[1] *AJA*, 51, 1947, 252, pl. LIXA. [2] *Fouilles de Delphes*, v, 124, fig. 466.

[3] For these reliefs in general, Payne, *Necrocorinthia*, 222 ff.

[4] Pausanias, 5, 17, 5 ff.; for gold overlays from archaic caskets see D. Ohly, *Griechische Goldbleche des 8 Jahrhunderts v. Chr.*, Berlin, 1953, 55 ff. A silver example in Richter, *Greek Collection*, 32.

silver of the Argive-Corinthian class of overlays, there was found among the fragments of silver from graves at Trebenishte (near Lake Ochrida) one with repoussé ornament thought to be part of a silver mirror showing a seated sphinx and a lion which Payne believed was strongly Corinthian in style though not pure 'Argive-Corinthian'.[1]

GREEK SILVER ABROAD

The finds from Illyrian graves at Trebenishte introduce some of the earliest examples of precious metalwork made by Greeks for the wealthy barbarians living on the fringes of their world. The people buried at Trebenishte were the chieftains of the tribe of the Dassaretioi who presumably controlled supplies of precious raw materials which by now were much in demand in Greece. The burials date mainly from

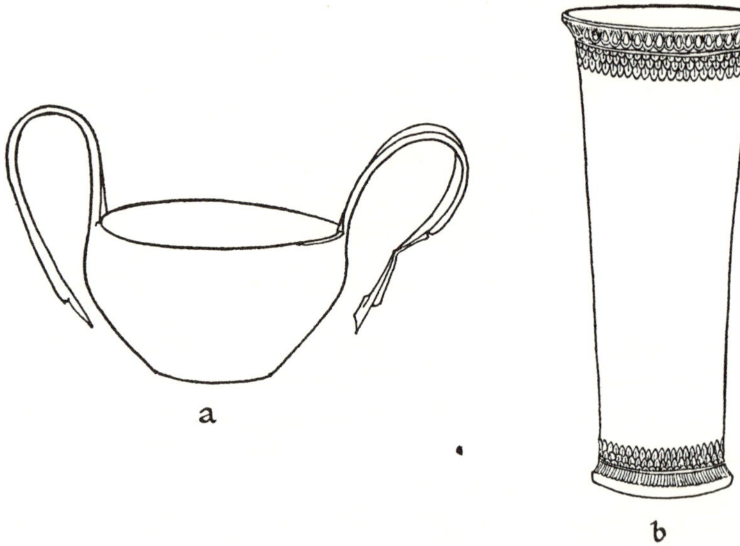

FIG. 14: (*a*) Silver two-handled cup and (*b*) Silver beaker from Trebenishte. Scale 1:3

the later sixth century B.C. The imported Greek objects include fine bronze vessels probably of Corinthian manufacture and also a number of silver vases of outstanding interest. Three silver *kantharoi* (e.g. fig. 14*a*) are generally thought of as pure Greek works.[2] The upright

[1] *ÖJh*, xxvii, 1932, 10, fig. 10.

[2] Filow, *Trebenischte*, 30, figs. 26–7; *ÖJh*, xxvii, 1932, 11 ff.

strap handles are made in one piece with the body of the vessel and the lower ends are soldered on to the body; the handles were once decorated with some kind of appliqué which has now disappeared.

Among the other silver vessels found at Trebenishte are some which were probably made to the order of the local tribesmen by Greek craftsmen. Both the long drinking horn[1] which seems to have been the principal drinking vessel of the Thracians and the tall cylindrical beaker (fig. 14*b*) are vessels of local form, but the ornamental patterns of overlapping leaves, fluting etc. are purely Greek in style and manufacture.

At Kelermes on the Kuban river, a series of Scythian barrows, mostly of the sixth century, contained some Greek-made or Greek inspired objects of gold and silver.[2] There was a silver-gilt mirror, of about the

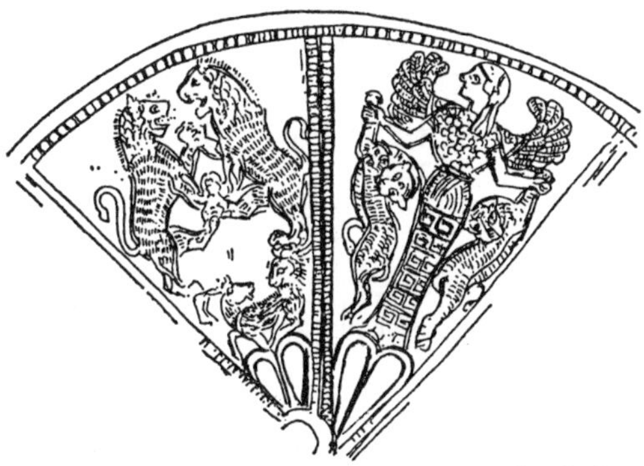

FIG. 15: Part of the decoration on a gilt mirror-back from Kelermes

middle of the sixth century, with a series of reliefs in segmental panels, including a Potnia Theron (fig. 15), the origin of which has been much debated; Curtius thought it was Corinthian,[3] Payne preferred Ionian and Rostovtzeff 'mix-Hellenic from one of the Black Sea colonies'. An engraved silver *rhyton* also from Kelermes is decorated with Greek mythological subjects and has recently been restored and published.[4] It is generally believed to be Ionian work, specially made for a Scythian patron whose normal drinking vessel was the *rhyton*. Schefold attributed the mirror and the *rhyton* to the same hand. A very curious bowl

[1] Filow, *Trebenischte*, 31, pl. VI, 1.

[2] Rostovtzeff, *I & G*, 49; *AA*, 1905, 58; K. Schefold, 'Der Skythische Tierstil in Südrussland', in *Eurasia Septentrionalis Antiqua*, xii, 1938, 1 ff.

[3] *Festschrift P. Arndt*, 40.

[4] *SA*, xxv, 1956, 215 ff.

on a stand from Maikop[1] seems to belong to the same class of silver made to local designs by Greeks of the S. Russian colonies.

CONCLUSIONS

The surviving gold and silver plate in Greece from the period down to 500 B.C. is very small in quantity. Nothing can be said about the principal centres of manufacture, though it is clear that Corinth and the cities of Ionia were producing fine work. Probably most of the principal cities were producing a few gold and silver counterparts of shapes popular in bronze and pottery for dedication at sanctuaries, and the special ritual vessels, like the *phiale mesomphalos,* were made everywhere. From the seventh century onwards Greek craftsmen were acquiring reputations for the quality of their work in gold and silver as in other materials, and their services were in demand far outside Greece. The contacts between Greek craftsmen and northern and eastern peoples they served led to the increase in their repertory of forms and decorative designs which was to play an important part in the later history of Greek plate.

ARCHAIC ETRUSCAN

I. SEVENTH CENTURY B.C.

Early Etruria provides a remarkable contrast with Greece in the quantity of precious plate that has survived, especially of the seventh century B.C. By the middle of that century, the Etruscans of central Italy were wealthy and powerful, and their wealth is represented by the contents of several lordly burials, the most famous being the Regolini-Galassi tomb at Caere (Cerveteri)[2] and the Bernardini and Barberini Tombs at Praeneste (Palestrina).[3] Gold and silver were plentiful and were used extensively for the manufacture of plate as well as for jewellery.[4]

The Tomb of the Warrior at Tarquinia, dating from the first half of the seventh century, contained what are probably the earliest silver

[1] *AA*, 1909, 151, fig. 11.

[2] Pareti, *Regolini-Galassi.*

[3] *MAAR*, iii, 9–90, and v, 9–52; the numbers given in the text refer to these two publications.

[4] On the jewellery see Higgins, *Jewellery*, chapter 13.

vessels found in Etruria.[1] One of the vessels is a two-handled cup without a foot (fig. 16*b*); it was hammered up from sheet and the handles were soldered on. The second vessel is a one-handled cup (fig. 16*a*) with a shallow footless body and a rather tall neck with slightly worked rim.

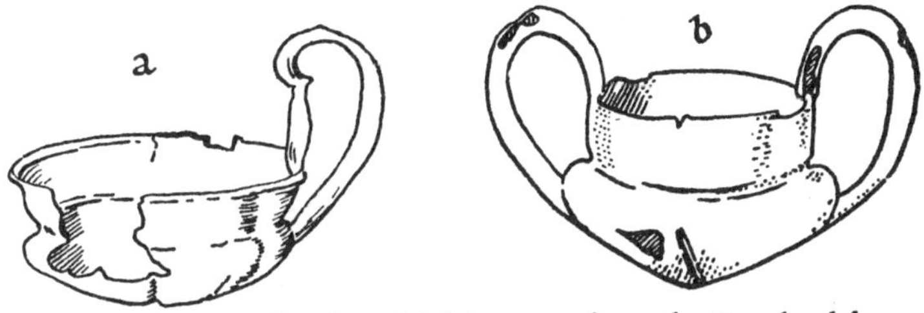

FIG. 16: (*a* & *b*) Silver drinking cups from the Tomba del Guerriero, Tarquinia. Scale 1:3

The body is decorated on the underside with engraved lines radiating from a central boss; the handle is of strip metal. The forms of both these vessels also occur in late 'impasto' wares of the period, illustrating the close connection that exists between metal vessels and the pottery of the seventh century.[2] It is generally believed that many of the characteristic shapes of the 'bucchero' pottery which superseded 'impasto' were also made in imitation of vessels of precious metal. In the Regolini-Galassi tomb dating probably around 650 B.C.[3] there was a little amphora (no. 164) (pl. 10A) with simple repoussé spiral decoration which is exactly matched in very early bucchero.[4] Of the shapes of vessels occurring in precious metals in seventh-century Etruria, several, including the Corinthian cup-*kotyle* and the narrow necked jug, are also found in pottery forms.

DRINKING VESSELS

Drinking vessels of various kinds form a large part of the gold and silver plate in seventh-century Etruscan graves. One of the simplest and most popular shapes is a deep, footless bowl, slightly closing at the top, which

[1] *AdI*, 1874, 254; *Monumenti Inediti*, x, pl. x; Randall-MacIver, *Villanovans*, pl. 30.

[2] J. D. Beazley and F. Magi, *La Raccolta Benedetto Guglielmi nel Museo Vaticano Etrusco*, Vatican City, 1939, i, Ceramica, pl. 46, nos. 34, 47.

[3] The date and building history of the tomb and its burials is obscure. See Pareti, *Regolini-Galassi*, chapter 2, and E. Richardson, *The Etruscans*, Chicago, 1964, 51–4.

[4] *MA*, iv, 1895, 230 ff.

was 'raised' from thin sheet metal and usually decorated below the rim with rows of incised semicircles. The shape is purely Etruscan and widespread. Examples have been found in the Regolini-Galassi tomb (no. 152 (almost complete) and nos. 153–6 (fragments only)), in several tombs at Marsiliana d'Albegna[1], in Vetulonia[2] and in the Bernardini (nos. 32, 33 and 39) and Castellani tombs[3] at Praeneste. One of the examples from the Regolini-Galassi tomb has a prominent inscription giving the name of its owner.

A number of the drinking cups found in tombs of the period are closely connected with Greek, mainly Corinthian, shapes. One of these is a deep cup with curving sides and a concave flaring rim equipped with two upturned loop handles set horizontally below the rim (pl. 11B); there were four well-preserved silver examples of this shape in the Regolini-Galassi tomb (nos. 157, 158, 159 and 162) and fragments of others. A shallow two-handled cup on a tall foot (no. 163) from the same tomb with vertical ring handles of strip metal is connected with a Protocorinthian form. The Protocorinthian deep cup or *kotyle* fitted with horizontal loop handles (pl. 11A) occurs in gold, silver and bronze as well as clay during the seventh century and was clearly among the most popular shapes of the period in Etruria. Of the examples in precious metals, some are plain, others have punched or incised ornament of circles and arcading round the rim or a narrow engraved frieze, like the one from the Circolo degli Avori at Marsiliana[4] and a few are decorated with elaborately engraved figured scenes and ornament and partly gilded. The cups were raised from sheet; the tubular handles were made separately, filled with resin and soldered to the body. Most of them must have been made in Etruria. Two examples found in a tomb at Fabriano (S. Maria in Campo, Tomb 3) in Picenum are Etruscan imports; they were associated with other imported Etruscan objects of the later seventh century B.C., a time when Etruscan influence was particularly strong on the eastern seaboard of Italy.[5]

Three richly engraved and gilded examples of this type of *kotyle*, all very fragmentary, have been found in Etruria, two in the Barberini Tomb at Praeneste (nos. 13 and 14: Villa Giulia Museum nos. 13226

[1] Minto, *Marsiliana*, 210 ff., pl. XV, 1–3.

[2] Falchi, *Vetulonia*, pls. XIV, 13; XVI, 3.

[3] *MA*, XV, 567, fig. 168.

[4] Minto, *Marsiliana*, 212, fig. 12. There are fragments of at least one plain *kotyle* of this type from Tomb XLVII of the Banditella cemetery.

[5] *MA* XXXV, 3, pl. XV.

and 13227) and one in the Tomba del Duce[1] at Vetulonia. The Vetulonia example (pl. 12B) now in the Archaeological Museum, Florence (Inv. no. 73582) is engraved with friezes of animals obviously inspired by oriental models such as the Phoenician bowls discussed below, but this is the work of an Etruscan not an oriental craftsman; it has been noted that while the figures are 'at one remove only' from their oriental prototypes, the versions of Egyptian hieroglyphs are a complete travesty of the originals.[2] The evidence of shape, style and craftsmanship all combine to suggest that the vessel was made by an Etruscan craftsman decorating a shape copied from Greek vessels with ornament based upon such oriental models as the Phoenician bowls. The two examples from the Barberini Tomb are decorated with similar engraved friezes of animals and floral ornament and were richly gilded with a fairly thick gold foil. A very fine cup of this form, made of pure gold, was found in the Bernardini Tomb at Praeneste (no. 20) (pl. 11A). On each of the handles are perched a pair of sphinxes which were made of plates of thin gold beaten into a mould and then soldered together.

GOLD GRANULATION

Some details of the sphinxes on this cup are composed of lines of gold granulation. The technique of decorating gold by soldering on tiny granules of gold is one in which the Etruscans achieved a very high degree of mastery during the seventh century B.C.; it was used mostly for the elaborate jewellery of which the Etruscans were so fond but there are also one or two surviving gold vessels decorated in this technique. The finest example is the deep bowl in the Victoria and Albert Museum (pl. 12A) which probably dates from about 650 B.C. The whole surface of the vessel is decorated with the geometric and floral patterns carried out in granulated lines.[3] Another example of the same technique is the little alabastron decorated with similar patterns in the British Museum, said to come from Palestrina.[4] Both these little vessels are probably 'toilet vessels' and this kind of decoration, so fashionable on contemporary jewellery, might seem especially appropriate to them.

[1] Falchi, *Vetulonia*, pl. x, 3.
[2] W. L. Brown, *The Etruscan Lion*, Oxford, 1960, 28 f.
[3] M. Pallottino, *Art of the Etruscans*, London, 1955, pl. 27.
[4] *BMCJ*, no. 1448.

BOWLS

The most numerous series of bowls found in seventh-century Etruscan contexts are the so-called 'Phoenician bowls';[1] examples found at Caere and Praeneste and elsewhere[2] are among the best and most ornate of their kind. The bowls are of silver, richly gilded and decorated with concentric rings of figured ornament carried out by engraving and low-relief repoussé in a mixed oriental style combining elements of Phoenician, Assyrian, Egyptian and Greek origin. The gilt silver dish from the Bernardini Tomb at Praeneste (no. 25) (pl. 13A) is a typical example of the decorative scheme. The central medallion shows a male figure in Egyptian dress, certainly an Egyptian Pharoah, overcoming his enemies; immediately round this medallion is a frieze of horses and birds perhaps inspired by Greek work. The main frieze illustrates a series of episodes connected with hunting which are Assyrian in derivation and the frame to the whole bowl takes the form of a snake's body coiled round, another Egyptian motif. The Etruscan tombs contain two varieties of these bowls – a shallow dish (e.g. Regolini-Galassi nos. 321–3) and a smaller hemispherical bowl (e.g. Regolini-Galassi, no. 324, pl. 13B).[3] 'Phoenician' silver bowls have been found in Cyprus and bronze versions in Greece and the eastern mediterranean. It is generally believed that most of the Etruscan bowls are imported from Cyprus or Phoenicia. A bowl from Cyprus in New York[4] is engraved with scenes very similar to those of the Bernardini bowl (pl. 13A). Another bowl (no. 26) from the Bernardini Tomb has a Phoenician inscription giving the name of one Eshmunyaad, son of Ashto, perhaps the maker or owner.[5] It is not possible to be precise about the centres of manufacture. A combination of Assyrian and Greek elements, as on the bowl pl. 13A, would seem to be most at home in Cyprus; other examples are more purely Egyptian and Syrian in

[1] There is a large bibliography on these bowls; see especially Poulsen, *Orient*, 20 ff.; Pareti, *Regolini-Galassi*, 316 ff.

[2] e.g. one found at Pontecagnano near Salerno (W. Fröhner, *La Collection Tyszkiewicz*, Munich, 1892, pl. II, *SE*, xxxi, 1963, 241–7) and now in the Petit Palais, Paris.

[3] There is a deep bowl of slightly different profile from the ones found in Etruria in the Museum of Fine Arts, Boston (*Greek, Etruscan, and Roman Art*, Boston, 1963, 36, figs. 31a and b).

[4] Myres, *Cesnola Collection*, no. 4556.

[5] There are inscribed examples from Cyprus, e.g. Myres, *Cesnola Collection*, no. 4552; cf. *JdAI*, 38/9, 1923–4, fig. 12.

style. Attempts have been made to distinguish the work of several different 'schools' among the bowls from Etruria and Cyprus.[1] It is perhaps unlikely that any of the seventh-century bowls found in Etruria were made there, though, in fact, the precise technique of the Etruscan bowls is not found anywhere else.

The technical details of the bowls are of some interest. The shallow bowl, no 323, from the Regolini-Galassi tomb is about 2 mm. thick and raised from sheet silver. The inside surface was first gilded all over, except for a strip outside the ornamental border of the figured friezes. The engraving on the inside was done after the gilding; the lines of the engraving would show through on the outside so that the repoussé could be done last. No. 322 was originally gilded all over on the inside, the engraving of the scenes followed, and then areas of the gilding were scraped away so as to leave gilt frames round the figures only. The whole of the central medallion remained gilt. A similar technique was employed for the deeper bowl (no. 324) which consists of two skins of silver, the outer lipping over the inner. The engraving of each part was done after gilding and this was followed by the repoussé; afterwards areas of the gilding were removed to leave the background of the figures in the colour of the silver. All the bowls were gilded with leaf. In the case of no. 321 a rather thicker leaf was used so that the engraving lines do not cut through it so obviously; there is much less repoussé on this example than on 322 and 323. The deep bowl from the Bernardini Tomb is gilded with thick leaf or foil covering the entire inner surface; the repoussé shows in negative on the outside. The bowl illustrated on pl. 13A, also from the Bernardini Tomb, is gilded over the whole inner surface except the strip outside the enclosing snake.

Another variety of shallow bowl in seventh-century Etruscan contexts has a low foot ring and a series of radial flutings, convex on the outside, framing a flat central zone. It is common in bronze. Like the Phoenician bowls it is oriental in origin, the closest parallels coming from Assyria.[2] There is one silver example, very fragmentary, from the Regolini-Galassi tomb at Caere (no. 167) (fig. 17) and fragments of another fluted bowl with zig-zag ornament below the rim were found in the Artiaco Tomb at Cumae.[3] The latter has been thought of as Greek not Etruscan but scarcely enough survives for a firm conclusion.

[1] *Opuscula Archaeologica*, iv, 1946, 1 ff.

[2] The type is discussed in *Klio*, 1937, 110.

[3] *MA*, xiii, 1903, 245, fig. 20.

The various forms of the Greek *phiale mesomphalos* do not occur in seventh-century Etruria though two little silver dishes from the Bernardini Tomb (nos. 34–5) have a little boss, hardly an omphalos, in

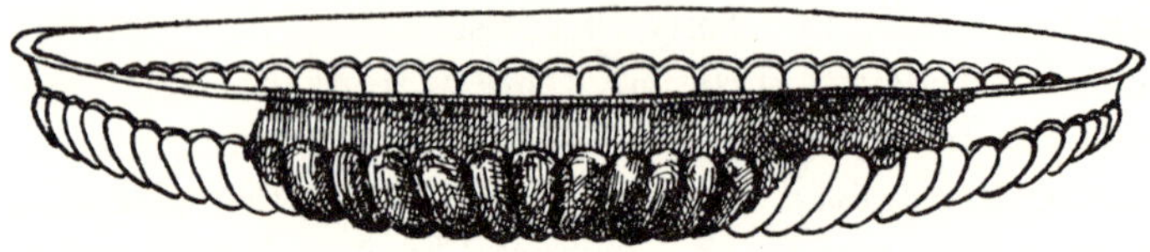

FIG. 17: Silver bowl from the Regolini-Galassi Tomb, Caere. Scale 1:2

the centre. By the sixth century the Greek types must have been well known. A detached omphalos framed by an ovolo moulding was found in the votive deposit of the temple of Mater Matuta at Satricum; it probably derives from an imported *phiale* of pure Greek form made in the second half of the sixth century B.C. A *phiale mesomphalos* found at Chiusi is now known only from old engravings;[1] it combined the Greek form with the concentric bands of figured ornament found on the Phoenician bowls. The scenes were, apparently, of Etruscan inspiration and the *phiale* was probably made in the first half of the sixth century B.C.

The repertory of Etruscan silversmiths was not confined to sacrificial bowls and drinking vessels. A large bowl from the Bernardini Tomb at Praeneste has a close fitting lid in the form of a strainer to which a silver ladle was attached (no. 30). The ladle and strainer have hooks at the end suggesting already the form of the duck's head into which they developed on later examples. The whole made up a kind of table set for serving wine. Another large bowl of gilded silver, similar in shape, but more open at the top is decorated with engraved bands in the same style and technique as the Phoenician bowls depicting warriors on horseback and on foot and hunting scenes (no. 23) (pl. 10B). Attached to the outside just below the rim are a series of six silver snakes' heads covered with thin gold foil; these seem to be additions to the original vessel perhaps made by a local craftsman to an imported piece. Another unusual vessel is a shallow bowl found in the Castellani Tomb at Praeneste.[2] The decoration consists of concentric circles of close-set

[1] Mühlestein, *Ursprünge*, no. 25.

[2] *MA*, xv, 1905, 565–6, fig. 166.

dots punched in from the outside and an engraved roundel on the bottom with figures in orientalising style.

JUGS

Another vessel of oriental origin popular in Etruria at this period is the jug illustrated in fig. 18. One fairly complete example and a fragment

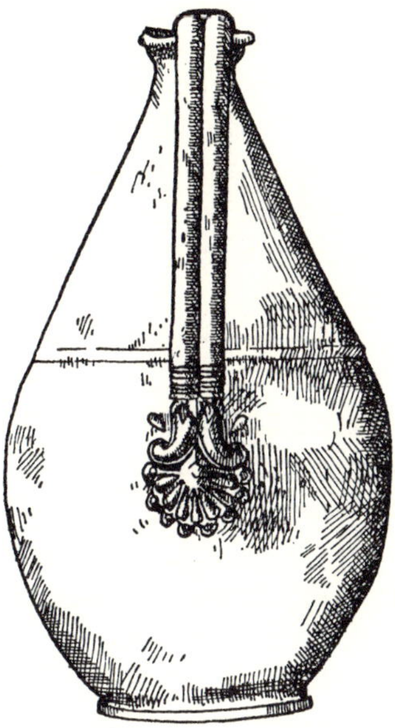

FIG. 18: Silver jug from the Regolini-Galassi Tomb, Caere. Scale 1:3

of another were found in the Regolini-Galassi tomb (no. 165-6); these jugs have a tapering neck with a little trefoil mouth and a handle composed of two tubes set together. They were made in four pieces. The body with its low foot was hammered from sheet; the neck and trefoil mouth were formed from a second piece which was then joined to the body, the junction being concealed by a metal ring, and the double tubular handle was soldered on, the lower joint being concealed by a gold repoussé plaque with lotus ornament. Other examples of this kind of jug have been found at Praeneste (Bernardini no. 36 and Barberini no. 17), Vetulonia[1] (Tomba del Duce) and Cumae[2] (Artiaco

[1] Falchi, *Vetulonia*, pl. x, 8.

[2] *MA*, xiii, 1903, 242, fig. 17.

Tomb) and versions were also made in bronze and bucchero. The eastern origin of this type seems certain and its distribution has recently been studied in some detail;[1] a very close parallel for the Regolini-Galassi jug is provided by a fragment of neck and handle with palmette plaque which was found at Curium in Cyprus.[2]

OVERLAYS

A common use for silver in seventh-century Etruria was for overlays on wooden or metal cores; these were generally cut out 'à jour' and the silhouettes were usually decorated with engraving and a limited use of repoussé comparable to that found on the Phoenician bowls. A typical example of this kind of decoration may be seen on a tall narrow cylindrical wooden bucket from the Regolini-Galassi Tomb at Caere (no. 151); the ornament is 'orientalising' with friezes of real and fantastic animals, palmette ornament and interlacing arcs. The handle is fluted and terminates at both ends in protomai of lions; similar protomai of lions support the rings into which the bucket handle is fitted. Another similar *situla* of rather more squat form was found in the Castellani Tomb at Praeneste (fig. 19);[3] in this example a female head rising from above a palmette supports the loop of the handle, a detail which is also found on a fragment from the Barberini tomb. The popularity of this type of ornamentation is shown by many finds; in the Bernardini Tomb there were many fragments of silver open-work strips, with ornament engraved or in low relief. Many of the fragments still have the nails by which they were fixed to the wooden buckets. The same technique and similar decorative themes were used to decorate a house-shaped urn or box made of bronze from the Tomba del Duce at Vetulonia;[4] silver and gold plaques were also used to overlay ivory objects.

2. SIXTH CENTURY B.C.

The finds from the seventh-century 'orientalising' tombs form a narrow group of comparatively few types with similar forms of decoration. Very few pieces later in date than these have survived. One of these few is the bucket or *situla* from Chiusi known as the Plicasnas *situla* from the

[1] *AEArq*, xxvi, 1953, 235–44.
[2] Cesnola, *Atlas*, iii, pl. XXXIX, 12.
[3] *MA*, xv, 1905, 562 ff.
[4] Falchi, *Vetulonia*, 149 ff., pl. XII; *AJA*, iv, 1888, pl. XI.

name, either that of the owner or the maker, which is inscribed on it twice.[1] The shape of the *situla* is unusual and may be inspired by a Corinthian model. The chief interest lies in the decoration which, while it is related to the style of the Phoenician bowls, seems to be an independent Etruscan development with scenes taken from Etruscan life. The zones of figured ornament are divided by bands of guilloche; on the main zone is depicted a religious procession to a sacrificial altar with athletes, pipers, dancers etc. In the lower scene is a shepherd and his flock. The *situla* was probably made in Chiusi between 600 and 550 B.C. A *phiale mesomphalos* of the same period which is also decorated with scenes of Etruscan inspiration has already been noted.

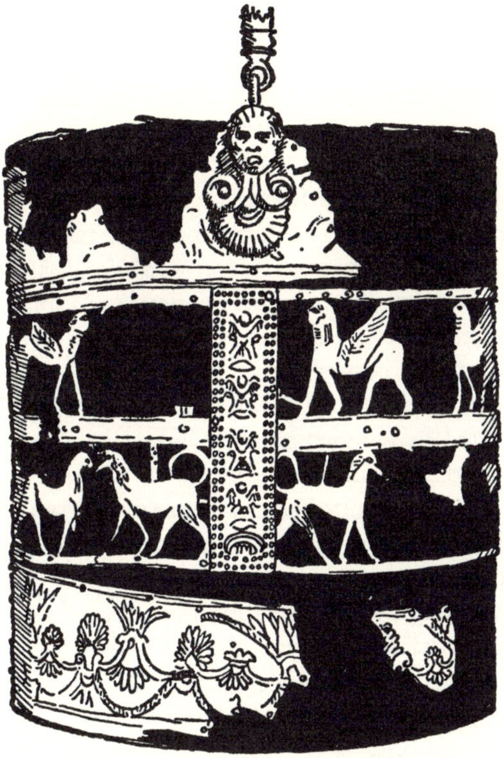

FIG. 19: Wooden bucket with silver openwork overlay; Castellani Tomb, Praeneste. Scale 1:3

[1] Milani, *Firenze*, no. 2594, pl. XIX.

No vessels of precious metal have survived from the later sixth century in Etruria. There is little doubt, however, that expensive plate was still being made and used. The reputation of the Etruscans for luxury, especially in gold and silver,[1] is confirmed, to some extent, by representations of metal vessels in sixth-century painted tombs. In the Tomb of the Lionesses at Tarquinia a scene of festivity shows an enormous wine bowl and ladle which, to judge from the colour is meant to be of silver.[2] In the Tomb of the Augurs at Tarquinia, the three bowls placed between the combatants in a wrestling match, which are usually interpreted as the prizes of victory, seem to be made of silver and gold.[3] The skill of Etruscan silversmiths in the later sixth century is shown by the fine repoussé relief from Castel S. Mariano, now in the British Museum;[4] the relief, which is of thin repoussé silver partly gilded with thick leaf, shows two lions attacking a boar with the figure of a sphinx to one side. Another silver relief from the same source shows two Amazons on horseback and a fallen comrade on the ground. The third piece is a charming openwork design of volutes and palmettes. All these three pieces were riveted to wooden backing and probably served to decorate furniture of some kind. It is difficult to say to what extent the bucchero of the sixth century had counterparts in metal vessels. In the seventh century, the close connexion between metal and pottery is certain; in the sixth, the relief bucchero (bucchero pesante) largely replaced that with engraved designs and this may reflect the popularity of repoussé metalwork in the period, though nothing of the kind in gold and silver has in fact survived. Metal originals for such vessels as the clay *kotylai* with punched ornament round the rim and reliefs on the body or the bucchero bowl with high-relief heads, both from one of the Montetosto Tombs at Caere, seem very likely.

CONCLUSIONS

The finds of gold and silver plate in the seventh-century tombs in Etruria give only a very partial idea of the output of Etruscan silversmiths. The practice of burying large quantities of expensive vessels with the dead does not seem to have outlasted the century. Much of the seventh-century plate was certainly imported from the eastern mediter-

[1] Diodorus, v, 40.
[2] M. Pallottino, *Etruscan Painting*, 43.
[3] *ibid.*, 39.
[4] *BMCP*, nos. 2–4; *JdAI*, 73, 1958, 9 ff.

ranean; local products, like the Greek-type *kotylai,* bowls etc., seem to have come from comparatively few workshops. They are almost all drinking or ritual vessels, and some may have been made solely as dedications to the dead. The goldsmiths who made the lavish jewellery of the period also seem to have turned their hands to the production of plate, like the two surviving gold vessels with granulation ornament. In the seventh century the themes chosen by the silversmiths follow very closely the orientalising repertory but towards the end of the century pure Etruscan themes begin to appear. After 600 we have no almost direct evidence for the history of Etruscan plate until the fourth century B.C.

CHAPTER FOUR

Classical Greece: 480–330 B.C.

In the period following the Persian Wars there was a considerable increase in the production of gold and silver plate in the Greek cities. For most of the fifth century no plate was manufactured for private domestic use in Greece, but ritual vessels and expensive versions of everyday vessels were dedicated at the sanctuaries of the gods. Almost none of this has survived the fate of those places in later times but some idea of what has been lost can be gathered from official inventories of temple-treasures.[1] The collections were stacked or stored in boxes and generally catalogued in batches[2] by a board of magistrates appointed to take stock. The plate was given for many different reasons – in atonement, to enrich the shrine, in gratitude for athletic victory,[3] as a memorial. A few of the objects were used in ritual, the rest were regarded as so much precious metal stored in an attractive form; sometimes old pieces were melted down or sold to meet costs. At Delos in the fourth century B.C., 60 different kinds of vessels appear in the Treasure Lists.

In Greece itself very little classical silver has been found. Our knowledge of it depends almost entirely on finds from the barbarian fringes of the Greek world. The wealthy members of rich and prosperous neighbours of the Greeks acquired some of the best products of Greek craftsmanship and were buried with them when they died. The richest finds come from Thracian tombs in S. Bulgaria and from Scythian burials in the valleys of the Dniepr, the Kuban, and elsewhere in S. Russia. The find in the tumulus of Baschova Mogila, one of a series of rich Thracian tombs in the area of Duvanli, S. Bulgaria,[4] the contents of which are now in the Museum at Plovdiv, is a typical example. The ashes of the dead man were collected in a *phiale mesom-*

[1] e.g. *IG* II, 699–701, 768. [2] F. Durrbach and P. Roussel, *Inscriptions de Delos*, 97.
[3] cf. the φιάλη νικοδρόμειος referred to in *BCH*, x, 1886, 462. [4] Filow, *Duvanlij*, 59 ff.

phalos of Attic (?) workmanship on which was inscribed in Greek letters the name of its Thracian owner, Dadaleme. Other silver vessels in the tomb included a stemless cup with an engraved scene on the inside, a horn *rhyton* ending in the foreparts of a horse and a little silver jug with reeded body, all of Greek, probably Athenian, workmanship. This particular burial dates from the last decades of the fifth century.

Until about the middle of the fifth century B.C. the repertory of Greek silversmiths was a comparatively limited one, consisting mainly of the traditional shapes of ritual vessel, such as the *phiale mesomphalos.* The finds of the second half of the century include a much greater variety of shapes and it seems certain that by this time most of the popular vase forms were also being made in silver. The influence of Achaemenid metalwork was strongly felt throughout the period. Enormous booty of Persian gold and silver was taken at the Battle of Plataea and divided among the allies.[1] The Achaemenid form of the *phiale mesomphalos* (see p. 76) and the popularity, if not the introduction of, the various forms of the *rhyton*[2] illustrate Persian influence on contemporary silversmiths in the Greek cities. Greek silversmiths also continued to make vessels of foreign shape to the order of their barbarian neighbours. The Greco-Scythian metalwork of the late fifth and fourth centuries, produced in the Black Sea colonies for Scythian patrons provides the finest examples of this class.

THE PHIALE MESOMPHALOS: earlier fifth century B.C.

The *phialai* of this period were commonly made of gold and silver.[3] A narrow band of ornament immediately round the omphalos, such as is found on archaic *phialai,* was often the only decoration. On an example from Maikop in Berlin[4] the ornament consists of a narrow band of overlapping leaves (pl. 14A); a lightly engraved duck's head was added at some time on the interior of the vessel. Relief decoration became more common during the century. On a *phiale* from the second kurgan of the group known as Seven Brothers in the Kuban (*c.* 450) a row of close-set silenus heads frames the omphalos.[5] An example from Zubov's Farm in the Kuban has a snake in relief on the

[1] Herodotus, ix, 80.

[2] See *AK,* 4, 1961, 21 ff., and Tuchelt, *Tiergefässe,* 73 ff., for two different points of view.

[3] cf. Pindar, *Nemean,* ix, 51 f.

[4] Berlin Inv. no. 30221a; *Berliner Museen,* 1964, 32.

[5] *CR,* 1876, 157, pl. 4, 9; Minns, *S & G,* 210, fig. 107.

omphalos, a narrow frame of fluting immediately around it, and a series of stamped deer heads in relief on the inside near the rim (pl. 14B).[1] The burial dates from the first century B.C. but the *phiale* which bears an inscription recording that it belonged to the shrine of Apollo at Phasis, was probably made around the middle of the fifth century. More elaborate designs of concentric bands of repoussé ornament were coming into fashion in the middle of the century. A clay *phiale* from Locri, obviously imitating a metal original has three concentric rings of negro heads, acorns and bees.[2] A fragment of a gold *phiale* from Marion, Cyprus,[3] with two rows of acorns and little palmettes as fillers may be as early as this but most of the examples of these more elaborate schemes belong to the later fifth and fourth centuries.[4] The type of *phiale* with a radiating pattern based on the forms of the lotus and palmette continued to be made. A fragment of one from Nymphaeum, south of Kerch, comes from a grave which also contained a red-figure *skyphos* of about 440 B.C.; the double range of lotus leaves and palmettes is a development on the earlier single row (e.g. pl. 9A)[5] reflecting the general trend towards concentric patterns on these *phialai*.

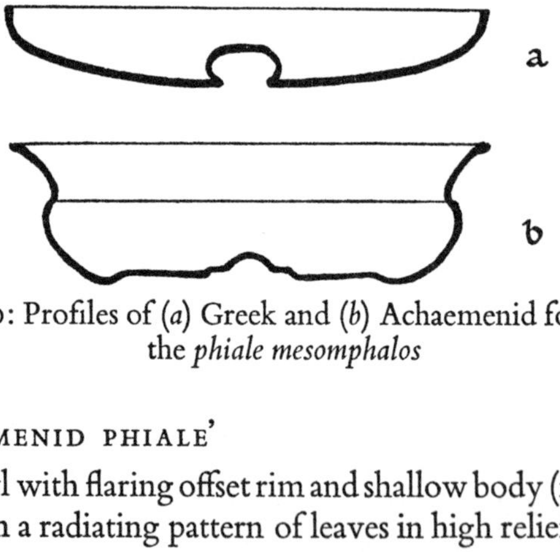

FIG. 20: Profiles of (*a*) Greek and (*b*) Achaemenid forms of the *phiale mesomphalos*

THE 'ACHAEMENID PHIALE'

A type of bowl with flaring offset rim and shallow body (fig. 20*b*) usually decorated with a radiating pattern of leaves in high relief was known in

[1] *AA*, 1901, 56. [2] *BMMA*, xxi, 1962, 154 ff.

[3] The fragment is in Warsaw (K. Michalowski, *Muzeum Narodowe w Warsawie, Sztuka starożytna*, 192, fig. 129). M. Ohnefalsch-Richter (*Kypros, The Bible and Homer*, London, 1893, 361–2) states that it was found at Marion in a tomb with objects of the late sixth century B.C.; W. Froehner (*Collections du Château de Gołuchów, L'Orfévrerie*, Paris, 1897, no. 39) says it was found near Smyrna.

[4] See below pp. 80–1. [5] *CR*, 1877, 233, pl. 3, 5. Minns, *S & G*, 215, fig. 114.

Greece as early as the sixth century B.C. A bronze example was found in the Sanctuary of Hera Limenia at Perachora,[1] and there is one presumably of silver, shown on a red-figured cup fragment by Euphronios.[2] The origin of the type is oriental and it is especially common in Achaemenid contexts, for example, the Treasure of Achalgori.[3] For this reason it may be called the 'Achaemenid phiale'. No silver examples of the period have actually been found in Greece. There are a number from graves in southern Bulgaria. The earliest, a rather deep version with pear-shaped bosses, was found in the Muschovitsa tumulus of the Duvanli group (late sixth-early fifth century) and is like the one from Perachora.[4] It may not be Greek. The example from Kukuva Mogila (first half of the fifth century) has a larger omphalos and a reeded body.[5] The three found in the Alexandrovo burial look Greek, and one of them has a Greek inscription giving the name of its owner, Kotys, King of the Engestai (pl. 16A).[6] This has a reeded body, and there is another similar one with some decoration on the omphalos; a third is plain except for a gilded omphalos overlaid with a silver rosette. It seems likely that this type of vessel achieved its popularity through Achaemenid imports and was being made by Greek craftsmen at least as early as 450 B.C. Two fine silver examples of the shape found in fifth-century graves at Ialysos on Rhodes must be Achaemenid work. They are decorated with a series of pear-shaped bosses between which are pairs of opposed S-spirals, each ending in birds' heads and filled out with palmette ornament.[7] An identical *phiale* was found at Kasbek in Georgia with an inscription in old Persian.[8] Achaemenid versions of the fifth century generally lack the omphalos and the form with a central rosette on the bottom and a radiating pattern of fluting, which is found, for example, in the Oxus Treasure,[9] seems to be the forerunner of the leaf *phiale* which is discussed below (p. 82).

CYPRUS: CLASSICAL SILVER

Phialai of both the Achaemenid and the Greek form have been found in Cyprus which, in the fifth century B.C., was open to imports and

[1] *Perachora*, i, pl. 56, 3–4.
[2] *BCH*, 54, 1930, 422, pl. 20, and *AA*, 1938, 762 ff.
[3] J. I. Smirnov, *Der Schatz von Achalgori*, Tiflis, 1934, pl. VIII, no. 61; see also *Stathatos Collection*, iii, 260 ff.
[4] Filow, *Duvanlij*, 88, fig. 110.
[5] *ibid.* 50, fig. 60.
[6] *RM*, 32, 1917, 52 ff.
[7] *Clara Rhodos*, 8, figs. 168–9; Luschey, 61 ff.
[8] Smirnov, *Argenterie Orientale*, iii, 13–14.
[9] Dalton, *Oxus*, pl. V, 19.

influences from the Greek and the oriental world. Plain silver *phialai mesomphaloi* of Greek form are common. An example from Curium with a band of repoussé gold overlay decorated with palmettes and lotus flowers immediately round the omphalos may date from the earlier fifth century.[1] The *phialai* of Achaemenid shape include one which is very like the example from the Muschovitsa tumulus at Duvanli and a leaf *phiale*, perhaps an early one.[2] Among the Cypriote silver of the classical period are various kinds of jugs and bowls, either of Greek or oriental derivation.[3] Silver spoons, found mostly at Curium, may also be classical. There are a number of round-bowled spoons of various sizes and one with a pear-shaped bowl;[4] the bowls tend to be shallow, almost flat, and one example has a double scroll, not unlike an Ionic capital at the junction of the bowl and handle. The purpose of these spoons is uncertain.

ENGRAVED VESSELS

About the middle of the fifth century, to judge at least from surviving examples, Greek silversmiths began to engrave silver vessels, especially drinking cups, with figure scenes and ornament, a comparatively short-lived fashion in the history of Greek plate which lasts into the fourth century. These engraved vessels are expensive counterparts of pottery vessels decorated in the prevailing and long-established fashion of line drawing in the red-figure technique. The output was probably not large and comparatively few shapes – the *kantharos*, the *kylix* and other cup forms – were decorated in this way. Details of shapes as well as decoration seem to follow the clay versions, a reversal of the more normal dependence of clay upon metal. It has been pointed out, for example,[5] that several details of the two fine *kantharoi* from the tumulus of Golemata Mogila at Duvanli are not, in fact, well-suited to metalwork. The knobs and the satyr heads are not integral parts of the handles while the cross-braces, necessary in clay vessels, do not seem to be required in metal.

The vessel illustrated on pl. 15A is one of the earliest examples of this kind of engraved silver; it was found in the main burial of the second kurgan (tumulus) of the Seven Brothers in the Kuban, a rich source of Greek metalwork.[6] The vessel is a fragmentary *kylix* with a medallion

[1] Cesnola, *Atlas*, iii, pl. XXXVII, 4. [2] *ibid.* pl. XXXVII, 3. [3] *SCE*, iv, 2, 409.
[4] Cesnola, *Atlas*, iii, pl. XXXIX, 1–6. [5] *AJA*, li, 1947, 253. [6] *CR*, 1881, 5 ff., pl. I, 3.

on the inside showing Bellerophon in combat with the chimaera, surrounded by a frieze of male figures. Another *kylix* found in the débris from a group of mounds not far from the Seven Brothers is very similar in style; the central medallion shows Dionysos and a Maenad in an animated twosome, surrounded by a frieze of sileni and maenads.[1] The scenes were engraved on the silver and then covered with a gold leaf which is described as being about the thickness of thick paper; after the leaf had been applied it was apparently burnished over the engraving so that the lines of the drawing showed through and then the surplus leaf was cut away from the outlines of the figures. It is difficult to establish the precise date of these vessels but by analogy with drawing on pottery the period around 450 B.C. seems most likely. A stemmed *kantharos* from the tumulus of Golemata Mogila at Duvanli belongs to about the same period.[2] Scenes are engraved on opposite sides of the body. On one a Naiad is bringing a fawn to Dionysos; on the other a satyr and a maenad are dancing. The style suggests the middle of the fifth century. The *kantharos* is one of a pair, each with an omphalos on the bottom of the bowl, satyr heads inside the handles looking into the vase, knobs on the outside, and cross braces to the lip. Three of the satyr heads were chased and gilded and the fourth, which is cast, may have been made to replace one broken off in ancient times.

A little later is an engraved *kylix* from the main burial of the fourth kurgan of the Seven Brothers with a central engraved medallion of Nike seated.[3] On another cup, from the sixth kurgan, the figured medallion is framed by a border of ivy-wreath and anthemion; the scene shows a bearded man with a stick to the left and two women, one seated and one standing, to the right. It has been interpreted as a family group or as an unidentified scene from Greek Tragedy.[4] The date is around 420 B.C. Another vessel of about the same date is a one-handled deep cup found in the tumulus of Solokha (near Melitopol).[5] The lower part of the cup is ribbed and the tall upper part is engraved with ritual scenes involving groups of women (pl. 16B). A stemless cup with gilded engraving from the tumulus of Baschova Mogila at Duvanli[6] has a central medallion surrounded by a laurel wreath and showing a female figure (Selene?) riding over the sea on a horse. Schefold was inclined to attribute this piece to the same hand as the cup from the sixth

[1] *ibid.* pl. I, 5. [2] Filow, *Duvanlij*, 106 ff., pl. VII. [3] *CR*, 1881, pl. I, 4.
[4] *RM*, 46, 1931, 119. [5] *RA*, xxiii, 1914, 164 ff. [6] Filow, *Duvanlij*, 65, pl. V.

kurgan of the Seven Brothers and Filow assigns it to the end of the fifth century B.C.

THE PHIALE MESOMPHALOS: Later fifth and fourth centuries B.C.

One of the finest pieces of engraved plate found at Duvanli is a *phiale mesomphalos* from the tumulus of Baschova Mogila (pl. 15B).[1] The subject is a procession or demonstration of skill by armed *apobatai* riding in four-horse chariots, each with its charioteer. The engraving is gilded and immediately round the omphalos there are bands of engraved ornament – anthemion and laurel wreath; the vessel probably dates from the last decades of the fifth century B.C. Another engraved *phiale* was found in a grave dating from the first half of the fourth century at Chmyreva Mogila in the Dniepr group of Scythian tombs. Immediately round the omphalos there is a band of ornament consisting of winged busts alternating with palmettes and on the inner surface of the *phiale* is engraved a Bacchic revel. The *phiale* was found with two others both decorated with bands of low-relief ornament immediately round the omphalos; one has a band of palmettes and winged busts, the other horned heads between palmettes.[2]

In the later fifth century *phialai* richly decorated with repoussé reliefs became common. The fashion had been developing in the earlier part of the century and by the end of it *phialai* with overall repoussé decoration were fashionable. A *phiale* with the popular design of concentric rows of acorns was shown in the hands of the Caryatids from the Erechtheum[3] and, according to Pausanias, the statue of Nemesis at Rhamnous held a *phiale* on which Ethiopians were represented. Some very elaborate relief *phialai* have been found in South Russian graves. A gold *phiale* from the barrow at Solokha is decorated over its whole surface with close-set groups of fighting animals, twenty-one altogether, arranged in three concentric rings and worked in relief on the outside.[4] There are Greek inscriptions on the rim and the style is Greek, but there is something un-Greek about the chaotic design. The *phiale* dates from the late fifth or early fourth century. Another gold relief *phiale* of about

[1] *ibid.*, 63, pl. IV.

[2] *AA*, 1910, figs. 16–17; *Materials*, 36, 1918, 53, figs. 52–4.

[3] Seen best in copies from Hadrian's Villa (S. Aurigemma, *Villa Adriana*, Rome, 1961, fig. 96) and a fragment from the Forum of Augustus.

[4] *RA*, xxiii, 1914, pl. XI; *SA*, xiii, 1950, 217–38.

the same period was found in the tumulus called the Kul Oba not far from Kerch.[1] The scheme of decoration is more formal, based upon the traditional *phiale* with radiating lotus and palmette patterns; but this basic design is overlaid with a profusion of ornamental motifs perhaps to suit the taste of Scythian patrons. Round the omphalos is a narrow frieze of dolphins and on the elements of the radiating leaf pattern are superimposed Gorgons' heads, grotesques, and filling ornament of scrolls and floral motifs.

A group of relief *phialai* with scenes depicting the Apotheosis of Herakles has been assigned to this period. The finest example, in the Metropolitan Museum, New York, is one of a pair said to have been found in a tomb at Spina together with a calyx krater by the Dinos painter (*c.* 425–400 B.C.) now in the Ashmolean Museum, Oxford.[2] The subject is treated in two scenes; on the narrow frieze round the omphalos (a traditional fifth century element) is shown the wedding banquet with Herakles and the other gods, while the main relief zone depicts the journey to Olympus with the four chariots, each shown in three-quarter view, of Herakles, Athena, Ares and Dionysos. Decoration and style permit a date from the late fifth century onwards and the discovery of a similar dish made of tin in a tomb at Spina has shown that the type was certainly current as early as the first half of the fourth century.[3] There are two similar *phialai,* less elaborate in design, found at Èze in the Alpes Maritimes and now in the British Museum (pl. 19A).[4] Not all of these are certainly original works of the late fifth century B.C.; we know that the type was popular and much copied in clay in the third century B.C. in S. Italy,[5] and it may be that the design originated in S. Italy or Sicily in the late fifth century and was later copied in various materials. In this connection it is interesting to note that the surviving examples were made by means of different techniques. Miss Richter[6] found that one of the London *phialai* was cast while the New York and second London pieces were hammered into matrices; both methods are suited to the kind of mass-production that takes place in an age of copying though they are not necessarily evidence for it. That the basic design of

[1] *SA*, xiii, 1950, 217–38.

[2] *AJA*, xlv, 1941, 363 ff; Beagley, *EVP*, 292; see also additional note on p. 89.

[3] *Hommages à Albert Grenier*, 1962, 84–103; 'terminus post quem non' of 340–330 B.C.

[4] *BMCP*, nos. 8–9; there is a fragment of another in Basel (*AK* 7, 1964, 97, pl. 31).

[5] *art. cit.* (note 2), 383 ff.; R. Pagenstecher, *Die Calenische Reliefkeramik*, Berlin, 1909, 159–64.

[6] *AJA*, liv, 1950, 364 f.

the *phialai* is appropriate to the later fifth century we have already seen from the evidence of the engraved *phiale* at Duvanli (see p. 80). There is another *phiale* with the same subject, very provincial in style, from Tivissa near Tarragona.[1] It is said to have been made by applying a sheet of silver over a negative mould and pressing it into the cavities. From the context in which it was found, the vessel is unlikely to have been made as early as the fifth century. It was probably manufactured in the third or second century B.C. perhaps with the aid of a clay version.

Other traditional forms of the *phiale mesomphalos* continued to be made in the late classical period. A fragmentary *phiale* from Ithaca in the British Museum[2] has two concentric bands of lotus and palmette like the one from Nymphaeum, and Luschey dates another example in Florence to the mid fourth century.[3] A *phiale* decorated like an open lotus flower was found recently at Populonia.[4] Two *phialai* of Greek type with radial fluting were found together with Achaemenid *phialai* in Thracian graves of the fourth century at Raduvene.[5]

THE ACHAEMENID PHIALE, later fifth and fourth century B.C.

One form of the Achaemenid *phiale* which became known in Greece in the late fifth and early fourth century is the so-called leaf *phiale* which is decorated on the underside with a series of close-set pointed leaves radiating from a central rosette. This scheme developed from the version with radiating flutes round a central rosette which is found in the Treasure of the Oxus. In the Treasure of Pithom (Tell el-Maskhuta) in Egypt the leaf *phiale* is found together with a number of other Achaemenid *phialai* of different designs; the treasure dates, apparently, from the first half of the fourth century B.C.[6] An example said to have been found in Akarnania and now in the Metropolitan Museum, New York, has a Greek inscription which has been dated to the fourth or third century B.C.[7] Another similar *phiale* was found together with objects of late fifth or early fourth century date at Boukiovtzi in Bulgaria.[8] It is probable that both the leaf *phiale* and a

[1] *AEArq*, 45, 1941, 534 f.; *AJA*, liv, 1950, 369.
[2] Reg. no. 1920, 5–29, 2; *Archaeologia*, 33, 1849, 12, pl. 2.
[3] Luschey, 97; Inghirami, *Monumenti Etruschi*, vi, pl. B.
[4] *NS*, 1961, 100, fig. 39.
[5] *RM*, 32, 1917, 55, fig. 53.
[6] *Brooklyn Museum, Five Years*; for the date *BSOAS*, xxiv, 1961, 190.
[7] Richter, *Greek Collection*, 97, pl. 76h.
[8] *Bull. Inst. Bulg.*, xii–xiii, 1938–9, 437–9.

variant on it which incorporates a series of egg-shaped bosses fitting into the spaces between the tips of the leaves were developed in the later fifth century. These and other Achaemenid forms continued to be popular in Hellenistic times and to exert a strong influence on Greek metalwork. The examples from Hellenistic contexts are discussed below (p. 99).

METAL RELIEFS: Later fifth century B.C.

In the cities of Greece during the latter part of the fifth century artists were acquiring great reputations in the craft of embossing metal. Miss Richter goes so far as to argue that when Pliny says of Pheidias that he 'opened up the art of *toreutice*'[1] this should be translated as 'showed the possibilities of the art of embossing' and that Pliny's source was specifically referring to the gold reliefs on various subsidiary parts of the chryselephantine statues – Amazons and Greeks on the shield of the Parthenos, Lapiths and Centaurs on the sandals. Miss Hill[2] interprets the passage as meaning that 'free repoussé' was invented by Pheidias, all previous reliefs having been hammered into matrices or carried out with punches, but this seems over-subtle. Miss Richter would argue, on the evidence of two passages in Martial,[3] that the great names of fifth-century sculpture – Myron, Polycleitus, Pheidias – also made relief vessels of gold and silver that were famous throughout antiquity and widely copied later.

Apart from the relief *phialai* the only evidence we have for the gold and silver repoussé work of the period is indirect: a few surviving clay moulds or reliefs which seem to be obviously copied from works in bronze or silver and the increasing popularity of relief ornament on painted vases made under the influence of metalwork. The purpose of the moulds and reliefs is uncertain;[4] they might serve for casting replicas of repoussé originals but other suggestions have been made, among them that they were used for identification and proof of ownership of fine metal originals. One such mould seems to have been taken from a silver cheekpiece of a helmet[5] and in quality it compares with the finest

[1] Pliny, *NH*, xxxiv, 54.
[2] *Hesperia*, xii, 1943, 87.
[3] Martial, viii, 51; iv, 39.
[4] see *Hesperia*, viii, 1939, 285 ff.; *Hesperia*, Suppl. 8, 1949, 365 ff.; *BCH*, lxxiv, 1950, 296.
[5] *JdAI*, xli, 1926, 191.

relief sculpture of the period. Rodenwaldt went so far as to say that work of this quality, by men like Mys who collaborated with Pheidias on the Athena Parthenos, must have exerted a strong influence on contemporary marble reliefs. Another mould found in the Agora at Athens suggests a silver original of the period around 415 B.C., the period when the Nike Temple parapet was being carved. Miss Richter has also argued that some of the plaster-casts found in the famous Mit Rahinet hoard and elsewhere[1] should be considered as copies of Greek fifth-century metalwork. Another interesting piece she discusses is a plaster *tondo* in the Vatican Library which she believes to reproduce a flat dish with a central medallion. The figures arranged in groups around the medallion depict an amazonomachy; Helios appears in the medallion itself. It is by no means certain that the piece is a straight copy of a fifth-century work but it shows the same basic scheme of decoration as the Herakles *phialai*. The references to copying of classical masterpieces in silver during the late Republic and early Empire has inspired a search for examples of pieces that seem to be derived from earlier work. None have been certainly recognised as direct copies and it must be remembered that however closely the style of a Roman piece, as for example the Hoby cups in Copenhagen, seems to be based upon classical originals, we have no reason to suppose that the original on which the work was based was a silver vessel.[2] On the other hand we are told that a certain Zenodorus made facsimiles of two cups by Calamis, presumably a classical master, which were so exact that scarcely any difference could be detected.[3]

PLAIN VESSELS: Later fifth and fourth centuries

Towards the end of the fifth century B.C. the use of gold and silver plate in private life was becoming rather more common. This increasing private wealth is reflected in the fact that many of the characteristic black-glazed vessels of Attic manufacture have counterparts in silver during this period. There is a bulbous jug with trefoil mouth in the Stathatos Collection that probably belongs to this period.[4] A little ribbed wide-mouthed jug from Baschova Mogila (pl. 17B) may be compared with clay examples from the Agora at Athens where the shape was especially popular, it seems, in the early years of the Peloponnesian

[1] *AJA*, lxii, 1958, 369 ff.
[2] See below p. 136.
[3] Pliny, *NH*, xxxiv, 47.
[4] *Collection Hélène Stathatos*, iii, no. 182.

War.[1] There is another similar vessel in the Vatican Museums. A jug with ribbing on the body and a handle ending below in a palmette was found at Boukiovtzi in Bulgaria.[2] A silver cup from Nymphaeum (Tumulus IV) in the Ashmolean Museum, Oxford (pl. 17A) may be dated by comparison with clay vessels to around 400 B.C.[3] Among the silver vessels found in the Vouni Treasure in Cyprus, which had been stored in a terracotta jar at the time of the destruction of the Palace in 380 B.C., was a cup-*kotyle* of silver with a slightly everted rim, a stand-ring base and two loop handles; the closest parallels for this cup are to be found among the thin-walled black-glazed cup-*kotylai* of the late fifth century in Athens.[4] The plain cup with a ribbed handle (pl. 18 centre) found in 1879 in a grave at Dalboki (Stara Zagora), Bulgaria has exact counterparts in Attic black-glaze of the late fifth century.[5] The contents of this find at Stara Zagora, which are now in the Ashmolean Museum, also included two beakers of local design with engraved ornament on the base and upper part. The engraving on one of these (pl. 18 left) looks as if it might have been made by a Greek craftsman while the second (pl. 18 right) is much less refined and skilful, perhaps an imitation by a Thracian metalworker. There is another beaker from the same source in the Hermitage Museum, Leningrad.[6] A horizontally ribbed beaker with a frieze of palmette ornament on the upper part was found at Boukiovtzi together with the jug and the *phiale* mentioned above.

In the first half of the fourth century B.C. the parallels between black-glazed pottery and plain silver ware continue to be close. A *kotyle* with the rim turning inwards slightly at the top, from a tomb at Kozani in Macedonia, may be dated just before the middle of the fourth century[7] and a similar piece in a poorer state of preservation comes from Chalke, near Rhodes and is now in the British Museum.[8] An elegant ribbed *kylix* which also has clay counterparts of around 350 B.C. was found in the Chmyreva Mogila (Dniepr Group); on the

[1] Filow, *Duvanlij*, 67; cf. *Hesperia*, iv, 508.

[2] *Bull. Inst. Bulg.*, xii–xiii, 1938–9, 437–9.

[3] *JHS*, v, 1884, 62–73; cf. *Hesperia*, xviii, 1949, pl. 86, 34, 33; *JHS*, lxiv, 1944, pls. 1 ff.

[4] *SCE*, iii, 278; cf. *Hesperia*, xviii, 1949, 343, no. 148.

[5] *Ashmolean Museum Department of Antiquities, A Summary Guide*, 1951, pl. XL; *Bull. Inst. Bulg.*, vi, 1930–1, 45 ff.

[6] Leningrad D 1903; *Fouilles et Recherches* (Sophia), iv, 1949, 207 ff.

[7] *AE*, 1948–9, 93.

[8] *BMCP*, no. 14.

inside is a gold repoussé medallion depicting a Nereid riding on a Hippocamp. The *kylix* seems to be the earliest surviving example of the use of an appliqué relief-medallion to decorate the inside of a vessel, a form of decoration which became very popular in the Hellenistic period.[1]

RHYTA AND HEAD VASES

The earliest surviving Greek silver vases with animal heads or *protomai* belong to the later fifth century. The two main forms are the animal-head cup (sometimes called a *rhyton*), of which clay examples are known throughout the fifth century, and the horn *rhyton* ending in the foreparts of an animal, which is not found in any material in the Greek world until the late fifth century. It was, however, a popular Scythian vessel, inspired by Achaemenid vessels with animal *protomai*.[2] The Greeks of the Black Sea colonies were probably making this kind of vessel for Scythian patrons earlier in the fifth century and the two gold horn *rhyta* which were found, together with a purely Persian piece, in the fourth kurgan of the Seven Brothers in the Kuban, (a burial that should be dated a little before 450), may, in fact, be the work of Greek craftsmen.[3] One terminates in a ram's head and the other in the foreparts of a leaping dog; the horns are decorated with chased geometric ornament. A Greek version of this type of *rhyton* seems to have been evolved at the end of the fifth century. The best example is the *rhyton* from Baschova Mogila at Duvanli (pl. 20A);[4] it is fluted down its length and ends below in the foreparts of a horse. There is a band of engraved lotus and palmette on the upper part of the horn and leaf ornament on the lip. The *rhyton* has been variously assigned to an Attic or east Greek workshop of the late fifth century. A little later, perhaps, is a very similar *rhyton* in the National Museum at Prague.[5]

The earliest Greek animal head cups in clay belong to the early fifth century B.C. but there are no metal examples before the end of the century.[6] The best known of these is the hind's head cup in the Museum at Trieste which is probably Attic or Ionian work of the first half of the

[1] *AA*, 1910, 219, fig. 18.
[2] On the relations between these forms see Tuchelt, *Tiergefässe*.
[3] *CR*, 1881, pl. I; Rostovtzeff, *I & G*, pl. XII.
[4] Filow, *Duvanlij*, 67, pl. VI.
[5] Svoboda and Cončev, *Neue Denkmäler*, pls. I ff.
[6] Tuchelt, *Tiergefässe*, 123.

fourth century;[1] the reliefs on the neck of the vase show a young woman and a bearded man (a rape scene?) and figures of Athena and an old man (Erechtheus?). A calf's head cup of the same period from Rachmanli in Bulgaria, now in the National Museum, Sofia, has reliefs of dancing satyrs and ivy-leaf ornament on the neck of the vessel (pl. 20B).[2] A very similar cup was found at Rozovetz in Bulgaria.[3] A Greco-Scythian boar's head cup of gilt silver was acquired recently by the Louvre;[4] the reliefs on the neck depict scenes connected with the life of Scythian warriors. There are two animal head cups of this period which do not look like Greek work. One was found in the Kul Oba tumulus[5] and another from Poroina is in Bucarest.[6] Both have repoussé figured reliefs in barbarous classicising style.

Head vases were made in clay throughout the fifth century. There is only one surviving silver example, very fragmentary, which belongs to the early fourth century; it was acquired recently by the British Museum. The vase is janiform with heads perhaps of Attis and Cybele back to back and a Judgement of Paris in relief on the neck. It is said to come from the Tell el-Maskhuta hoard in Egypt which consisted of Attic coins and Achaemenid silver plate, datable in the first half of the fourth century B.C.[7] The inscriptions explaining the figures in the Judgement are in Lycian script and the style of the figures is close to that of the hind's head cup in Trieste. It is almost certainly Ionian work, but of Attic inspiration, like so much of the art of Asia Minor in the first half of the fourth century.

GRECO-SCYTHIAN SILVER

A number of fine silver vessels were made by Greek artists in Panticapaeum (Kerch) for Scythian patrons and are generally decorated with scenes in relief relating to Scythian life. The main output of this school seems to be concentrated in the period from 400–350 B.C. The shapes of these vessels are often local ones but the craftsmanship is purely Greek. Two common shapes are a deep bowl narrowing towards the top with a pair of downward sloping lug handles, and a small bulbous flask with a

[1] Wuilleumier, *Trésor*, 60, pl. IX; *ÖJh*, v, 1902, 112. Some good details in G. Hafner, *Ein Apollon-Kopf in Frankfurt*, 1962, figs. 24–6.

[2] Filow, *Duvanlij*, 167, pl. X, figs. 182–3.

[3] *Bull. Inst. Bulg.*, xii–xiii, 1938–9, p. 208, fig. 56.

[4] *La Revue des Arts*, 1962.

[5] *ABC*, 87, pl. XXXVI, 1 and 2.

[6] Odobesco, *Petrossa*, 498 ff., figs. 202, 205.

[7] Reg. no. 1962, 12–12, 1, *BMQ* 28, 1964, 95–102; on the hoard, see above, p. 82.

tall concave neck. One of the bowls, from the Solokha barrow, has a reeded lower part separated from an upper, figured, zone by a band of guilloche;[1] the reliefs in repoussé, chased and gilded, represent Scythian horsemen out hunting. Another of these lug-handled bowls, found in the tumulus of Chmyreva Mogila has a main frieze of water birds and fish.[2] On little flasks from Častye Kurgan, Voronež[3] and Kul Oba,[4] the lower part is reeded and the friezes show Scythian warriors in everyday activities (e.g. pl. 19B) – in conference, instructing a youth in the use of the bow, in scenes of war and campaigning. Rostovtzeff has this to say of the artists who made the vessels; 'The whole atmosphere is that of the Russian steppes; the artist must have known the steppes, must have studied the life of the Scythian camp and must have been thoroughly well-acquainted with the little horses of the steppes.'[5]

The masterpiece of this school is the famous Chertomlyk *amphora* (pl. 21)[6] found in a chamber of a large barrow in that place. The proposed dates for this vessel have differed widely but it can hardly be much later than 350 B.C.[7] The vase is a large *amphora* standing 70 cms high with three outlets in its body each equipped with a strainer; the principal outlet is in the form of a horse's head while the side outlets have lion's heads. On the shoulder are two bands of relief, the upper showing animal groups in low relief and the lower, which goes right round the vessel, Scythian warriors breaking in a horse. The figures in the latter scene are in high relief; they were cast separately and then soldered on. The body of the vase is covered with an overall design of scroll ornament and palmettes; on the main side the design is worked in repoussé relief while on the back it shades off into engraving. Minns[8] suggests that the vase was specially designed to be used for *kumys*, a local drink with dregs that would require the use of such strainers.

[1] *RA*, xxiii, 1914, pls. III–IX; Ebert, *Reallexikon*, s.v. Solocha.

[2] *AA*, 1910, 219, figs. 20–1.

[3] Rostovtzeff, *I & G*, 108; *Materials*, 34, 1913, 75 ff.; *SA*, viii, 1946, 11–50.

[4] Rostovtzeff, *I & G*, pl. XXII.

[5] ibid. 109 ff.

[6] *AD*, iv, 83–90; P. Jacobsthal, *Ornamente Griechischer Vasen*, Berlin, 1927, pls. 142–3; Becatti, *Oreficerie*, pl. CXXVII.

[7] The Chertomlyk burial is not dated, though it has a *terminus post* of about 350. The amphora has been dated as late as third century B.C. (*BABesch*, xxx, 1955, 50 ff.) but this seems to separate it too far from the main series of Greco-Scythian vessels which belong to the early fourth century. On the other hand, the engraved dish found with the amphora (see below p. 106) is probably not earlier than 300 B.C.

[8] Minns, *S & G*, 288–9.

CONCLUSIONS

By 330 B.C. Greek craftsmen were using almost all the techniques of the silversmith, except those connected with mass-production. The fact that silver plate had by now come into domestic use greatly increased its variety. Though there are no surviving examples of the silver dishes occasionally referred to, most of the everyday drinking vessels had their expensive counterparts in silver. It is curious that little 'toilet vases' – unguentaria, pyxides etc. – and mirrors do not seem to have been made of silver in the classical period. There was a great revival of the art of repoussé in the later fifth century which seems to have put an end to the comparatively short-lived fashion for engraved plate. The class of Greco-Scythian silver includes some of the finest surviving products of Greek repoussé work for which we have so very little direct evidence in Greece itself.

Note: While this book was in the press, Mr Brian F. Cook informed me that an analysis of one of the New York *phialai* referred to on p. 81 has shown that it consists almost entirely of tin with a little silver which was perhaps originally on the surface. The other New York *phiale* is, no doubt, also made of tin.

CHAPTER FIVE

The Hellenistic Age I: Early Hellenistic, 330–200 B.C.

In the period discussed in this and the following chapter there was a vast increase in the quantity of gold and silver plate in the hands not only of rulers but also of private individuals. The supplies of precious metals had greatly increased. Philip II owed much of his success in expanding the power of Macedon to his exploitation of the gold and silver mines in Macedonia and Thrace and to prospecting activities elsewhere. Alexander followed his father's policy in the eastern territories that came under his rule and brought back great quantities of treasure as booty from his campaigns.[1] His successors, notably the Ptolemies and the Seleucids, had in their territories rich sources of precious metals. Wealthy businessmen of the period hoarded gold and silver vessels as suitable form of reserve capital and from the time of Alexander onwards the fashion for collecting expensive tableware became more and more general. The temples of the gods continued to be enriched with dedications of gold and silver plate; the dedications of the Ptolemies and Seleucids to the Treasury of Apollo at Delos and other temple treasures show how the Hellenistic Kings vied with one another in ostentatious present giving.[2] The period ends when the Romans, who had acquired the taste for gold and silver plate from their contacts with the Greek world, took the place of the Hellenistic Kings and gave their patronage to the metalworkers of the Hellenistic World.

In view of the remarkable wealth in gold and silver suggested in the written sources for the period, the actual finds of plate from Hellenistic times, though they are incomparably larger than those for the classical period, are still small. S. Russia and the peripheral regions of the Greek

[1] Rostovtzeff, *SEHHW*, 129 ff.
[2] *IG*, xi, 4, 6; *OGIS*, 214; *Inscr. de Delos*, 287.

world continue to supply the main evidence for the history of silver plate but new areas of the expanded Greek world, especially Egypt, become important. Down to 330 B.C. there were perhaps only a few important centres for the manufacture of high-class silverware. All the engraved plate of the fifth century B.C. was probably made in Athens or by Attic craftsmen, and the silversmiths of S. Russia working for Scythian chiefs formed one of the few clearly recognisable schools. In the Hellenistic period the shops of the silversmiths multiplied everywhere and regional styles developed, but the freedom with which craftsmen moved from one centre to another and the widespread trade in plate produced a common tradition that makes it very difficult to isolate the products of particular places. Only a few centres, such as Tarentum, are comparatively well known; as for the rest, discoveries so far have been insufficient to build up a picture of their characteristic products.

A grave in the Sellenskaya Mountains on the Taman peninsula[1] contained a collection of plate which is typical of early Hellenistic finds; the grave included coins of Alexander the Great and probably dates from the end of the fourth century. The plate consisted of a ladle and a strainer, both with handles terminating in ducks' heads, a fragmentary plain stemmed *kantharos,* a plain cup-*kotyle* with two loop handles, a *phiale* of Achaemenid type with fluted body and a straight offset rim, a small long-necked flask with scroll decoration and fluting on the body, a jug, a little plain flask and a curious bucket-shaped container with a lid and loop handle. Some of the vessels seem to be of local shape and use; others are pure Greek. The find illustrates the increasing repertory of the silversmiths who were turning out objects designed for domestic use; we get for the first time what look like collections of domestic plate sometimes covering a wide variety of uses. (See also Appendix IV.)

LADLES

Silver ladles and strainers become common in this period. The form of the ladle differs hardly at all from the Mycenaean (p. 47) and Etruscan (p. 68) examples already noted. The bowl is rather shallow, the handle is straight or slightly curved backwards and widens to a shoulder from which springs a narrow loop ending in a duck's head (fig. 21*a*). The ladle from the Sellenskaya find is of this form and an identical one was

[1] *AA*, 1913, 184 ff.

found in the contemporary burial at Karagodeuashk.[1] A similar ladle (pl. 22A) was part of a find said to have been made at Prusias in Bithynia, the contents of which are now in a private collection in New York.[2] Another was found with several silver vessels at Montefortino in North Italy and is now in the Metropolitan Museum, New York; the context of this find suggests that the objects must be earlier than 290 B.C.[3] A ladle of this kind, perhaps of the later third century, said to have been

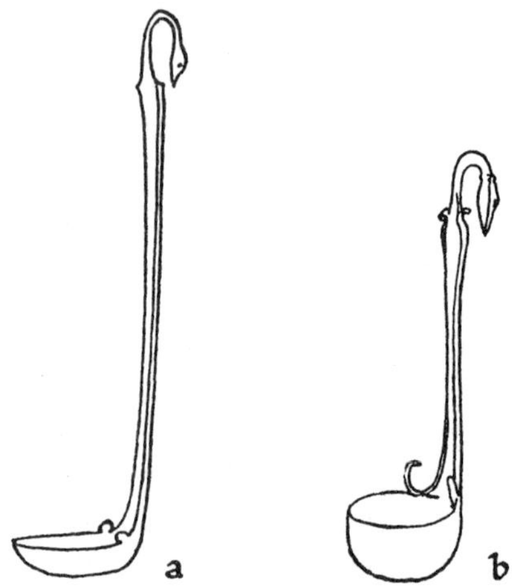

FIG. 21: Silver ladles; (*a*) early Hellenistic (*b*) late Hellenistic

found in Akarnania, was bought in Athens in 1938;[4] it bears an inscription giving the ancient name of this utensil, the *kyathos*. A good example of this earlier Hellenistic type, found in a third-century grave in Thessaly, is in the Walters Art Gallery, Baltimore; it was found together with a strainer.[5] Several examples from undated contexts are known, including two from Kerch.[6]

STRAINERS

The earliest surviving silver strainer from the Greek world seems to be the one found in a fifth-century grave at Duvanli;[7] it takes the form of a

[1] *Materials*, xiii, 1894.

[2] Neugebauer, *Privatbesitz*, 47, no 213; von Bothmer, *Private Collections*, no. 266.

[3] *MA*, ix, 1899, 695 ff., 766 ff.; Richter, *Greek Collection*, 127, pl. 107.

[4] *AJA*, xlvii, 1943, 209 ff.

[5] *Journal of the Walters Art Gallery*, i, 1938, 41 ff.

[6] *ABC*, pl. xxx, 1; *CR*, 1863, 49; for these ladles in general Robinson, *Olynthus*, x, 194–8.

[7] Filow, *Duvanlij*, 133, fig. 157.

small bowl with the holes punched in a whirligig pattern. The Hellenistic examples are more elaborate and are usually equipped with handles. The one from the Sellenskaya find has a shallow round bowl with patterned perforations, and a broad flat handle in the same plane as the rim; like the handles of the ladles, this handle has a loop at the end with a duck's head finial. There is also a horizontal loop on the side of the

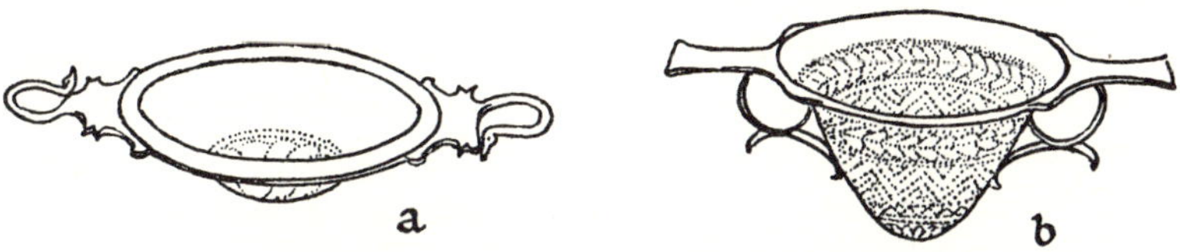

FIG. 22: Silver strainers; (*a*) early Hellenistic (*b*) late Hellenistic

bowl opposite the handle which could rest on the lip of the container when liquid was being poured. There is a ladle almost identical with this one from Karagodeuashk[1] and a somewhat later version in the Walters Art Gallery, Baltimore[2] (fig. 22*a*) which has two shorter handles of the same basic type as the Sellenskaya strainer. A strainer from the Prusias find has its perforations punched in a whirligig pattern and a single handle made of thick wire bent round and ending in a duck's head (pl. 22c). A similar strainer from S. Russia[3] is equipped with a single *kylix* handle and perhaps represents a slightly earlier type than the Sellenskaya one. The strainer found in Akarnania with the ladle mentioned above is an elaborately decorated version of this type. The strainer itself is oval and surrounded by a horizontal frame with an elaborate border of acanthus leaves; at one end there is a duck's head handle in the same plane as the rim of the strainer.

DRINKING CUPS

Plain silver drinking cups of classical pedigree are found in a number of early Hellenistic contexts. The cup-*kotylai* with loop handles from the Sellenskaya and Prusias finds have high cavetto foot and flaring rim which may be compared with Attic clay vases of about the end of the fourth century. The Prusias cup is decorated on the inside with a series of stamped palmettes, a form of decoration which seems more appropriate to clay vessels than to metal.[4] A deep cup in the Walter C. Baker

[1] *Materials*, xiii, 1894, pl. VI, 3.
[2] Found with the ladle mentioned above.
[3] *ABC*, pl. XXXI, 4.
[4] *Hesperia*, xxiv, 1955, 172 ff.

collection[1] also has parallels in Attic black-glaze around 300 B.C.; the bowl is almost hemispherical and stands upon a high foot and there are two high-swung loop handles fixed to the body by means of long tongue-shaped soldering plates. A similar cup from Kul Oba lacks one of its handles, it is inscribed with the word *ΕΡΜΕΩ*.[2] An odd feature is its silver-gilt lid engraved with a design of linked palmettes, alternately upright and inverted, round a central rosette.

A tall-stemmed *kantharos,* similar in shape to the one from the tumulus of Golemata Mogila, was part of the Sellenskaya find and there was a tall-stemmed *kylix* in the Karagodeuashk burial.[3] An interesting *kantharos* was found in a man's grave at Gornyani in Bulgaria in 1936.[4] The vessel has a round bowl and a tall upper part with flaring rim, a moulded foot and two high-swung handles with horizontal projecting thumb rests. Its shape compares with Attic black-glaze vessels of the turn of the fourth-third century and it was found together with tetradrachms of Philip of Macedon. Two similar *kantharoi* were found together with several other silver vessels at Dherveni in Macedonia in a tomb dating from the later fourth century B.C.[5] A stemless *kylix* from Montefortino[6] belongs to an important group of silver drinking vessels of this period which are decorated on the inside with engraved ornament (pl. 24A). The *kylix* has loop handles and a central boss on the inside, around which is engraved a frieze of palmette and leaf ornament. The concentric lines on the inside of the bowl suggest that the vase was finished by turning on a lathe and the heavy silver indicates that the bowl was first cast, a normal practice in contemporary bronze drinking vessels. A very similar *kylix,* said to come from Boscoreale, is in the British Museum;[7] the central boss is gilded and in the engraved anthemion pattern that surrounds it are some letters of the Greek alphabet which may be the signature of the man who made the vessel. There are two other *kylikes* of this kind in Berlin which were part of a find made at Paternò near Katana in Sicily (pl. 24B).[8] The provenance of all these *kylikes* is Italy or Sicily and it seems likely that they were made in western Greek workshops around 300 B.C. A fine cup-*kotyle* not unlike

[1] von Bothmer, *Private Collections*, no. 270.

[2] *ABC*, pl. XXXVII, 4, 5.

[3] *Materials*, xiii, 1894, 45, fig. 12.

[4] *Bull. Inst. Bulg.* xi, 1937, 209, figs. 188–9.

[5] *Arch. Rep.*, 1961–2, 15; see Appendix 4.

[6] Richter, *Greek Collection*, pl. 107d.

[7] *BMCP*, no. 15.

[8] *Stephanos T. Wiegand*, pls. 9–10; see below note 2, p. 98.

the Prusias and Sellenskaya ones, which was acquired recently by the Louvre, is elaborately decorated on the inside.[1] It has a central boss with six stamped palmettes arranged round it. Two concentric rings of ovolo form the borders for a frieze of engraved and gilded floral ornament. The combination of stamped ornament and engraving is odd and one wonders whether they are contemporary. The engraving, in any case, is not much earlier than around 250 B.C. Two shallow *kylikes* found with other silver in a woman's grave near the Quarantine Road at Kerch[2] are decorated on the inside with appliqué medallions representing Helios in his chariot. This form of decoration, which was also coming into fashion on various kinds of bowl, must have been common on the drinking cups of the period and is imitated in clay vessels. The Quarantine grave seems to belong to the period around 200 B.C.[3]

Towards the end of the period discussed in this chapter, drinking cups decorated with chased ornament on the outside were becoming fashionable. A good example comes from the Quarantine grave mentioned above (pl. 30B). The vessel is a developed form of the classical cup-*kotyle* with only a trace of the everted rim of earlier examples, the form being intermediate between the cup-*kotyle* and the deep cups of the second and first centuries B.C. This cup is engraved on the outside with a chased and gilt necklace stretching between the handles, a popular form of ornament in the period,[4] and the moulding of the foot is also decorated. It is clear that this vessel is rather earlier than the ovoid cup in the Benaki Museum[5] which is decorated with guilloche on the outside below the rim and has loop handles with horizontal finger grips, or the similar cup with *kylix* handles in New York.[6] These two are typical of the later Hellenistic period and all the drinking cups with rich repoussé and chased decoration on the outside belong to the period after 200 B.C.

One of the most striking pieces from the so-called Treasure of Tarentum is a tall *kantharos* standing on a broad foot and a high moulded stem enriched with acanthus ornament.[7] The lower part of the cup

1 *La Révue des Arts*, 1960, 133 f.

2 *ABC*, xxxviii, 5.

3 For the find in general see *AdI*, 1840, 13; Minns, *S & G*, 384–5, thinks that the plate is of different periods.

4 cf. the clay examples, *AM*, 26, 1901, 74.

5 Segall, *Benaki*, no. 39.

6 Richter, *Greek Collection*, pl. 107.

7 Wuilleumier, *Trésor*, pls. V–VI.

springs from a calyx of leaves and is decorated with vertical ribbing; the upper part is concave and ornamented with a garland in low relief. Two upright loop-handles rise from the ribbed section of the body and below each of the handles is a figure of Eros carrying an amphora. The cup has a heavy moulded rim and a removable case is fitted to the inside. A very similar tall *kantharos*, without the 'plastic' decoration was found in a tomb at Kerch (pl. 26A).[1] In other materials, the closest parallels to these vessels are a faience *kantharos* said to come from Tanagra and a West Slope *krater* from the Athenian Agora.[2] The date of the Tarentum Treasure is much disputed. A *pyxis* in the find (see below p. 104) contained coins struck at Tarentum between 315 and 272 and the vessels were originally assigned to that period. More recently they have been dated to the second half of the third century and, by one student, as late as 100 B.C.[3] The most probable date seems to be around 200 B.C.[4] The *kantharos* and other vessels in the find exhibit the same taste for baroque shapes and ornament as the find from the Quarantine Road which is generally assigned to that period.

BOWLS

One of the most characteristic pottery vessels of the Hellenistic period is the hemispherical bowl without a foot, known as a Megarian bowl.[5] These bowls are richly decorated with relief ornament and made in moulds, and it has long been recognised that in form and decoration they are closely related to contemporary metalwork. A common form of decoration consists of a calyx of leaves issuing from a central rosette, the calyx being composed of acanthus leaves and various forms of the *nymphaea* leaf; reeding, overlapping leaves, a calyx combined with a frieze of figures are among other popular forms. The earliest clay examples of this type of bowl belong to the period just after 300 B.C. The only silver example of such an early date is a very battered one from the tumulus of Karagodeuashk, the details of which cannot be made out clearly.[6] All the other surviving examples in precious metal seem to be later than 200 B.C. and are discussed in the following chapter.

[1] *ABC*, pl. XXXVIII, 2.
[2] *BABesch*, xxxiii, 1958, 49 ff., figs. 12–14.
[3] Kuthmann, *Toreutik*, 23 ff.
[4] *BABesch*, xxxiii, 1958, 43 ff.
[5] There is a vast literature on this type of bowl. For the relations with metalwork see especially *Hesperia*, iii, 1934, 311–480; *BABesch*, xxviii, 1953, 1 ff.; *JdAI*, 70, 1955, 129 ff.
[6] *Materials*, xiii, 1894, 43, fig. 8.

Various other forms of footless bowl, including the ovoid *mastos*, also belong in general to the period after the one discussed in this chapter.

A pair of bowls or cups decorated on the inside with relief medallions showing heads of Dionysos and a Maenad kissing were found in the Treasure of Tarentum.[1] Such relief medallions on cups and bowls, usually made separately and soldered on, were coming into fashion in the third century and are one of the most characteristic features of late Hellenistic silver. Medallion bowls and cups, imitated from metal originals, are among the common types of Calene black-glazed ware made in Campania between 250 and 180 B.C.[2] They are also found on Attic vessels of West Slope fabric.[3] A deep bowl not unlike the later *mastos* in shape was found in Lokris and is now in the National Museum at Athens;[4] it has an omphalos on the inside which is decorated with an engraved rosette and there are two concentric bands of gilded ornament consisting of a wave pattern and a floral scroll on the inner surface of the bowl. It also has close parallels in clay vases.

THE PHIALE MESOMPHALOS

A magnificently decorated gold *phiale* was found in the recently discovered treasure of gold vessels from Panagyurishte in S. Bulgaria, which seems to belong to the late fourth century B.C.[5] The decoration on the *phiale* consists of three concentric rows of negro heads in repoussé relief with a row of acorns immediately round the omphalos; the spaces between the heads and the acorns are filled with palmette ornament in low relief and there is a narrow band of ornament immediately round the omphalos. The *phiale* has an inscription giving its weight expressed in the Attic system and its equivalent in Persian darics (100);[6] its actual weight, 845·7 grammes, is close to that of the *phiale* from Solokha mentioned above. A very similar gold *phiale* was recently acquired by the Metropolitan Museum, New York (pl. 23A).[7] The ornament consists of three concentric rings of acorns diminishing in size towards the centre and a row of beech nuts immediately round the omphalos; the spaces between are filled with low-relief ornament

[1] Wuilleumier, *Trésor*, pl. 1.

[2] Pagenstecher, *Calenische Reliefkeramik.*

[3] *AM*, 26, 1901, 81, no. 31.

[4] *ibid.* 90.

[5] Svoboda and Cončev, *Neue Denkmäler*, 115 ff.; *AK*, 3, 1960, 3 ff.; for a heretical dating *RM*, 65, 1958, 121. See below p. 102.

[6] I. Venedikov, *The Panagyurishte Gold Treasure*, Sofia, 1961, 22–3.

[7] *BMMA*, xxi, 1962, 154 ff.

of little bees and motifs based upon palmette designs. This *phiale* has a weight inscription in Punic characters dating from the third century B.C. and a short Greek graffito; it must have been made by a Greek for a Carthaginian or soon came into the latter's possession. The design of the New York and Panagyurishte *phialai* is one which had been developed in the later fifth century B.C. (see above p. 80).

A fragmentary *phiale* found in the tumulus of Karagodeuashk[1] has a series of ornamental bands round the omphalos, very like the *phialai* from Chmyreva Mogila. The popularity of the lotus *phiale* in clay presupposes their existence in metal though, in fact, no silver or gold examples can be assigned with certainty to this period. A form of the *phiale* found in Greece from the fourth century onwards is the so-called egg *phiale* which appears, for example, in the frieze of the Tholos at Epidaurus. A good example is the silver-gilt *phiale* which formed part of the hoard of silver from Paternò (see above p. 94) and is now in Berlin (pl. 26B);[2] by analogy with clay vessels it may be assigned to a workshop in Apulia of the third century B.C. By the rim of the vessel, between the eggs, there are little repoussé heads wearing pointed caps and between them half-palmettes and scrolls. The omphalos is gilded and the surface around it is overlaid with gold sheet decorated with anthemion ornament in repoussé. The *phiale* once in the Museum at Bari[3] which is said to have been found at Tarentum is really a shallow plate with a low concave rim. Its basic design is strongly influenced by late Achaemenid bossed *phialai* such as those from the Prokorovka Kurgan of the third century B.C.[4] The egg-shaped bosses in relief on the outside are reduced to a very minor feature. On the inside a large relief medallion is fitted and this is surrounded by the zone of little egg-shaped recesses alternating with little theatrical masks which are also separately made and applied. The medallion and masks conceal the reverse of the low-relief repoussé on the outside of the *phiale* which consists of a formal design of stems and tendrils radiating from a central rosette, and a series of low-relief lions' heads between the bosses. A comparable vessel is the

[1] *Materials*, xiii, 1894, pl. VI, 4.

[2] Bruns, *Schatzkammer*, 30, fig. 24. The hoard, found in 1909, was quickly dispersed; it is described from hearsay evidence in *NS*, 1912, 412. Surviving objects believed to have belonged to it include the two *kylikes* in Berlin (p. 94) and a shell-shaped *pyxis* also in Berlin (p. 104 note 3).

[3] *RM*, 33, 1918, 104 ff.; Wuilleumier, *Trésor*, pl. VIII; *AD*, iii, 256.

[4] Rostovtzeff, *I & G*, pl. XXIV.

silver-gilt *phiale* from Maryinskaya in Moscow; this also has a large central medallion and a ring of small pear-shaped bosses divided by simple leaf motifs.[1] The medallion consists of a rosette surrounded by a collar of leaves and from this spring four systems of scrolls between which are winged siren-like creatures, each wearing a polos. Similar foliate winged creatures appear on other metalwork of the third century B.C.[2]

THE ACHAEMENID PHIALE

A *phiale* in the Prusias find belongs to the type with flaring offset rim decorated on the underside with a series of long, pointed leaves radiating from a central rosette (the so-called leaf *phiale*). It has already been suggested that the type derives from Achaemenid fluted *phialai* of the fifth century and was perhaps known in Greece by the early fourth century. The leaf *phiale* is commonly found in Egypt, as for example in the hoard of Tell el-Maskhuta[3] and Luschey is inclined to attribute al Hellenistic examples to workshops in Ptolemaic Egypt where the influence of Persian metalwork was particularly strong.[4] A variant introduces a series of egg-shaped bosses (e.g. pl. 25A) fitting into the spaces between the tips of the leaves, a scheme which is obviously inspired by the various forms of bossed *phialai*.[5] A characteristic group of early Ptolemaic silver vessels found in Egypt in 1917 and now in the Metropolitan Museum, New York includes one of these leaf *phialai* with bosses, and a lotus *phiale*, also bossed.[6] In the Hellenistic period there was a complicated interaction of Greek and Achaemenid forms of *phiale* upon one another and there are many problems connected with the various forms which still remain to be solved.

THE ACHAEMENID DEEP BOWL

Another vessel of Achaemenid origins which becomes popular in Greece in the early Hellenistic period is the little bowl with a hemispherical body and a concave upper part with flaring rim (fig. 23). Examples of this basic shape occur in the fifth century in Achaemenid contexts[7] but not, apparently, in the Greek world until the fourth

[1] *GA*, 1887, pl. 23.
[2] *PBSR*, xviii, 1950, fig. on p. 4, pl. II.
[3] Brooklyn Museum, *Five Years*, pls. 68–74.
[4] Luschey, 128 ff.
[5] *BSOAS*, xxiv, 1961, 190.
[6] *BMMA*, 33, 1938, 199.
[7] e.g. a plain silver one from Gordion (*AJA*, 66, 1962, pl. 41, fig. 1a) and an elaborately decorated gold bowl in the Teheran Museum, inscribed 'Xerxes the Great King' (*ILN*, July 21st, 1956.)

century. The earlier examples are either plain or decorated very simply with an ovolo moulding dividing the two parts of the body. There are two good examples with the ovolo moulding in the Archaeological Museum at Istanbul (nos. 87 and 5411). In Hellenistic times the vessel,

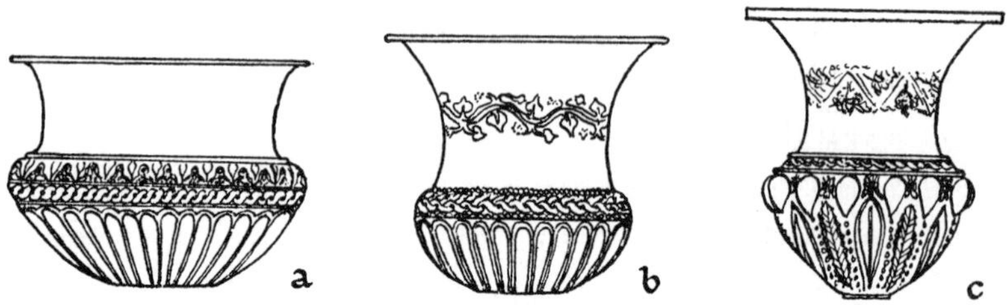

FIG. 23: Three forms of the 'Achaemenid deep bowl'
Scale 1:3

which is essentially a deep form of the Achaemenid *phiale,* is similarly decorated with the upper part plain and the lower ornamented with fluting, ribbing, or leaf ornament. It was common in Egypt during the early Hellenistic period as was the Achaemenid *phiale* itself. A good example comes from the Treasure of Tukh el-Qaramous which is dated by coins to the first half of the third century B.C.[1] It occurs in Attic black-glaze around 300 B.C. and during the Hellenistic period develops in increasing richness with the addition of decorated mouldings dividing the two parts and more elaborate ornamentation on the body. Among the early silver examples, dating perhaps around 300 B.C., is one from Mezek in Bulgaria[2] with a ribbed lower body and a row of beading dividing it from the concave upper section. Another similar one was found at Karagodeuashk.[3] More elaborate, but still perhaps fourth century, is one from Nikisiani in Macedonia[4] found with coins of Philip of Macedon; the lower body is fluted and divided from the upper part by several bands of decorated moulding – guilloche, cable, leaf-and-tongue and cable again. This vessel was found together with a plain one of the same type and a silver *skyphos*. Another from Sedes Tomb G at Salonika,[5] usually assigned to the late fourth century B.C., is almost identical. A fragment from Zlokoutchéné in Bulgaria, with overlapping leaf ornament on the lower body instead of ribbing,

[1] *Le Musée Egyptien*, ii, 1907, 57–62, pls. XXVII, XXVIII, 2.
[2] *Bull. Inst. Bulg.*, xi, 1937, 134, fig. 122.
[3] *Materials*, xiii, 1894, pl. V, 2.
[4] *BCH*, lxxxiv, 1960, 799.
[5] *AE*, 1937, iii (1956), 884, figs. 18–19.

belongs to the third century B.C.[1] A taller version (fig. 23*b*) found in a tomb at Varbitza in Bulgaria[2] has been dated to the late Hellenistic period,[3] although its comparatively simple decoration, consisting of a central rosette and ribbing on the lower part and an engraved frieze of ivy leaf on the tall upper wall, is hardly much later than the mid-third century.[4] A much more elaborate example of the tall form is the cup from Ithaca in the British Museum (fig. 23*c* and pl. 25B)[5] which has a calyx of leaves on the lower part combined with egg-shaped bosses and an engraved and gilded vine wreath on the upper part of the body. This combination of leaves and bosses, like that on the shallow lead *phialai*, had been popular in Egypt from early Ptolemaic times. The fleshy naturalistic leaves suggest a date not much earlier than 200 B.C. An example from Egypt in Brooklyn[6] is decorated with a calyx of leaves similar to those found on Megarian bowls of the second century B.C. One in the Cabinet des Médailles, Paris, is simpler in decoration and might date from the third century B.C.; it is said to have been found in Greece and bears a graffito inscription with the word *ΠΑΤΡΟΚΛΕΟΣ*.

RHYTA AND HEAD VASES

Rhyta of various kinds are frequently shown in scenes of Hellenistic origin and seem to have been particularly popular in Ptolemaic Egypt. A fine Greco-Iranian drinking horn was found in the Egyptian Treasure of Tukh el-Qaramous (*c.* 300–250 B.C.) together with other pieces of close Achaemenid connections; the horn terminates in the protome of a winged griffin.[7] A very fragmentary drinking horn from Karagodeuashk is similar in form to the Scythian horns of the fifth century (see above p. 86); it ended in a little animal head and the whole surface was decorated with engraved figures and ornament including a wide frieze of horsemen near the rim.[8] The workmanship is obviously Greek and

[1] *Bull. Inst. Bulg.*, vi, 1931, 256, fig. 187.

[2] Filow, *Duvanlij*, 171 ff.

[3] Kuthmann, *Toreutik*, 91.

[4] Other examples, without provenance, in Hamburg (H. Hoffmann, *Kunst des Altertums in Hamburg*, Mainz, 1961, pl. 98), Boston (*Archaeology*, 12, 1959, p. 4) and the British Museum (*BMCP*, 84).

[5] On loan from the Society of Antiquaries: Reg. no. 1920, 5–29, 1; *Archaeologia*, 33, 36–54, pls. II, III.

[6] Brooklyn Museum, *Five Years*.

[7] *BSRAl (ns)*, x, 1938–9, 336 ff.; Maspero, *Le Musée Egyptien*, ii, 57–62.

[8] *Materials*, xiii, 1894, 144 ff.

related to Greco-Scythian work of the late fifth and fourth centuries. The Treasure of Panagyurishte[1] included, apart from the *phiale mesomphalos* mentioned above, four gold *rhyta,* three head vases and a richly decorated amphora. Of the *rhyta,* three are animal head vases with heads of a stag (pl. 23B), a bull and a ram, while the fourth is a bent *rhyton* ending in the foreparts of a goat. The upper parts of all four are decorated with repoussé reliefs depicting Greek mythological subjects – a Judgement of Paris, Dionysos and Maenads, Herakles and Theseus, and a group of Hera, Apollo, Artemis and Nike. The handles of the head vases take the form of animal figures resting their forepaws on the rims of the vessels and surmounting a fluted columnar stem. The three jugs in the form of women's heads have similar handles with sphinxes at the top. One of the heads is helmeted and all three have been interpreted as Amazons. The *amphora,* really an *amphora-rhyton,* is a tall-necked vessel, the body decorated with repoussé reliefs representing the episode of the Seven against Thebes; a band of anthemion divides the relief from the plain neck and on the bottom there is a rosette and a pair of negro heads with open mouths through which liquid could be drunk. The handles take the form of figures of centaurs surmounting a short, fluted stem.

The date of the Panagyurishte Treasure is disputed; on present evidence the period around 300 B.C. seems most probable. The influence of Achaemenid art is particularly strong in the shapes and decoration of the vessels. The *amphora* is closely paralleled in form by a silver *amphora* of Persian origin found in the region between Sinope and Trebizond on the Black Sea which also has spouts on the bottom for drinking the liquid.[2] The centaur-handles and other details of design and ornament also suggest strong Persian influence and it seems likely that these vessels were made in some part of the Greek east where such influence would be particularly strong during the early Hellenistic period. The conclusion is confirmed by the fact that some of the weight measurements on the vessels are given both in the Persian and the Attic system. Presumably the collection represents the possessions of a religious shrine; it is hard to suppose any other use than a ritual one for these vessels.

[1] Svoboda and Bončev, *Neue Denkmäler*; D. Zontschew, *Der Goldschatz von Panagurischte*, Berlin, 1959; I. Venedikov, *The Panagyurishte Gold Treasure*, Sofia, 1961.

[2] *AK*, ii, 1959, pl. 24.

TOILET VESSELS

The manufacture of silver 'toilet vessels' of various kinds was an important part of silversmith's work in Hellenistic times. Perfume vases, little trinket boxes (*pyxides*), and mirrors were often made of silver; silver strigils and other toilet implements became common.

A] *Perfume vases*

A common type of perfume vase or *unguentarium* has a bulbous body tapering downwards to a narrow stem and usually having a tall narrow neck. One of the earliest silver examples, found in a tomb in Boeotia, is now in Berlin.[1] The lower part of the body is ornamented with a calyx of leaves, alternately plain and serrated, surmounted by a band of guilloche; the bulbous part of the body is vertically ribbed and there is a band of anthemion ornament on the shoulder below the narrow neck. The *unguentarium* is probably not much later than 250 B.C. Variations on this form remained in fashion throughout the Hellenistic period. A similar vessel, perhaps used as an oil flask, was found together with a silver strigil, ladle, spoon and other toilet instruments in a tomb of the third century B.C. by the Quarantine Road at Kerch;[2] it is decorated with chased ornament on the body and the characteristic calyx of leaves on the narrow stem. One of the most attractive examples of this kind of vessel was found in a tomb of the same period at Bolsena and is now in the Metropolitan Museum, New York;[3] it has leaf ornament on the lower part, a necklace-garland chased and gilded on the body and two handles giving it the appearance of a little amphora (pl. 28A). Although it has an Etruscan inscription the vessel was probably made in S. Italy, perhaps Apulia, in the late third century. There is a very similar vessel in the Louvre probably from Italy, and fragments of another, from S. Paolo di Civitate, in the Museum at Taranto.

B] *Pyxides*

The *unguentarium* from Bolsena was found together with a little cylindrical *pyxis* illustrated in pl. 28B. The pyramidal lid ends in a

[1] *BABesch*, xxxiii, 1958, 48, fig. 9; *AA*, 1899, 129, fig. 11.

[2] *ABC*, pl. XXXI, 3.

[3] Richter, *Etruscan Collection*, figs. 163–4; A. Furtwängler, *Kleine Schriften*, ii, 515, figs. 16–18.

moulded finial and is decorated with leaf ornament; the body of the *pyxis* is attractively decorated with a band of chased scroll ornament and decorated mouldings. This is one of the best examples of a very common type in the period which continues to be made throughout Hellenistic times. There is another similar piece from Taman, now in the Hermitage Museum, Leningrad.[1] A very elaborately decorated *pyxis* formed part of the Treasure of Tarentum. It consists of a cylindrical box standing on three feet in the form of foreparts of sphinxes. The lid of the box is decorated on the outside with a repoussé roundel showing Artemis, Apollo and Zeus, and on the inside with a rich pattern of leaves radiating from a central rosette. The artist signed his name, Mikon, on the top of the lid. The style of the relief may be compared with a number of other pieces attributed to Tarentine workshops of the third century B.C.

c] *Mirrors*

The box mirror with a hinged lid decorated with repoussé relief on the outside was at the height of its popularity during the third century B.C., having superseded the open disc mirror of archaic and classical times. The finest silver example is one found in a grave at Demetrias with relief on the outside of Selene and Endymion (pl. 29A).[2] A number of small mirrors of this type, probably made in Tarentum, have been found in Apulia. One was found with a jewel case in the form of a shell in a tomb of the late third century at Canosa.[3] A medallion from Tarentum, now in the British Museum (pl. 29B), is probably from the lid of one of these mirrors; the relief depicts the toilet of Aphrodite.[4] Two silver medallions said to have been found at Tarentum and now in the Princeton Art Museum, may have served the same purpose.[5] It is interesting to note that a number of little box-mirrors with rather poor reliefs on the lids have been found in central Italian tombs of the third and second century B.C.; they seem to be local products, imitating better quality work imported from S. Italy during the period. The products of S. Italian silversmiths were well known to the Romans and

[1] *CR*, 1880, 71; *ABC*, pl. XXXVII, 3.

[2] W. Züchner, *Griechische Klappspiegel*, Berlin, 1942, 63; *Polemon*, I, 1929, 7 ff.

[3] *Iapygia*, 6, 1935, 225 ff.; *Ori e Argenti*, nos. 383 ff.; Becatti, *Oreficerie*, nos. 446–8. A similar jewel-case in Berlin is believed to have belonged to the Paternò Treasure (see p. 98 note 2).

[4] *BMCP*, no. 71.

[5] *Archaeology*, 7, 1954, 241.

their neighbours after the sack of Tarentum in 272 B.C. A group of silver objects in the Museum of Fine Arts, Boston, which is said to come from a tomb at Chiusi,[1] includes two hinged mirrors with poor repoussé reliefs on the lids showing Dionysos between a Silenus and an Eros. A similar group appears on a mirror cover in the British Museum.[2]

OTHER SILVER VESSELS

There is not enough evidence to attempt to classify the various types of silver vessels in use during the period. Jugs have been found in the Sellenskaya grave and at Montefortino; a pair[3] with very rich ornament came from the large silver find in the woman's tomb by the Quarantine Road at Kerch (see above p. 95). The necks of these vessels are decorated with floral wreath ornament and the shoulder with scrollwork; the handle, in the form of a twisted rope, is attached below by a soldering plate in the form of a satyr head. There was a bucket with a pair of loop handles attached to the side in the Montefortino find and a bucket-shaped container with a lid and loop handles in the Sellenskaya grave. A silver bucket of a type common in the Greek world and Etruria during the third century was found at Pilaf Tepe in Thessaly;[4] the attachment for the double-loop bucket handles surmounts a mask of Herakles attached to the side and there was presumably a spout formed of two heads (satyr and maenad or the like) on the opposite side, as there is on a number of bronze examples of this type of bucket. A spout of this kind appears on a strange vessel from the Quarantine grave which consists of a biconical container on a high foot with the lid rising to a tall finial (pl. 27A). The lower part of the body is ribbed and the upper part decorated with repoussé scrollwork and chased ornament. The handles take the form of satyr figures bending over backwards and the heads of a silenus and a nymph combine to make the spout. The decoration is richly gilded. A handsome little *hydria* from Thessaly is in the Benaki Museum.[5] Its rope handle with soldering plate decorated with a female head in relief and the necklace-garland hanging between the handles remind one of vessels from the Quarantine find. Like them it was probably made in the late third century B.C.

[1] *AJA*, xxii, 1918, 251 ff.
[2] *BMCP*, no. 70.
[3] *ABC*, pl. XXXVIII, 3; *AdI*, 1840, suppl., pl. B 3.
[4] *JHS*, xx, 1900, pl. V; now in the National Museum at Athens.
[5] Segall, *Benaki*, no. 38, pl. 15.

The incense-burner (*thymiaterion*) from the Treasure of Tarentum stands on a decorated base and a tall fluted stem; the container is a low cylindrical drum with a tall domed lid decorated over its whole surface with chased overlapping leaves. Two other incense-burners were found in the Egyptian Treasure of Tukh el-Qaramous;[1] they resemble the Tarentum piece only in general form. The bases and fluted stems are similar to those on a pedestal basin from the Quarantine tomb, and they have low domed lids. There are two vessels of the same general form in the Hermitage Museum, Leningrad.

Silver dishes must have been in fairly general use by this time but few examples have survived. There is a magnificent silver-gilt piece found together with the Chertomlyk vase (see above p. 88) but certainly later in date, probably of the mid-third century B.C. The dish stands on three bobbin-shaped feet and has two loop handles, each attached to it by means of an elaborate plate decorated with a calyx of acanthus leaves from which rises the head and shoulders of a female figure wearing a calathos. A large palmette hangs down from the calyx and the design is framed on either side by leaves and scrolls. The dish is fluted on the inside around an engraved medallion of scroll ornament radiating from a central rosette and a collar of acanthus leaves, the whole design being not unlike the relief on the underside of the Bari *phiale*.[2]

CONCLUSIONS

In this period a greater variety of domestic utensils is added to the traditional forms of ritual and domestic plate most of which continue in use. The whole class of 'toilet silver' is now an important part of the silversmith's repertoire. The very early Hellenistic plate for domestic use is comparatively plain but there is a developing tendency towards elaborate ornament during the period. Medallion dishes and bowls were becoming fashionable and drinking cups with exterior ornament were appearing around 200 B.C. As a result of Alexander's conquests the influence of Achaemenid silver was strongly renewed.

[1] Maspero, *Le Musée Egyptien*, ii, 57–62.
[2] *Pantheon*, 1942, 56–62; *BABesch*, xxx, 1955, 52 ff.

CHAPTER SIX

The Hellenistic Age
Late Hellenistic, after 200 B.C.

The Hellenistic period in the historical sense ends in 31 B.C. with the death of Cleopatra VII but this date has no special significance in the history of ancient plate. By that time the Romans had become ardent collectors and much of the plate that was produced was made for the Roman market so that the 'Hellenistic' merges completely with the 'Roman' in the late Republic. Moreover, many silver vessels made by Greek craftsmen in the second and first centuries B.C., and perhaps earlier, were treasured by Roman families for many generations and are found in the Roman hoards of the first century A.D. In this chapter, therefore, it seems best to deal with silver made in the Greek and Roman world down to the end of the first century B.C. excluding what has been found in the later hoards; the specific question of survival of earlier plate will be dealt with in discussing the contents of those hoards.

There are very few fixed points in the history of silver plate during the period now under review, and neither the riches of Hellenistic kings nor the great enthusiasm of the Romans as collectors during the late Republic is truly reflected by the quantity of surviving plate. One problem of Hellenistic art in general has always been to distinguish regional styles deriving from the main divisions of Alexander's Empire in an artistic tradition which, despite these political divisions, is surprisingly homogeneous. It therefore seems worthwhile to attempt as a conclusion to this chapter a regional survey of surviving silver from Hellenistic times. A second important problem for this period is to establish the chronological and stylistic development of the various types of silver vessel that were popular in the early years of the Roman Empire and were coming into fashion during this time.

BOWLS

The footless bowl, probably used as a drinking vessel, is one of the most characteristic vessels of this period. The two main forms, a deep hemispherical bowl and a deep conical bowl, may be given the generic name of *mastos* (see fig. 24). The *mastos* is usually quite plain on

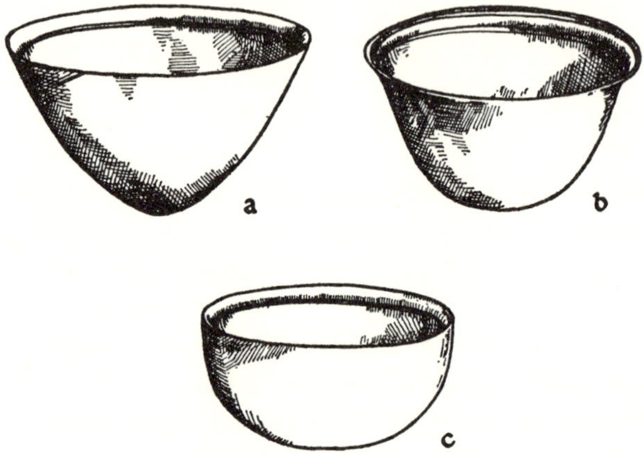

FIG. 24: Three forms of the Hellenistic footless bowl

the outside; on the inside there is, sometimes, a turned disc at the bottom and a little convex moulding at the rim. Most of these bowls were probably made by spinning (see above p. 8). They have been found all over the Hellenistic world, a number in approximately dated contexts. Three deep hemispherical and two conical bowls were found with coins of the late second century B.C. in the Cemetery of S. Bernardo at Ornavasso in N. Italy.[1] Another conical one was found in a late Hellenistic tomb on Euboea,[2] and one with Roman coins of the third to first centuries B.C. at Torre de Juan Abad (Cuidad Real) in Spain.[3] They are especially common in the Spanish[4] and Balkan[5] Treasures of this period (see below p. 122). A *mastos* found at Ancona has a punched inscription below the rim giving the name of its owner,

[1] Willers, *Neue Untersuchungen*, 16, fig. 11.

[2] G. Papabasileios, *ΠΕΡΙ ΤΩΝ ΕΝ ΕΥΒΟΙΑ ΑΡΧΑΙΩΝ ΤΑΦΩΝ*, Athens, 1910, pl. 1e.

[3] *AEArq*, xviii, 1945, 205 ff.

[4] e.g. the Cordova Treasure in the British Museum (P. Dixon, *The Iberians of Spain*, Oxford, 1940, pl. 23).

[5] *Bull. Inst. Bulg.*, xii–xiii, 1938–9, 445, fig. 238; *Dacia*, xi–xii, 1945–7, 35 ff.

Zopion;[1] one in Dumbarton Oaks seems to have been a votive offering and two other bowls in the same collection are said to come from Syria.[2] A few vessels of *mastos* shape with the internal moulding decorated with chased ornament are known; two rather shallow examples, one in Kansas City[3] and the other in a private collection in New York[4] came from Māzandarān in Persia and there is a third from a burial of the first century B.C. at Aktanizovskaya Stanitza in the Taman peninsula.[5] An example from Santisteban del Puerto has beading on the inside and outside of the rim.[6]

DECORATED BOWLS

The decorated forms of the footless bowl have been mentioned (p. 96) as coming into fashion around 300 B.C.; the surviving examples in precious metal almost all belong to the late Hellenistic period. The two outstanding examples, now in the National Museum at Naples (nos. 25284–5), formed part of the large find of silver made at Civitá Castellana in 1811, most of which was quickly dispersed or melted down.[7] The scheme of decoration on both (pl. 31A) is that of the so-called Pergamene bowls consisting of a rich calyx of leaves radiating from a central rosette; the leaves are alternately those of the acanthus and the nymphaea caerulea, the latter enriched with finely chased stems and flowers with little birds and animals in low relief. Little garnets are inserted at the centre of the main rosette and some of the subsidiary rosettes on the bowls, and the detail is richly gilded. The bowls are composed of an outer repoussé case and an inner lining; some of the higher-relief parts, such as the rims of the nymphaea leaves, seem to have been applied separately. Although the bowls were found in central Italy and one of them has a name and weight inscription in Latin, there can be little doubt that both are of Greek workmanship; the form of the bowls and the rich realistic modelling of the ornament suggest that they may have been made in Pergamon in the time of Eumenes II. Indeed, the only other surviving piece from the Civitá Castellana find, the protome of a Centaur perhaps from a *rhyton,* is in a style which is

[1] dall'Osso, *Guida*, 309 ff.
[2] Richter, *Dumbarton Oaks*, nos. 27, 29–30.
[3] *Survey of Persian Art*, i, 459, pl. 136.
[4] von Bothmer, *Private Collections*, no. 45.
[5] *CR*, 1900, 105 ff.
[6] Alvarez-Ossorio, *Tesoros Españoles Antiguos*, pl. XXXVI.
[7] *Atti Accad. Rom. Arch.*, i, pt. 2, 303 ff.; Wuilleumier, *Tarente*, 362.

remarkably close to that of the Great Altar of Pergamon (pl. 27B).[1] As is known from literary sources, 'Asian' silver flooded into Rome in 133 B.C., and it is possible that Cività Castellana hoard was a collection of plate belonging to that time. A similar scheme of decoration occurs on other surviving bowls including one in a private collection said to have been found in Bulgaria[2] and another in the collection of G. F. Reber in Luzern,[3] which comes from the Treasure of Nihawand, between Hamadan and Isfahan, a hoard of precious objects discovered in 1902 and then dispersed.[4]

Several other decorated silver bowls were contained in the Treasure of Nihawand. A bowl now in Berlin is decorated with four groups of close-set fluting diametrically opposed on the body, the space between the groups being taken up with a tall pointed leaf flanked by engraved vine-stems.[5] An identical bowl with the word ARTAFAR in Parthian script punched on the rim is now in the collection of the King of Sweden. The design is related to early clay examples, such as a bowl from the Agora at Athens,[6] but these bowls are unlikely to be earlier than the second century; they were made either in Seleucid Syria or in the Greco-Bactrian kingdom. A fine gold bowl richly decorated with leaves and tendrils rising from a small calyx of acanthus leaves at the base was found in Siberia as long ago as 1727 and is now in the Hermitage, Leningrad.[7] To judge from its free overall design the bowl was made in the first century B.C. Some parts of the repoussé design are decorated with coloured inlays, a technique that seems to have been popular in the eastern Hellenistic world;[8] the bowl has an Aramaic inscription. There is a bowl related in style in the Metropolitan Museum, New York; flying *erotes* are incorporated in an overall floral design. The bowl is said to come from Olbia.[9]

A number of decorated bowls in the National Museum at Naples

[1] Arneth, *Gold- und Silber-Monumente*, s vi.

[2] T. Kraus, *Megarische Becher im Römisch-Germanischen Zentralmuseum zu Mainz*, Mainz, 1951, 18, pls. IV and V.

[3] *Survey of Persian Art*, i, 461, pl. 122; *Mnemosynon Th. Wiegand*, 1938, 57.

[4] E. Herzfeld, 'The hoard of the Kâren Pahlavs' in *Burlington Magazine*, 52, 1928, 21.

[5] Rostovtzeff *SEHHW*, i, 534, pl. 60, 2.

[6] *Hesperia*, iii, 1934, 351.

[7] Smirnov, *Argenterie Orientale*, pl. VIII.

[8] Plate with precious stones inlaid (*διάλιθα, λιθοκόλλητα*) are frequently referred to (e.g. Athenaeus, v, 197c) and Cicero (*Verr.*, iv, 62) associates the fashion especially with Syria.

[9] Richter, *Greek Collection*, pl. 106*b*; *BMMA*, xvii, 1922, 134, fig. 2.

which are mainly from Pompeii and Herculaneum must have been made in the last two centuries B.C. One is a deep bowl with spiral flutings on the outside radiating from a moulded disc at the bottom (Inv. no. 25286); the shape is like some of the *mastoi* of the first century B.C. A fragmentary bowl (Inv. no. 25373), composed of inner lining and outer case, was decorated in a very similar way to the bowls from Nihawand: fluting divided by tall pointed leaves. Another bowl (Inv. no. 25678) has a flaring rim and chased ornament over its whole surface: overlapping leaves on the lower part surmounted by bands of leaf ornament and guilloche.

MEDALLION BOWLS

Bowls and dishes ornamented with relief *emblemata* or medallions on the inside had been coming into fashion in the earlier Hellenistic period and were very common in the last two centuries B.C. The *emblemata* were generally made separately and soldered on to the vessel, and although very few bowls have survived complete, detached *emblemata* have been found all over the Hellenistic world. Two fine examples, one depicting a satyr and maenad and the other Herakles and Auge, were found in Syria together with an appliqué disc decorated with a pattern of stems and flowers radiating from a central rosette.[1] Another *emblema,* which seems to show a portrait of Antiochus VII Sidetes wearing Parthian headdress and torque, perhaps belonged to a bowl in a set made in commemoration of the King's exploits.[2] Four *emblemata* were found in the Nihawand hoard.[3] A satyr head in high relief and a portrait of Demosthenes found at Miletopolis, not far from Pergamon, are probably Pergamene work of the second century B.C.[4] The *emblemata* of the first century B.C. are often framed by elaborate floral ornament. A silver-gilt one of Medusa from Aktanisovskaya Stanitza is framed by a floral wreath.[5] A similar *emblema* from Centuripe shows Artemis and two wild goats.[6] Relief *emblemata* are the most commonly copied pieces in the collections of plaster casts of metalwork found in Egypt and elsewhere (see below p. 120). A recent find of late Hellenistic silver from Novocherkask[7] includes two bowls with medallions show-

[1] *GA*, 1880, pls. 23–4.
[2] *Le Musée*, iii, 1906, 75 ff., pl. XII.
[3] R. Zahn, 'Silber-emblem der Sammlung Loeb' in *Festschrift James Loeb*, 131–41.
[4] 68 *Berlin Winckelmannsprogramm*, 1908.
[5] *CR*, 1900, 105 ff.
[6] *NS*, 1947, 272; *Ori e Argenti*, no. 290.
[7] *Antiquity*, xxxvii, 1963, 256 ff.

ing erotes and chased ornament of overlapping leaves on the inside surface; a third bowl is flanged and similarly decorated.

PHIALAI

Few examples of the traditional forms of the *phiale mesomphalos* in silver or gold can be attributed with certainty to this period. Several traditional designs were copied in clay by potters in Campania during the third and second centuries B.C. and it is possible that some of the silver *phialai* in late fifth-century style, which have already been mentioned (see pp. 81-2) were actually made in this period. An interesting silver *phiale*[1] from Santisteban del Puerto (Jaén) was found with objects of the third or second century B.C. The scheme of decoration is basically similar to some of the fifth-century *phialai* but the *omphalos* has become an *emblema* of a wolf's head holding in its jaws a human head. There is a narrow frieze of erotes around it while the main frieze shows centaurs and centauresses in a lively revel.

The egg-*phiale* was by now a well-established form. A fragmentary silver example, similar in design to the one from Paternò was found with other late Hellenistic silver at Ancona;[2] on the edge, between the eggs there is a series of little heads wearing conical caps and in the centre a medallion of Artemis framed by bands of ornament. A miniature egg-*phiale* decorated entirely with floral ornament, is in the Louvre;[3] it has a central rosette surrounded by a zone of overlapping leaves, a bead-and-reel, the row of eggs and an outer frame with engraved zig-zag ornament. There is another very similar one in Ancona (no. 5601). *Phialai* with little pear-shaped bosses like the one from the Treasure of Tarentum also continued to be made; there is a plaster cast of one from Mit Rahinet.

DRINKING CUPS

The types of drinking cups in general use in late Hellenistic times are well illustrated in finds from Ancona (fig. 25):

(*a*) is a deep, straight-sided cup on a tall turned stem equipped with two handles; the handles may be Greek *kylix* handles set vertically and with very angular overhang at the top, or ring handles with a horizontal thumb-plate at the top. The Ancona example (no. 5257) has *kylix*

[1] García y Bellido, *Esculturas Romanas*, 492.

[2] dall'Osso, *Guida*, 347.

[3] de Ridder, *Bijoux*, no. 1965.

handles while a similar vessel from Artiukhov's Barrow (Taman), which is now dated to the later second century B.C.,[1] has ring handles.

(*b*) has a wide shallow bowl standing on a low base ring and may be equipped either with *kylix* handles or ring handles (Ancona nos. 5590 and 5491, and a good example from a find at Megara Hyblaea[2]).

(*c*) is a deep cup of ovoid shape not unlike a *mastos* which stands on a fairly tall foot and may have handles of either type.

The handles of these cups are attached with leaf-shaped soldering

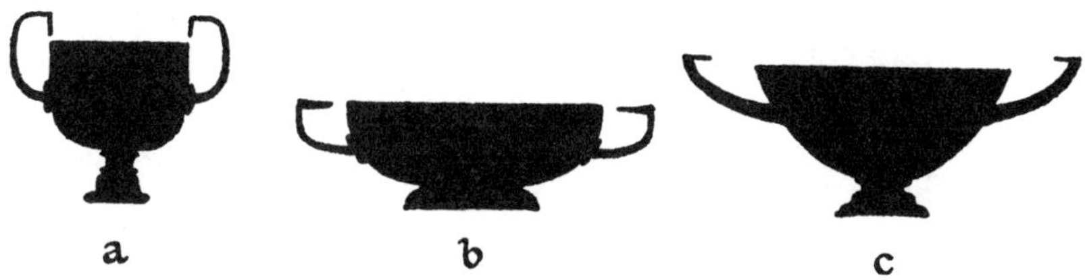

FIG. 25: Shapes of late Hellenistic drinking cups

plates; there is a fashion for little coils of metal flanking the thumb grips surmounting the ring handles. An ovoid cup from Ancona is decorated with a band of guilloche below the rim, a cyma reversa moulding on the foot, and the soldering plates are in the form of acanthus leaves.[3] There is a very similar cup with some engraved ornament on the upper part of the bowl in the Metropolitan Museum, New York.[4] The tall *kantharos* and a number of other traditional Greek shapes were popular in this period. Two deep cups with *kylix* handles also in New York formed part of the find said to have been made at Tivoli (see p. 19) which looks like a collection of late Republican plate. The ornament consists of a band of cyma reversa ornament below the rim and a narrow band of guilloche round the body. There is a pair of almost identical cups from a Belgic grave at Welwyn, Herts, now in the British Museum.[5] Both pairs might have been made as early as the first half of the first century B.C. but they could be as late as Augustan.

DECORATED DRINKING CUPS

The fashion for decorating the outside of drinking cups with more elaborate ornament usually carried out by repoussé and chasing seems

[1] *CR*, 1880, 5 ff.; for the dating *JRGZM*, 5, 1958, 94 ff., and *SA*, 1960, 346–58.
[2] *Ori e Argenti*, no. 287.
[3] dall'Osso, *Guida*, 349 ff.
[4] Richter, *Greek Collection*, pl. 107*c*.
[5] *Archaeologia*, 63, 1911–12, 1 ff.

to have begun in the second century B.C. The earliest surviving examples are from Artiukhov's Barrow and belong to the second half of the second century B.C.[1] A two-handled deep cup (pl. 31B) with decoration similar to that found on the Pergamene bowls – a radiating pattern of acanthus and nymphaea – was found in Grave 2 of this barrow. The cup stands on a moulded foot enriched with decoration and the handles are made of stout wire knotted in the middle and surmounted by a long horizontal thumb-grip. The ornament is in low relief and was probably done by chasing from the front. The second cup is a *kantharos* from Grave 3 with a concave upper part surmounted by a thickened rim and a bowl-shaped lower section. Foot and handles are similar to those on the other cup. The ornament on the body consists of a low calyx of leaves on the bottom with a band of guilloche on the upper part of the bowl and a band of tendril ornament on the concave section.

It seems fairly certain that by the early first century B.C. it had become fashionable to decorate drinking cups with high-relief figured scenes as well as floral decoration of various kinds and it is arguable that many of the drinking cups of this kind found in the Campanian hoards were, in fact, made as early as 100 B.C.[2] But outside these hoards there are very few pieces that can be assigned to such an early date. As soon as high relief came into fashion the cups had to be made in two parts – an outer repoussé case and an inner plain lining which fitted closely together. The types of cup that appear in the Roman hoards are shown in fig. 27 and it is likely that all these types were known in Hellenistic times. Such cups were, as we know from literary sources, ardently collected by Romans of the Republic. Although none of these cups can be certainly assigned to this period it may be taken as certain that they represent perhaps the most popular type of luxury vessel from about 100 B.C. onwards.

Here it may be worthwhile to mention a few relief cups outside the Campanian hoards to which a Hellenistic date has been attributed. A silver *kantharos* found in the Delta and now in the Walters Art Gallery, Baltimore[3] has been thought of as Alexandrian work of the first century B.C. The lower part of the vessel is ribbed and on the concave upper section is represented the Indian Triumph of Bacchus. The squat

[1] See above p. 113 note 1.

[2] On this question see, especially, Kuthmann, *Toreutik*, passim.

[3] Inv. no. 57929; *AA*, 1907, 385 ff.

silver *kantharos* dredged from the bed of the River Meuse near Stevensweert[1] has ivy-leaves and branches decorating the lower part of the vessel and a frieze of satyr heads and other Bacchic attributes on the concave section. Although the arguments, based on graffiti on the cup, for dating it to the second century B.C. are unconvincing,[2] there is nothing about its decoration and design to preclude a date around 100 B.C. The cup found at Alesia, now in the Museum of St-Germain (pl. 33B), illustrates[3] the kind of naturalistic ornament of fruit and flowers which we know to have come into fashion in late Hellenistic times, and if it is accepted that the cup was lost at the time of Caesar's siege in 52 B.C. – though this has been seriously doubted – we should have a fixed point in considering the development of these relief cups.

The problems connected with the dating of these 'Hellenistic-Roman' drinking cups are well illustrated in the case of three cups recently acquired by the British Museum.[4] One of the cups is a tall *kantharos* decorated on its shallow bowl with low-relief floral ornament and on the high wall with a scene from Greek legend, perhaps derived from a lost play of Sophocles. The other two cups are a pair decorated with floral ornament of fruit and flowers in a delicate naturalistic style. All three have lost their feet and handles. Although there are no firm grounds for assigning these pieces to the first century B.C., all three must represent types already popular in the period, and the two floral cups are closely connected in style and detail with the cup from Alesia. All one can say is that such vessels have a possible date-range between about 75 B.C. and the time of Augustus. These problems are discussed further below (pp. 137–9).

LADLES

The ladles of the late Hellenistic period keep the duck's head handle of earlier examples but the bowl is usually much deeper, almost hemispherical (see fig. 21*b*). The handle is sometimes curved backwards and at its junction with the bowl there are often metal coils like the ones flanking the handles on drinking cups of the period. A typical example of the late Hellenistic form is the ladle from Arcisate in the British Museum (pl. 34); the Arcisate find has been dated around 75 B.C.[5] Many

[1] L. H. M. Brom, *The Stevensweert Kantharos*, 1952; *Mon. Piot*, 46, 1952, 39–67.

[2] *JHS*, lxxvi, 1956, 140; *Journal of the Warburg and Courtauld Institutes*, xxvii, 1964, 307 ff.

[3] *Mon. Piot*, 9, 1902, pl. XVI; *CRAI*, 1949, 189–95.

[4] *BMQ*, xxiii, 1961, 68–86.

[5] *BMCP*, nos. 126–30.

similar ladles have been found, for example, in a small hoard of Republican silver said to come from Boscoreale,[1] in a hoard from Menjíbar (Jaén) in Spain of the time of the Sertorian War,[2] and in a small hoard from Megara Hyblaea.[3] Many examples are known from Greece and the Greek East.[4]

STRAINERS

The strainers of the period are generally cup-shaped with the holes punched in floral and geometric patterns. The strainer from Arcisate (pl. 34, left) is a deep straight-sided bowl with ornamental perforations, another from Lake Trasimene[5] is in the shape of a *mastos* (fig. 22b) equipped with two loop handles like the cups of the period, and one from Boscoreale is a shallower, straight-sided vessel with a flat bottom and is equipped with a single handle.

JUGS

The little round-necked jug from Arcisate illustrated on pl. 34 is a characteristic vessel of the hoards of the first century B.C. and is found together with ladles and strainers of the types described above. There are good examples from Aktanizovskaya Stanitza, Boscoreale and Ancona. One of the Ancona jugs has a figured handle[6] and two others are fitted with an extra loop handle on the opposite side of the jug. This type, or a related type, was still fashionable in the early Roman Empire (see below p. 141). Although this is the only type of jug that can be certainly associated with the late Hellenistic period, it is probable that richly decorated jugs of various kinds, like those found in the Roman hoards, were already being made.

OTHER DOMESTIC PLATE

Most of the small hoards of the late Hellenistic period consist of silver used in the service of liquids. The Arcisate hoard is typical and looks like a little 'drinking set' consisting of a jug, a shallow bowl or cup, a

[1] *RM*, 38–9, 1923–4, 124 ff.

[2] J. C. Baroja, *España Primitiva y Romana*, Barcelona, 1957, figs. 341–2.

[3] *Ori e Argenti*, nos. 287–9.

[4] e.g. one from Syria in Dumbarton Oaks (Richter, *Dumbarton Oaks*, no. 26).

[5] *Sale Catalogue, Sammlung Ruesch*, 171–4; now in Walters Art Gallery, Baltimore (*BMMA*, 1964–5, 177–185).

[6] dall'Osso, *Guida*, 348.

strainer and a ladle (pl. 34). Other forms of domestic silver are rare. One of the few finds that gives some idea of the variety of domestic silver utensils now in use was made at Gabalon in Aetolia.[1] The find contained a number of the common late Hellenistic vases, a *mastos,* a cylindrical *pyxis,* some small pots, and a few more unusual pieces including plain oval dishes and basins, a curious bowl on a high pedestal and a jug shaped rather like a modern decanter. An oval basin with a horizontal rim and a rimless basin were found in Grave II of Artiukhov's Barrow.[2] Another vessel of the period is a handle-less calyx-bowl with a chamfered rim standing on a conical foot rim; examples have been found at Menjíbar and Megara Hyblaea. A similar type of vessel is found in the hoards of the first century A.D. There is very little evidence for silver spoons and other eating implements in this period, though they must have been coming into general use, especially in Italy. Late Republican silver spoons may be represented by the examples in New York from the find said to have been made at Tivoli. The little round-bowled spoons are just like the Imperial examples discussed below, but the larger spoons (*ligulae*), of which there were originally ten, look different and earlier. They have wide bowls with very simple attachment to the handle and a duck's head finial at the end of the handle. This latter feature is not found on Imperial spoons.

TOILET VESSELS

Cylindrical *pyxides* with flat or conical lids and *unguentaria* with more or less bulbous body and narrow neck and foot are the most common types of toilet vessel in the late Hellenistic hoards. A typical group of plain vessels of this kind was found in a tomb at Goritza in Thessaly together with a duck's head ladle, a strigil and other small silver objects.[3] A good example in silver of the late Hellenistic fusiform unguentarium is one from Artiukhov's barrow found in the same tomb (no. 3) as the silver *kantharos* mentioned above (p. 114); the vessel is decorated with a calyx of leaves rising from the foot and bands of wreath ornament and wave pattern. Another popular shape of small toilet vessel is the little pot illustrated in fig. 26; the characteristic feature is the decorated cyma reversa profile dividing the neck and the body. There are many

[1] *AE*, 1906, 67 ff.
[2] *CR*, 1880, 5 ff.
[3] *BCH*, 55, 1931, 490.

examples, including one in the British Museum,[1] one in New York,[2] and a third in the Stathatos Collection in Athens.[3]

The *pyxis* and *alabastron* from Palaiokastron in Thessaly (pl. 32A and B)[4] are the finest surviving toilet vessels of the period; their date is

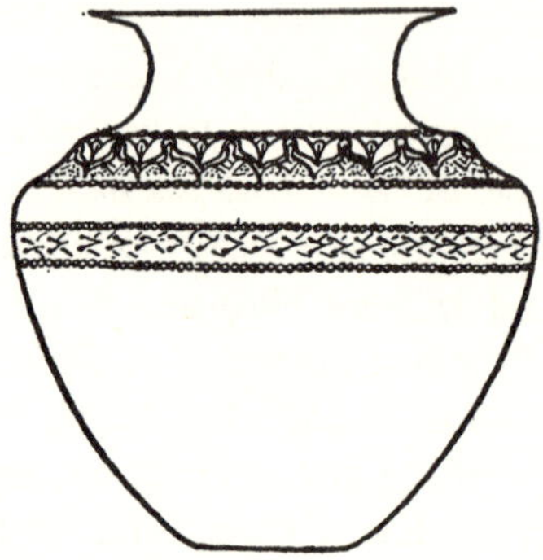

FIG. 26: Silver pot in the British Museum. Scale 1:2

probably around 100 B.C. Both are richly decorated with the kind of repoussé ornament that was becoming the fashion on drinking cups and other vessels. The *alabastron* is rounded at the bottom, tapers towards the top and has a narrow round neck. The whole vessel is ornamented with repoussé and chasing – a little calyx of leaves at the base, a principal scene with figures in high relief representing the childhood of Dionysos, and a narrow frieze of Erotes above that. Bands of wreath ornament between beading divide the scenes from one another. The *pyxis* is cylindrical and has a pyramidal lid surmounted by a pomegranate; the body is decorated with figures of dancing maenads in high relief and on the lid is a rich garland of fruit supported by theatrical masks and bukrania. The style and themes of the vessels suggest the work of the neo-Attic school which grew up in Athens during the first century B.C. in response to the Roman demand for works of decorative art in Greek style. Another elaborately decorated *alabastron* was found at Ancona (no. 5600).[5] The lid takes the form of a tall finial and the body is decorated with repoussé and chased ornament with a central figured zone bordered by bands of ornament.

[1] *BMCP*, no. 80.
[2] von Bothmer, *Private Collections*, no. 274.
[3] *Stathatos Collection*, iii, no. 172.
[4] *AM*, 37, 1912, 87 ff.
[5] dall'Osso, *Guida*, 345.

Late Hellenistic, after 200 B.C.

Silver box-mirrors continued to be made in this period but no examples can certainly be assigned to it. The open mirror with baluster handle, often decorated with relief on one side, which is characteristic or early Imperial hoards (see below pp. 157–8) must have come into fashion in the first century B.C. in Italy, combining the forms of the Greek box-mirrror and the Etruscan open hand-mirror. There is also a small group of wall-mirrors which may belong to the late Hellenistic period. These consist of a bronze or bronze-alloy disc, backed with wood and framed with a border of open-work or relief in silver gilt. Their date is very difficult to establish but there are no strong arguments for assigning them to the Roman period.[1]

REGIONAL SURVEY OF HELLENISTIC PLATE

GREECE

Early Hellenistic finds in Macedonia and N. Greece reflect the wealth of the region in the time of Philip II and Alexander. After Alexander Greece may have lagged behind the newer centres of the Hellenistic world but fine work, like the mirror from Demetrias, was being produced throughout the period. The close connection between the silverware from the Quarantine find at Kerch and Attic West Slope vases suggests that Athens continued to be a main producer of plate, and the *alabastron* and *pyxis* from Palaiokastron almost certainly represent the 'neo-Attic' revival of art in Athens that took place around 100 B.C. The strong influence of 'neo-Attic' style may also be seen in silver vessels from the Roman hoards of the first century A.D.

ASIA MINOR

The cities of Ionia were the principal mixing-places of Greek and Achaemenid forms in this period. The Treasure of Panagyurishte which shows a mixture of the two traditions was probably made somewhere in western Asia Minor. Of the main centres, Pergamon is the best known. The centaur-protome and bowls from Cività Castellana may well be Pergamene work and the two *emblemata* from Miletopolis are probably from the same source. Almost nothing is known of work in other cities. Here, as elsewhere, Roman influence of the last two

[1] *AJA*, li, 1947, 221 ff.

centuries B.C. produced a revival and we hear, for example, of a Posidonius of Ephesus who made silver vessels in the time of Pompey the Great.[1]

EGYPT

The Treasures of Tukh el-Qaramous and Tell Tmai[2] give a fair idea of the output of Egyptian silversmiths in early Ptolemaic times. The influence of Achaemenid silver was particularly strong. The later Hellenistic period is poorly represented. The silver *kantharos* in the Walters Art Gallery and a little silver pot with fishing scenes in the British Museum[3] are two examples of late Hellenistic repoussé work from Egypt. Alexandria has generally been thought of as a chief creator of fashions in Hellenistic art and the attribution of silver vessels to Alexandrian workshops is a hazardous activity that has been freely indulged. But there are grounds for thinking that some of the shapes of vessel popular in Roman hoards, for example the *kalathos* or *modiolus* (fig. 27*g*) originated there. Some indirect evidence for Alexandrian metalwork may be gained from the series of plaster casts made from fine metalwork found in 1907 at Mit Rahinet and now in the Pelizaeus Museum at Hildesheim.[4] They are believed to be the stock of a working silversmith and are probably of the Roman period. But the vessels from which they are taken are mainly Hellenistic – *emblema* dishes, egg-*phialai*, Megarian bowls etc. Some of the originals, such as the medallion portraits of the Ptolemies, were certainly made in Egypt.[5] Egyptian themes also appear on the plaster casts from another large find at Begram in Afghanistan.[6]

SYRIA

The riches of the Seleucid kings of Syria were proverbial and they were enthusiastic collectors of plate.[7] Antioch and other Syrian cities were certainly important centres of manufacture. A few relief *emblemata* from Syria have been mentioned and there are grounds for thinking that some of the silver found in the Greco-Bactrian area was, in fact, made in Syria. The whole series of cup *phalerae* decorated with calyxes

[1] Pliny, *NH*, xxxiii, 156.
[2] von Bissing, *Metallgefässe*, pl. III.
[3] *BMCP*, no. 76.
[4] Rubensohn, *Silbergerät.*
[5] *ibid.* no. 32, pl. VI; *BSAAl*, 32, 1938, 77 ff.; *RA*, 1961, 113 ff.
[6] J. Hackin, *Nouvelles recherches archéologiques à Begram*, Paris 1954, 137 ff.
[7] Cicero, *Verr*, iv, 62; cf. Athenaeus, v, 193d.

of leaves and bands of chased ornament are closely related to Megarian bowls.[1] The bowls and *emblemata* from the Nihawand hoard may also be of Syrian manufacture. The inlaid gold bowl found in Siberia has been attributed to Syria. On the other hand, some of the Greco-Bactrian plate shows elements of local iconography and must have been made in the Greco-Bactrian Kingdom. In addition, plain silver of most of the standard Hellenistic types – *mastoi,* wine ladles, plates – are reported to have been found in the Seleucid kingdom.

REPUBLICAN ITALY AND SICILY

There is hardly any surviving Etruscan silver from the sixth to the third century B.C. A silver beaker with engraved bands of ornament said to have been found at Cività Castellana and now in the Metropolitan Museum, New York dates from the fifth century B.C.;[2] no other silver plate can certainly be assigned to this period. Etruscan tombs of the third and second centuries, especially at Chiusi have produced a good deal of silver, mostly rather poor in quality and imitating contemporary Greek fashions. The stimulus to this local production must have been the influx of plate from S. Italy as a result of Roman campaigns. A high proportion of the silver consists of small toilet vessels (see above p. 103). It is interesting that the Greek type of box mirror is more common than the Etruscan open mirror in these finds though both types occur and one of the finest pieces of Etruscan silver of this period is the open mirror with low-relief figured scene on the back of the disc which was found at Bomarzo.[3]

The finds in Apulia, which include the famous Treasure of Tarentum give a fair idea of the output of Tarentine workshops, which were setting the fashions in central Italy from the third century onwards. Some relics of the huge influx of gold and silver from the Hellenistic kingdoms may be seen in the survivors of the Cività Castellana hoard. Tombs at Ancona have provided a good cross-section of the plain silver popular in the last century of the Republic and a number of small finds in various parts of Italy shows that taste was remarkable homogenous. Possibly large producing centres, such as Capua, were already responsible for most of the output of plain vessels. Almost no decorated silver of this period has survived.

[1] For this plate in general, Trever, *Monuments.*

[2] Richter, *Bronzes,* no. 579.

[3] Milani, *Firenze,* pl. XXXVII.

WESTERN ROMAN PROVINCES

A find from Tivissa, near Tarragona in Spain includes two *phialai* and three little flasks which seem to be copied from Hellenistic vessels of the third century B.C. One of the flasks is closely related to the vessel from Ithaca in the British Museum (fig. 23*c*) and one of the *phialai* is of the Apotheosis of Herakles type (see above p. 81). A stemmed goblet of Hellenistic form decorated with chased acanthus ornament was found with the *phiale* from Santisteban del Puerto (p. 112). Several of the other Spanish hoards date from the time of the Sertorian War. The *mastos* is the commonest silver vessel in these hoards.[1] The small find at Menjíbar (Jaèn) consists of plain silver vessels – a deep strainer, a ladle and a bowl – of the same types as those found in late Republican Italy. The only find of the period in Gaul is the Alesia cup which may have been lost there in 52 B.C. (see above p. 115).

S. RUSSIA AND THE BALKANS

In the early Hellenistic period the finds at Sellenskaya and Karagodeu-ashk are among the most important for the history of Greek plate. After about 350 B.C. it is no longer possible to recognise the work of S. Russian centres. The plate is precisely like that found elsewhere in the Greek world and in the third and second centuries most of it was probably imported. Throughout Hellenistic times, the S. Russian finds continue to provide the basis of our knowledge of Greek plate.

Macedonia and Thrace are rich sources of early Hellenistic plate. The Panagyurishte Treasure is the most remarkable find of all. Late Hellenistic plate has also been found in the western Balkans. Nine *mastoi* and a small bucket were found in Bohot in Bulgaria.[2] The Geto-Dacian treasures are also rich in late Hellenistic plate. The outstanding find is the hoard of silver vessels from Sîncrăeni in Transylvania;[3] these are mainly decorated drinking cups of Greek type but not, certainly, pure Greek work. Where they were made is uncertain; parallels have been drawn with two late Hellenistic deep cups with chased ornament from the tumulus of Tersiyeköy near Adapazari in Turkey.[4] They may be Greco-Sarmatian work from the Olbia region.

[1] *AEArq*, xii, 1936, 151 ff.; Alvarez-Ossorio, *Tesoros Españoles Antiguos.*

[2] *Bull. Inst. Bulg.*, xii–xiii, 1938–9, 445.

[3] *Dacia* (n.s.), ii, 1958, 157–206; *Antiquity and Survival*, ii, Hague, 1957, 21–8.

[4] *AJA*, 64, 1960, pl. 14, figs. 15–16.

CHAPTER SEVEN

The Roman Empire

For much of her early history, Rome had been poor in precious metals. She did not issue a silver coinage until the third century B.C. and until about 200 B.C. silver plate was rare in the city. The temple treasuries had been swelled by booty derived from the capture of Etruscan cities and we hear that in 296 B.C. the aediles Cn. and Q. Ogulnius had vessels made from confiscated silver to decorate the tables in the Temple of Jupiter Capitolinus.[1] There are some references to domestic silver in the third century. A certain P. Cornelius Rufinus in 275 incurred the displeasure of the censors for possessing over 10 lb.[2] and towards the end of the century references in Plautus show that silver was coming increasingly into fashion. In the course of the Second Punic War an appeal could be made for domestic plate as a contribution towards the funds for the War.[3] But the only domestic silver in common use were the salt (*salinum*) and dish (*patella*) that were the essential instruments of sacrifice to the gods[4] and this state of affairs is, no doubt, reflected in the story, which presumably refers to the third century, of the Carthaginian embassy to Rome who found the same service of plate in every house they dined at.[5]

The Second Punic War was the real turning point. Not only were the rich sources of silver in Spain made available for Roman exploitation[6] but immense booty of gold and silver from the cities of Magna Graecia, of which Syracuse and Tarentum were two of the richest, began to flow into the city.[7] In the following century, the Triumphs of Roman generals,[8] those, for example, of T. Quinctius Flamininus in 194 B.C.,[9]

[1] Livy, x, 23, 11.

[2] Pliny, *NH*, xxxiii, 142.

[3] *Aulularia*, ii, 4, 64; *Pseudolus*, i, 2, 29; Livy, xxvi, 36, 5.

[4] Scholiast on Horace, *Odes*, ii, 16, 14.

[5] Pliny, *NH*, xxxiii, 143.

[6] Silius Italicus, *Punica*, lxv, v, 496–8.

[7] Livy, xxvii, 16, 7.

[8] See, especially, O. Vessberg, *Studien zur Kunstgeschichte der römischen Republik*, 26 ff., 59 ff.

[9] Livy, xxxiv, 52, 4–5.

and L. Scipio Asiagenus[1] in 188 B.C. were adorned with the captive treasures of the Hellenistic Kings. Plutarch's account of the Triumph of L. Aemilius Paullus over Perseus specially mentions the *kraters, rhytons, phialai* and *kylikes* of immense size and superb craftsmanship.[2] The Bequest of Attalus in 133 B.C. produced an enormous influx of Pergamene silver and, according to Pliny it was the public auction of the king's effects that did most to foster enthusiasm among wealthy Romans for collecting silver.[3] Diehards like Q. Aelius Tubero might still refuse to use any silver except what L. Aemilius Paullus had given him[4] but by the end of the second century B.C. the collecting of silver plate had become an established part of patrician life. In the Sullan proscription lists single dishes of 100 lb. weight were apparently mentioned.[5] Huge prices were paid for collector's pieces; L. Licinius Crassus (*cos.* 95 B.C.) bought two cups by Mentor for 100,000 sesterces.[6] Others, like the notorious Verres, used less legal means to acquire old silver by Greek craftsmen and the collecting of plate aroused incredible covetousness. Verres was said to have set up his own factory for remounting on plate the medallions (*emblemata*) he had filched from wealthy provincials.[7] In the last century of the Republic, craftsmen all over the Hellenistic world were called upon to supply the Roman demand for fine silver; Pliny singles out the period of Pompey the Great, who was himself a keen collector,[8] as one in which several notable artists were making silver plate for Roman patrons.

The importance of silver plate in the domestic, political and economic life of the Roman Empire cannot be overestimated. The evidence of literary and legal texts gives proof of the vast quantity of silver in private hands, the changes in fashion, the enthusiasm of collectors, the ostentation of owners. A middle-class family of the Empire would probably have a complete set of table silver for dining besides a quantity of show-plate acquired as heirlooms, wedding presents, and so on. There was hardly any family that did not possess some item of table silver and to have been brought up in a family that had none was a sign of the most abject poverty.[9] Rich patrons would give substantial

[1] Pliny, *NH*, xxxiii, 148.
[2] Plutarch, *Aemilius Paullus*, xxiii.
[3] Pliny, *NH*, xxxiii, 149.
[4] *ibid.* 142.
[5] *ibid.* 145.
[6] *ibid.* 147.
[7] Cicero, *Verr.* ii, 4, 54.
[8] Pliny, *NH*, xxxiii, 148.
[9] Suetonius, *Domitian*, i.

gifts of plate to their clients and Martial[1] mentions five pounds of silver ware as a reasonable present at the festival of the Saturnalia. We hear of a slave of the Emperor Claudius who possessed a huge collection of plate[2] and in large households several slaves were fully occupied with the task of maintaining the silver. There were collectors who accumulated every kind of silver, old and new.[3] The collections of Temple Treasuries and Town Councils[4] swelled the amount of Roman plate to immense proportions and a trade highly organised for mass-production was needed to satisfy the demand.[5]

The few finds of Republican silver in Italy which have already been mentioned give very little idea of the immense 'luxe de service' of a Roman nobleman in the last century of the Republic. The earliest large finds of Roman plate have been made in the towns of the Bay of Naples which were buried by the sudden catastrophic eruption of Vesuvius in A.D. 79. The earlier finds of small collections of plate at Pompeii were completely overshadowed by the discovery in 1895 of a hoard of fine table-silver – 109 pieces in all – stored away in a wine vat below a villa at Boscoreale.[6] The hoard is a typical collection of plate in the possession of a prosperous middle-class Roman during the first century A.D. and includes both show-pieces, such as would have adorned the side tables and cabinets in the house, and pieces in more general use. The second large Campanian hoard was discovered in the Casa del Menandro at Pompeii, on the 5th December, 1930, wrapped in cloth inside a bronze-bound wooden chest;[7] it consisted of 118 pieces of fine table silver of all kinds. These two hoards and a number of other smaller but important finds provide a good cross-section of the plate in use in the first century A.D. But it should be remembered that the hoards do not represent the possessions of the very wealthy but of successful business-men in an Italian provincial town.

The later periods in the history of Roman silver are by no means so well represented by surviving plate although a large number of finds over the whole Roman Empire and even outside its frontiers have been made during the last 200 years. Most ancient plate went into the melting-pot in the collapse of the Roman Empire, nor, indeed, has all the ancient silver discovered in comparatively modern times escaped the same fate.[8]

[1] vii, 53.
[2] *CIL*, vi, 5197.
[3] Martial, iv, 39.
[4] cf. Livy, xxii, 32.
[5] See above pp. 15–16
[6] de Villefosse, *Boscoreale*, 31 ff.
[7] Maiuri, *Casa del Menandro*, 245 ff.
[8] See above p. 18.

The hoards that have come to light, mostly in the western provinces of the Empire were buried in some time of crisis to prevent them falling into the hands of the enemy. A recently discovered (1962) hoard of first-century silver from Hockwold in Norfolk[1] has been connected with Boudicca's rebellion and most of the major finds have some similar historical explanation. The two main groups of hoards are those connected with barbarian invasions in the late third century and those buried in the late fourth and early fifth centuries when the Roman Empire in the West was collapsing.

One of the largest and most important hoards of the third century is the Treasure of Berthouville near Bernay which was found in 1830 at a spot which later proved to be the site of a Temple of Mercury destroyed at that time.[2] The Berthouville silver consists of ritual plate and dedications from the domestic plate of wealthy benefactors who included Roman citizens, Gauls and Romanised Gauls. Another large hoard is the Treasure of Chaourse (near Montcornet, Aisne), a large find of domestic plate, now in the British Museum,[3] which was found in 1883 in a field where it had been buried wrapped in cloth. The latest coins found with the silver belonged to the reign of Postumus (A.D. 267) and the Treasure was probably buried during the reign of Gallienus. A more recent find of very similar silver, buried at the same time, was made at Graincourt-lès-Havrincourt.[4] Most of the third-century finds come from Gaul and the fact that no comparable finds have been made in Italy perhaps gives a somewhat false picture of the plate of the period. On the other hand, what evidence we have suggests that fashions were remarkable uniform throughout the Empire.

In the case of the fourth- and fifth-century hoards, Britain has been one of the richest sources.[5] The Mildenhall Treasure, found during the Second World War includes some of the finest and most ornate examples of silver plate from the ancient world, the property of a wealthy provincial who had buried them for safety.[6] The Treasures of Traprain Law in Scotland[7] and of Coleraine[8] in Ireland both consist mainly of fragments of silver vessels destined to be melted down as

[1] The contents of the hoard are in the British Museum; Toynbee, *Art in Britain*, 301 ff.

[2] Babelon, *Berthouville*, 14–32.

[3] *BMCP*, nos. 144–82.

[4] *Galerie Charpentier, Sale Catalogue*, 10th June, 1958.

[5] For late Roman hoards in Britain see Dohrn, *Spätantikes Silber*.

[6] Brailsford, *Mildenhall.*

[7] Curle, *Traprain.*

[8] *BMCP*, nos. 195–223; *Antiquity*, ii, 1937, 39 ff.

bullion. The famous picture dish found in the Tyne at Corbridge, known as the Corbridge *lanx*, seems to have been part of another hoard of the period.[1] The hoards of the fourth and fifth centuries, though mainly confined to the west are a good deal more widely distributed than those of the third century. They include the recently discovered Treasure of Kaiseraugst in Switzerland and the Treasure found on the Esquiline Hill in Rome, and they combine to give a fairly thorough idea of the silver fashions in the late Empire.

A large number of important discoveries have been made outside the confines of the Roman Empire. Fine table silver played an important role in Roman trade and diplomacy abroad. Tacitus refers to Roman silver in use among the chieftains of Germanic tribes which had been given to them as diplomatic presents.[2] Two fine silver cups were buried in a Belgic chieftain's grave at Welwyn, Herts., long before the Roman invasion of Britain.[3] In eastern trade, worked plate was among the commodities most in demand.[4] and it was eagerly sought by the barbarians on the northern frontiers of the Empire.[5]

The largest find of Roman silver made outside the frontiers came to light in 1868 at Hildesheim near Hannover and has been explained as the plate belonging to some Roman commander that was lost on campaign against Germanic tribes,[6] although it is difficult to connect the loss with any definite campaign. From the first century B.C. onwards Roman silver, acquired as a result of trade, robbery or diplomacy turns up in burials of barbarian chiefs in places as far apart as Denmark and Pomerania.[7] Two relief-decorated cups of very fine quality made in Augustan times,[8] were found buried in a rich chieftain's grave at Hoby on Laaland. Extensive finds of Roman silver have also been made outside the eastern boundaries of the Empire, especially in S. Russia. One interesting group of such silver from tombs at Armazis-khevi in Georgia includes a dish of Roman make with an inscription recording that it was presented to one of the local princes by a certain King Faldad (?).[9]

[1] *JRS*, iv, 1914, 1 ff.

[2] Tacitus, *Germania* 5.

[3] *Archaeologia*, 63, 1911–12, 1 ff.

[4] Fabricius, *Der Periplus*, 24 and 28.

[5] cf. Dio Cassius, lxvii, 7.

[6] Pernice and Winter, *Hildesheim*, 12 ff.

[7] For these burials in general see Wheeler, *Rome Beyond the Imperial Frontiers*, 31 ff.

[8] *Nordiske Fortidsminder*, ii, 3, 1923, 119 ff.

[9] A. Mongait, *Archaeology in the U.S.S.R.*, Moscow, 1959, 238 ff.; *Mzkhetha* I, pls. LIV–LV.

The contents of the surviving hoards of Roman silver, although they represent some areas and periods far better than others, give a fair idea of the principal kinds of plate throughout the period of the Roman Empire. Before discussing the development of Roman plate it seems worthwhile to begin with a general account of what is known from literary sources about the most important items of domestic and religious plate in use.

A complete set of domestic plate, known as a *ministerium,* comprised *argentum escarium* (eating silver) and *argentum potorium* (drinking silver). Sacrificial implements used in domestic cult would also be included in the inventory of silver plate, and many articles of domestic furniture (*suppellectilis*) and toilet vessels used by the women (part of the *mundus muliebris*) might also be made of silver.

ARGENTUM ESCARIUM

The Romans ate their food from dishes, plates and bowls of various kinds. In the early Imperial period these were generally round, varying in size from large plates (*lances*) to little shallow dishes (*scutellae*); they were often made in sets of different sizes. Certain special shapes of dish and bowl were made for particular kinds of food; oval plates were obviously suitable for eating fish[1] and the popular shell-shaped bowls, not unlike modern jelly-moulds in shape, obviously served a special use. A large number of names for dishes have come down to us.[2] A *missorium* was a large plate for serving meat, fruit or cake, a *paropsis* a small side plate. Sometimes the different kinds are distinguished by their decoration, as *lances filicatae, paterae pampinatae, disci corymbiati.* Large trays (*fercula*) are used for bringing food to the table. The table itself would be equipped with salt-cellars (*salina*) pepper castors (*piperatoria*) and various vessels to hold sauces. An unusual group of little vessels in the Casa del Menandro hoard (nos. 48–51) are the little cups on narrow stems standing on a wide base which look as though they must have been used for eating eggs (pl. 42B).

An inventory of the plate in the possession of a wealthy Roman in Egypt is preserved in a Berlin papyrus.[3] The plate had been packed in

[1] Some surviving examples have fish engraved on them (e.g. *GA*, 1885, 108).

[2] For names of Roman dishes etc., *Germania*, xi, 1928, 56 ff.; *BJ*, 130, 1925, 80 ff.; *AM*, xxxviii, 1913, 193 ff.

[3] *RM*, 36–7, 1921–2, 34 ff.

chests and deposited in various hands for safe-keeping. The text shows that the basic *σύνθεσις* (ministerium) was made in sets of 4 *πινάκια* (dishes) *παροψίδες* (side plates) and *οξύβαφα* (bowls) for which the Latin equivalents would seem to be *catinus, paropsis* and *acetabulum*; finds at Pompeii (see below p. 148) have confirmed the general use of sets of this number. The same inventory mentions many other kinds of domestic plate – large dishes (*lances*) of which one weighed over 21 lb., and vessels of special use like the *gararia* (for the sauce *garum*) and *boletaria,* dishes for mushrooms. It also refers to different kinds of decoration and details of design, and distinguishes between 'old' and 'new' plate.

The food was brought to the table in ready-prepared portions and table knives were not necessary. Nor, it seems, were forks used at table; some silver forks found in Rome were once thought to be Roman but are not now generally believed to be ancient.[1] The only eating implement in common use was the spoon of which there were two popular shapes. The smaller of the two usually has a circular bowl and the handle ending in a point that could be used for extracting shellfish; this is the *cochleare* whose uses are nicely described in one of Martial's epigrams.[2] The larger is a dessert spoon (*ligula* or *lingula*),[3] used, for example, in eating cereal foods; the bowl is pear-shaped, the handle generally ends in a finial and is continued down the bowl as a rat-tail. A number of larger spoon-like utensils probably for serving have been found in the early hoards and there is a series of little eating implements with leaf-shaped ends, perhaps used for shellfish, in the late hoards (e.g. Kaiseraugst nos. 17–18).

ARGENTUM POTORIUM

Argentum potorium (drinking silver) includes a rich variety of vessels connected with the serving and drinking of wine. The *simpulum* for ladling liquids, is a utensil with the handle set perpendicular to the bowl while a second form of ladle has a horizontal handle. Amphoras and jugs (*urceus, lagona*) of many different kinds were used for holding and pouring wine. The drinking cups themselves are of many different shapes, some inherited from the Greek world, others of modern and sometimes short-lived taste. A list of drinking vessels mentioned in the

[1] *BCom.*, 2, 1874, 116 ff.
[2] Martial, xiv, 121.
[3] *ibid.* 120.

Digest includes *trullae, scyphi, modioli, phialae.*[1] It has been suggested that the *trulla* is the very popular saucepan-shaped vessel which is found throughout the period of the Roman Empire; *scyphus* and *phiala* probably describe a number of different kinds of cup like those illustrated in fig. 27, many of which are of ultimately Greek origin. The *modiolus* must be the drinking cup of the shape illustrated in fig. 27*g*. A strainer (*colum*) was used for straining the wine, either at table or in the kitchen.

SHOW PLATE

Apart from the domestic silver in use, a separate class of show plate is found among the hoards of the Roman Empire. This would be exhibited on side-tables (*abaci*) in the triclinium of the house and would include such pieces as the Athena dish of the Hildesheim Treasure and the Africa dish from Boscoreale which could never have served a useful purpose. A large display of drinking silver is shown set out on a side table in a painting from the Pompeian tomb of C. Vestorius Priscus.[2] It includes two horn *rhyta,* three bulbous jugs on a high foot, a shallow *patera* with fluted handle ending in an animal head, and cups of various kinds. Among the objects found in the Casa del Menandro hoard was a stand for exhibiting a piece of show-plate (no. 117).

FURNITURE AND OTHER DOMESTIC SILVER

In wealthy households the tripod table supports (*delphica*), candlesticks (*candelabra*) and many other items of domestic furniture (*suppellectilis*) would also be made of silver.[3] Pliny refers to silver baths, banqueting couches and beds. *Aquiminaria* for washing before meals are referred to in the *Digest*[4] and in exceptional cases even some of the cooking utensils could be of silver. Another large class of domestic silver are the mirrors, toilet vessels, trinket boxes etc. which go to make up the *mundus muliebris.*[5] Silver mirrors were especially popular.[6] Children, too, had little miniature vases made of precious metal.[7]

[1] *Digest,* 34, 36. [2] *Mem Acc. Lincei,* Series 3, 1943, 237 ff.
[3] Pliny, *NH,* xxxiii, 146. [4] *Digest,* 34, 2, 19, 12. [5] *ibid.* 34, 2, 25.
[6] Pliny, *NH,* xxxiii, 130; they came into fashion in the first century B.C.
[7] cf. the contents of the so-called 'Child's Grave' now in Berlin, *JdAI,* 65–6, 1950–1, 264 ff.

RELIGIOUS PLATE

Apart from domestic table silver, some of the Roman hoards contain examples of plate that was particularly associated with the worship of the gods. The *patera* (dim. *patella*) was the principal libation vessel, generally preserving the forms of the Greek *phiale* and its derivatives; it is frequently shown on religious and funerary monuments, sometimes equipped with a handle.[1] The jug for pouring sacrificial wine was called a *guttus*. The *simpulum* also served for ladling sacrificial wine; Varro[2] who describes the various utensils used in sacrificial rite in the late Republic comments that these same forms when used domestically acquired the Greek names of *epichysis* and *cyathos* but that in religious usage the old Roman names were preserved. The *lanx*, generally a shallow dish, was used for sacrificial meats and other purposes connected with religious rite. Several of the big picture dishes with elaborate religious scenes are probably ritual plate; examples are the Corbridge *lanx* with its scenes of the worship of Apollo on Delos or the Parabiago dish with its representation of the cult of Cybele.[3] The presence of religious subjects on any particular vessel does not itself show that it served a religious purpose but the notably large number of religious scenes on the handles of surviving saucepan-shaped vessels suggests that the type had an important place in religious cult. Apart from the plate specifically used in religious ritual the shrines of the Roman Empire also contained large treasuries of silver of the kind found at Berthouville; these were not ritual objects but dedications of domestic plate made to the god. Sometimes a special kind of vessel was dedicated at popular sanctuaries like the cylinder-shaped vessels dedicated at Aquae Apollinares (Bagni di Vicarello) near Bracciano.[4] Mirrors were considered as especially appropriate dedications to goddesses.[5]

The following chapters discuss what has survived of this vast accumulation of plate from the time of the Roman Empire, and it has seemed best to divide the period into three main divisions, the first dealing with the Campanian hoards of the first century B.C. and related

[1] von Schaewen, *Opfergeräte*, pl. V, 1.

[2] *De lingua latina*, v, 125.

[3] Levi, *Parabiago*.

[4] Marchi, *La stipe tributata alle divinità delle Aquae Apollinares*, Rome, 1852; *REA*, liv, 1952, 27–38.

[5] Pliny, *NH*, xxxiii, 45.

silver found elsewhere in the Empire, the second with the hoards of the third century which may contain a good deal of silver of earlier date, and the last with the fourth and early fifth-century hoards which consist almost entirely of late Roman silver. An attempt is also made in each section to discuss systematically the development of various shapes and forms of decoration during the period under review.

CHAPTER EIGHT

The Roman Empire: First Century A.D.

The first century A.D. is the best documented period in the history of ancient plate. The collection in the National Museum at Naples, consisting of silver found mainly at Pompeii and Herculaneum, provides a fairly complete cross-section of the plate in use during the early Empire. The eruption of Vesuvius in A.D. 79 gives a *terminus ante quem* for the Campanian silver but many of the pieces must have been old, some very old, when they were buried. The wide date-range of the objects in the Berthouville Hoard, which includes pieces certainly as early as the first century A.D. and as late as the third century, is a reminder that plate was preserved for a long time both in temple treasures and in private collections. In general, it seems that at Pompeii and Herculaneum most of the plate in use was made in the first century A.D., whereas the 'show plate' may be very much earlier. Apart from the Campanian finds, there are very few closely dated finds of Roman silver and individual pieces are not generally datable on internal evidence. No precise date can be given, for example, to the Hildesheim Treasure though most of the plate is of the early Empire.[1] In these circumstances it is not possible to attempt any systematic account of the development of particular shapes within the period, except in a few special cases.

DRINKING CUPS

Silver drinking cups were in very general use at this time. The most popular shapes are Greek in origin and developed from late Hellenistic versions. Cups that generally have handles include the shallow or deep ovoid or hemispherical two-handled cup, standing on a moulded stem

[1] Kuthmann, *Toreutik*, 92, thinks the Treasure is Augustan.

with spreading foot (fig. 27*a–c*); a broader, shallower, two-handled cup with straight sides set on a low base ring (fig. 27*e–f*); a one-handled beaker-shaped vessel with straight or slightly concave sides which seems to be the *modiolus* of ancient texts (fig. 27*g*); and the Greek *kantharos*

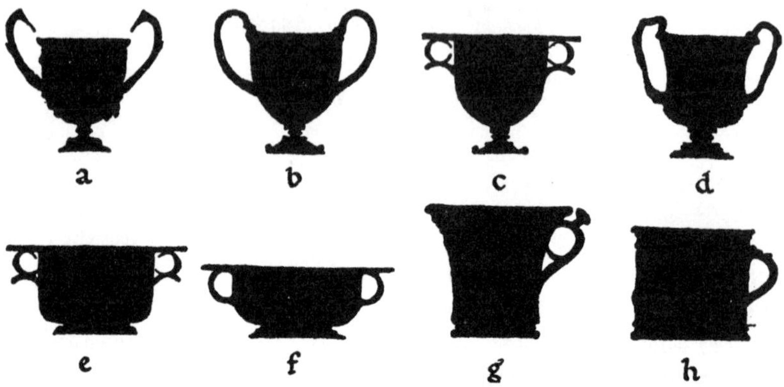

FIG. 27: Shapes of decorated drinking cups in hoards of first century A.D.

shape with a concave upper part and a shallow bowl (fig. 27*d*). A vessel of *kantharos* profile standing on a base ring instead of a foot is also found. The commonest types of handle are the ring handle with horizontal thumb plate at the top, and the high-swung loop handle attached to the rim and body of the vessel; the latter type also occasionally has a horizontal thumb plate. Late forms of the Greek *kylix* handle are also found (e.g. Naples nos. 116329–116332, from Pompeii). Cups generally without handles include beakers of various shapes and a large number of bowl-shaped vessels, like the footless and footed calyx-bowls which are so popular at Pompeii.

The richly decorated versions of these various types of early Imperial cups are discussed below; the plainer versions are sometimes enriched with decorated mouldings on the foot and rim and some chased or engraved ornament. Two pairs of deep cups in New York and London have already been mentioned (p. 113); they may be late Republican or early Imperial. Several cups with similar ornament which seem to be imitations, perhaps Gaulish imitations, of Roman cups of this period have been found in a number of barbarian graves outside the northern frontiers of the Empire, in Denmark,[1] Poland[2] and elsewhere.

[1] *ActaA*, xix, 1948, 252.

[2] Majewski, *Importy*, pls. VIII, X*a* and *b*.

A pair of cups found with a ladle in a tomb of the first century A.D. at Olbia are *kantharos*-shaped on a low foot ring; the only ornament is a decorated ovolo below the rim.[1] Reeding and fluting of various kinds often appear on the cups of this period. At Pompeii the *kantharos* shape was sometimes decorated in this way (e.g. Naples nos. 2560–2). There is a vertically fluted tall beaker and a spirally fluted two-handled cup in the Vatican Museums. A pair of tall beakers of thin metal (nos. 25 and 26) in the Casa del Menandro treasure have a series of concave ovals beaten into the sides. Cups of the period were sometimes decorated with chased or engraved ornament of overlapping leaves (e.g. Naples no. 11778), scrollwork or the like.

DECORATED DRINKING CUPS

The most characteristic vessels of the first-century hoards and the most prized possessions of their owners are the drinking cups richly decorated with repoussé reliefs that served both for use and for show in Roman households.[2] The main shapes that occur are illustrated in fig. 27. They were generally made in pairs decorated with similar ornament or related subjects. Each consists of an outer case in which the reliefs were worked and a plain lining to which the mouldings at the top are attached. The two parts were generally soldered together and the feet and handles which were made separately were also soldered on. The reliefs on the outer case were normally made by repoussé. In the soft alloys used for these cups it was possible to achieve a remarkably high relief; the berries on the olive cups from the Casa del Menandro (nos. 7 and 8) are almost in the round and they had to be filled up with lead to give them solidity. A few little details like the stems of the berries were made separately and soldered on. On the pair of cups with ivy-leaf ornament in Naples from Herculaneum (Naples nos. 25378–9)[3] it looks at first sight as though the silversmith must have used separate pieces of silver to achieve the almost free-standing parts of the leaves but a closer examination shows that he has punched out the metal until he broke through and was then able to draw out the exposed edges and finally solder them together to form the leaf. Some of the cups of this period

[1] Minns, *S & G*, 383, fig. 284.

[2] For these cups in general see *Varia Historica* (dedicated to A. W. Byvanck), Assen, 1954, 71–82.

[3] Pesce, *Oreficeria*, fig. 24; Spinazzola, 234.

were probably cast though this technique has not been noticed by the present author on any of the cups from early contexts that he has examined. It is claimed by one authority that this technique was used for the Stevensweert *kantharos* (see above p. 115). The handles and feet of the cups were generally cast; they, too, were frequently decorated with relief ornament and decorated mouldings.

It is impossible to discuss in detail the vast variety of decorative themes and figure subjects that appear on these cups. Naturalistic floral ornament was especially popular. The fine cup with myrtle branches from Alesia, the olive cups from the Casa del Menandro and the ivy cups from Herculaneum have been mentioned; to these may be added the pair with arabesques incorporating clusters of shrubs, fruit and flowers which were recently acquired by the British Museum,[1] a pair with vine ornament from Herculaneum and many others. Cups with birds and animals, landscape and 'genre', Bacchanalian themes, Centaurs, Tritons and Nereids, scenes from Greek mythology and literature, religious rites and erotic scenes illustrate the vast range of the figured subjects. The two famous cups with historical scenes found at Boscoreale represent an important class of silverware which was produced under the aegis of the imperial court.[2] On one of the cups Augustus is shown in two scenes illustrating his rule in peace and war; on the other Tiberius in a triumphal procession, accompanied by a scene of sacrifice. The cups which seem to have been made in the Tiberian period are probably officially inspired works of propaganda made by court silversmiths and were perhaps distributed as gifts on a special imperial occasion, like the anniversary plates in the fourth century and later (see below pp. 199–201).

Cups of this class have been found all over the Roman Empire and outside its frontiers. Two of the finest, now in the National Museum at Copenhagen, were discovered in a local chieftain's grave at Hoby in Denmark; the cups were made as a pair of which one is decorated with a scene (pl. 35B) showing Priam making his appeal to Achilles for the body of Hector, and the other with two episodes from the story of Philoktetes.[3] A cup showing sea horses comes from another chieftain's grave at Goslawice in Poland.[4] These decorated cups were probably a

[1] *BMQ*, xxiii, 1961, 77 ff.

[2] de Villefosse, *Boscoreale*, pls. XXXI ff.

[3] *Nordiske Fortidsminder*, ii, fasc. 3, 1923, 119 ff.

[4] Majewski, *Importy*, pls. XXXIV–V.

popular form of diplomatic present much in demand among friendly and client kings outside the frontiers. A painted tomb in a tumulus at Vize in eastern Thrace contained four deep cups decorated with figures of storks in marsh landscape;[1] this was a popular theme in the period and there are two similar stork cups in the Pierpont Morgan Library, New York[2] and two others (nos. 13 and 14) in the Boscoreale Treasure. A *modiolus* with reliefs showing satyrs and with a handle in the form of a putto was found with the Vize cups.

Decorated cups were probably made throughout the main centres of the Empire, especially in eastern provinces. A cup from Meroe in Egypt, now in the Museum of Fine Arts, Boston, which is decorated with a scene of Egyptian inspiration showing the king passing judgment on a man, may be thought of as a local product of the Augustan period.[3] Another cup found at Lyon is decorated with scenes connected with local religious cult.[4] Two cups, one a tall beaker showing *erotes* with the attributes of Hercules and the other a deep cup with plane branches and leaves, are said to have been found at Eretria in Euboea and may have been made in Greece.[5] A cup with scenes of homosexual love recently on the London Market[6] is said to have been found in Palestine together with coins of Claudius. Very recently a battered cup with olive branches and vine was found in the small silver hoard, probably of the Neronian period, at Hockwold.[7]

As had been stated already, the fashion for drinking vessels richly decorated with repoussé seems to have come in soon after 100 B.C. and it lasted for the greater part of the first century A.D. (see also p. 163). In the present state of knowledge it does not seem possible to decide when, within this period, particular cups found in the first-century hoards were made. The detail of the chased floral ornament on the Mars and Venus cups from the Casa del Menandro (nos. 5 and 6) suggests the mid first century B.C.; the form of the handles on the pair of olive cups in the same find (nos. 7 and 8) is Hellenistic rather than

[1] *Bull. Inst. Bulg.*, xii–xiii, 1938–9, 154–89.

[2] G. M. A. Richter, *Art in America*, iv, 1918, 171 ff.; *Ancient Italy*, 59.

[3] *BMFA*, 23, 1925, 10; found in the debris of the pyramid of the King of Meroe who reigned *c.* 45–25 B.C.

[4] *RA*, viii, 1936, 46–53.

[5] de Ridder, *Bijoux*, nos. 1927 and 1930.

[6] *AK*, 6, 1963, pl. IX; R. V. Nicholls informed me about its provenance.

[7] The find is in the British Museum; Toynbee, *Art in Britain*, pl. LXXb.

Roman. The big goblet with floral arabesques in the Boscoreale hoard (no. 9) has been plausibly attributed to the mid-first century B.C. The Neo-Attic style of such pieces as the Tritons and Nereids cup from Pompeii might be found at any time from about 100 B.C. onwards.[1] On the other hand, the decorated mouldings and the handles in the form of twisted branches on two *kantharoi* decorated with Bacchic masks and attributes in the Hildesheim treasure seem to be typical of developed first century A.D. taste.[2] Cups like nos. 15 and 16 from Boscoreale which have cast handles with low-relief ornament related to that on the handles of the saucepan *paterae* (see below p. 145 ff.) must belong to the first century A.D. A few vessels like the historical cups from Boscoreale, the Hoby cups and the cup from Palestine mentioned above may be firmly dated to the Augustan and Julio-Claudian periods on grounds of subject matter or style. A recent attempt to assign dates to all the best-known cups in the first-century hoards within the period 75 B.C.–A.D. 50 has not been completely convincing.[3]

The problems will not be satisfactorily solved until we know a great deal more about the technique as well as the style of the most important pieces. In the first century B.C. a number of master-craftsmen in silver had acquired great reputations in the manufacture of these drinking cups.[4] In the early years of the Empire the vastly increased demand for fine silver led to the development of mass-production and an inevitable decline in creative craftsmanship. There was, indeed, a very great difference between the artistic climate of the first century B.C. and that of the first century A.D. In the earlier period there were artist-craftsmen capable of producing original masterpieces for their Roman patrons whereas in the later period the laws of supply and demand tended to drive out the educated artist and produce in his place the craftsman not at all inferior in the skills of the metalworker but lacking real creative ability. These craftsmen resorted to basing their work upon, or directly copying, earlier prototypes and we hear, for example, of the clever Zenodorus who copied two cups by Calamis with such skill that it was scarcely possible to tell the difference. It has been suggested that the well-known cup from Anzio, now in the Corsini Palace, Rome, which

[1] *BdA*, 7, 1927–8, 433 ff.; *RM*, 49, 1934, 282 ff.

[2] Pernice and Winter, *Hildesheim*, 37 ff., pls. XIII–XVII; cf. the handles found in the Hockwold hoard.

[3] Küthmann, *Toreutik*.

[4] See above p. 114.

depicts the episode of Athena casting her lot for Orestes, is a copy of one of the cups mentioned by Pliny the Elder as the work of a certain Zopyrus.[1] The process of copying well-known works was greatly aided by the practice of making plaster casts from them which could be distributed to silversmiths. A large number of these plaster-casts have been found; the most famous hoard, that from Mit Rahinet (Memphis) which has already been mentioned, probably belonged to a working silversmith of the early Roman Empire, and the casts had been taken from a wide range of late classical and Hellenistic metalwork. Finds of similar plaster casts have been made in other parts of the Roman Empire.[2] The craftsman might use the casts in a number of different ways. If he were working in repoussé, the cast would serve as a guide to be copied as closely as the technique allowed and, as already mentioned, most of the surviving cups seem to be made by this technique. He might use the cast for preparing a mould in which to cast a copy of the original, but although it is clear that, in the early Empire, silversmiths had become very skilled in making thin silver castings[3] it is not yet known to what extent this method was actually used on drinking cups. A detailed technical examination of all the cups of the period is badly needed.

The use of plaster models is strongly suggested in the case of the Hoby cups which were made by repoussé, since there exist fragments of moulds and pottery of Arretine fabric showing parts of the same scenes which are very similar but not identical in detail.[4] It is a reasonable inference that while the potter was reproducing a model by some mechanical means (e.g. making a mould from a plaster cast), the silversmith was working with the aid of the same model which he could not copy with absolute precision and had to adapt to the shape of the vessel he was decorating. There is also an Arretine version[5] of the scene on the Orestes cup in the British Museum but it differs in a number of details.

The fashion for these relief-decorated cups flourished until about the

[1] A. Michaelis, *Der Corsinische Silbergefass*; G. Hafner, *Iudicium Orestis* (113 Berlin Winckelmannsprogramm), 1957; *RM*, 20, 1905, 289 ff. and 21, 1906, 280 ff.

[2] Apart from the Mit Rahinet and Begram casts, an important find was made in Chersonnesus (*Materials*, 7, 1892).

[3] Ippel, *Guss- und Treibarbeit.*

[4] *ActaA*, i, 1930, 273 ff., and xxxi, 1960, 185.

[5] A. Stenico, *La Ceramica Arretina*, Milan, 1960, pl. 16, no. 87.

middle of the first century A.D. Pliny says that the art of repoussé was very little practised in his own day; 'all of a sudden', he writes, 'this art so declined that it is now valued only in old specimens and authority attaches to examples worn with use even if the very design is invisible.'[1] Pliny's remarks are confirmed by the fact that very few relief cups can be attributed to the last quarter of the first century and later, and the evidence suggests that the thin repoussé vessels of the Hellenistic-Roman class went out of fashion in favour of more solid relief bowls and cups, cast in heavy silver. A good example of the latter type is the Ingolstadt vase in Munich;[2] a cup with reliefs showing an Amazonomachy now in Turin[3] and another cup in Belgrade with reliefs of Dionysos and a Maenad on a hippocamp belong to the same category.[4] Storks and water-birds appear on solid cast cups or bowls from Calafat (Donau) in Rumania[5] and in the British Museum.[6] With the general use of more solid metal for vessels of this kind, the practice of cutting the ornament in the soft metal seems to have come in. This technique was apparently used on a silver beaker from Hermopolis, assigned to the Flavian period; the ornament shows putti vintaging amid an overall design of vine branches.[7] The same technique has been suggested for the Ingolstadt vase. It is one which was much used later in the workshops of Gaul (see below p. 180) and perhaps Pliny is describing its beginnings when he speaks of a fashionable technique that involved 'wasting as much of the silver as possible'.

JUGS

Three jugs of domestic use from the hoard of the Casa del Menandro are illustrated in fig. 28*a–c*. The tall, round-necked jug, fig. 28*a*, is 24 cm. high and equipped with a solid cast handle decorated with floral ornament in low relief and duck's head arms attaching it to the neck. There is another jug of this form, also with a relief-decorated handle, in the Boscoreale Treasure (no. 44). This type of jug was popular in the period and there are six of them with plain handles in the National Museum at Naples. One of these (Inv. no. 25694) has a leaf-shaped thumb rest at the top of the handle; another has a soldering plate in the

[1] *NH*, xxxiii, 157.
[2] *RM*, 67, 1960, 111.
[3] U. Hausmann, *Hellenistische Reliefbecher aus attischen und böotischen Werkstätten*, Stuttgart, 1959, pl. 46.
[4] *RA*, 1903 (i), 18.
[5] *Germania*, xxxvii, 1959, 238.
[6] *BMCP*, no. 72.
[7] Adriani, *Gobelet*.

form of a palmette at the base of the handle. The little squat, bulbous jug (fig. 28*c*) standing on a low base ring is another popular type of the period. The example from the Casa del Menandro (no. 21) has a cast handle which is surmounted by a female head, looking into the vessel –

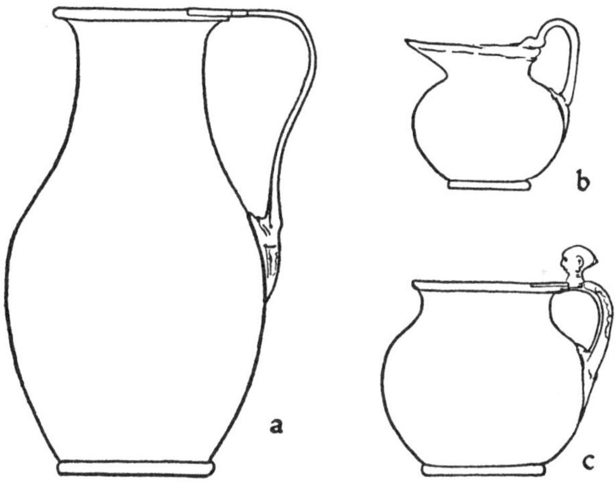

FIG. 28: Three types of domestic jug; first century A.D.
Scale 1:4

a common feature of this type of jug. In the National Museum at Naples there is another similar jug (no. 25680), one with spiral flutings on the body (no. 25372), and another with a plain body and a decorated handle. The last of these has a soldering plate in the form of a frontal head and the handle is surmounted by a satyr head looking upwards (Inv. 25370). There is a jug of this type with spiral flutings and a female head on top of the handle from Boscoreale in the Field Museum, Chicago.[1] Together with the jugs of this type may be mentioned a little spouted bowl in Munich with a decorated handle surmounted by a female head and two little ear-handles on either side.[2] The third jug illustrated in fig. 28*b* is a less common type – a small, bulbous vessel with a spouted neck; there are two in the Casa del Menandro find (nos. 23–4), one in the Antiquarium at Pompeii (1948/4), and another in the Boscoreale Treasure (no. 96). It is surprising that a number of other

[1] H. F. de Cou, *Antiquities from Boscoreale in Field Museum*, Chicago, 1912, no. 24668 (p. 197).

[2] Schreiber, *Toreutik*, no. 48.

jug-forms of the period, like the trefoil oinochoe which is so common in bronze, are not represented in the surviving silver.

DECORATED JUGS

The decorated jugs of this period are very different in form from the domestic jugs described above. These decorated jugs usually have oval or pear-shaped body, a trefoil or spouted neck, a high foot and a handle which arches above the top of the vessel. The handles usually have cast ornament, a decorated soldering plate at the base, a leaf thumb grip at the top, and often a head or figure between the arms attaching the handle to the neck of the vessel. This type of jug is frequently shown on sculptured monuments of the period as a sacrificial vessel,[1] and the surviving examples all belong to the class of show-plate. Two of the finest come from the Treasure of Berthouville (nos. 4-5) (pl. 53A); the reliefs represent Homeric subjects: on one, Achilles mourning and the ransoming of Hector: on the other, the dragging of Hector's corpse and the death of Achilles. The style is Hellenistic and the jugs, like some of the figured cups, may be as early as the first century B.C. Lehmann-Hartleben[2] prefers to think that the scenes were copied from cups of the late Hellenistic period by a silversmith of the Flavian period who, he says 'kept alive some of the artistic spirit of the first century B.C. when art was produced by educated artists for an educated public familiar with mythology, moral philosophy, and the history of Greek art'. A pair of richly decorated jugs with sacrificial scenes were found in the Boscoreale Treasure (nos. 3-4) and there is a fine jug in Munich said to come from Naples which is decorated with a Centauromachy.[3] A very fragmentary example with leaf ornament on the body comes from the Hildesheim Treasure; its handle is very ornate, arches high above the neck of the vessel and ends below in a satyr head.[4]

AMPHORAE

The silver *amphorae* from Pompeii and Herculaneum are similar in form to the tall jug illustrated in fig. 28*a*. A little one from the Casa del Menandro hoard (no. 22) is very close to the jug. Two very large

[1] von Schaewen, *Opfergeräte*, 16 ff. The fine inlaid bronze examples of this type of jug from Egyed in Hungary was found with a sacrificial *patera* (*JdAI*, xxiv, 1909, 28 ff.).

[2] *AJA*, xlii, 1938, 82 ff.; see also *CRAI*, 1948, 95–111; *Mon. Piot*, xx, 1950, 13 ff.

[3] Sieveking, *Antike Metallgeräte*, fig. 8.

[4] Pernice and Winter, *Hildesheim*, 46.

amphorae in the National Museum, Naples, are of the same general shape but lack the moulded lip; one of these (Inv. no. 111768) is 44 cm. high and was probably used for serving wine at table. One of the very few surviving pieces of gold plate belonging to this period seems to have been an *amphora* of this type. The vessel was found somewhere off the west coast of Asia Minor and is now in the British Museum;[1] it has a weight inscription giving a figure considerably greater than its present weight and the discrepancy can be easily explained by the loss of its two handles. A number of charming little *amphorae* have been found at the site of Aquae Apollinares (Bagni di Vicarello) where silver of various kinds was dedicated by those who had come to take the curative waters of the spa.[2] There is one with cast ornament on the handles and body in the British Museum,[3] (pl. 39B) another in the Victoria and Albert Museum[4] and another in the Vatican Museums. These little *amphorae* were probably made in the second half of the first century A.D.

LADLES (*simpula*)

The round, flat-bottomed ladle with a short vertical handle which is one of the commonest vessels connected with the service of liquids in the first-century hoards must be identified with the *simpulum* of domestic and religious use (fig. 29 and pl. 39A). It apparently superseded the long duck's head ladle of the Hellenistic period which did not survive in common use into the first century A.D. although there is one plain one in the Antiquarium at Pompeii (no. 1148/4) and a very ornate one in the Museum of Fine Arts, Boston with a decorated bowl and a panther head at the end of the handle which on grounds of style may be attributed to the early Empire.[5] The *simpulum* in its basic form is a shallow, flat-bottomed bowl with slightly curving sides and an upright handle of strip metal made in one piece with it. The two commonest types of handle among surviving silver examples from Pompeii and Herculaneum are shown in fig. 29*a* and *b*; the 'knobbed' variety is the more popular of the two. Occasionally the handle is bent over at the top either in a curve or completely looped round (e.g. Naples no. 118984, from Pompeii). A typical *simpulum* found in the Bursa Treasure is now

[1] *BMCJ*, no. 3168. [2] See above p. 21. [3] *BMCP*, no. 79.

[4] *Burlington Fine Arts Club Exhibition of Ancient Greek Art*, 1904, D 88.

[5] *AK*, 6, 1963, 33, pl. 15; this ladle is said to have been found with the three cups in the British Museum (see p. 115) and a cup with Bacchic subjects now in the Toledo Museum of Art.

in the British Museum. Decorated handles, some very elaborate, were fitted to these ladles. One found in the house of Trebius Valens at Pompeii (fig. 29*d*) has a plain handle surmounted by a pelta (Antiquarium no. 429/4)[1] and this seems to have been a common motif in the

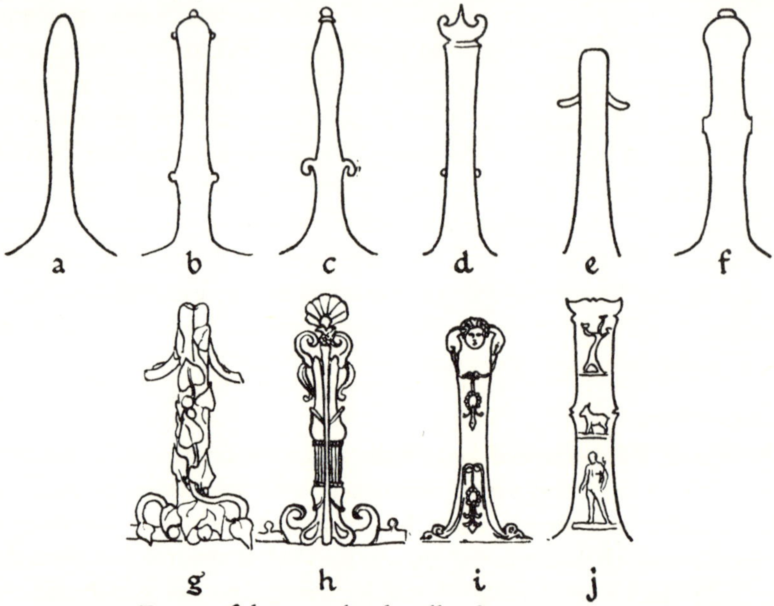

FIG. 29: Forms of the *simpulum* handle; first-second century A.D.

period. A very elaborate cast handle in the form of branches with leaf decoration is found on a *simpulum* in the Hildesheim Treasure (pl. 39A); another handle from this Treasure in the form of a double stem surmounted by a palmette probably comes from a similar vessel (fig. 29*h*). A *simpulum* found in a small hoard of objects at Tekija in Yugoslavia, dated by associated finds to the period A.D. 80–90, is decorated with low-relief ornament of tendrils and scrolls like that found on the saucepans of the first century A.D.[2] In the find at Vize in Thrace there was a *simpulum* with a cast handle decorated with leaf ornament.

STRAINERS

It is remarkable that very few silver strainers have been found at Pompeii and Herculaneum. There are two examples in the National

[1] *NS*, 1915, 339.

[2] *Travaux de Conservation et de Recherche*, Belgrade, 1956, 174–8; D. Mano-Zisi, *Nalaz iz Tekije*, Belgrade, 1957.

Museum at Naples of which one, in the shape of a little cup with a single cup handle with horizontal thumb grip, is indistinguishable from the type in use under the Republic. The second strainer has a wider perforated bowl and a long horizontal handle, a smaller version of the typical bronze strainer of early Imperial finds.[1] The rarity of silver strainers in early Imperial hoards is perhaps to be explained by a change in the method of preparing wine for the table. In the late Republic, a wine strainer was, apparently, a necessary piece of table equipment; it may be that under the Empire wine was strained in the kitchen with bronze utensils and brought ready to the table. Wine was both strained and cooled by means of strainers in the period.

'SAUCEPANS'

The *patera* in the shape of a saucepan is a vessel which, like the *simpulum*, appears first in hoards of the first century A.D. and is thereafter one of the most characteristic vessels of the Roman period. Its uses are by no means clearly established. The bronze examples, which are extremely numerous, are often found in conjunction with ladles and strainers and this suggests that the main use was in the service of liquids. The alternative suggestion that it was used for the slow cooking or warming of foods is highly unlikely although one or two examples do seem to show some traces of the action of heat.[2] The existence of examples in glass would seem to rule out this alternative. The saucepan which seems to have begun as a domestic vessel was probably used later in religious cult; religious themes are commonly represented on the handles of silver saucepans and they were often dedicated at sanctuaries. The ancient name for the vessel is not known.[3]

In its simplest form the vessel consists of a flat-bottomed bowl with gently curving sides, a moulded rim and a horizontal handle of metal strip made in one piece with the bowl. The handle is about the same length as the diameter of the bowl; its sides curve inwards from the bowl and widen again towards the end which is usually rounded. There may be holes for hanging up the vessel near the end of the handle. This basic form of which there are many examples in bronze is comparatively

[1] For this see Radnóti, *Bronzegefässe*, pl. XXIVf.
[2] Maiuri, *Menandro*, 354.
[3] Heron de Villefosse identified this vessel as the *trulla* which seems to be referred to in ancient texts as ladle and drinking vessel.

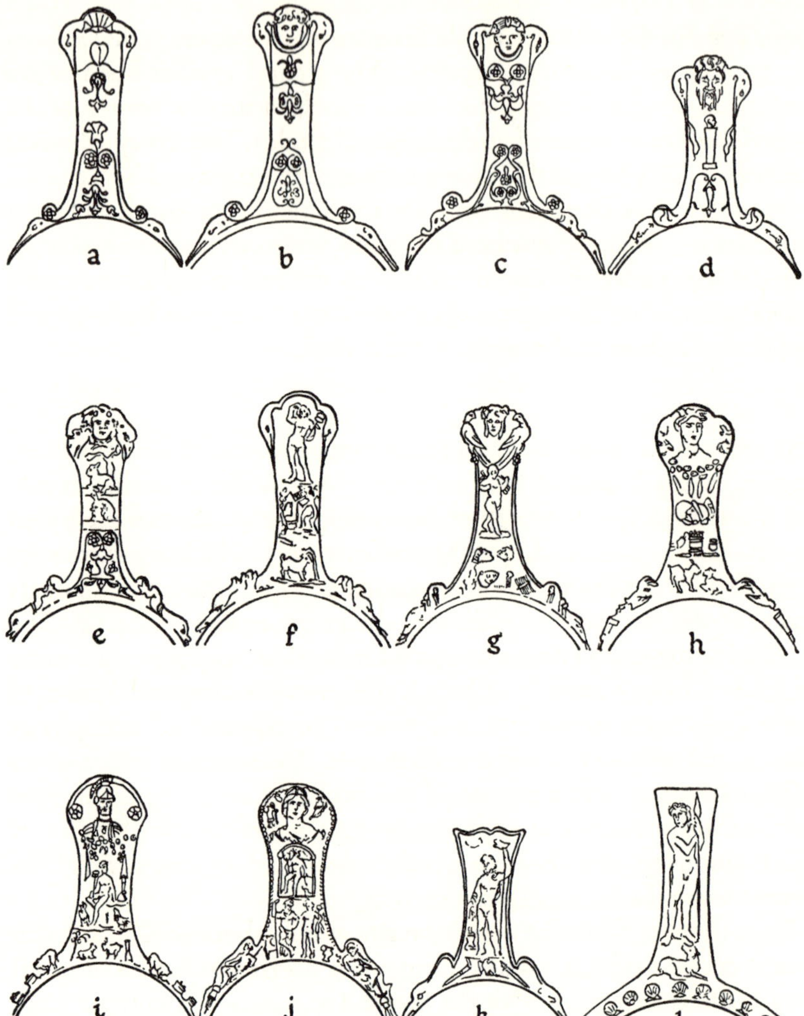

FIG. 30: The development of Roman 'saucepan' handles; first–fourth century A.D.

rare in silver. There is one completely plain one from Pompeii in Naples (no. 25339) and one in the Antiquarium at Pompeii (no. 1135/4) with three holes for suspension near the end. Another example in the Antiquarium of Pompeii has some simple engraved ornament on the surface of the handle. It is probable that the other forms of handle which are found in bronze had silver counterparts in the period.[1]

The silver saucepans of the first century A.D. generally have handles which are decorated with low-relief ornament on the upper surface; these were cast separately and soldered on to the bowl with the aid of two curving arms following the contour of the bowl on either side. Saucepans were usually made in pairs with matching handles; the two handles of a pair are not usually identical in detail and probably not, therefore, cast in the same mould. The decoration follows certain standard patterns (see fig. 30). The arms attaching the handle to the bowl take the form of swans' heads with long beaks; two swans' heads flank the end of the handle and there is often a shell or similar motif placed at the end between them. Scroll ornament, following the curve of the handle, and little low-relief floral motifs fill the rest of the space (fig. 30*a*). A good example of this early scheme of decoration is the saucepan from Boscoreale illustrated in pl. 38A. There is an almost identical pair in the collection at Munich[2] and others in Naples. Two similar ones found 'near the Black Sea' are in the collection of Gideon N. Stieff snr.[3] A Medusa head between the swans' heads at the end of the handle, as on a pair from the Casa del Menandro (nos 18–19), was commonly introduced (fig. 30*b*). On a pair of saucepans found in the Rhine near Oberkassel[4] little elephant heads appear in conjunction with the swans' heads on the arms of attachment (fig. 30*c*); elephant heads also occur on a pair found in a small hoard of silver at Ruffieux near Bourgoin (Isère) and now in Lyon.[5] The introduction of a standing figure, generally of a god, as the main decorative motif on the handle appears first in this period, perhaps not much before A.D. 79. There is one example from Pompeii (Naples Inv. no. 25338) with a figure of Mercury occupying most of the space; and a related piece in the Berthouville hoard (fig. 30*d*) has a tall herm in this position.

The bowls of first-century saucepans were generally raised from sheet or spun on a lathe; a few may have been cast. They usually have

[1] Radnóti, *Bronzegefässe*, 19 ff.

[2] Munich nos. 650, 651; Schreiber, *Toreutik*, 326, nos. 32, a and b.

[3] Fogg Museum, *Private Collections*, no. 322, pl. LXXXIX; *Bulletin Walters Art Gallery*, iv, 1952, 2–4.

[4] *BJ*, 151, 1950, 194; H. von Petrikovits, *Das römische Rheinlande; Arch. Forschungen seit 1945*, 117, pl. 8; now in Rhein, Landesmuseum, Bonn.

[5] Schreiber, *Toreutik*, 327, no. 34. *GA*, 1884, 344.

a series of turned concentric rings on the bottom. The shapes vary a good deal; the sides curve gently and the bowl may be deep or shallow. One or two unusual shapes occur, like the one with concave sides in the Hildesheim Treasure.[1] The bowls are almost always plain; exceptions are the pairs from the Casa del Menandro and Oberkassel which have a series of convex ovals on the body and one in Naples with a series of close set concave circles. A rare decorated example from this period is a saucepan in the Boscoreale Treasure with a bowl of *kantharos* profile decorated on its upper part with vertical fluting like the cups described on p. 135. A similar one was found at Pompeii.

Apart from the orthodox decorated handles of the period there are a few with unusual designs. One of the finest is the handle from the Casa del Menandro (no. 17) illustrated on pl. 38B which is decorated with a hunting scene, the detail of which is richly gilded. A popular design in the Campanian hoards consists of a steering oar as the main motif with the rest of the field filled with sea-creatures. There is one in the Boscoreale hoard and two in the Museum at Naples (nos. 175262 and 11115). The Treasure of Hildesheim, which represents the products of different workshops from the Campanian ones, contained a number of unusual handle forms; the arms attaching the handles are in the form of swans' heads but the rest of the decoration is very different. One has a vine tendril in low relief down the length of the handle, one is apparently a bundle of leaves bound in the middle, and a third suggests the branches of a tree.

PLATES AND DISHES

In the Casa del Menandro find there is a complete service of plates all made to the same pattern (nos. 27-43), consisting of one large serving dish and sixteen smaller plates, four of 16 cm. diameter, four of 11·1 cm., four of 10·1 cm. and four of 7·5 cm. The plates are all round, of shallow curved section with a pronounced convex rim and each is equipped with a pair of segmental flat handles decorated with cast ornament in low relief, the decoration consisting of a head of Silenus flanked by geese whose necks stretch out to form the arms by which the handle is soldered to the rim of the dish (pl. 40A-B).

These dishes with ear handles have been found in large numbers at

[1] Pernice and Winter, *Hildesheim*, 72.

Pompeii and Herculaneum.[1] Examples occur with shallow curved interior and a central boss, usually decorated with a gilded rosette. There are also flat-bottomed dishes with gently convex sides, flat-bottomed dishes with concave sides and a narrow flat rim with decorated mouldings, and a number of other slightly variant forms. The decoration of the handles is fairly standard; one large dish found in the Boscoreale Treasure has two swans' heads emerging from below two heraldically opposed dolphins flanking a shell, the space between being taken up with floral ornament. These dishes were also made in sets with bowls of similar form. We find bowls with concave sides, with straight sides and horizontal decorated rim, with curved sides and central boss decorated with rosettes, all corresponding with the forms of the dishes. Dishes with concave upright sides and a series of concentric turned circles as the interior decoration occur in the Collection at Naples. The shallow dishes (e.g. Inv. no. 116345) have a broadish convex rim decorated with cast floral ornament in low relief. Oval dishes were probably rare in this period though some with ear handles are reported to have been found at Pompeii. They become common later.

One exceptionally large and richly decorated dish perhaps of the first century A.D. is the so-called Bizerta dish, one of the largest surviving pieces of Roman plate.[2] The plate was dredged up from the sea off the harbour of Bizerta together with another, very fragmentary dish. With its two ear handles its maximum length is 92 cm. and it weighs 9 kilos. The rich decoration illustrates several techniques used by the silversmiths of the first century A.D. There is a central medallion of Apollo and Marsyas with the figures inlaid with gold and electrum. A narrow frieze of putti and animals is engraved on the surface of the dish and the frieze round the rim shows Bacchanalian scenes in low relief. The handles, richly decorated with reliefs, were cast separately and soldered on. The style of the reliefs suggests a date in the second half of the first century or in the early second century A.D.

A number of large plates in the Hildesheim Treasure illustrate forms common in the first century A.D. outside the Campanian hoards. Two of these are large flat plates (about 30 cm. in diameter) with a broad

[1] This type of handle is referred to in the Egyptian inventory of plate mentioned above (p. 128); ὠτάρια σατύρια are presumably handles with satyr heads.

[2] *Mon Piot*, ii, 1895, 77.

slightly raised flange decorated with acanthus-scroll ornament in relief and edged with an ovolo (pl. 41B).[1] A third example, of the same size, had vine-leaf ornament on the flange and was once fitted with handles, presumably of the ear-type. Another flat plate simply has a narrow rim with fluting which also seems to have been fitted originally with handles; these must have been let into the rim and at some later date they were removed and the rim made good. This plate is also patched underneath. A large plate, 37 cm. in diameter, is plain with a moulded rim and was probably made to be set on the handsome silver folding tripod illustrated in pl. 41A.[2] A set of three little oval plates equipped with handle-grips at either end are better described as dishes than trays though they probably served exactly the same purpose as the rectangular trays described below (pp. 154–5)[3].

PICTURE DISHES

Picture dishes belong to the class of show-plate. The idea of making the whole surface of a dish the field for a relief picture is Roman and the earliest examples belong to the first century A.D. One of the earliest is the so-called Aquileia *patera* in Vienna[4] (pl. 44A) which belongs to the class of propaganda court silver like the historical cups from Boscoreale. The whole surface of the dish which is 29·5 cm. in diameter is decorated with a scene showing a Roman Emperor or prince (Claudius?) as Triptolemus, the bringer of prosperity and fertility to the earth. Another 'picture' dish which may be as early as the first century A.D. is in the Antonio de Otañes collection at Castro Urdiales where it was found;[5] the reliefs on the surface refer to the medicinal spring at Umeri which was a flourishing health resort at the time. The dish is presumably some kind of souvenir. The date of a small picture dish found at Lameira Larga in Portugal and showing Perseus slaying Medusa is much disputed; it has been put as early as Augustan by some authorities.[6]

[1] Pernice and Winter, *Hildesheim*, 57.

[2] *ibid.* 59.   [3] *ibid.* 60.

[4] Rostovtzeff, *SEHRE*, pl. XIII; Arneth, *Gold- und Silber-Monumente*. H. Möbius ('Der Silberteller von Aquileja' in *Festschrift für Friedrich Matz*, Mainz 1962) identifies the main figure as Mark Antony.

[5] Rostovtzeff, *SEHRE*, pl. XXXV (with bibliography); García y Bellido, *Esculturas Romanas*, no. 493.

[6] *AA*, 1910, 332, fig. 26; *Bol. de la real Accad. de la Storia*, 1909, 4; García y Bellido, *Esculturas Romanas*, no. 491.

MEDALLION DISHES AND BOWLS

Dishes and bowls with figured relief-medallions on the inside belong generally to the class of show-plate, the medallion often occupying the larger part of the bowl or dish and making it useless for any practical purpose. As in the case of the decorated cups, the *emblema* dishes found in the Campanian hoards may be considerably earlier than the date they were buried, having been treasured in the family for generations.[1] As we have seen, the fashion for *emblema* dishes had originated in the third century B.C. and examples were enthusiastically collected by Romans of the late Republic. A typical heirloom is the bowl found in the Boscoreale Treasure (no. 2) which is decorated in the centre with the bust, modelled in the round, of an elderly man of the time of Augustus, probably an ancestor of the last owner. The bowl had a counterpart with a portrait of his wife, and this portrait which became detached from its bowl and from the rest of the treasure is now in the British Museum.[2] One of the finest surviving *emblema* bowls is the Africa bowl, also from the Boscoreale Treasure (pl. 36B), which is decorated with a high-relief medallion showing a personification of Africa wearing an elephant headdress and carrying a cornucopia. The bowl is really a silver picture which would stand prominently among the display silver and it may be as old as the first century B.C.[3] It has an elaborate weight description giving the details of the *emblema* and bowl separately and together (see above p. 22). A bowl in the Hildesheim Treasure with a high-relief medallion of Hercules strangling two snakes has very similar chased ornament round the inside and looks like a work of the same period. Another fine medallion-vessel from Hildesheim is a shallow bowl fitted with two cup handles and decorated with a superb seated figure of Athena in high relief (pl. 36A). To judge from the ornament this vessel was made in the early Empire but the medallion is probably copied from a Hellenistic one. The technique of this vessel and the Hercules bowl has been studied in detail;[4] the Athena medallion was apparently cast whereas the Hercules bust was made by repoussé. One might imagine that the Athena medallion was made with the aid of a plaster cast of the type found at Mit Rahinet and elsewhere. These

[1] Such dishes were often bequeathed to favourite relations (cf. *CIL*, vi, 10229).

[2] *BMCP*, no. 26.

[3] The head has been identified as a portrait of Cleopatra VII (*Libyca*, ii, 1954, 49 ff.).

[4] Ippel, *Guss- und Treibarbeit*.

medallion dishes were often made in pairs with related subjects. Two dishes in the Hildesheim Treasure have medallions of Attys and Cybele[1] and two others found at Hermopolis in Egypt have female profile busts facing in opposite directions.[2] A silver bowl from the Casa del Menandro (no. 14) has the only surviving gold medallion of the period which shows a bust of a city-goddess wearing a turreted crown. A silver medallion showing a silenus with a wine-cup which probably came from a bowl of this kind was found as far afield as Taxila; it had been mounted on a silver stand to serve as a table-ornament and was associated with a silver spoon of early Roman type.[3] Many other detached *emblemata* have survived.

BOWLS

Apart from the various kinds of bowl made to the same pattern as the popular form of 'eared' dish, which have already been mentioned, an infinite variety of bowls large and small formed part of the table service in the first century A.D. and no attempt can be made here to describe all the different kinds. Small bowls, with various profiles, and with or without feet, would be used for eating cereal foods and drinking soup; some are scarcely distinguishable from plain drinking cups. In the Casa del Menandro find there occur the following types; two sets of four (nos. 48–55), one larger, one smaller, of a two-handled bowl with a heavy cast hanging rim decorated with ovolo: a set of four calyx bowls, plain, on low foot rings (nos. 90–93): a set of four similar bowls, smaller, on tall feet (nos. 94–97): a set of four conical bowls with convex sides, and seven shallow curved bowls with feet. Another popular bowl, of which eleven examples of various sizes occur in the Museum at Naples is a conical bowl with concave sides decorated with vertical fluting and a scalloped rim. There are five concave-sided conical bowls with a vertical rim and two curious shallow bowls of biconical section with a wavy flange dividing the two parts (Inv. nos. 144804, and 19331). The shell bowl was clearly very popular. The orthodox form is shaped like a conch shell and may stand either on a low foot or on three knobs. Variants have complicated designs of spiral and transverse fluting with scalloped rims (e.g. no. 110863) or a central boss on the

[1] Pernice and Winter, *Hildesheim*, 26 ff.

[2] Adriani, *Gobelet*, pls. IV–V.

[3] Wheeler, *Rome beyond the Imperial Frontiers*, 159, pl. XXVII*b*.

inside. Shell-shaped bowls were used for various foods, perhaps as the shape suggests for shellfish. A big fluted serving bowl from Pompeii has two heavy bucket handles to carry it, like the very large shell bowl from the Casa del Menandro (no. 83). In the Hildesheim Treasure there were three calyx bowls, not unlike examples from Pompeii but with heavy rims, a shallow tripod bowl with a band of leaf ornament inlaid in niello (see p. 12) and two sets of footed bowls with inlaid vine ornament, one set of four larger, and three smaller examples of the same pattern.

A number of large vessels for liquids were found in the Hildesheim Treasure. One of the finest is a *krater* or mixing bowl, 36 cm. high, consisting, like the decorated cups of the period, of an inner lining and an outer case which is decorated with low-relief tendril ornament. The *krater* is equipped with two loop handles. Two other vessels which probably served as wine containers are an enormous *kantharos* 52·5 cms. high and a big bucket 36·2 cms. high. There are no comparable vessels in the Campanian hoards.

OTHER TABLE SILVER

A large number of other silver objects of various kinds would decorate the table of a wealthy Roman in the first century A.D. Hot dishes and bowls would be placed on little stands. There is a charming set of four such stands in the Casa del Menandro hoard consisting of a flat plate with hanging rim supported on three feet in the form of elephant heads (nos. 56-9); the rim is decorated with ovolo ornament and the top has a pattern of scroll ornament round a rosette, both of which are inlaid in gold. There are four plain, slightly concave stands with animal feet in the same find, and a number of other plain stands in the collection of the National Museum at Naples. Little shallow cups, used presumably for eggs, stand on stems joined to a large flat base plate. An example from Boscoreale has a large rectangular plate decorated on the underside. It may have served a dual purpose as an egg-cup and, when inverted, a stand. The series of four little egg-cups on stems with broad flat bases from the Treasure of the Casa del Menandro (nos. 48-51) have foot plates of complicated shape with a semicircular and a rectangular part (see pl. 42B) with a small semicircle cut out of the latter; Maiuri suggests that the set was fitted into a wooden tray, very much like a modern egg-cruet. There are four more egg-cups in the collection of the Naples Museum (Inv. nos. 116349 and 116350–2) standing on large lozenge-shaped bases.

The two little vases from the Casa del Menandro illustrated in fig. 31 are pepper pots, the earliest from Roman times. The use of Indian

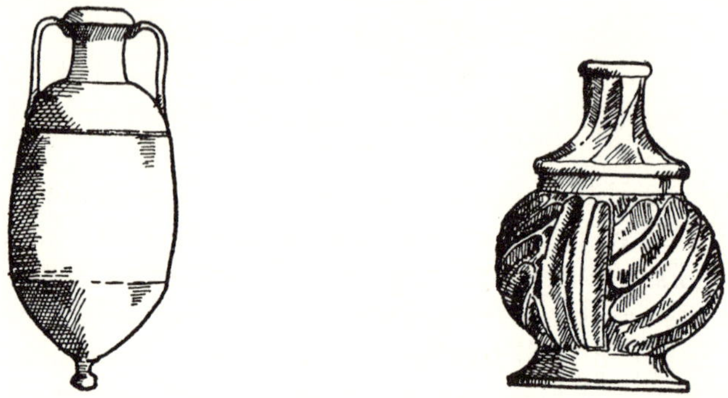

a b

FIG. 31: Silver pepper pots from Casa del Menandro, Pompeii; National Museum, Naples. Scale 1:2

pepper seems to have been introduced in the first century A.D. and Pliny comments on the strangeness of the taste; it never lost its popularity and was used to flavour both food and drink. Pepper vases (*vasa piperatoria*) never seem to have acquired standard forms. One of the Casa del Menandro vessels is in the form of a little amphora with the holes punched in the base and the other is a little fluted pot also with the holes at the bottom. There are two similar pots with punched bases in the Museum at Naples (Inv. nos. 116354 and 133332).

TRAYS

Trays for bringing dishes and foods from kitchen to table were a necessary part of domestic equipment. The largest may be described as portable tables which were set down in the triclinium and used as serving tables. In Naples there is a fairly well-preserved example of a large rectangular tray (*ferculum*) 53·5 cm. long and 35·7 cm. wide, equipped round the edge with sixteen little projecting ear handles triangular in shape and decorated with lotus flowers flanked by ducks' heads. There is a reference to another one being found in 1754 and a large fragment of sheet silver apparently for overlaying a similar *ferculum* was found in the Casa del Menandro (no. 118). A series of grotesque figures of slaves found at Pompeii are shown carrying rectangular silver trays with borders of chased floral ornament. The Hildesheim Treasure contained a very large rectangular bowl, 53 cm. long and 30·7 cm. wide, with a flange at either end equipped with two semi-circular projections as grips; the body of the bowl is transversely fluted. It was presumably made as a serving bowl or tray.[1] In the same treasure there were two sets of 3 little trays, basically rectangular in shape with ornamented handles at the two ends.

SPOONS

Spoons were the only eating implement in common use during this period and they were often made of silver even in the poorest families. Before the first century A.D. there is no evidence for their use at table. There were, apparently, only two basic types of spoon in use during

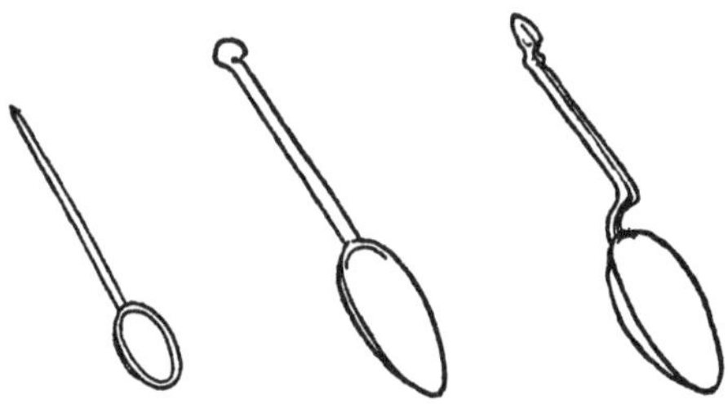

a b c

FIG. 32: Silver spoons; first century A.D.

the first century A.D. (see fig. 32). The little round-bowled spoon (*cochleare*), used for eating eggs and shellfish,[2] usually has a thin handle of round section tapering to a point. This type very occasionally had an ornamental handle.[3] The larger spoon with pear-shaped bowl (*ligula*) has a thicker handle, short in proportion to the size of the bowl. This is often linked with the bowl by means of a downward curving arm set at an angle to it, which continues in the form of a rat's tail down the back of the spoon (fig. 32*c*). The handle may be of circular section and end in a simple knob or it may be moulded, fluted or facetted through its length, and end in a more complicated finial. A finial in the form of a

[1] Pernice and Winter, *Hildesheim*, 66.
[2] See above p. 129.
[3] e.g. *BMCP*, no. 101.

cloven hoof was very popular on the spoons of the period (fig. 32*c*); examples have been found in Syria, S. Russia and elsewhere. Examples from Pompeii in Naples include the following types – a round handle with knob, round handle with cloven hoof, fluted handle with knob, facetted handle with moulded finial.

OTHER SILVER IMPLEMENTS

There are a number of silver implements found in the Campanian hoards which must have served special uses on the table (fig. 33). There

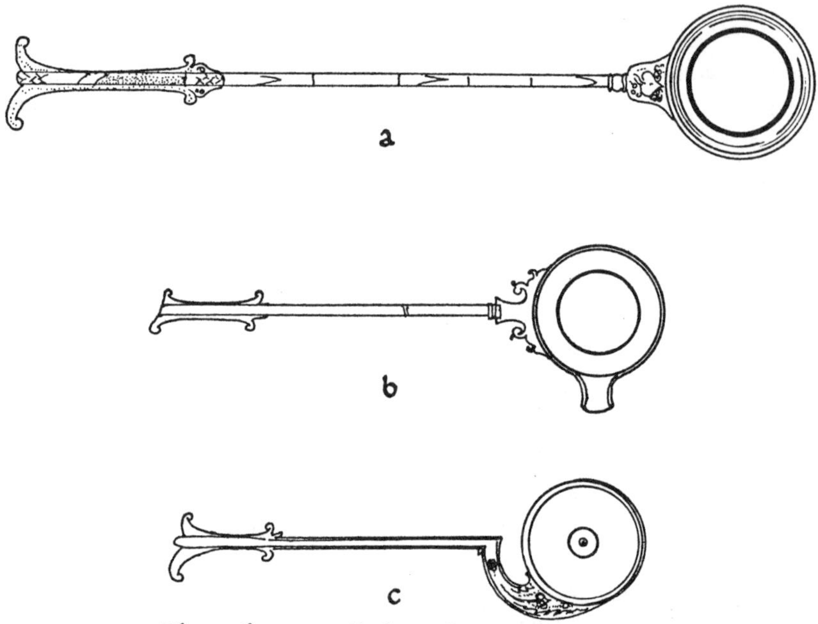

FIG. 33: Three silver utensils from the Treasure of Boscoreale; Musée du Louvre, Paris. Scale 1:5

is a pair of little ladles with flat-bottomed spouted bowls, long handles, and finials in the form of steering oars (fig. 33*b*) from the Boscoreale Treasure (nos. 53-4). The same treasure contains a device consisting of a ring on the end of a handle with a steering oar finial (fig. 33*a*) which may have been used for stirring wine (no. 56). There is also a spoon or ladle with a round bowl attached to the handle by an arm curving from the straight stem (no. 51) (fig. 33*c*). A large spoon from the Casa del Menandro (no. 64) is described by Maiuri as a 'cucchiaio grande da portata'. It has a handle in the form of a steering oar and a leaf-shaped bowl with one sharp edge that could have been used for cutting portions of cake or sweet; the 'spoon' is 41 cm. long. The steering-oar handle which was also used for ordinary spoons seems to have come into fashion in the first century B.C.; a silver handle of this form was found at Vulci (Necropoli dell' Osteria, Tomb 18) in association with late Hellenistic pottery.

'TOILET SILVER'

The possessions of the lady of the house formed an important part of the domestic silver. The wealthy lady would have a wide range of small implements – ear picks, cosmetic sets – made of silver and she would keep her jewellery and other possessions in silver boxes. The contents of a woman's tomb of the first century A.D. found at Bursa and now in the British Museum[1] includes a cylindrical *pyxis*, a little straight-sided bowl, a little spoon with a looped handle ending in a swan's head, probably used for cosmetics, a mirror and a spindle. In the National Museum at Naples there is a silver basket-shaped vessel with a flat lid decorated overall with imitation basket-work and equipped with a chain for suspension. An attractive little *pyxis* with repoussé reliefs of putti racing *bigae* was found in a cremation burial of the late first century A.D. at Draguignan (Aix-en-Provence). Silver oil flasks and strigils were common in this period.

MIRRORS

Silver mirrors were widely used at this time. The popular form of hand mirror consists of a disc with the reflecting surface on one side and decorated on the back with concentric circles turned on a lathe and a frame of decorated mouldings. The mirrors are equipped with long handles attached by arms to the disc of the mirror, rather like the 'saucepan' handles; a baluster handle is the commonest type and Hercules' club was popular at Pompeii. Intertwined branches and other designs are also found. A very popular variant on this type of mirror has a star-like border round the disc of the mirror. There are two examples from the 'Child's Grave' in Berlin[2] and one in Naples from Pompeii (Mus. no. 119679). There are several hand mirrors of the period the backs of which are decorated with appliqué roundels with

[1] *BMCP*, nos. 119–25.

[2] *JdAI*, 65–6, 1950–1, 264 ff.

relief decoration. One of the most striking is the mirror from the Casa del Menandro hoard with a relief medallion showing a female head in profile (no. 15) (pl. 37A). There are two mirrors of this kind in the Boscoreale Treasure; no. 21 has a star border, a bust of a Maenad on the back (pl. 37B), and an inscription with the name of its maker M. Domitius Polygnos; no. 22 is a round mirror with ovolo border, a medallion of Leda and the Swan and a baluster handle. Some of these mirrors may be as early as the late Republic when Pasiteles, for example, acquired a reputation for making them.[1]

Plain disc mirrors without handles were also in use, and mirrors with rings for suspension could be moved easily from room to room. One from the Casa del Menandro (no. 16) is 13·8 cm. in diameter with the ring attached by a pelta-shaped soldering plate. There are two others in Naples, one with pelta attachment and the other with ivy-leaf (Inv. nos. 110628 and 124791).

RITUAL PLATE

Roman ritual vessels are frequently shown on sculptured monuments of the period.[2] The Greek *phiale mesomphalos,* serving as the Roman sacrificial *patera,* appears frequently with elaborate leaf ornament on the inside and is sometimes equipped with a horizontal handle. Surviving examples in silver are very rare. A lotus *phiale* in the National Museum at Naples could conceivably be Roman and there is a small fluted *phiale mesomphalos* in the same collection. Egg *phialai* have been found in the Boscoreale Treasure and at Pompeii (Naples no. 109691); they are probably Hellenistic survivals. A handsome fluted *phiale* in the Treasure of Berthouville (no. 11) has a central medallion, which shows Omphale reclining on Hercules' lion skin (pl. 43A); this *phiale,* dating from the first half of the first century A.D., looks on the outside not unlike a Hellenistic egg *phiale.* Another bowl with central omphalos decorated with a rosette and four large oval bosses around it was found at Bori in Georgia, apparently with an early relief-decorated cup.[3] The *patera* with central omphalos or medallion and a horizontal handle is commonly found in bronze;[4] the handle is usually a fluted tube

[1] Pliny, *NH,* xxxiii, 128–30.
[2] von Schaewen, *Opfergeräte.* [3] *CR,* 1908, 183–4.
[4] For the type Radnóti, *Bronzegefässe,* pls. XXVI–XXVIII.

ending in an animal head. No examples in silver can certainly be attributed to this period. The *simpulum* which was certainly used in religious ritual is shown on the sculptured monuments. Sacrificial jugs are like the decorated jugs discussed above (p. 142).

FURNITURE

A number of references to the use of silver furniture in the wealthier Roman households have already been noted.[1] Silver tables and couches were by no means uncommon throughout the Roman period but, in fact, very few examples have survived. The middle-class families of the Campanian towns used mainly bronze and wooden furniture, but in the Hildesheim Treasure a few interesting small items of furniture in silver are preserved. There is a small silver tripod table with richly decorated animal legs, a folding tripod serving as a stand for a large dish (pl. 41A), and the ornate base of a candelabrum stand.[2] Some little silver lamps, found in the 'Child's Grave', are in Berlin and there is a very handsome gold lamp in the National Museum at Naples.[3]

[1] See above p. 130.
[2] Pernice and Winter, *Hildesheim*, 50, 53, 54 f.
[3] *Ori e Argenti*, no. 523.

CHAPTER NINE

The Roman Empire: Second and Third Centuries A.D.

In contrast to the wealth of evidence for the first century A.D., the finds of second-century silver are disappointing. There are no large hoards of the period and only very few closely dated finds. A small hoard from Backworth in Northumberland, now in the British Museum, contained coins down to A.D. 139[1] and the Lovere hoard in the Castello Sforzesco, Milan dates from around A.D. 170.[2] A few hoards belong to the early third century, and in the second half of the third century, as a result of barbarian attacks on the Empire, a lot of silver was buried for safety, especially in the western provinces. One series of hoards in northern France seems to lie on a Germanic invasion route from the frontier towards Amiens and Rheims; two of these are the Treasure of Chaourse (Aisne) in the British Museum[3] and the smaller contemporary hoard of very similar silver recently discovered at Graincourt-lès-Havrincourt (Pas de Calais)[4] in the Louvre. They are fairly closely dated to the period around A.D. 270.[5] Other important hoards of about this date have turned up elsewhere in the Gaulish provinces[6] and in the frontier regions on the Rhine and the Danube; the Treasures of Berthouville[7] and Notre-

[1] *BMCP*, nos, 183–7.

[2] *NS*, 1908, 4 ff.; A. Frova, *Kunstschätze der Lombardei*, Zurich, 1948, 38–9.

[3] *BMCP*, nos. 144–82.

[4] *Galerie Charpentier Sale Catalogue*, 1958; *Art de France*, 2, 1962, 46–56; *Mémoires de la Commission Départmentale des Monuments Historiques du Pas-de-Calais*, IX^2, 1958.

[5] Picard (*RA*, 1959, i, 229) mentions another hoard from the same area, now in America.

[6] For the Gaulish finds in general see *GA*, 1884 and 1885; I have omitted the treasures of Leyris in the Louvre, and of Chalon-sur-Saône in the Musée de S. Germain which I do not accept as ancient. For these treasures see *L'Art dans l'occident romain* (Exhibition Paris 1963). I have also omitted the gold Patera of Rennes.

[7] Babelon, *Berthouville*.

Dame d'Allençon[1] are in the Cabinet des Médailles and the Louvre respectively. Two smaller hoards from Caubiac and Chattuzange-le-Goubet (Drôme) are in the British Museum.[2] The treasures of Wettingen[3] and Trier[4] which have not survived since their discovery although something is known of their contents from old drawings or descriptions, were buried in the early fourth century. Apart from the Gaulish provinces, Britain has yielded one or two small finds of the second and third centuries of which the third-century Capheaton hoard is probably the most important.[5] In Italy itself, although there have been no very large finds, many important single pieces and small groups have turned up from time to time.[6] In the eastern provinces finds of plate have been made in Egypt including the important hoard from Karnak now in Berlin, dated by its coins to the first half of the third century;[7] outside the frontiers, in Poland, S. Russia and the Balkans plate exported from the Roman world continues to be found in this period.

Most of the third-century hoards contain plate of the period in which they were buried. Fashions in domestic silver had changed and much older silver had probably gone into the melting-pot to make pieces in the latest style. Thus, in the Treasure of Chaourse which is the nearest approach to a complete *ministerium* of silver among the third-century hoards, all the pieces would seem to be of this date. A most important exception is the Treasure of Berthouville which is not, like the Chaourse Treasure, a collection of domestic plate but the contents, or part of the contents, of a religious shrine, the Temple of Mercury at Canetonum, collected over a period of many years. The find of 63 pieces of plate altogether, represents the ritual and dedicated plate of the sanctuary and in date it covers a period from the first century A.D. to around A.D. 275 when it was buried.

The predominance of finds from the western part of the Roman Empire, especially Gaul, gives a rather one-sided picture of the total production of silver plate in this period. Most of the pieces in the

[1] de Ridder, *Bijoux*, 188 ff.; the silver is not catalogued as a group.
[2] *BMCP*, nos. 131–6 (Chattuzange), 137–43 (Caubiac).
[3] *ZSAK*, 8, 1946, 1 ff.; *MAGZ*, 15, 1864, 133 ff., pl. XIV.
[4] See appendix I.
[5] *BMCP*, nos. 188–94; Toynbee, *Art in Britain*, 304–5.
[6] e.g. the Treasure of Bosco Marengo (Bendinelli, *Marengo*).
[7] *AA*, 1902, 46; 1904, 43 ff.; Köster, *Antikes Tafelsilber*, pl. XVI.

Treasures of Chaourse and Graincourt are the products of Gallic workshops. Shapes like the Hemmoor bucket and probably the flanged bowl are peculiar to the west, and the style of niello inlay on dishes and bowls suggests the product of a few closely related factories in the big towns. Gaulish plate was extensively exported outside the frontiers, as for example, to Poland where it may be recognised in the find from Zakrzow,[1] and many fine pieces of second and third-century silver found in Britain and other western provinces probably derive from the factories of Gaul. These include a saucepan from Backworth with relief scroll ornament and a dedicatory inscription to the Mother Goddesses on the handle, and, most probably, the saucepan handles from Capheaton.

Not all the silver from the Gaulish hoards will have been made locally. Most of the 'Hellenistic-Roman' silver in the Berthouville hoard presumably comes from Italy and such a fine piece as the Hunting Dish (no. 15) (pl. 49) is probably an import. This dish is closely matched by one from the Treasure of Karnak in Egypt.[2] There are other examples of very similar pieces being found widely scattered over the Empire and generally in style and detail of ornament there is a surprising uniformity throughout the Roman world. Attempts to discover the major centres that were the creators of fashion have been unsuccessful; undue prominence has been given to centres in the eastern Mediterranean, especially in Syria and Egypt,[3] for whose metalwork there is very little direct evidence. In the first century we may be fairly sure that Rome and Italy were setting fashions but there is very little to be said about Italian factories in the second and third centuries, since finds of silver in Italy itself are comparatively rare. Only very occasionally do we get from the eastern provinces examples of silver plate of distinctive character like the little pot with a frieze of masks and vine scroll from Dura Europos[4] or the dishes from Daphne by Antioch (see below p. 174). In this period there were silversmiths everywhere and although, like the metalworkers of Gaul, every centre will have had some peculiarly local designs, a remarkable uniformity was created by the freedom with which plate, designs and models passed about the

[1] Majewski, *Importy*, pl. XXXVIII.

[2] Adriani, *Coppa Paesistica*, pl. XXV.

[3] e.g. in Schreiber, *Toreutik*, a view corrected by *BJ*, 118, 176 ff.

[4] *The Excavations at Dura-Europos*, IV Season, 1933, pl. XII.

Empire. In the main it seems that fashions were created in Rome and Italy though it is not at all unlikely that the continued popularity of traditional forms like the medallion bowls may be due to the influence of Hellenistic centres.

DRINKING CUPS

In general, silver drinking cups were less common in this period. There are no plain examples of the traditional Hellenistic goblets and beakers

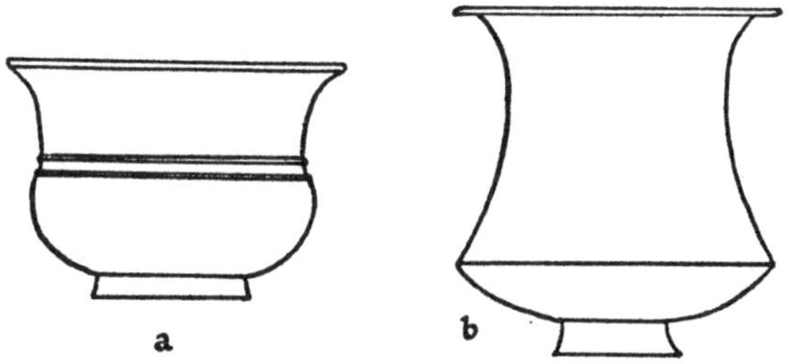

FIG. 34: (*a* & *b*) Beakers from Chaourse; British Museum. Scale 1:3

that can be assigned to this time and it is probable that glass drinking vessels were generally favoured.[1] In the Chaourse Treasure there are two tall beakers (fig. 34*b*) with concave upper part and shallow bowl standing on a high foot ring and a set of four silvered bronze cups with a profile ultimately derived from the old Greek *kantharos* form (fig. 34*a*).[2] None of these cups have handles. It is probable that many of the smaller conical and hemispherical bowls of the period (see below pp. 174–5) also served as drinking vessels.

DECORATED DRINKING CUPS

A number of drinking cups decorated with reliefs continue the tradition of the early Empire. Unlike the earlier cups, examples of the second and third centuries are usually cast solid and not made by repoussé; they do not require the use of an inner lining. This technique of solid casting is one feature that distinguishes the cups of the period; the relief is usually lower and Bacchanalian themes are used almost to the exclusion of all others. One of the finest examples, which must have been made some time in the second century A.D., is the cup from Ostropataka (Hungary),

[1] Cf. Lampridius, *Alex. Sev.* 34, 1.
[2] For the shape, La Baume, *Kunstgewerbe*, 106–7.

now in Vienna (pl. 43B),[1] which represents a developed form of the early Imperial cup illustrated on fig. 27*f*. The handle consists of horizontal grips soldered by means of arms to the rim; the loop of the handle is dispensed with. Bacchic masks, animals etc. in low relief decorate the body of the cup and there is relief decoration on the upper surface of the handles. A pair of handles from Armazi-Msheta in Georgia,

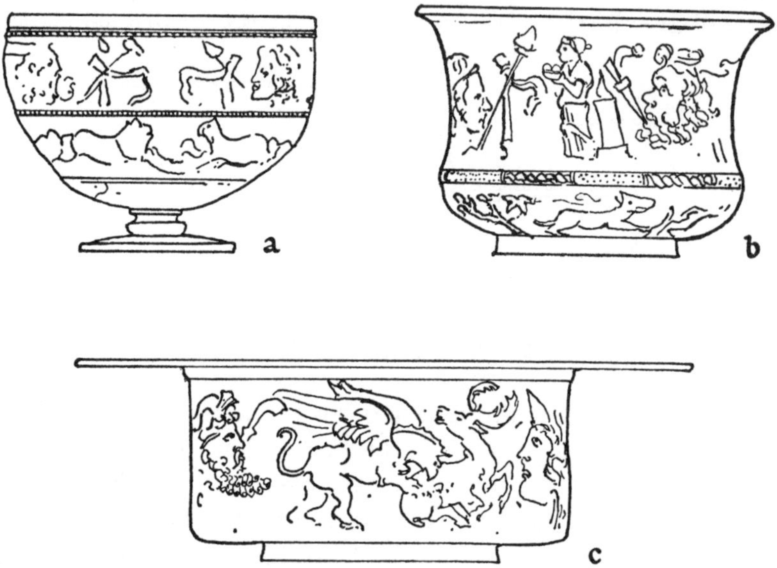

FIG. 35: Silver decorated drinking cups; second and third centuries A.D.

each with a figure of Meleager in low relief are closely similar to the handles of the Ostropataka cup and probably derive from a similar vessel.[2]

Decorated cups, without handles, of the shape illustrated by the plain vessel from Chaourse (fig. 34*a*) were in fashion during the third century. There is one in the Museo Poldi-Pezzoli, Milan with a double frieze – masks and Bacchic attributes on the upper part and a frieze of animals on the lower (fig. 35*b*).[3] A cup of similar shape and decoration from Arras is in Vienna,[4] and there is another with reliefs, showing groups of

[1] Arneth, *Gold- und Silber-Monumente*, pl. S III, no. 88.

[2] *AA*, 1934, 1 ff.

[3] *BJ*, 118, 1909, pl. VIII, 4, 5.

[4] *L'Art dans l'Occident Romain*, no. 99; *Mém. Soc. Nat. des Antiq. de France*, lxx, 1911, 135.

fighting animals on the upper part only in the Cabinet des Médailles, Paris.[1] The latter is made of heavy cast silver with the highest parts of the relief cast separately and fitted into beds, a technique that has been noted on a number of silver vessels of the third century A.D. A cup from S. Donnino in Bologna[2] belongs to this same group of drinking vessels and in Vienna there is a hemispherical cup on a moulded foot which is decorated with two friezes, a broad upper one with masks, *thyrsi* etc. and a narrow lower one with animals (fig. 35*a*).[3] Cups with similar scenes were found at Troia in Portugal, Nîmes, and Castro Urdiales.[4] There is a fragmentary one in the Archaeological Museum, Florence (Inv. no. 15731).

A cup from Varpelev in Denmark, found together with a coin of the late third century A.D., consists of an elaborate openwork silver case with vine ornament and a good luck inscription in Greek, which has inside it a cup of blue glass.[5] The silver handles consist of a horizontal thumb grip with a tail of metal below which is not looped to join up with the sides of the cup; this type of handle is also found on a drinking cup from Marwedel.[6] This technique of using openwork silver as a frame for a glass vessel, of which the earliest example seems to be the little pot in the British Museum (p. 13), continued to be popular in the later Roman Empire.

JUGS

Very few jugs have been found in the hoards of the second and third centuries. The three best known are all similar in form. One, from the Chaourse Treasure (no. 147) is a slim vessel on a low base ring of the same basic type as the first-century jug illustrated on fig. 28*a*, with a rather angular handle equipped with a curving thumb piece at the top. The neck is ornamented with a convex band decorated with guilloche ornament. A similar vessel was found in the Tomb of the Queen with the Golden Mask at Kerch together with a little decorated *pyxis* and a large plate with niello ornament (pl. 63A); the soldering plate at the

[1] *BJ*, 118, 193, fig. 5.

[2] *AdI*, 1832, 304–11; *Mon. dell'Inst.*, i, pl. XLV B,C,D; *Ori e Argenti dell' Emilia Antica*, nos. 131–3.

[3] *BJ*, 118, 1909, pl. VIII, 3.

[4] E. Hübner, *Die antiken Bildwerke in Madrid*, Berlin, 1862, 233–4.

[5] Wheeler, *Rome beyond the Imperial Frontiers*, 71, pl. V, B.

[6] Eggers, no. 1058.

base of the handle is decorated with a Medusa head in low relief.[1] Another jug similar in general shape to the Chaourse example was found together with two silver plates and a silver statuette at Daphne by Antioch;[2] this jug has a sharply angular handle and stands on a low foot rim. The form of the handle relates it to the jugs of the fourth century A.D. and it can hardly be earlier than the end of the third century. It is probable that several other kinds of jug were made in this period but no examples have survived. In the Berthouville Treasure there is a trefoil necked jug (no. 34) standing on a rather high foot which, to judge from the detail of the handle probably dates from the second or third centuries.

AMPHORAE

No large *amphorae* of this period have been found. In the Berthouville Treasure there was found a little *amphora* (no. 36) with the whole body covered with bands of dots punched in from the outside, a form of ornament that was very popular in the period. A plain *amphora* from Limes has handles in the form of dolphins.[3] Some of the little *amphorae* with relief ornament from Bagni di Vicarello may belong to the second century A.D. (see above p. 143).

SIMPULA

The ladle with short vertical handle (*simpulum*) continued in use during the second century A.D. but lost popularity; it does not occur in bronze after the second century. Silver examples are rare. There are three in the Treasure of Berthouville all with shallow bowl and each with a different kind of handle. One of these (no. 12), which has a pelta-shaped finial on top and relief decoration with a figure of Mercury, a goat and a tree arranged like the designs of saucepan handles (fig. 29*j*), belongs to the second century A.D. The rough vestigial bosses on the second *simpulum* (fig. 29*f*) suggests a late version of the popular first-century type.

SAUCEPANS

A large number of surviving examples of this vessel belong to the second and third centuries, but while it is possible to give some account

[1] *ABC*, XXXVII, 2.
[2] *Archaeology*, vi, 1953, 39 ff.
[3] *GA*, 1885, 106, fig. 1.

of its development during the period, the rarity of closely dated pieces rules out any attempt at absolute chronology. Plain handles of the period are usually straight ended or waved as shown in fig. 30*k*; examples with disc ends, like the popular bronze form, occasionally appear in silver.[1] Of these three forms the handle with waved end was most popular in the third century but occurs in the second, the disc-ended type is probably not later than the second, while the straight-ended variety may occur throughout the period. Plain or very simply decorated examples of the first type have been found in the hoards from Lovere,[2] Manching[3] and Rudnik.[4] A disc-ended handle with a shell as its decorative motif was found at Berthouville (no. 29) and another with a rosette from St. Genis is in Geneva.[5] A pair with plain, straight-ended handles comes from Berthouville (nos. 26–7) and there is another of the same type, with an engraved leaf on its upper surface, in the find at Notre-Dame d'Allençon.[6] In this period there is a good deal of variety in the shapes of the bowls. The form with a straight-sided conical bowl is frequently found, e.g. at Notre-Dame d'Allençon and Marwedel.[7] The bowls with curved sides tend to be narrower and deeper than those of the earlier period.

A rich variety of figured subjects and decoration occurs on the relief-handles of the period. The standard first-century form with swans' heads flanking the end of the handle and also forming the arms of attachment to the bowl and with floral scroll-work as the main decorative motif, is modified and elaborated in various ways. The swans' heads at the end of the handle are often replaced by other animal heads, for example, eagle heads (fig. 30*e*) or they are omitted in favour of rosettes (fig. 30*i*). The mask or head at the end of the handle often becomes the head or bust of a deity. Figures and figured scenes occupy the main space on the handle and may be arranged in a number of ways. Sometimes a single figure occupies most of the handle, or there may be a number of little scenes divided from one another by horizontal ground-lines. The differences extend to the arms of attachment where the swans' heads are often replaced by other motifs e.g. dolphins, elephant heads etc.; this was already beginning to happen in the first

[1] e.g. Arneth, *Gold- und Silber-Monumente*, pl. S I, 92, with inlaid inscription.
[2] *NS*, 1908, 4.
[3] *Neue Ausgrabungen in Deutschland*, Berlin, 1958, 199 ff.
[4] *RA*, 1903, 19, fig. 4.
[5] *L'Art dans l'Occident Romain*, no. 27.
[6] de Ridder, *Bijoux*, 1992.
[7] Eggers, no. 1058.

century A.D. The space, which tends to become wider could also be used to continue the theme of the figured decoration. The last feature occurs especially on third-century saucepans where the arms are almost always much broader.

There are three examples in the Archaeological Museum, Turin, which illustrate well the main features of the saucepans of this period.[1] On one a bust of Mercury between animal heads decorates the end of the handle; below are masks, vases and a bird and animals, arranged in separate registers. The same theme of decoration extends to the arms of attachment. The second is round-ended and decorated with a figure of Mercury and the child Bacchus, between rosettes; a ground line separates the figure from a zone with Bacchic masks and animals. On the arms are baskets of fruit and other attributes. The third saucepan is simpler in design, with a figure of Mercury between swans' heads at the end and a rustic shrine and a tethered goat in register below; there are baskets of fruit and dolphins' heads on the arms. A closely related example is the saucepan from Chattuzange-le-Goubet in the British Museum (pl. 45A).[2] The handle is rounded at the end, with a figure of Felicitas between rosettes; below this is a rustic shrine and below that again a woman sacrificing at an altar. The soldering arms have baskets of fruit, goats and pipes in low relief. Examples of similar saucepans of the second and third centuries may be cited from Nijmegen,[3] Mecklenburg,[4] Berthouville (no. 25), Aigueblanche,[5] and Reignier.[6] A particularly fine example is the saucepan found at Vindonissa;[7] at the top of the handle is a bust of Mars between rosettes and below that a figure of Hermes resting in a rustic setting amid animals and birds. Each arm of attachment has the figure of a bull, an altar and a basket which are cut round the outline so as to leave them freestanding. The details of the relief are richly gilded.

It is difficult to suggest a stylistic development for the handles within

[1] Schreiber, *Toreutik*, 316–17; Adriani, *Coppa Paesistica*, pl. XI, 33, 35, 36.

[2] *BMCP*, no. 136; Toynbee, *Art in Britain*, 303.

[3] *400 Jahr Romeinse Bezetting Noviomagus Batavorum*, 1961, no. 1957, pl. 38.

[4] H. Willers, *Die römische Bronzeeimer von Hemmoor*, Hanover, 1901, 198, fig. 75; Sieveking, *Antike Metallgeräte*, pl. 13. The vessel is in the Schwerin Museum.

[5] *L'Art dans l'Occident Romain*, nos. 23–4; R. Lantier, *Guide Illustré du Musée des Antiquités Nationales au Château de Saint-Germain-en-Laye*, 118, fig. 49A.

[6] *ibid.*, no. 26.

[7] O. Hauser, *Vindonissa*, 1904, pl. 62; the saucepan is said to be in America.

this period. In general, those which retain elements in common with the early types, e.g. swans' heads flanking the ends, are probably early. A pair from Tarascon in the Musée Calvet, Avignon[1] may be cited as examples. A few saucepans can confidently be assigned to the third century, for example, the Vindonissa saucepan and those found at Capheaton in Northumberland.[2] Two of the latter have a frame of beading round the relief scenes and the arms of attachment are very wide as they usually are in late examples. On one of them reclining figures of a water nymph and a river god occupy the space. It seems fairly certain, too, that the handles with waved end incorporating a single figure of a deity occupying most of the main part, like the ones from Cullera near Valencia[3] and Wettingen (fig. 30*k*), belong to the third century A.D. Examples of relief-decorated handles which follow a completely different scheme of decoration occur throughout the period. One of the finest is the saucepan from Chattuzange-le-Goubet which is decorated with handsome acanthus ornament.[4] The upper surface of the handle often had an inscription to the deity at whose shrine it was used or dedicated. The Backworth saucepan in the British Museum combines acanthus ornament and a gilded inscription to the Mother Goddesses[5] and probably came from a Gaulish workshop. Poor versions with roughly engraved ornament based on the popular schemes also occur.

The bowls of saucepans made in this period were sometimes decorated. A plain wave-handled saucepan found at Manching is vertically fluted on the body. One from Debe in Poland has a band of guilloche ornament on the outside just below the rim.[6] The saucepan with acanthus ornament on the handle from Chattuzange has decorated ribbing on the outside of the bowl and another one in the British Museum, said to come from Syria, has spiral fluting on the body and a roundel of the Three Graces in the centre on the inside;[7] the handle of the latter example has a bust of Diana (?) between eagles at the top and below that, figures of Mars and Rhea Silvia sleeping. Figured scenes on the outside of the bowls appear in the third century. The example from the lost Wettingen Treasure showed the deities of the seven days of the week on a straight-sided bowl; the handle, waved at the end, had

[1] *L'Art dans l'Occident Romain*, 17–18.
[2] *BMCP*, nos. 188–92.
[3] Schreiber, *Toreutik*, 319.
[4] *BMCP*, no. 135.
[5] Toynbee, *Art in Roman Britain*, no. 109, fig. 129.
[6] Eggers, 2025, pl. 13, 151.
[7] *BMCP*, no. 73.

figures of Victory and Mercury.[1] The reliefs on the outside of the saucepan from Cullera show Leda and the Swan and the figure of Zeus occupies most of the surface of the handle (fig. 30*k*).[2]

PATERA WITH TUBULAR HANDLE

The shallow *patera* with horizontal tubular handle which is common in bronze throughout the first two centuries A.D. (see above p. 158) is represented by a silver example with a fluted handle ending in a ram's head from Armazis-khevi[3] and there is part of a plain handle of this type in the Treasure of Berthouville (no. 59). A number of detached animal heads, for example a dog's head in the British Museum,[4] may once have decorated *paterae* of this kind.

STRAINERS

One of the most interesting vessels in the Chaourse Treasure is a combined strainer and funnel (pl. 46B). The strainer fits into the bowl of the funnel and the two are hinged together; the holes are punched in geometric and floral patterns. The piece is unique and bears no relation to the standard bronze forms of strainer in the Roman period. A charming little circular casket (pl. 46A) found on the site of the Walbrook Mithraeum in London[5] contains a cylindrical strainer or filter with patterned holes on the bottom which is lifted out by means of crossing bars at the top. A very similar strainer was found at Strážе in Czechoslovakia. The outside of the Walbrook casket is richly decorated with cast and chased reliefs showing hunting scenes in a style which seems to relate to the medallions on the hunting dishes from Berthouville and Karnak and the casket was probably made in the early third century A.D. It is suggested that the strainer had some special use in Mithraic cult.

PLATES AND DISHES

Many different kinds of dishes and plates were made in silver during this period, and matching services of plates and bowls were still in

[1] Schreiber, *Toreutik*, 319.

[2] In the Exhibition, *L'Art dans l'occident romain*, Paris, 1963, the bowl of this vessel (no. 117) which is now in the Petit Palais, was exhibited without its handle.

[3] A. Mongait, *Archaeology in the U.S.S.R.*, Moscow, 1959, 240; *Mzkhetha* I, pl. LXVII.

[4] *BMCP*, no. 59.

[5] J. M. C. Toynbee, *A Silver Casket and Strainer from the Walbrook Mithraeum in the City of London*, Leiden, 1963.

fashion. Oval dishes came into general use. Dishes with ear handles of the type popular in the early hoards continued to be made and the same type of handle was often applied to oval dishes. But this handle was losing popularity and probably went out of general use in the third century. Dishes with beaded rims were very popular. Relief decoration was applied to flat or convex friezes round the edges of the dishes and to central medallions; a combination of framing frieze and central medallion was especially in fashion. Niello came into gencral use in the decoration of plates. Flat dishes with upright rims decorated with relief on the outside also occur in this period.

DISHES WITH EAR-HANDLES

A few large and elaborately decorated 'ears' from dishes of this kind may be assigned to the second century A.D. The Birth of Venus is depicted on a fine example from Bondonneau in the Musée du Louvre[1] and a handle in the Metropolitan Museum, New York, shows hunting scenes.[2] Another handle with a scene showing the Indian Triumph of Bacchus was acquired recently by the Metropolitan Museum.[3] The reliefs on these handles are cast, chased and gilt; in the last example, the highest parts of the relief were cast separately in a different alloy and fitted into beds left in the main casting.[4] The gilding on both New York handles was done with leaf. It is impossible to say whether these handles belonged to round or oval dishes but the ear handle seems to have been especially popular on oval dishes during this period. One of the finest examples is the dish in the Archaeological Museum, Turin (pl. 47A) which is decorated with a typically second-century border of animals, masks, trees etc.[5] A very similar dish was found together with a cup and two spoons in a tomb at Lillebonne (Seine Inférieure), which has been dated to the Antonine period.[6] Plainer versions of the oval dish with ear handles have been found at Manching (third century),[7]

[1] *L'Art dans l'Occident Romain* no. 22, pl. III.

[2] *BMMA*, ii, 1907, 124, fig. 5; its weight is given as 1438.53 grammes and it measures 37 cm. across.

[3] *BMMA*, xiv, 1955–6, 64 ff.

[4] For the technique see also p. 165.

[5] *Ori e Argenti*, no. 692, pl. LXXX.

[6] *BJ*, 118, pl. VII; *GA*, 1884, 346; *Antioch-on-the Orontes*, i, 1934, 51 fig. 5, illustrates a clay copy.

[7] *Neue Ausgrabungen in Deutschland*, 199 ff.

at Saulzoir near Bavai,[1] St Chef, Limes,[2] Karnak[3] and Basayrt in Bulgaria.[4] The dish from Saulzoir, probably of the third century A.D. has elaborate ear handles and engraved swans' heads and pelta ornament decorating the flat surface.

OVAL DISHES

Apart from the dishes with ear handles, other kinds of oval dish were being made. In the Wettingen Treasure there were two oval dishes, one having an edging of bead and reel and a small central decorative motif, probably inlaid in niello, and the other a framing frieze of animals, Bacchic attributes and masks in the typical style of the period. There is a little oval dish with a masks-and-animals frieze in the Walters Art Gallery, Baltimore (Inv. no. 57, 1815). Plain oval dishes also occur, for example, in the Rudnik hoard.[5]

DISHES WITH RELIEF ORNAMENT

Dishes in practical use were often decorated with low-relief medallions in the centre. A good example is the dish with a medallion of the goddess Fortuna from Batum which belongs to the late second or third century A.D.[6] A smaller dish, showing a figure of Mercury richly gilt, from the Chaourse Treasure, is illustrated on pl. 48B. The reliefs were generally cast, or, as in the case of the Mercury dish, cut in the solid metal. A fairly wide relief border round the outside of the plate was another popular form of decoration in this period; the ornament is generally Bacchic in inspiration but floral designs and other kinds of decoration are found. In the Caubiac Treasure, now in the British Museum, there is a little flat plate,[7] probably part of a large service made to the same pattern, which is decorated on a slightly raised border with Bacchic masks etc. There are other examples of the same type in the Kunsthistorisches Museum, Vienna[8] and the Louvre in Paris.[9]

Some of the finest dishes of the period combine the two features of central medallion and framing frieze. One of the best is the dish from the Treasure of Berthouville (no. 15) illustrated on pl. 49; the central

[1] *L'Art dans l'Occident Romain*, no. 89; in the Valenciennes Museum.
[2] *GA*, 1884, 346; Odobesco, *Petrossa*, 105.
[3] Köster, *Antikes Tafelsilber*, pl. XVI.
[4] *Bull. Inst. Bulg.*, vii, 1919–20, 150, fig. III.
[5] *RA*, 1903 (1), 22, fig. 11.
[6] *AA*, 1908, 163–4, fig. 8.
[7] *BMCP*, no. 139.
[8] *BJ*, 118, pl. VIII, 2.
[9] de Ridder, *Bijoux*, no. 1955.

medallion, cast in low relief, shows a hunting scene and the framing frieze is decorated with animals, Bacchic masks and other attributes. Round the central medallion is engraved an inscription to the god Mercury of Canetonum. A very similar dish, 43 cm. in diameter, was found in the Egyptian Treasure of Karnak which consisted of 16 pieces of plate together with 1200 gold coins running down to Elagabalus. The central medallion shows a lion hunt and the decorated border has hunting scenes and animals divided from one another by masks. The plate probably dates from the second century A.D. A similar plate is mentioned among the silver of the lost Treasure of Trier.[1] At Graincourt-lès-Havrincourt two fine dishes with the same basic scheme of decoration were found. One is 33 cm. in diameter and combines a central medallion of Leda and the Swan with an outer frieze of animals and masks; on the other, which is 35 cm. in diameter, both the medallion and the border are decorated with fish and other sea creatures. A fine dish from Hassleben with a formal floral motif in the centre and scroll ornament on the border, dates from about A.D. 250;[2] there was a very similar dish in the Wettingen hoard and another was found in a burial vault of the Eristavis at Armazis-khevi in Georgia,[3] with coins down to Trajan Decius.

DISHES WITH UPRIGHT RIMS

The Caubiac Treasure contains one very large dish, 38·75 cm. in diameter with an upright curved rim decorated with Bacchic masks and attributes in low relief. Large dishes, perhaps serving dishes, with this kind of rim were probably coming into use in the third century. There is a curious dish with upright fluted rim and elaborate niello medallion in Vienna which seems to have been found with the Ostropataka cup referred to above (p. 163).[4]

DISHES WITH CHASED AND ENGRAVED ORNAMENT

A fine engraved dish with a central roundel showing a fisherman, surrounded by a broad band of fish and other sea creatures, was found in the late second-century hoard from Lovere in N. Italy. A dish

[1] Appendix 1.
[2] W. Schulz and R. Zahn, 'Das Fürstengrab von Hassleben' in *Röm-Germ Forsch*, vii, 1933.
[3] Mongait, *Archaeology in the U.S.S.R.*, 241.
[4] Arneth, *Gold- und Silber-Monumente*, pl. S III.

from Berthouville (no. 20) is decorated all over with lightly engraved arabesques. Flat chasing is used to make floral and figured designs on another dish in the same treasure (no. 16). A style of flat chased ornament which became common in the later Roman Empire makes its earliest appearance on two plates found at Daphne by Antioch together with the silver jug referred to on p. 166. One of the plates is decorated with an eight-pointed star in the centre, and a border of fluting, and the other has a star and feather design in the middle and overlapping leaves around the rim. These plates are perhaps not earlier than about A.D. 300.[1]

NIELLO DISHES

One of the most popular kinds of dish in the third-century hoards is a flat dish with a beaded rim and a central decorative motif inlaid in niello. One of these, 38·3 cm. in diameter, was found in the Treasure of Chattuzange (pl. 48A); the central motif is a swastika. The same motif also appeared on one of the lost dishes in the Wettingen Treasure. There are a number of dishes of this kind in the Chaourse Treasure; one has a swastika, another a rosette while the third is plain except for the beaded rim. More elaborate niello motifs appear on some examples of the period. A design of leaves and scroll ornament inside a border of wave pattern decorates the centre of a large dish, 43 cm. in diameter, from the Treasure of Graincourt; a similar design, also inlaid in niello occurs on the dish with upright fluted rim in Vienna. A dish from Berthouville (no. 24) has a little bird enclosed in a wreath as the central motif.

BOWLS

The wide variety of bowls made in silver during the second and third centuries are difficult to classify. Some were made to the same pattern as the dishes, to form part of the same service. Four hemispherical bowls in the Chaourse Treasure have beaded rims and a central niello motif on the inside matching the dishes found in the same treasure; similar bowls have been found at Graincourt, Niederbieber on the Rhine frontier,[2] and Nicolaevo in Bulgaria.[3] An example dredged from the bed of the Saône has an inlaid niello rosette in the centre.[4] To judge from the Gaulish finds, one of the most popular shapes in the second

[1] *Archaeology*, vi, 1953, 39 ff.

[2] *BJ*, 120, 281 f.

[3] *Bull. Inst. Bulg.*, iv, 1914, 1 ff.

[4] *L'Art dans l'Occident Romain*, no. 41.

and third centuries was the conical flat-bottomed bowl found in various sizes, for example, in the Treasures of Berthouville and Notre-Dame d'Allençon. The same shape appears in the saucepans of the period. The bowls are generally made of thin hammered metal and often have engraved ornament on the bottom of the inside. Another very common form of decoration on these conical bowls is punched in from the outside. One from Notre-Dame d'Allençon has a knobbly omphalos in the centre and around it six circles with the intervening space filled with punched dots. Another from the same hoard has a central boss surrounded by six similar bosses and floral patterns in the spaces between. There is a bowl like this in the Berthouville Treasure. The same kind of punched ornament was used on vessels of a number of different shapes. In the Chaourse Treasure there are two hemispherical bowls or cups in thin silver decorated with bands of punched dots, bead and reel, and ovolo; a bowl in the lost Treasure of Wettingen had punched lozenges and ovals on the body. It is thought that these thin silver vessels with punched ornament imitate the appearance of contemporary glass-ware; the vessel in the Wettingen Treasure must have been very like a glass cup formerly in the Niessen collection, Cologne.[1]

Bowls with separate cast or repoussé relief *emblemata* in the fashion of the first century A.D. continued to be made. There are a number of these bowls in the Berthouville Treasure (nos. 17–19); the *emblema* is usually let into a recess in the bottom of the bowl, a feature that distinguishes these later examples from the earlier. The bowl with high-relief busts of Mercury and Maia in the Berthouville Treasure dates from the Antonine period and belongs to a tradition that goes back to the second century B.C.[2] Two detached *emblemata* found in the Treasure of Notre-Dame d'Allençon were probably made in the third century. Several interesting *emblema* bowls were discovered at Armazis-khevi. A bowl with a medallion of Antinous came from a tomb of Hadrianic date; two others, one with a man's bust in high relief and another with a female bust holding a cornucopia, were found in a tomb of the late second century.[3] Fluted bowls were popular throughout the period. Two fine examples, one a large bowl with a star-pattern

[1] Loeschke, *Sammlung Niessen*, pl. 27, no. 328.

[2] H. Jücker, *Das Bildnis im Blätterkelch*, 2 vol., Lausanne, 1961, fig. 44.

[3] Mongait, *Archaeology in the U.S.S.R.*, 242; *RA*, 1961, 72; *Mzkhetha* I, pls. XLI, LXVIII, LXIII.

engraved in the roundel on the bottom (pl. 51A), were found at Chaourse. A spirally-fluted bowl with a low-relief central medallion of Aphrodite is one of the pieces from Caubiac, and a remarkable bowl in the form of a lotus flower with a central medallion of the Three Graces comes from Chattuzange-le-Goubet. A big shell bowl was discovered at Graincourt-lès-Havrincourt.

FLANGED BOWLS

A form of bowl which seems to have become popular in the second century A.D. in Gaul is the flanged bowl, examples of which have been found at Chaourse, at Graincourt and in Champagne.[1] One of the bowls from Chaourse is illustrated on pl. 51B; it stands on a foot ring, the flange is curved downwards and decorated with floral ornament, and surmounted by a vertical rim. The bowl from Champagne, whose present whereabouts seem to be unknown, has a frieze of masks and animals on the flange. The Graincourt bowl is very similar to one of the Chaourse bowls. The variant form of flanged bowl without the vertical rim, which is characteristic of the fourth and fifth-century hoards (see below p. 203) seems to be a later development, based on the third-century type.

HEMMOOR BUCKETS

A type of vessel peculiar to the Gaulish hoards of this period is the so-called Hemmoor bucket which is a deep hemispherical bowl on a low foot with single or double bucket handles (pl. 52 right) swivelling in vertical ring-attachments on opposite sides. This type of bucket is common in bronze between A.D. 150 and 250; five silver examples are known.[2] Two of these come from the Treasure of Chaourse; one is plain and the other decorated with a narrow frieze of scroll ornament below the rim. The bronze examples often have a frieze of animals and Bacchanalian themes between decorated mouldings in this position and a similar design seems to have been used for a silver bucket in the lost Treasure of Trier which is described as a 'situla aureis hominum ferarumque simulacris aspera'. A bucket of this kind from Tourdan near Vienne which is now in the British Museum[3] has the body decorated

[1] *GA*, 1880, pl. I.
[2] The type is fully discussed by H. Willers, *Die römischen Bronzeeimer von Hemmoor*, Hanover 1901.
[3] *BMCP*, no. 74.

with low-relief figures of the Four Seasons; although the style of the reliefs suggest the earlier first century A.D. it is unlikely that this form of bucket was in use so early. The silversmith seems to have been using early models in casting the reliefs and some of the coarse detail of the figures is probably due to subsequent chasing by his or someone else's less experienced hand. Another bucket of this kind, plain except for a decorated moulding below the rim was found in a third-century burial (Tomb I) at Zakrzow in Poland.[1]

SPOONS

Of the two standard types of spoon used in the first century A.D., the little round bowled *cochleare* with its handle ending in a point became

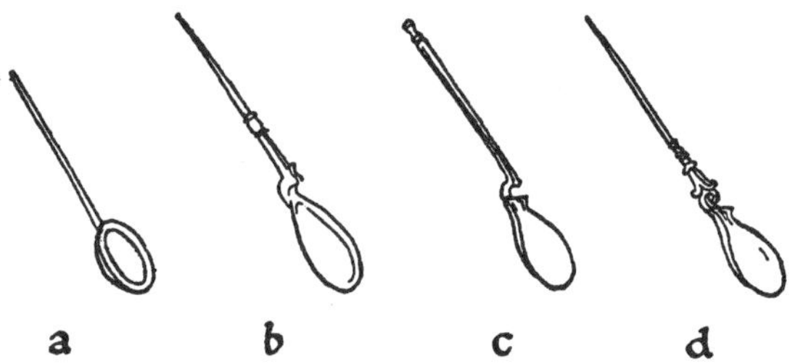

FIG. 36: Silver spoons; second-third century A.D.

much less common in the second century A.D., though it is found in several hoards of the period. The second century form of bowl is easily recognisable by the convex moulding on the inside which may be seen on examples from the Backworth hoard (fig. 36*a*) and from Muswell Hill, also in the British Museum;[2] the bowl rests on top of the handle which is continued in the form of a rat-tail. The *ligula,* with its large pear-shaped bowl, also seems to have lost popularity in the period though it does occur in second and third century hoards (e.g. Manching, Berthouville). Two new types of spoon came in. One of these has a fiddle-shaped bowl (fig. 36*c* and *d*) which is usually offset from the handle and connected with it by a curving arm like that on the old *ligula*; in other versions the arm is adapted into an openwork scroll (fig. 36*d*). The handle may either taper to a point or be moulded throughout its length and this suggests that the type was made to serve the uses of the *cochleare* and the *ligula*. In the find of eleven such spoons

[1] Majewski, *Importy*, pl. XIX*a*.

[2] Registration, 1928, 10–20, I.

at Rudnik in Yugoslavia, six have pointed ends and three have handles of square section ending in a finial.[1] The popular steering-oar handle also occurs on this type of spoon. One of these spoons with a moulded stem and a scroll at the junction with the bowl was found in a group of burials at Vermand assigned to the time of Gallienus.[2] It must have been especially popular in the third century but continued into the fourth. Another type of spoon with a pear-shaped bowl attached to the handle at its pointed end, usually by means of a curving arm, came into use in the second century. In the second-century examples, e.g. Backworth (fig. 36*b*), this spoon also has the characteristic convex moulding on the inside of the rim. It is usually quite a small spoon, unlike the later examples of this same shape.

A few decorated and inscribed spoons occur in this period. A fiddle-spoon found at Zakrzow in Poland in a third-century context[3] has the back of the bowl decorated with scroll ornament and a framing band of wave pattern, all inlaid in niello. At the same time it was probably becoming more common to inscribe or decorate the inside of the bowl; there is a fiddle-spoon in the Petit Palais, Paris which has an inscription on the inside framed by an engraved wreath. It probably belongs to the third century. Two spoons from Köln-Bickendorf,[4] dated 270–80, are short-handled spoons, one pear-shaped the other fiddle-shaped; both have some chased ornament on the inside of the bowl. These spoons have animal heads at the junction between bowl and handle, and suggest that this form of embellishment, which is common in fourth-century spoons, was coming into fashion at the end of the third century.

PEPPER POTS

A little pepper pot in the form of a squatting negro boy was found in the Chaourse Treasure; the holes for the pepper are punched in the boy's head. The theme was obviously a popular one. A similar piece found at Nicolaevo near Pleven in Bulgaria,[5] and now in the Sofia Museum, is in the form of a negro boy holding a puppy; there is a

[1] *RA*, 1903, (i), 23, fig. 15.

[2] T. Eck, *Les deux cimetières gallo-romains de Vermand et de Saint-Quentin*, Paris — St Quentin, 1891, 206, pl. xx.

[3] Majewski, *Importy*, pl. xxx.

[4] *Germania*, 1927, 39–40.

[5] *Bull. Inst. Bulg.*, iv, 1914, 10, pl. 1.

similar one in the de Clercq Collection.[1] Unlike the early Roman pepper pots, these examples would stand neatly on the table and serve also to decorate it.

'TOILET SILVER'

There is not much toilet silver of this period surviving. Silver mirrors were certainly still in common use but the mirror with long handle seems to have gone out of fashion. There is a mirror from the Backworth hoard in the British Museum consisting of a plain disc with turned rings on the back to which a handle seems to have been attached with arms in the form of leaves. Mirrors from Chaourse are simply plain discs with turnings on the back, but the mirrors of the period often had a handle fixed to the back like the example, probably of the early third century, found at Wroxeter.[2] On the back it is decorated with a frame of wreath ornament and the handle consists of two pieces of substantial silver wire tied in a reef-knot and ending in leaf terminals as soldering plates. Little rosettes are soldered on to the wire near the soldering plates.

Little pots of various kinds were used to keep cosmetics and various implements for applying them were also made of silver. A popular type of little pot with bulbous body and low concave neck may have been used for cosmetics. There is one with punched circles on the body in the Berthouville Treasure (no. 35) and another with cast low-relief scroll ornament on the body of the Vatican Museums (no. 12131).

FURNITURE

Although silver furnishings of various kinds must have continued in common use, very few examples have survived. The late second-century Treasure of Bosco Marengo near Turin[3] contained one fine fragment of the *pulvinum* of a silver couch decorated in gilt repoussé with a panel of acanthus scroll ornament rising from a leaf-calyx on which the figure of a nymph is reclining (pl. 53B). The Bosco Marengo Treasure also contained many pieces of thin silver plate which served to overlay wooden furniture; many of these pieces are decorated with chased ornament and repoussé reliefs. Another of the rare examples of

[1] *de Clercq Bronzes*, 106, no. 164.

[2] D. Atkinson, *Report on Excavations at Wroxeter*, 1923–7, Oxford, 1942, 196 f.; now in Shrewsbury Central Library (Toynbee, *Art in Britain*, 334–5, pl. LXXVIII C).

[3] Bendinelli, *Marengo*, pls. IX–X.

household furnishings is the *candelabrum* now in the British Museum from the Treasure of Beaurains near Arras[1] which included a number of pieces of silver plate and many coins and medallions down to the time of Constantine I. The *candelabrum* has a double stem of square section that can be extended and locked by means of a locking pin inserted into holes at intervals. The stem is inlaid with a niello pattern of wave ornament similar to that found on Gaulish plate of this period and area.

TECHNIQUES

The changes in techniques during the second and third century A.D. which can be followed out fairly well in surviving examples of silver plate are worth summarising. Repoussé ornament had been on the decline in Pliny's day and the later examples of repoussé work are generally inferior to those of the first-century hoards. The medallion dishes from Berthouville and Notre-Dame d'Allençon are poor in comparison with earlier pieces. In the manufacture of drinking cups casting almost completely superseded work in repoussé. Casting was the prevailing technique both on eating and drinking vessels. A curious technical detail on several vessels of the period is the casting of the highest parts of the relief separately and then inserting them into prepared beds. In the second century the low-relief decoration on dishes, such as the hunting dish from Berthouville, was normally cast but in the third century increasing use was made of the technique of cutting the design out of the solid metal. It seems to have become very common in the Gaulish workshops of the third century A.D. and the little flat dish from Caubiac and the bucket and flanged bowls from Chaourse were certainly made by this method. The use of the technique was facilitated by the very soft alloys favoured by Roman silversmiths but, even so, the detail of ornamental bands made in this way is often very harsh and rough in comparison with the softness of cast detail first modelled in wax. Formal ornamental patterns which were fashionable in the third century lend themselves to this kind of treatment much more than the delicate naturalism of ornament in the first century A.D. (see pl. 52). Figured subjects like the Mercury medallion on the dish from Chaourse (pl. 48B) were also worked by this method of carving and chasing in the third century.

[1] Reg. no. 1924, 5–14, 1; for the date *Numismatic Chronicle*, xiii, 1933, 268–348.

The popularity of niello inlay, which had come into use during the first century A.D.[1] was increasing and was to culminate in the elaborate niello and gilt designs of the dishes made in the fourth and fifth centuries. In the third century the niello designs remained very simple and generally confined to small motifs on dishes and ornamental bands. Gilding was generally applied to ornamental patterns and figured reliefs; mercury gilding was in general use but leaf-gilding is also attested on a number of pieces.[2] Chasing and engraving of high quality was carried out in some workshops and attention has been drawn to the punched patterns, apparently imitating contemporary glass technique, on a number of vessels from the Gaulish hoards. Openwork designs in silver acting as casings for glass vessels were also popular. Throughout the period discussed in this chapter, the silversmiths of the Roman Empire maintained a very high standard in the basic techniques of manufacturing silver plate. They 'raised' complicated shapes and shapes demanding a high degree of accuracy with the utmost skill; the fluted silver bowl from Chaourse is one of the most attractive pieces of Roman silver that has survived to us. The various parts of vessels are so skilfully soldered together by the use of hard silver solder that it is hardly possible to detect the joins. There is, however, a marked poverty of creative inspiration as is clear from the repetition of similar patterns and figured designs on the plate of the period. The friezes of heads or masks and animals seem to follow standard designs wherever they are found.

[1] See above p. 12.

[2] e.g. the big ear-handles in New York (see above p. 171).

CHAPTER TEN

The Roman Empire: Fourth and Fifth Centuries A.D.

A large number of important hoards of Roman silver plate date from the later fourth and fifth centuries, the period of the final collapse of the Roman Empire in the West. Together they give a clearer picture of the silver of this period than we have of any other, except the earlier part of the first century A.D. The hoards illustrate vividly the fate of most of the best products of Roman silversmiths. Some, like the Mildenhall Treasure,[1] which contains some of the richest and most lavishly decorated pieces of ancient plate, represent the possessions of wealthy provincials hurriedly buried in times of desperate emergency and never again recovered by their owners. The most recently discovered of the big hoards of the late Empire, that of Kaiseraugst near Basel,[2] had been buried for safety within the walls of a Roman fort some time between A.D. 350 and 360. Other hoards of the period, of which the most important is that from Traprain Law in lowland Scotland dating from the early fifth century,[3] consist of silver bullion much of which is broken-up table silver destined for the melting-pot. In the Traprain hoard there were fragments of over 100 silver vessels, many of the finest quality. Similar, but smaller, finds have been made at Coleraine in Ireland,[4] Gross Bodungen,[5] Høstentorp in Denmark,[6] and elsewhere.[7]

Most of the late hoards contain only late Roman silver. In the Esquiline Treasure of the late fourth century, now in the British

[1] Brailsford, *Mildenhall.*

[2] Laur-Belart, *Kaiseraugst.*

[3] Curle, *Traprain.*

[4] *BMCP*, nos. 195–223; for the date *Antiquity*, 1937, 39 ff. The coins range from Constantius II to Honorius.

[5] Grünhagen, *Gross Bodungen.*

[6] *ActaA*, xxv, 1954, 171 ff.

[7] e.g. a small find from Balline, Co. Limerick (S. P. O'Riordain, 'Roman Material in Ireland' in *PRIA*, 51C, 1945, 43–54).

Museum, there are one or two pieces which may be survivals from an earlier period but most of the objects must have been made within about 50 years of the time when they were buried. It is worth noting here that, although so much was destroyed or buried in this period, a fair amount of late Roman silver must have survived above ground for many generations. The Cesena dish (pl. 58) of the fourth century was not apparently buried until the sixth; the Risley *lanx* remained for a long time in a Church Treasury, and a bowl which might be as early as the fifth century was found in the Sutton Hoo burial of the seventh.[1]

As in the case of the third-century hoards, the great majority of late Roman finds have been made in Italy and the western provinces, especially Gaul and Britain. Late Roman silver from the eastern provinces does scant justice to the importance of such cities as Antioch and Alexandria in the production of silver-plate but Syria, especially, has yielded some interesting finds. Important finds of the period have been made in the Danube provinces and S. Russia. A large hoard of silver from Carthage, now in the British Museum, is one of several finds from Roman North Africa.[2] Single pieces of high-class plate have turned up in every province of the Empire.

CENTRES OF MANUFACTURE

Many attempts have been made to establish the main centres of production of silver plate in this period. After the founding of Constantinople and the partitioning of the Empire, there were many capital centres – Rome, Constantinople, Antioch, Trier, Milan, Ravenna – and many centres where first-class silverware was turned out for members of the court and wealthy citizens. Any of these might be expected to have set fashions in this period but there are very few hard facts to aid the attribution of particular pieces.

Some light is thrown on the problem by the stamps which occur on a few surviving vessels of the fourth and fifth centuries. It seems that silver plate was taken to be stamped with a guarantee of quality, usually after the piece had been formed but before it was decorated, to an office of the *argentarii comitatenses*, a department of the *Comes Sacrarum Largitionum*.[3] Only five examples of this early period are known. One of these, which is a flanged bowl of the fifth century found in Syria and

[1] *The Sutton Hoo Ship Burial*, London, 1947, 47, pl. 15.
[2] *BMECA*, nos. 356–75.
[3] Dodd, *Silver Stamps*.

now in Berlin, was stamped in an eastern city, almost certainly Constantinople; the stamp is rectangular with a figure of Tyche closely resembling that on a coin of Valentinian II (383–92) and an inscription reading *ΑΒΑΛΑΤΟϹ ϹΦΡΑΓΙϹΕΝ* ('Abalatos stamped it') (pl. 56B).[1] A second example on a small fluted bowl,[2] also has a seated Tyche figure to be compared with coins of Theodosius II and Valentinian III. An important set of three stamps on the Cesena dish which is discussed below, cannot unfortunately be read or interpreted, and it is clear that many more examples must be found before any useful general conclusions can be drawn from these early stamps.

On grounds of style, the attribution of surviving silver to centres of manufacture seems at present impossible. A large number of dishes and bowls of the period are decorated with chased formal ornament of an easily recognisable kind (fig. 39) and it is tempting to assign them to one, or a few, centres of manufacture. Most of them have been found in the west but works in the same style are widely distributed[3] and one such dish (no. 5) from the Treasure of Kaiseraugst has a careful pointillé inscription giving the name of Euticius of Naissus (Niş) who is almost certainly its maker. The richly decorated Achilles dish (no. 1) from the Treasure of Kaiseraugst is inscribed by its maker Pausylypos of Thessalonike and a number of other late Roman dishes have maker's names, occasionally with the place of origin as well. But in most cases there is no inscriptional evidence and the widely differing opinions that have been held about the origin of such pieces as the Theodosius dish in Madrid illustrate how difficult it is to solve such problems on any other evidence.

Apart from the plate produced within the Roman Empire, the work of silversmiths on the fringes of the Roman world and outside its frontiers was strongly influenced by Roman forms and modes of decoration. Roman influence is particularly strong in work of Sassanian origin and Sassanian metalwork must have played a part in the development of Roman plate, especially in the eastern provinces. On the northern fringes of the Empire silver plate was being produced which followed prevailing Roman fashions but contained strong elements of

[1] Dodd, *Silver Stamps*, no. 81; *Amtl. Berichte*, xxxviii, 1917, cols. 263–304.

[2] Dodd, *Silver Stamps*, no. 83.

[3] The style is discussed in *PBSR*, xv, 1939, 33 ff.; many more examples could now be added.

local style. The gold jug and dish from the Treasure of Petrossa are both closely related to Roman fifth-century designs but some of the ornament is of local inspiration. The remarkable *amphora* from the Concesti hoard (pl. 57) with its apparent Greco-Persian affinities looks like the work of a silversmith outside the main stream of Roman metalwork.[1]

CHRISTIAN SILVER

In the hoards of this period have been found the earliest examples both of domestic plate with Christian subjects or inscriptions and of plate used in Christian worship. At this time owners who had embraced the Christian faith often had chi-rho monograms and other Christian symbols engraved on their silver though its decoration might be purely pagan in inspiration, like the silver from the Esquiline Hoard. They also collected plate decorated with Christian themes, like the fine silver-gilt flask with scenes from the Old and New Testaments in the Treasure of Traprain Law (pl. 55A). A good deal of plate was also being made for religious use in the fourth century and from the time of Constantine the Churches were vastly enriched with precious vessels. Constantine himself gave a dish (*patena*) weighing 15 lb., 5 *scyphi* and four other vessels to the Basilica of SS. Peter and Marcellinus.[2] A wide variety of vessels would be used in the churches. Jugs were used at the Mass both for pouring wine and for washing hands; incense burners, lamps and candlesticks were also to be found in the churches. It has been suggested that the Treasure of 24 silver vessels found at Canoscio in Umbria all belonged to a Christian Church;[3] it included dishes, bowls, cups and spoons, some of which are certainly as early as the fifth century A.D.[4]

The rectangular *lanx*, which was found at Risley Park in Derbyshire in 1729 and has since been lost, has a definite connection with a Christian Church.[5] It bore an inscription which read EXSVPERIVS

[1] Matzulewitsch, *Byzantinische Antike*, pls. 36 ff.; *RM*, 31–2, 1921–2, 108 ff.

[2] cf. Duchesne, *Liber Pontificalis*, i, 79.

[3] *Rivista di archeologia cristiana*, xii, 1935, 313 ff.; E. Giovagnoli, *Il Tesoro Eucaristico di Canoscio*, Città di Castello, 1940.

[4] For Christian ritual plate in general see Volbach, *Metallarbeiten*, and J. Braun, *Das christliche Altargeräte*, Munich, 1932.

[5] Odobesco, *Petrossa*, 110, fig. 141; *Mélanges*, 18, 1898, 363 ff.; Cabrol, *Dictionnaire*, 9, col. 1405.

EPISCOPVS ECCLESIAE BOGIENSI DEDIT XP, recording its dedication by Bishop Exsuperius to an unidentified church. The decoration, with hunting scenes, heads etc., followed pagan traditions. A number of other surviving vessels of the fourth and fifth centuries A.D. have Christian subjects and are probably church silver and these include a number of fine silver jugs (*amulae*). An example in the Vatican Museums of the slim jug popular in this period (see fig. 37*a*) is decorated with horizontal bands of rope ornament dividing the body into zones, the middle one of which has a series of repoussé medallions enclosing heads of Christ, Saints Peter and Paul, and two apostles.[1] A little jug with religious scenes, formerly in the Collection of Count Leo Strozzi, is now in the British Museum.[2] Some of the spoons punched or engraved with chi-rho monograms may have served religious uses. Those found in domestic contexts, like the spoons in the Mildenhall Treasure, have been thought of as christening spoons.[3]

RELIQUARY CASKETS

The reliquary caskets form an important little group among the surviving Christian silver of the fifth century. One of the best known is the little casket found near the high altar of the Basilica at Grado in 1871.[4] The casket is a small elliptical box with a convex lid, decorated with repoussé reliefs. On the lid are represented lambs adoring the Cross and on the body of the box are three roundels of which the centre one encloses a frontal head of Christ and the others heads of Peter and Paul in profile. The bands of wreath ornament at the base and on the rim of this vessel are characteristic of the repoussé vessels of the period. A very similar casket is the so-called 'capsella africana' which was found in the ruins of a Christian basilica at Henchir-Zirara (Numidia) and is now in the Vatican;[5] on one side of the body is a frieze of lambs with the Cross, on the other two deer drinking from rivers at the foot of the Cross. The figure of Christ appears on the lid. A casket found at Castello di Brivio, Lombardy, now in the Musée du Louvre,[6] is of similar shape

[1] Discussed in *The Art Bulletin*, xx, 1938, 193 ff.

[2] *BMQ*, xvii, 1952, 16–17, pl. v, a.

[3] For early Christian spoons in general, Cabrol, *Dictionnaire* s.v. Cuiller; J. Braun, *Das Christliche Altargeräte*, 265 ff.

[4] G. Brusin, *Aquileia e Grado*, Udine, 1950, 155 ff.; *Bull. Arch. Christ*, 1872, 41 ff.

[5] *Art Bulletin*, 1938, 216, figs. 24–5.

[6] Volbach, *Early Christian Art*, 120.

and decoration. The Adoration of the Magi appears on one side of the box and the Three Hebrews in the Fiery Furnace on the other; on the lid is the miracle of the Raising of Lazarus.

The rectangular reliquary box from the Church of S. Nazzaro Maggiore in Milan shows Christ among the Apostles on the lid and scenes from the Old and New Testaments on the four sides.[1] The little six-sided casket (pl. 54A) found on the south side of the Duomo at Pola on the site of what had been the Altaresepulchrum of the former Basilica[2] has figures of Christ and Apostles on the facets of the body and busts on those of the lid. Fragments of a very handsome octagonal casket, probably a reliquary casket, were found in Room 3 of Tomb 3 at Ballana in Nubia.[3] On the panels of the box are shown Christ and Apostles and on the eight triangular panels of the lid there was repoussé floral ornament. The lid was surmounted by a finial. All these caskets probably date from the fifth century A.D.

CUPS

Silver drinking cups are not common in the late hoards but a number of new and attractive shapes are found. Three cups found at Canoscio are similar to the vessels from Chaourse illustrated in fig. 34*a*, though they stand on a rather higher foot, a characteristic of the cups, bowls and dishes of the period. Two plain conical beakers (no. 16) on low foot rings were found in the Treasure of Kaiseraugst. A silver vessel found in a small hoard at Great Horwood, Bucks., is a version of the long-necked beaker common in pottery of the third-fourth centuries, and a related beaker, found in the River Tyne near Bywell in 1760, is believed to have formed part of the Corbridge Hoard.[4]

The shallow goblet on a baluster stem and wide base plate (no. 13) from the Treasure of Traprain (pl. 54B) seems to represent a type popular in the period. There were fragments of six such goblets from Traprain and a pair of similar goblets was found in the Mildenhall Treasure (nos. 16 and 17); on the latter the baluster stem is enclosed by four bars of square section converging at top and bottom. It has been suggested that the wide base plates could be used as miniature dishes or

[1] *ibid.* 110–15.
[2] Volbach, *Metallarbeiten*, 25 ff.; Noll, *Vom Altertum zum Mittelalter*, no. B 13.
[3] Emery and Kirwan, *Ballana and Qustul*, pl. 68, 279, fig. 97.
[4] *JRS*, iv, 1914, 1 (see below p. 198 note 3).

stands, and they are, in fact, decorated with chased leaf ornament on the underside. A similar dual purpose had been served by the 'egg-cups' from the Campanian Hoards (pl. 42B). The rims of the Mildenhall cups and the edges of the base plates are beaded, like so many other vessels of the period.

Decorated drinking cups are rare. In the Walters Art Gallery, Baltimore, there is a beaker with straight sides sloping inwards towards the top, decorated with Bacchic masks and figures in low relief in a style which may well belong to the fourth century A.D.[1] A fine example of the technique of openwork silver and glass is the *kantharos* found near Tiflis.[2] The inside is of violet glass and the outer case is decorated with hunting scenes. The shape is based on the Greek *kantharos* but has the ball stem above the foot which is a common feature of metal vessels in this period (cf. fig. 37). The same detail appears on the so-called 'Chalice of Antioch', a deep cup which consists of a bowl of silver set inside an openwork case on which are represented Christ, the Four Evangelists, and six saints, set in an overall pattern of vine with birds, animals and other motifs.[3] A technique related to the openwork silver and glass is found on the two elaborate multangular gold cups with animal handles in the Treasure of Petrossa. Here the openwork gold was filled up with semi-precious stones, producing two of the most ornate examples of late Roman metalwork.

JUGS

There were three main types of silver jug in this period.

The first is a tall slim vessel (fig. 37*a*) with ovoid body and long tapering neck and flat circular mouth with upright rim. The lower part of the body may either narrow downwards and widen out again for the foot or there may be a ball stem between body and foot. The foot is sometimes edged with heavy beading. The shape in general is not unlike the Hellenistic fusiform unguentarium. The handle may either arch above the level of the rim or may run horizontally from the rim and bend downwards at a sharp angle to join the body of the vessel. There are good examples of this kind of vessel in Berlin, one of which

[1] *WAG Exhibition*, 1947, no. 361 (Inv. no. 57.1411).

[2] *CR*, 1872, 143–54.

[3] *WAG Exhibition*, 1947, no. 388. J. J. Rorimer, 'The Authenticity of the Chalice of Antioch', in *Studies in Art and Literature for Belle Da Costa Greene*, Princeton, 1954, 161–88.

is decorated with horizontal bands of ornament,[1] and there are two in the Vatican Museums[2] of which the smaller, decorated with roundels of Christ and the Apostles, has already been mentioned (p. 186). The second jug is fragmentary and plain except for a Christian inscription

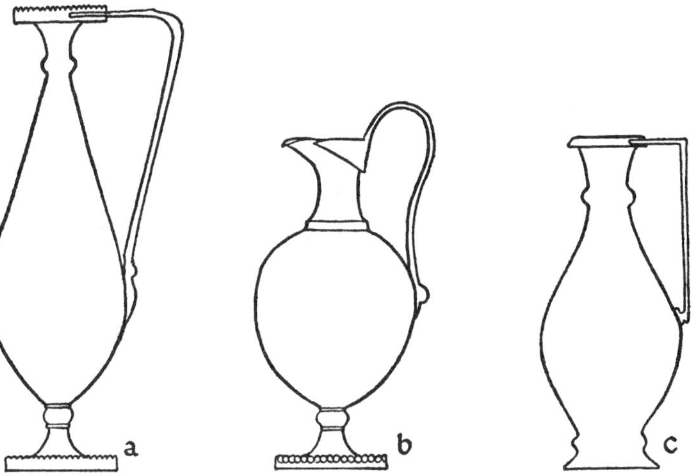

FIG. 37: Forms of late Roman silver jugs

in two lines round the neck. Three jugs of similar shape were found in the tombs of Ballana and Qustul in Nubia.[3] A fine gold example of this form from the Treasure of Petrossa is decorated on the body with wavy fluting and there is a roll moulding round the narrow part of the neck; the handle is of the angular form and there is a ball stem above the foot.[4]

The second type of jug (fig. 37*b*) has a bulbous body, a narrow tapering neck sometimes with a roll moulding and a horizontal spout which may be fitted with a hinged lid; there is often a ball stem between the body and the foot and the handle may either arch above the level of the mouth or curve downwards from it to join the body at its widest point. The example from Syria in Berlin (pl. 56A) has the handle attached by means of two leaf-shaped soldering plates and there are knobs at intervals on the handle itself; the foot is rimmed with beading.[5]

[1] Schlunk, *Spätantike*, 106, pl. 26.

[2] Odobesco, *Petrossa*, ii, 16, fig. 18; *The Art Bulletin* 1938, 193 ff.

[3] Emery and Kirwan, *Ballana and Qustul*, pl. 64B.

[4] Odobesco, *Petrossa*.

[5] Schlunk, *Spätantike*, no. 104, pl. 25.

There is a similar vessel in the Cabinet des Médailles, Paris with a hinged lid and the inscription VIVAS IN CHRISTO QUINTA in nielloed letters on the neck.[1] A handle from a jug of this type was found in the Esquiline Treasure;[2] the arms by which the handle was soldered to the rim are decorated with openwork designs and the soldering plate below is engraved to represent a leaf. A jug of this type and one of the slim jugs which were found together in the catacombs of Kerch[3] with commemorative dishes of Constantius II described below are illustrated in fig. 37*a* and *b*.

The third type of jug has an ovoid body standing on a foot ring, a narrow neck, usually decorated with a roll moulding, and a round mouth with vertical rim (fig. 37*c*). The handle rises vertically from the widest part of the body and is attached to the rim by a horizontal plate with arms closing on the rim. The shape is a direct development of the third-century jugs mentioned above (p. 166). A good example of the shape decorated with niello and gilt geometric ornament on the neck and upper part of the body was found at Trier;[4] a facetted jug of this kind was found at Aquincum.[5]

A number of other types of jug occur in the period. There is one in a find of silver said to come from Syria and now in the Cleveland Museum of Art, which looks like an earlier form.[6] The jug has a trefoil mouth and a squat bulbous body on a low base ring; the heavy beading on the handle suggests the late Roman period to which the rest of the silver in this find belongs. Jugs with facetted bodies came into fashion with other facetted vessels. A jug in the Esquiline Treasure has a long horizontal spout hinged for a lid and a facetted body standing on a foot rim;[7] the handle arches above the top of the jug. Ovals on the facets of the shoulder contain letters making up a complete inscription – PELEGRINA VTERE FELIX. Two jugs from Apahida in Transylvania both have four-sided bodies decorated with repoussé reliefs;[8] the necks are rectangular with semicircular spouts and the handle is of the angular type with upright thumb grip ending in a knob.

[1] Odobesco, *Petrossa*, ii, 16, fig. 18*a*.
[2] *BMECA*, no. 344.
[3] *AA*, 1905, 61, fig. 6.
[4] La Baume, *Kunstgewerbe*, 41, fig. 33.
[5] *ibid.* 44, 36, Radnóti, *Bronzegefässe*, pl. XLV.
[6] *Bulletin Cleveland Museum*, 1958, 35–41.
[7] *BMECA*, no. 307.
[8] *Arch Ert.*, 9, 1889, 306 ff., pls. 1–2.

FLASKS

A popular vessel of this period is a flask without handle, related in shape to the jugs of the third type, which was usually decorated with rich ornament of some kind. The flask has an ovoid body resting on a low foot rim, a narrow neck which is often decorated with a heavy roll moulding, and a wide round mouth with vertical rim. One of these flasks, decorated with repoussé scenes from the Old and New Testaments, was found at Traprain Law (pl. 55A); the foot rim, as on a number of other flasks is formed by heavy beading. There were fragments of two other flasks decorated with scenes from classical mythology in the same treasure; one (no. 7) shows the figures of Pan and a Hermaphrodite and the other (no. 8) the discovery of Achilles among the daughters of Lycomedes. A fine, well-preserved example from Syria in Cleveland is decorated with a Bacchic thiasos on the main zone and subsidiary friezes of animals.[1] Another from Bolshoi Kamenets (Dniepr Basin) is one of the few pieces of stamped silver belonging to the fourth/fifth centuries; the figures of the Nine Muses are represented in relief on the body.[2] Like the jugs, these flasks were sometimes facetted and fluted. The upper part of a very large one in the Treasure of Traprain (no. 3) shows that the body was treated with alternately fluted and flat panels; the neck which is decorated with a heavy roll moulding has ten flat panels richly decorated with chased and nielloed ornament and gilded borders. Another flagon (no. 4) was decorated with bands of ornament incorporating roundels with heads and figures in a gilt and niello technique like that found on the dishes of the period (see p. 195).

There are several surviving flasks of this period which differ from the standard type. A tall slender vessel in the Esquiline Treasure (pl. 55B) is almost identical in shape with the body of one of the slim jugs described above, but seems never to have had a handle;[3] the vessel is decorated with formal scroll medallions diminishing in size towards top and bottom and framing groups and figures of animals and putti. A plain flask in the Traprain Treasure (no. 2), with pear-shaped body standing on a splayed foot rim, has a rounded moulding marking the junction

[1] *Bulletin Cleveland Museum*, 1958, 39 f.

[2] Dodd, *Silver Stamps*, no. 84.

[3] *BMECA*, no. 306.

between the body and the tapering neck. There is a very curious flask in the Vatican Museums which seems to belong to this period; the body is round, and flat on both sides, like an *ampulla,* but it has a long slender neck and foot. The body is decorated with repoussé roundels and scroll ornament.[1] There was a silver *ampulla* in the Treasure of Ténès.[2]

AMPHORAE

Two plain *amphorae* with arching handles were found in the Esquiline Treasure,[3] but this type of vessel was probably rare in the period. The silver *amphora* (pl. 57) found together with a bucket and a dish at Concesti (Moldavia) and now in the Hermitage Museum is one of the most remarkable pieces of late antique plate.[4] The repoussé reliefs on the body represent an Amazonomachy on the main frieze with a subsidiary frieze of Nereids and sea-monsters separated from it by a band of ornament. There is a heavy roll moulding round the tall neck and the handles (not shown in the plate) are in the form of centaurs. In many ways this *amphora* seems to hark back to Greco-Persian vessels of the fourth century B.C. and it was probably made in some eastern workshop where such early vessels might still be a source of inspiration.

SAUCEPANS AND HANDLED PATERAE

Saucepans of the traditional form were certainly being made in this period and continued in use a lot later. A pair found in the Valjevo district, now in Belgrade, have straight-ended handles edged with a decorated moulding and leaf ornament on the surface; they probably belong to the fourth century. One example, though it falls outside the period discussed in this chapter, probably illustrates the more elaborately decorated versions of the fourth and fifth centuries. This saucepan, which comes from Cherchel and is now in the Louvre, is dated by its stamps to the first half of the sixth century.[5] A single figure (of Neptune) occupies most of the space on the handle, as on some third-century saucepans, and the wide and rather ugly arms of attachment end in eagle heads; the rest of the space is taken up with two dolphins flanking a shell. The inside of the bowl is plain while on the outside there are fishing scenes in relief. A similar form of handle (fig. 30*l*) appears on a shallow *patera* from the Esquiline Treasure which is now in the Petit

[1] Odobesco, *Petrossa*, ii, 17, fig. 19.
[2] J. Heurgon, *Le Trésor de Ténès*, Paris, 1958
[3] *BMECA*, no. 308–9.
[4] Matzulewitsch, *Byzantinische Antike*, pls. 36–43.
[5] Dodd, *Silver Stamps*, no. 14.

Palais, Paris.[1] The vessel consists of a shallow bowl with a narrow horizontal rim; the rim is decorated with a series of little scallop-shells in relief and the inside of the bowl is treated as a large scallop-shell in which appears Venus attended by two *putti,* one holding a lotus flower and the other a mirror. The handle is occupied by the single standing figure of Adonis with a dog at his feet. This form of *patera* continued to be popular in later times. An example from Perm in the Hermitage Museum is decorated on the rim and the inside with Nilotic scenes and on the handle with a figure of Neptune very like that on the Cherchel saucepan.[2] It dates from around A.D. 500. There is a smaller *patera* from the Carthage Treasure with the figure of a frog, perhaps a Christian motif, in high relief on the centre of the inside; the horizontal handle is in the form of a knotted branch.[3]

LADLES

There are a number of small ladles with horizontal handles in the late hoards. The Mildenhall Treasure contains five (nos. 18-26) with the handles cast in the form of dolphins and joined to the bowl with arms of attachment terminating in birds' heads (pl. 67B); the bowls are similar in shape to the bowls of the saucepans and are plain except for a series of turnings on the bottom of the inside. There is a similar ladle in the Traprain Treasure with the handle in the form of a dolphin holding the rim of the bowl in its mouth (no. 106). A series of seven little ladles or large spoons in the Carthage Treasure have a shallower, rounded bowl;[4] the handles are octagonal in section widening towards the end and with a square panel at the junction of the handle and the arms of attachment. The panel is decorated with a cross between two scrolls inlaid with niello. There is a very similar ladle in the hoard from Canoscio and a pair with inscriptions on the panel from the Desana hoard in Turin.[5] An unusual ladle, probably from Carthage and now in the Louvre,[6] has the rim of the bowl formed into a star pattern with

[1] Gusman, *L'Art decoratif,* 1, pl. 26.

[2] Dodd, *Silver Stamps,* no. 77.

[3] *BMECA,* no. 360.

[4] *BMECA,* nos. 364–70.

[5] *Ori e Argenti,* nos. 806–10.

[6] de Ridder, *Bijoux,* no. 1985; the vessel is one of 5 pieces of silver formerly in the Tyszkiewicz Collection which are said to come from Torre del Greco or Carthage. The others are a bowl (no. 1921 *bis*) with a lid (see below p. 204), another bowl (no. 1922) and two little ladles like the seven in the Carthage Treasure. Clearly the Louvre silver also comes from Carthage.

little knobs on the points. The bottom is decorated with palmettes and rosettes and the handle is in the form of a dolphin.

PLATES AND DISHES

A] *Shapes and schemes of decoration*

In general design the dishes of the period follow the fashions of the third century. The biggest dishes, however, tend to be larger than those of the earlier period. The two dishes found at Cesena are 62 and 63 cm. in diameter, the Oceanus dish (no. 1) from Mildenhall is 60 cm., and the diameters of the large dishes in the Treasure of Traprain ranged from 45-60 cm. Enormous serving dishes are shown on wall paintings of the period.[1] One or two characteristic details distinguish the later plates from the earlier; the beading of the rims is much heavier and they usually rest on a higher but smaller foot rim. The round dishes may have a raised flat border with a beaded edge, a moulded rim, or an upright rim of some kind. The main innovations of the period are the fashion for angular shapes, including rectangular dishes, dishes with multangular outline, and round dishes within a square frame, and for dishes with openwork borders of various kinds. The schemes of decoration are similar to those of the earlier period; the flanges and central roundels are often decorated and sometimes the whole surface of the plate is decorated with chased ornament. Simpler dishes have a small decorative motif in the centre or they may be completely plain, except for the beaded or moulded rim. The characteristic decorative techniques of the period are an elaborate use of gilt and niello for decorative and figured designs, formal floral and geometric ornament carried out by chasing, and relief work, either cast or hammered.

B] *Niello Dishes*

Plainer dishes of the period were often monogrammed with the name of their owner in the niello and gilt technique. There were two sets of small dishes in the Esquiline Treasure, four round with moulded rim and four rectangular with openwork border, both of which had the monogram of Projecta in gilt and niello letters within a gilt and niello wreath. A large round dish from the Tomb of the Queen with

[1] e.g. the Lateran paintings (*Mem. Pont. Accad.*, vii, 1944, 282, fig. 222) and the scenes shown on mosaics from Antioch (Glanville Downey, *Ancient Antioch*, Princeton, 1963, figs. 37 ff.).

the Golden Mask at Kerch[1] has a similar wreathed monogram in the centre and gilt and niello ornament on the rim (pl. 63A). It dates perhaps from about A.D. 300 and a pointillé inscription shows that it had come into the possession of the Bosporan King, Rhescuporis. Some of the plates in the Canoscio hoard are simply decorated with a niello cross or chi-rho monogram in the centre.

Elaborate use of gilt and niello is characteristic of the period, both for floral geometric ornament and for figured scenes. Geometric ornament decorates the fine niello dish from the Mildenhall Treasure (no. 4) which has a central roundel with complex geometric pattern of circles and squares and similar geometric and floral patterns on the broad, slightly raised, flange round the edge. The dish is edged with heavy beading. Another dish with geometric niello patterns on flange and medallion was found at Kaiseraugst (no. 9). A somewhat later example of the same style and technique is the Anastasius dish found in the Sutton Hoo Treasure.[2] The best-known example of the use of niello and gilding for figured scenes is the dish (pl. 58) found near Cesena (Bolognese) and now in the Bibliotheca Malatestiana there.[3] The dish has a central roundel, framed by a band of close-set fluting on which is represented, in the upper half, an open-air banquet and, in the lower, a building before which there stands a horse and his groom. The frieze on the border of the plate shows, alternately, pastoral and hunting scenes divided from one another by medallion heads. The figures and other details are engraved and gilded against a niello background. The dish from Cesena has control stamps on the back and, as already noted, it seems to have survived above ground for a long time until it was buried at the time of the Gothic War between A.D. 538 and 553. A dish with similar decoration on the rim and geometric ornament in the roundel was found at Concesti with the amphora mentioned above (p. 192). Another masterpiece of the same technique was discovered recently in the Treasure of Kaiseraugst (no. 2); the central medallion shows a walled town by the sea with Cupids fishing in the foreground, and on the flange there are hunting scenes separated by bands of geometric interlace. The popularity of this technique is shown by numerous fragments from other sources. There are two with figured

[1] Minns, *S & G*, 434.

[2] *The Sutton Hoo Ship Burial*, London, 1947, 47, pl. 14.

[3] *Annuario*, xxiv–xxvi (viii–x), 1946–8, 309–44.

scenes from Hammersdorf[1] and several from Traprain. Among the latter there is one fragment of a large dish or bowl (no. 44) consisting of a medallion of Venus Anadyomene. Two fragments of the rim of a big circular dish are decorated with wreathed medallions enclosing human heads, separated by geometric designs. Three fragments of another dish show a bead-and-reel edging and interlaced patterns of geometric shapes enclosing floral motifs. The Treasure of Kaiseraugst also contained a most elaborate rectangular dish or tray (no. 3) with a design of openwork scrolls and scallops round the edge. Its surface is richly decorated with relief and gilded and nielloed engraving; in a rectangular panel in the centre, Ariadne is shown enthroned between a satyr and Bacchus, and in the panels round the outside there are cupids playing with animals.

c] *Dishes with chased ornament*

The characteristic chased ornament of this period is very distinctive. The designs, some of which are illustrated in fig. 39, are patterns of leaf ornament, diapers, interlace etc., carried out in a rough but effective technique of chased lines and grooves worked in the soft metal. As already noted, the standard repertoire seems to occur over a wide area and is frequently used to decorate dishes and plates of various kinds. The Euticius dish from the Kaiseraugst Treasure has a broad flange edged with beading and decorated with chased leaf pattern in this style; the surface of the dish is covered with close-set wavy fluting, another popular motif of the period which is found on dishes from the Carthage Treasure, Canoscio and Traprain Law. Another example of the same style of chasing is provided by the great gold plate from the Treasure of Petrossa[2] which is 56 cm. in diameter and weighs over 7 kilos; the central medallion is decorated with a wave pattern and the border with zig-zag leaf ornament. Three dishes with chased ornament of a similar kind were found in Moesia.[3] A dish from Mileham[4] in the British Museum (pl. 62A) combines a circular recess with a square flange edged with beading; the flange is decorated with chased leaf ornament. There are fragments of similar dishes from Traprain Law, Coleraine, Balline

[1] Rosenberg, *Niello*, ii, 69, figs. 58–60. [2] Odobesco, *Petrossa*, pl. II.

[3] *Jelentés a Magyar Nemzeti Muzeum*, 1908, 42 ff., figs. 2 & 3; *Folia Archeologica*, 7, 1955, 97–109; Pierce and Tylor, 55, pl. 61*b*.

[4] *BMCP*, no. 87, pl. XIV.

and elsewhere. A round dish in the Esquiline Treasure has an upright scalloped rim[1] and a medallion trellis pattern chased on the flat surface. Another elaborate dish found at Soissons,[2] with an upright rim decorated with openwork designs based on the *pelta* shape, has on the inside a complicated pattern of square frames and lozenges enclosing rosettes; some of the details are nielloed and gilt.

D] *Dishes with relief ornament*

Cast or hammered relief ornament was much used in the period, especially for the picture dishes which are discussed below. It also served to decorate the roundels and borders of dishes. One of the finest examples of this technique is the eight-sided dish (no. 1) from the Treasure of Kaiseraugst (pl. 59) which has a central roundel showing the discovery of Achilles among the daughters of King Lykomedes and a wide border divided up into a series of panels representing various episodes in the life of Achilles. Another popular form of relief decoration on the rims of dishes consists of animal figures or hunting scenes combined with human heads and busts. This scheme of decoration which also appears frequently on the flanged bowls of the period (see below) follows the tradition of the third-century dishes with masks, animals etc.

E] *Picture dishes*

Several magnificent picture dishes have been found in the late hoards. The outstanding example is the so-called Oceanus dish (no. 1) in the Mildenhall Treasure (pl. 60), a large dish 60·5 cm. in diameter with a heavy beaded rim, decorated in low relief with two concentric bands of figured ornament round a central medallion. The central medallion shows a frontal head of Oceanus which is immediately surrounded by a narrow frieze showing Nereids riding on sea-monsters; outside this there is a broad frieze with a lively scene of satyrs and maenads in energetic revel. The whole scheme of decoration is strangely reminiscent of the classical relief *phialai* (see p. 81). Maryon, who studied the technique of the dish reached the conclusion that it had been worked by hammering and chasing from the front after the dish had been cast

[1] *BMECA*, no. 311.
[2] *L'Art dans l'Occident Romain*, no. 87.

without decoration.[1] Two little platters with dancing satyrs and maenads in the same hoard (nos. 2–3) were probably made as a set with the large dish. The style of these dishes may be compared with that of a dish from Baku in the Caucasus which shows a Nereid riding a hippocamp surrounded by Tritons and Nereids.[2]

Probably the most famous of all the late Roman picture dishes is the rectangular dish (pl. 61) found in the Tyne near Corbridge in the eighteenth century, which seems to be the only survivor of a largish hoard.[3] The dish is framed by a raised border decorated with running scroll that encloses a relief scene showing a group of deities worshipped on the island of Delos. It has been suggested that the subject was chosen to commemorate the sacrifice offered to Apollo at Delos by Julian the Apostate in 363 and that the dish should be interpreted as a product of the pagan reaction to Christianity under that Emperor.[4] The rectangular picture dish from Risley Park (see above pp. 185–6) was decorated with a panel in the centre showing a hunting scene and there were hunting scenes and heads on the broad frieze round the margin in a style similar to that of the Heracles bowl from Traprain Law (no. 36). The inscription referring to Bishop Exsuperius was inscribed on the back of the dish. A fragment of a similar dish on which the main scene was the Rape of Hylas framed by a wide band with fishing scenes and a heavy beaded rim was found in the Gross Bodungen Hoard.

A number of other picture dishes may be assigned to the fourth and early fifth centuries. The magnificent Parabiago dish in Milan[5] is certainly a work of this period to judge both from its form and its decoration. The whole surface is taken up with a scene showing the goddess Cybele with Attis in a chariot drawn by lions and surrounded by symbolic figures of the Sun, Moon, Earth and Ocean. Related to it in style is a smaller dish showing an Amazon out hunting in the Dumbarton Oaks Collection. Another dish found at Lampsacus[6] is decorated in low relief with a magnificent seated figure of India

[1] Maryon, *Metalwork*, 115; *Man*, 1948, 25.

[2] *Enciclopedia dell'Arte Classica*, s.v. Caucaso; *CR*, 1896, 114, fig. 410.

[3] *VCH Northumberland*, 517 ff.; *JRS*, iv, 1914, 1 ff.; *JHS*, 35, 1915, 66 ff.; *JdI*, xxx, 1915, 192. Between 1731 and 1736, 4 pieces of silver plate were found in the same general area at Corbridge, and another vase found in 1760 at Bywell, 4 miles from Corbridge, is believed to come from the same source; see also Toynbee, *Art in Britain*, 306 ff.

[4] See *JRS*, xxxi, 1941, 100 ff.; *AA*, 1955, 259–63.

[5] Levi, *Parabiago*.

[6] *GA*, 1877, 119–22; *JdAI*, xv, 1900, 210 ff.

surrounded by beasts and birds. The plate is framed by an ornamental border of geometric pattern inlaid with niello, closely comparable with that on the niello dish from Mildenhall. It is suggested that the plate may have formed one of a set representing Africa, Asia, India and so on. Another characteristic picture dish of the period is the Diana dish in Berlin[1] (pl. 62B) which may also be compared with the dish showing Apollo Alexikakos from Ballana (Nubia).[2]

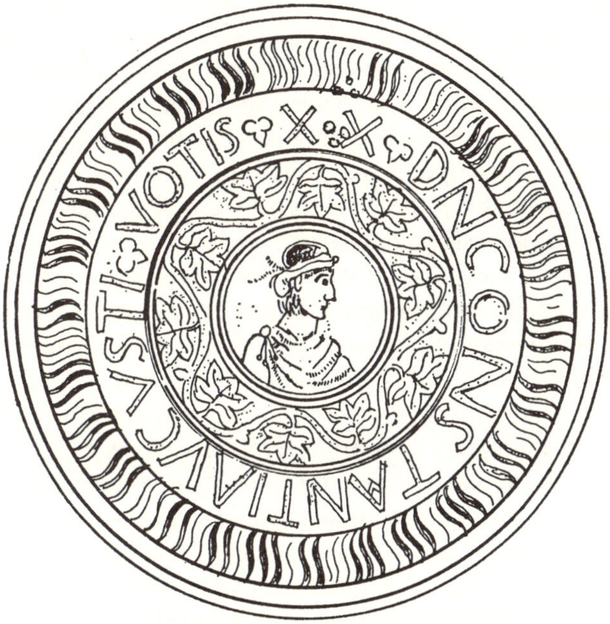

FIG. 38: Silver dish commemorating the *Vicennalia* of Constantius II in A.D. 343, from Kerch; Hermitage Museum, Leningrad. Scale 1:3

Anniversary dishes

The so-called *largitio* plates which were distributed on the occasion of imperial anniversaries form an important class of late Roman silver. The earliest of the late Roman series are the dishes commemorating the *Decennalia* of Licinius in A.D. 317. Two examples in Belgrade, one in Vienna (pl. 63B), and another in a private collection in Luzern were

[1] Schlunk, *Spätantike*, pl. 29, 107.

[2] *AA*, 1939, 571; Emery and Kirwan, *Ballana and Qustul*, pl. 65.

found together;[1] all four have an engraved inscription running round the inside near the rim with the words LICINI AUGVSTE SEMPER VINCAS and in the centre SIC X SIC XX enclosed in a wreath. They were made at Naissus (Niş). A dish from Svirkovo in Bulgaria has an engraved portrait of the same emperor and a pointillé inscription;[2] it was found together with a silver ingot. Two dishes found at Červenbreg in 1952 have upright fluted rims and are decorated in the centre with relief medallions of the emperor taken from the obverse of his coins. The inscriptions surrounding the portraits read LICINIVS INVICT AVG OB DIEM X SVORVM; on the back they are marked by Flavius Nicanus, *magister bisellarius nummulariorum*.[3] All the Licinius dishes seem to have been made in the areas where they were found. Two plates of Constantius II (fig. 38) each with a chased and nielloed portrait and commemorative inscription were found in a tomb at Kerch and were probably presented by the Emperor to the Bosporan King on the occasion of his *vicennalia* in A.D. 343.[4]

The finest of the imperial commemorative plates are the picture dishes with reliefs representing the Emperor and other members of the ruling house. A dish of Valentinian I, showing the Emperor flanked by his soldiers, was probably made for the Emperor's *Quinquennalia* in 369 or his *Decennalia* five years later; it is now in the Musée de la Ville, Geneva.[5] A fragmentary plate from Gross Bodungen found with coins of Magnentius to Constantine III shows an Emperor seated with attendants. The best known of all these Imperial picture dishes is the Plate of Theodosius I found in 1847 near Mérida and now in Madrid[6] which shows the Emperor and his two co-regents Arcadius and Valentinian II seated before a temple or tribunal together with attendants and soldiers (pl. 64). The inscription reads D(OMI)N(VS) THEODOSIVS PERPET(VVS) AVG(VSTVS) OB DIEM FELICISSIMVM X, referring to the Emperor's ten year anniversary in the year A.D. 388.

[1] *RA*, 1903, 26 ff.; R. Noll, *Vom Altertum zum Mittelalter*, 1958, pl. 12 (A 23); see also *Oud. Meded*, xlii, 1961, 63 ff.

[2] *Archeologiya* (Sophia), iii, 1961, 47 ff.

[3] *Bull. Inst. Bulg.*, xix, 1955, 233–43; *Folia Archaeologica*, xii, 1960, 133–43. An inscription of Flavius Nicanus was also found on a plate from Srem in Yugoslavia.

[4] Matzulewitsch, *Byzantinische Antike*, 95 ff., pls. 24–5.

[5] *GBA*, (series 5), i, 1920, 173 ff.; *Pierce and Tyler*, i, pl. 43.

[6] J. R. Mélida, *El disco de Teodosio*, Madrid, 1930; García y Bellido, *Esculturas Romanas*, no. 494.

Another of these commemorative plates which just comes within the scope of this book is the dish of Ardaburius Aspar in Florence (Inv. no. 2588) which is dated to the year A.D. 434,[1] and there is an interesting engraved dish with an Emperor on horseback found in one of the catacombs at Kerch which belongs to the same class of commemorative silver.[2]

BOWLS

The bowls of the period continue, with variations, most of the forms in use in the third century and one or two new and very characteristic types are introduced. The flanged bowls, which were very popular, differ in a number of details from their predecessors and the shallow scalloped bowl is a new type. Like the dishes of the period, the bowls usually stand on higher foot rims and a fashion for lidded bowls was coming in. The techniques of chasing, cast and hammered relief and niello inlay were generally used to decorate these vessels.

A] *Fluted and scalloped bowls*

There are a number of bowls with close set fluting on the outside. A good example comes from the Esquiline Treasure (no. 321) and a similar one found in Rumania has a control stamp of the fourth or fifth century.[3] The Cleveland hoard contains a fine fluted bowl on a tall base ring typical of the period. Bowls with fluting on the inside were also common, the fluting being often combined with a central decorated medallion. A bowl in the Kaiseraugst Treasure has a series of wide radial flutes around a central medallion; the medallion and the narrow horizontal rim are decorated with chased ornament. The bowl of very similar shape in the Sutton Hoo burial which has a central medallion with a profile female head in relief may not be much later than the Kaiseraugst example. A fragment of a shallow bowl with radial fluting and a central medallion decorated with a reticulated diaper pattern was found in the Treasure of Traprain (no. 32). Spiral fluting is also found on the interiors of bowls. A large deepish bowl on a high foot rim from Traprain (no. 19) is decorated in this way and had a central roundel with a head (?) in relief surrounded by a zone of punched dots. On the rim,

[1] Volbach, *Early Christian Art*, pl. 109.
[2] Matzulewitsch, *Byzantinische Antike*, 95 ff., pl. 23.
[3] Dodd, *Silver Stamps*, no. 84.

spaced between chased leaf ornament, are single capital letters forming a long inscription that went round the bowl.

A characteristic bowl of the period is the shallow bowl, usually of fairly large size, which has on the inside a series of alternate broad flutes with rounded ends and flat, straight-ended panels which are usually decorated with chased leaf ornament (pl. 65A). In the centre there is usually a roundel which is also richly decorated with chased or engraved ornament. The Esquiline Treasure contained a fine example of this kind of bowl; the flat panels are ornamented with leaf patterns and in the central roundel is set a square with diaper pattern, the intervening space being filled with leaf ornament. A similar, smaller, bowl was found at Traprain with fragments of another (nos. 30–1). There was one in the Mildenhall Treasure (no. 13) (pl. 65A) and another, from Weiden near Cologne, is in Berlin.[1] The bowl from Traprain has an engraved scene on its roundel, showing a Nereid riding on a sea-monster. The Mildenhall and Traprain bowls were both equipped with swing handles soldered on to the underside of the bowls by means of pear-shaped mounts. There was also a pair of handles ending in swans' heads in the Esquiline Treasure and these very probably belonged to the scalloped bowl.

FIG. 39: Chased patterns on late Roman silver dishes and bowls

B] *Flanged bowls*

The flanged bowls continued to be popular in the period. Several examples were found in the Mildenhall Treasure; one of these (no. 5) takes the same form as the bowls of the third century which are characterised by a vertical rim and a broad down-curved flange.[2] The flange of this example is decorated with a scroll pattern, which was

[1] Schlunk, *Spätantike*, no. 103, pl. 27.

[2] There is a bowl of this type in the fourth-century hoard of pewter from Appleshaw in the British Museum (*Archaeologia*, lvi, 1898, 9 ff.). It is worth noting here that the finds of later Roman pewter in Britain throw a good deal of light on fashions in contemporary silver. The pewter, as a cheaper substitute for silver tableware, follows its forms fairly closely.

once inlaid with niello, and it has a bead-and-reel border. The bowl which may be one of the earliest pieces in the Treasure was given a domed lid with relief decoration in a different and later style. The typical decorated forms of the late hoards are represented by four other examples in the Mildenhall Treasure (nos. 7-10); there is no vertical rim, the flange is broad and flat and edged with heavy beading. All four have decoration on the flange consisting of a frieze of animals in relief divided up by human heads and there is a central medallion head on the bottom of the bowl. The heads on nos. 9 and 10, which were made as a pair, are a veiled woman and a man wearing a helmet (Alexander and Olympias?) There are two very similar bowls in the Carthage Treasure (pl. 66B)[1] and two others form part of a find at Kostolac, now in the Museum at Belgrade.[2] An example with animals and masks on the flange, but lacking the central medallion, is in Vienna.[3] Two others of the same shape (nos. 11-12) in the Mildenhall Treasure are decorated with vine scroll on the surface of the flange while the inside of the bowl is decorated with curved fluting radiating from a central rosette. Niello ornament of geometric patterns occurs on the flange of a little bowl found at Aquileia.[4] An example found at Corbridge had scroll ornament and a series of chi-rho monograms on the flange and a central rosette on the inside of the bowl. Plain examples are also common. There were six (nos. 22-7) small examples in the Treasure of Traprain and one larger one (no. 21). One of these bowls in Berlin which has a control stamp on the underside has already been mentioned.[5] There are several plain flanged bowls in the Treasure of Kaiseraugst, one in the Cleveland hoard, and one from a tomb at Qustul. Sometimes the flange was given a multangular outline and there is a curious little bowl in the Traprain Treasure (nos. 35) which is triangular in shape and edged with heavy beading. Another bowl in the same treasure has a four-sided flange edged with beading and engraved with foliate designs (no. 34); this latter type was probably made to match the square dishes, like the Mileham dish described above. A very odd flanged bowl found at Kaiseraugst (no. 13) is basically rectangular in shape with two semicircular projections at the

[1] *BMECA*, nos. 356–7. [2] *RA*, 1903 (i) 26, fig. 19.

[3] Arneth, *Gold- und Silber-Monumente*, pl. S IVG.

[4] G. Brusin, *Aquileia Nostra*, xxix 1958, cols. 45–52; *FA*, xiii, 1958, no. 6202.

[5] See above p. 183.

ends. On the bottom of the dish is engraved a fish and there is some engraving on the flange.

c] *Other types of bowl*

The Carthage Treasure contains a small hemispherical bowl on a tall foot rim which is equipped with a lid looking like a shallower inverted bowl (pl. 66A); the body of the bowl is slightly facetted. There is another exactly like it in the Louvre,[1] probably from Carthage. A very similar bowl was found at Canoscio and another bowl of the same basic shape, decorated with a band of chased ornament below the rim is in the Cabinet des Médailles, Paris. A related form on a slimmer pedestal was part of a find made at Kostolac, now in Belgrade.[2] A bowl from the Coleraine Treasure is a late example of the thin metal bowls with punched ornament which apparently became fashionable in the third century. The ornament consists of bands of dots and ovals, lozenges and floral motifs as filling ornament, a design not unlike that on a bowl which has already been mentioned (p. 175) from the lost Treasure of Wettingen. Another bowl of this kind was found at Leuna in Saxony,[3] and there are other examples of the technique, which seems to imitate contemporary glass-ware, from Haagerup in Fyen and Nordrup in Zeeland.

SPOONS

The characteristic spoon of the late hoards has a pear-shaped bowl joined to the handle at its pointed end by means of a pierced scroll

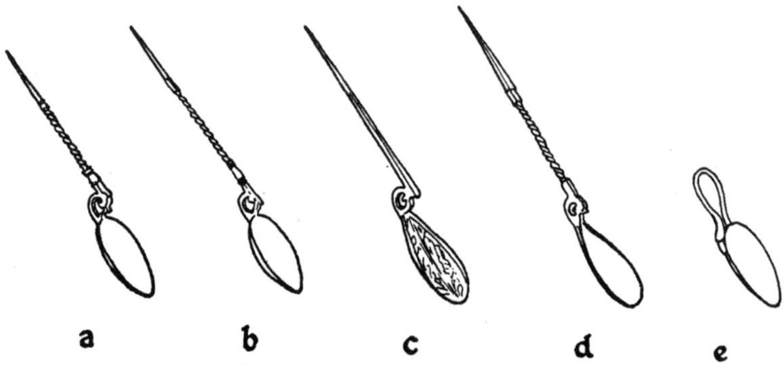

FIG. 40: Silver spoons; fourth-fifth century A.D.

[1] See above p. 193 note 6.
[2] *RA*, 1903 (i), 26.
[3] Eggers, no. 1539, pl. 14, 179; cf. pl. 15, 218 ff.

attachment (fig. 40*c* and *d* and pl. 67C); the handle is generally square in section and tapers to a point. The bowl is sometimes canted at an angle to the handle. This basic shape had appeared in the second century A.D. (fig. 36*b*) but the later spoons are larger and more elaborate in the detail of the attachment. There were 22 spoons of this kind in the Treasure of Kaiseraugst and they are found in most of the hoards. A second type of spoon, used in the period but less common, preserves the basic shape of the old *ligula* with a pointed oval bowl joined to the handle at its more rounded end (fig. 40*a* and *b*); the handle of this type is often moulded or twisted and is usually attached to the bowl in the same way as the handle of the first type. A spoon of this shape in the Mildenhall Treasure and another from a hoard at Dorchester (Oxon)[1] have moulded and twisted stems. A third type of spoon (fig. 40*e*) has the same shape of bowl as this but the handle is formed of thick wire looped round in some way and ending in a swan's head. There were 14 of these spoons from Kaiseraugst (no. 21) with the handle looped so that the swan's head rests against the rim of the bowl on one side (e.g. pl. 67D). On two examples in the Canterbury hoard[2] the handle is looped back to touch its point of juncture with the bowl and then curves upwards so that the swan's head is looking away from the bowl. Other variants are found; one from Traprain Law ends in the head of a swan holding a fish in its beak and the handle seems to have been looped back above the bowl. Most of the older forms of spoon seem to have gone out of general use in this period though there is a little round-bowled *cochleare* in the Carthage Treasure and some examples of the fiddle-spoon were found in late contexts, for example, the Esquiline Treasure. A little *cochleare* and an early *ligula* were found in the Tomb of the Queen with the Golden Mask near Kerch, which may be dated to the late third or early fourth century A.D.[3]

The spoons of the period are characterised by richer ornamental detail than their predecessors. One important feature is the elaborate ornamental treatment of the junction between bowl and handle. The curving arm joining stem and bowl in the old *ligula* form was often combined with a scroll curving towards the bowl; in the late spoons

[1] In the British and Mediaeval Department, British Museum (Registration 72 7–25 1–5); *VCH*, Oxon, I, 294.

[2] Unpublished; the contents are now in the Canterbury Museum.

[3] *ABC*, pl. XXX, 3, 5.

this scroll is a normal feature and it is not infrequently converted into an animal head, as on the spoons in the Canterbury hoard and others from Dorchester (Dorset).[1] The bowls of the spoons were now frequently decorated, especially on the inside. Three spoons from Mildenhall have chased floral patterns on the interior in the style of the period. Two other spoons with chased interiors formed part of a small hoard from Great Horwood near Aylesbury, Bucks.[2] and two chased spoons, one pear-shaped, the other of *cochleare* form, were found in the Carthage Treasure. There is a spoon in the Treasure of Traprain (no. 104) with a niello pattern inlaid on the inside, and a number of other chased and engraved examples. Inscriptions are very common on spoons. Of those in the Mildenhall Treasure, three have chi-rho monograms between alpha and omega engraved on the inside. Two others have good wish inscriptions PASCENTIA VIVAS & PAPPITEDO VIVAS, and it has been suggested that spoons with such inscriptions may have been given as christening presents. Several of the swan's head spoons have chi-rho monograms on the inside of the bowl; there is one from Mainz[3] and one from Canoscio where the dots of the inscription are punched through the metal so that it could serve as a strainer. The inscription on a spoon from Vermand has already been mentioned (p. 21). A find of late Roman spoons at Cuicul in Algeria included examples with the bowls decorated with Christian symbols.[4]

OTHER EATING IMPLEMENTS

A series of intriguing little eating implements were found at Kaiseraugst (pl. 67A). Three of these, with leaf-shaped ends tailing off to a sharp point are thought to have been used for eating such foods as snails or shellfish. The leaf is decorated with openwork ornament, in one case taking the form of a chi-rho. A plain example of this implement with a little 'ear pick' at the other end of the handle was found at Richborough.[5] A fine decorated spoon found at Kerch is fitted with a similar leaf-shaped finial at the end of the handle, suggesting that it

[1] *AntJ*, ii, 1922, 89 ff.

[2] Unpublished.

[3] *Art Sacré Rhenan* (Exhibition 24th June–30th September 1956), no. 6, pl. 3.

[4] *FA*, ii, 1947, no. 2807.

[5] J. P. Bushe-Fox, *Richborough*, iv, 1949, pl. XXXVII, 126–7. Similar bronze examples have been identified as medical probes (cf. *Instruments de chirurgie greco-romains*, N. Rauch Geneva Sale Cat., 1961, nos. 2 and 86) and as 'toilet implements'.

served a similar use to the more normal point.[1] The bowl of this spoon is chased with the figure of a peacock and there is a hawk's head at the attachment between bowl and handle. One of the leaf-shaped implements from Kaiseraugst has a little round bowl at the opposite end pierced to form a little strainer. Another strainer in the same treasure has a partly twisted stem and a little hook at the opposite end; there is a similar implement in the Canoscio Treasure which may have served some ritual purpose. A little strainer with a leaf-shaped finial at the other end was also found at Richborough; there is a hole through the finial fitted with a ring for suspension. A little strainer in the Treasure of Traprain (no. 111) has perforations forming the name 'Iesus Christus' in Roman capitals.

'TOILET SILVER'

One of the best-known pieces in the Esquiline Treasure is the large Casket of Projecta (no. 304), an oblong box with the lid in the form of a truncated pyramid and a body of similar shape; the whole box is decorated with repoussé reliefs in panels framed by bands of formal ornament. The casket was a wedding present to Projecta and bears the inscription SECVNDE ET PROIECTA VIVATIS IN CHRISTO, preceded by a chi-rho monogram; a roundel on the centre of the lid shows the husband and wife and scenes connected with the rites of marriage appear on the panels of the lid and the arcading on the body. The flat plates of the hinges on the casket are decorated with the characteristic late Roman chased ornament. A second casket in the Treasure (pl. 68) is a cylindrical box with a high-domed lid, the dome being formed with alternate flutes and flat panels, a combination of straight lines and curves that is wholly typical of the silver in the late hoards. On the flat panels are vine scrolls, issuing from vases and forming a series of roundels or medallions which again are characteristic of the late Roman ornamental repertoire. The sides of the casket are also alternately concave and flat and are decorated with repoussé ornament showing figures of Muses beneath arcading. Inside the casket is a thin bronze plate with holes cut in it to contain cylindrical boxes with lids, presumably containing cosmetics.

[1] *AA*, 1908, 175, fig. 11; found with two jugs (p. 190) and the Constantius plates (p. 200). A similar spoon was also found at Kerch in 1891 with a flanged bowl (*Materials*, 8, 1892, 2).

'Toilet silver' is rare in the other hoards of the period. A few silver mirrors have been found. The prevailing form seems to have consisted of a disc of metal, sometimes decorated with concentric turned circles and fitted with some kind of loop handle on the back. There is a mirror in the Cleveland Hoard with a handle of coiled wires ending in leaf-shaped soldering plates; a similar handle in the British Museum may come from a mirror.[1] Small flasks and pots used for scents, oil etc. are found from time to time. A little bulbous flask from Boroczyce[2] found with a gold medallion of Flavius Jovianus (A.D. 364) is decorated on the body with repoussé leaf-ornament. Another bulbous flask hinged in two parts and standing on a beaded foot was found in the Desana Treasure; a series of circles was cut out of the metal and filled in with cut amethysts. A little flask with figured repoussé ornament was found at Kerch in the Tomb of the Queen with the Golden Mask. A number of little silver *pyxides*, cylindrical in shape with domed lids and finials, were found in the tombs at Ballana and Qustul; they look very similar to Hellenistic examples.[3]

FURNITURE

There is not much silver furniture in the late hoards. In the Cleveland hoard there is a little pricket lampstand of a type which is common in bronze during the period. A fine *candelabrum* richly decorated with gilt and niello inlay was found at Kaiseraugst (no. 4); it stands on a tripod and takes the form of a six-sided column surmounted by a horizontal plate and cup with openwork borders. In the cup there is a thin stake for holding a candle. Some silver fittings from very ornate furniture formed part of the Esquiline Treasure. These include the silver-gilt figures of personifications of Rome, Antioch, Constantinople, and Alexandria, which probably adorned the pole-ends of a *sedia gestatoria* or a chair, and two other silver-gilt ornaments in the shape of a forearm holding an upright cylinder surmounted by a pomegranate. A very elaborate folding tripod of the same basic form as the one from Hildesheim was found at Polgardi in Hungary;[4] the legs of the tripod are decorated with griffin-protomai and surmounted by groups of Tritons and Nereids. The tripod is 114 cm. high and weighs 10 kilos;

[1] *BMECA*, no. 396.
[2] Grünhagen, *Gross Bodungen*, 50, fig. 3.
[3] Emery and Kirwan, *Ballana and Qustul*, pl. 66.
[4] *Arch. Ert.*, xlv, 1931, 1 ff.

to judge from the style of the figures, the detail of the chased ornament, and the heavy beaded edges, it dates from the fourth century A.D. There is a silver fragment in the Archaeological Museum in Florence (Inv. no. 2589) which seems to have been part of a chair; it is decorated with hunting scenes in the niello and gilt technique.

There is no really convenient point at which to end this account of classical silver. If the end of the fourth century also marks the end of the true spirit of pagan antiquity, the pagan traditions in iconography and style lived on in the decoration and design of vessels made for Christian usage. The Diana dish in Berlin has been mentioned as a work of the fourth century A.D. but in style and character it is difficult to distinguish from plates with pagan subjects which are known from their Byzantine control marks to have been made in the sixth century A.D. Many echoes of earlier types and conscious archaising occur among the masterpieces of Byzantine silver work during the sixth and seventh centuries. Classical models continue to serve as a source of inspiration and the techniques discovered and used under the Roman Empire continue to be practised in the centuries following the collapse of the Roman world.

Appendix I

THE TREASURE OF TRIER

The Treasure of Trier referred to on p. 18 was discovered in 1628 and melted down; the following account of the discovery with descriptions of some of the pieces was published in the *Epitome annalium Treverensium* 1676.[1]

'Quo tempore Societatis Jesu domus Probationis Treveris magno aucta Novitiorum numero, et alimentis impar, divini numinis providentia reconditum in horti agro per Tyrones suffosso thesaurum, necessitati levandae invenit. Vas lapideum inter eruta fodientium rudera compertum, quod submoto operculo, cibariam claudere supellectilem visum. Lances in hac magnae ex argento fuere decem, illusae auro, variisque emblematum ex antiquitate figuris, una grandior XXIV librarum effigiem in umbilico Caesarei capitis, alia venationem sparsis etiam ferarum per marginem formis exhibebat, cum inscriptione AVDENTIA NICETIO. Tertia binas facies viri ac feminae in medio sociabat, ut connubiale donum fuisse autumen. Quarta in umbilico pugiles, in margine alia gentilium aenigmata complectebatur. Praeter has decem, octo aliae lances concavae poeticis intus emblematibus, foris parergis illustratae; tum situla aureis hominum ferarumque simulacris aspera, disci recentioris operis gemini, quorum caelati margines quatuor sibi opposita exhibuere capita, cum epigraphe *Petrus et Paulus: Justus et Hermes*, ut priora sub gentilibus, haec sub Christianis, et illa quidem nuptialibus *Audentiae et Nicetii* muneribus destinata viderentur. Minora ex argento vasa omisero, universa suppellex ad ducentas quinquaginta libras pervenit, et quatuor imperialium milibus aestimata suo fuit pondere: maius longe habitura pretium, si integra cum figuris suis Principum manus pervenisset cum temere liquatione transfusa sit, ut *praesenti necessitati* consuleretur *quae optimi non semper consilii est capax*.'

From this description it seems likely that the hoard was buried in the fourth century but contained several pieces of the third century.

[1] Quoted in F. Wieseler, *Der Hildesheimer Silberfund*, Bonn, 1868, 4.

Appendix II

LIST OF DECORATED DRINKING-CUPS OF THE HELLENISTIC–ROMAN CLASS

TYPE	PROVENANCE	MUSEUM	PUBLICATION
deep cup: myrtle ornament	Alesia	St-Germain-en-Laye	*Mon. Piot.* 9, 1902, 179
deep cup: Orestes & Athena	Anzio	Rome, Corsini Palace	A. Michaelis, *Der Corsinische Silbergefässe*
various	Berthouville	Paris, Cabinet des Médailles	Babelon, *Berthouville*
shallow cup: leaf ornament	Bori (Georgia)	Tiflis	*CR*, 1908, 183-4
various	Boscoreale	Louvre	*Mon. Piot*, 5, 1895
kantharos: Triumph of Dionysos	Egypt	Walters Art Gallery, Baltimore	*AA*, 1907, 358 ff.
conical beaker: Erotes deep cup: plane branches	Eretria	Louvre	de Ridder, *Bijoux*, 1927 & 1930
cup: sea horses	Gosławice (Wichulla)	Warsaw	Majewski, *Importy*, pl. XXXIV
2 deep cups: ivy leaf ornament	Herculaneum	Naples	Spinazzola, 234
various	Hildesheim	Hildesheim	Pernice & Winter, *Hildesheim*

List of Decorated Drinking-Cups

TYPE	PROVENANCE	MUSEUM	PUBLICATION
2 cups: Homeric scenes	Hoby	Copenhagen	*Nordiske Fortidsminder*, ii, 1923, 119 ff.
cup: olive branches & fruit; other cups and fragments	Hockwold, Suffolk	London, British Museum	Toynbee, *Art in Britain*, 301 ff.
shallow cup: Homeric scene	Ingolstadt	Munich	*RM*, 67, 1960, 111 ff.
deep cup: religious scene	Lyon	Lyon	*RA*, vii, 1936, 46–53
deep cup: Judgment scene	Meroe	Boston	*BMFA*, 23, 1925, 10
deep cup: erotic scenes	Palestine	London Market 1963	*AK*, 6, 1963
2 deep cups: Centaurs	Pompeii	Naples	nos. 25376–7
deep cup: Tritons & Nereids	Pompeii	Naples	*BdA*, 7, 1927–8, 433 ff.
2 tall beakers: Isiac scenes	Pompeii	Naples	*NS*, 1939, pls. XII–XIII
various	Pompeii, Casa del Menandro	Naples	Maiuri, *Casa del Menandro*
various	Pompeii & Herculaneum	Naples	Spinazzola; Pesce, *Oreficeria*
kantharos: Bacchic subjects	Stevensweert	Amsterdam, Library of Dutch Academy	*Mon. Piot*, 46, 1952, 44
deep cups: storks *modiolus*: satyrs, masks, etc.	Vize (E. Thrace)	Istanbul	*Bull. Inst. Bulg.*, xii–xiii, 1938–9, 154–189
straight-sided cup: vine leaves	Farnese Coll.	Naples	Spinazzola, 237
straight-sided cup: vine leaves	Blacas Coll.	London, British Museum	*BMCP*, no. 82, pl. 11

Appendix II

TYPE	PROVENANCE	MUSEUM	PUBLICATION
kantharos: Orestes, Pylades & Iphigeneia pair of deep cups: floral ornament	Not known	London, British Museum	*BMQ*, xxiii, 1961, 77 ff.
deep cup: Bacchic scenes	Not known: found with above	Toledo Museum of Art	*AK*, 6, 1963
deep cup: plane-branches & leaves	Bought in Milan	Oxford, Ashmolean Museum (no. EF. B200)	*Mon. Piot.*, 46, 1952, 44
2 deep cups: storks	Not known	New York, Pierpont Morgan Library	G.M.A. Richter, *Art in America*, iv, 1918, 171 ff.
shallow two-handled cup: Dionysos on hippocamp	Not known	Belgrade	*RA*, 1903 (1) 18
fragment from a cup (?): scene of the cult of Artemis	Not known	Bologna, Museo Civico	*Ori e Argenti dell'Emilia Antica*, no. 303

Appendix III

ANALYSES OF ANCIENT SILVER PLATE

Mycenae, Shaft Grave; Schliemann, *Mycenae*, p. 368 ff.	Part of a vase	Silver 95·59 per cent, Gold 0·30 per cent, Copper 3·23 per cent, Lead 0·44 per cent, Iron 0·12 per cent
Enkomi, Cyprus; Schaeffer, *Enkomi-Alasia* I, 384	Inlaid bowl	Silver 86·5 per cent, Copper 9 per cent, Gold 3·4 per cent
British Museum; *BMQ*, xxviii, 1964, 95–101	Head-vase, fourth century B.C.	Silver 97 per cent, Copper 2·5 per cent ± 0·3 per cent
British Museum; *BMQ*, xxiii, 1961, 77 ff.	Cup, Augustan	Silver 98 per cent
Hildesheim; Wieseler, *Hildesheimer Silberfund*, 9	Part of a cup	Silver 94·78, Gold 3·18, Copper 1·92 per cent
Gideon N. Stieff Coll.; *Fogg Private Collections*, no. 322	'Saucepan' 1st C. A.D.	Silver 95·76 per cent, Gold and Copper present
British Museum; Crowland, 'The Metals in Antiquity' in *JRAI*, 1912, 235-7	'Saucepan'	Silver 95·76 per cent, Copper 3·44 per cent, Gold 0·47 per cent, Lead 0·33 per cent
Wroxeter; D. Atkinson, *Report on Excavations at Wroxeter*, Oxford, 1942, p. 196 ff.	Mirror	Silver 86·6 per cent, Copper 12·2 per cent, Lead 1·2 per cent
Svirkovo (Bulgaria); *Archeologiya*, iii, 1961, p. 47 ff.	Licinius dish	Silver 97 per cent
Cesena (Bolognese); *Annuario*, viii–x, 1946–8, 309 ff.	Niello dish	Silver 95–96 per cent, Copper 1–2 per cent, other metals 1–2 per cent

Mildenhall; Brailsford, p. 16	Dish	Silver 95·3 per cent, Copper 2·3 per cent, Gold 0·5 per cent
Traprain Law; Curle, *Traprain*, p. 92 ff.	(1) 'odd fragment'	Silver 94·08 per cent, Copper 4·97 per cent
	(2) No. 28	Silver 96·2 per cent
	(3) No. 87	Silver 95·3 per cent
Corbridge Hoard; Toynbee, *Art in Roman Britain*, 172	The *lanx*	Silver 92·6 per cent
Great Horwood; unpublished: information from Miss Helen Waugh	Beaker	Silver 93·6 per cent, Gold 1·00 per cent, Lead 1·0 per cent (approx.), Copper 4·4 per cent

Appendix IV

THE FINDS FROM DHERVENI

A number of fine silver vessels made in the late fourth century B.C. were discovered recently in tombs at Dherveni in Macedonia.[1] They are now in the new Museum at Salonika and have not yet been published in detail. Among the finds are a duck's head ladle of the early Hellenistic type with shallow bowl, and a strainer with two horizontal duck's head handles opposite one another, like the example in the Walters Art Gallery. The bowl of the strainer is framed by a chased and gilded wreath of leaves. The finds also included two leaf-phialai, very similar to the one from Akarnania in New York, and four Achaemenid deep-bowls – two plain ones with tall upper section and two squatter examples which are richly decorated. On both the decorated examples the lower part of the body is reeded and surmounted by decorated mouldings consisting of a guilloche and a cyma reversa. Each has a rosette at the bottom on the outside and an appliqué medallion-head in high relief on the inside; a fine Medusa head appears on one and a head of Silenus on the other.

The Dherveni finds also contained a good example of a type of jug which seems to have been popular in the period. The type is characterised by an ovoid body and a tall neck with splayed rim, the neck and body being divided by an ovolo moulding. The handle is soldered to the rim and to the body by means of a decorated soldering plate. The form seems to be Achaemenid in origin, the basic shape being similar to that of the Achaemenid amphora with animal handles found at Kukuva Mogila, Duvanli. The Duvanli example has gilded leaf-ornament on the body surmounted by a gilded anthemion. A jug of similar type found at Çastambol in Paphlagonia is decorated with the same scheme as is found on the 'Achaemenid deep bowls' – a row of upright leaves occupying most of the body with two bands of ornament, a guilloche and cyma reversa, above it. Another from Kirklareli in Thrace has a more elaborate design of upright leaves covering most of the body and probably dates from the third century B.C. An example in the Museum of Fine Arts, Boston, was found with one of the 'Achaemenid deep bowls', somewhere in S.W. Asia Minor.[2]

The other vessels from Dherveni include a unique silver askos with spout fitted with a strainer, two tall *kantharoi* like the one from Gornyani (p. 94) with upright cylix handles, and two cylindrical vessels with concave sides fitted with an inner semicircular container which probably served as salt-cellars. There were also three dishes, two large and one small and four bowls which may have been made in a set with the dishes. The dishes have convex rims between narrow mouldings.

[1] *Arch. Rep.*, 1963–4, 19, fig. 21; the find is to be published in *A Delt*, 18. I saw these pieces too late to be able to include them in the main text.

[2] *Greek, Etruscan and Roman Art*, Boston, 1963, 142, figs. 134–5.

Plates

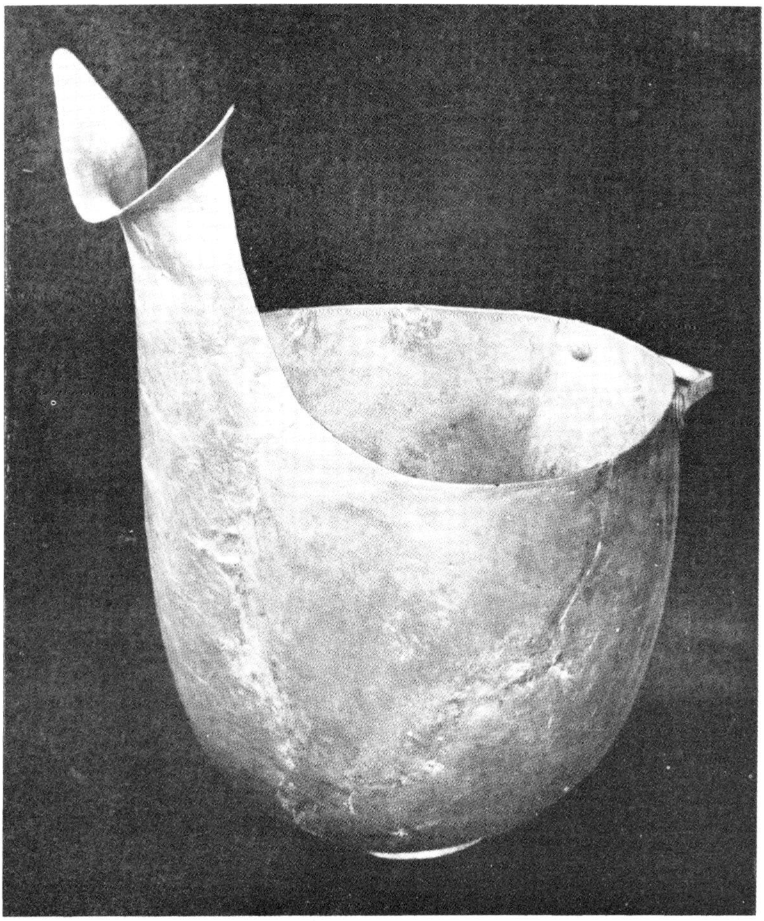

PLATE IA Gold 'sauceboat' from Arcadia; Paris, Musée du Louvre (p. 27). *h* 9·8 cm

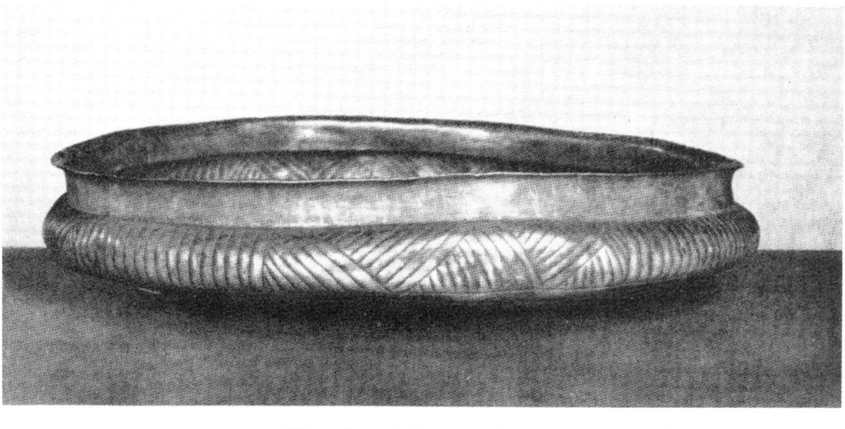

PLATE IB Silver bowl from Euboea; New York, Metropolitan Museum (p. 28). *h* 5·8 cm

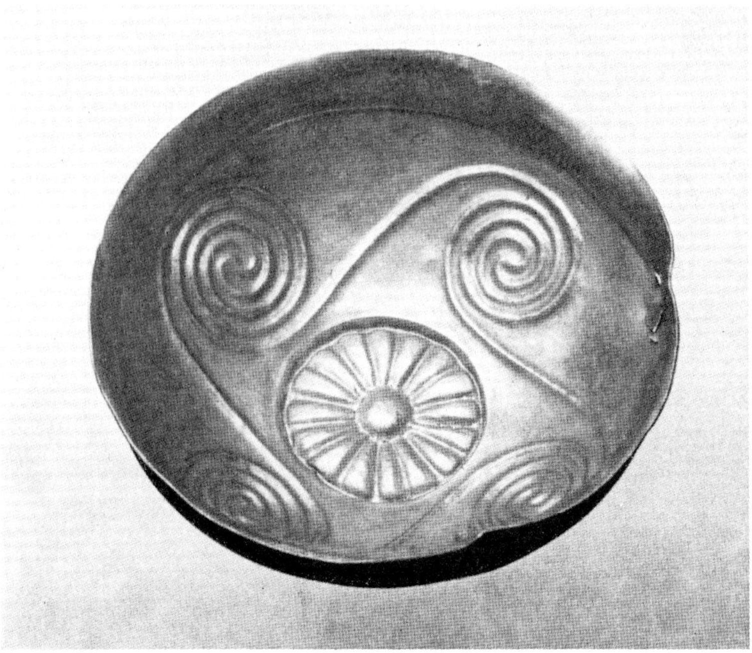

PLATE 2A Gold bowl from the 'Aegina Treasure'; London, British Museum (p. 32). *d* 9·7 cm

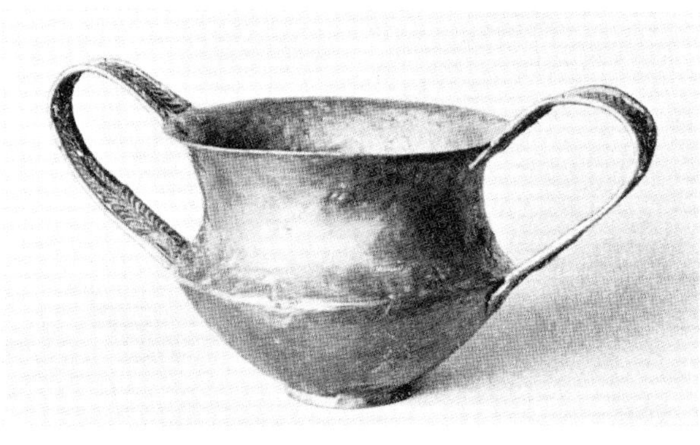

PLATE 2B Gold *kantharos*; New York, Metropolitan Museum (p. 38). *h* 7·3 cm

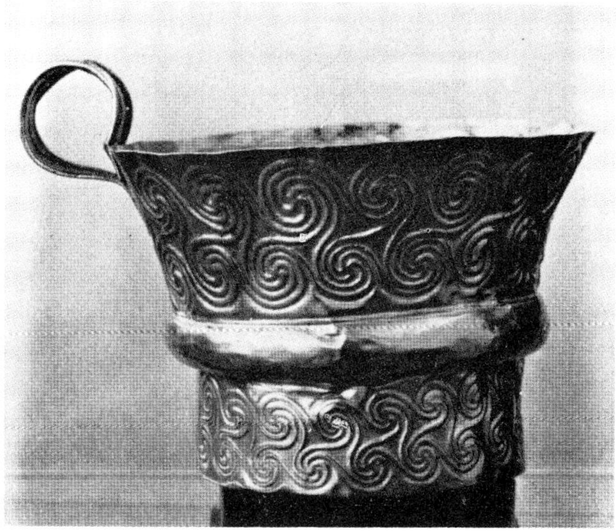

PLATE 3A Gold cup from Shaft Grave V, Mycenae; Athens, National Museum (p. 37). *h* 11 cm

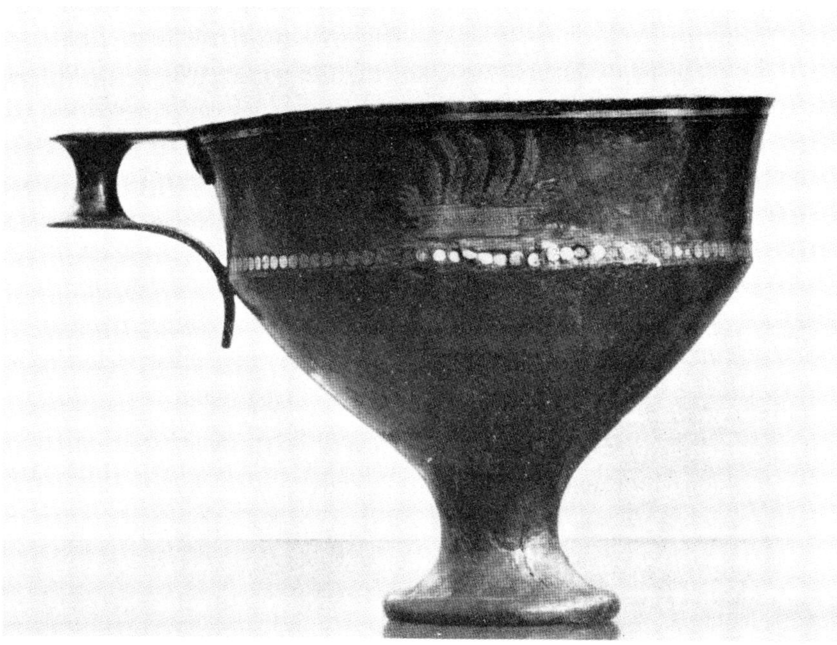

PLATE 3B Silver inlaid cup from Shaft Grave IV, Mycenae; Athens, National Museum (p. 37). *h* 15·5 cm

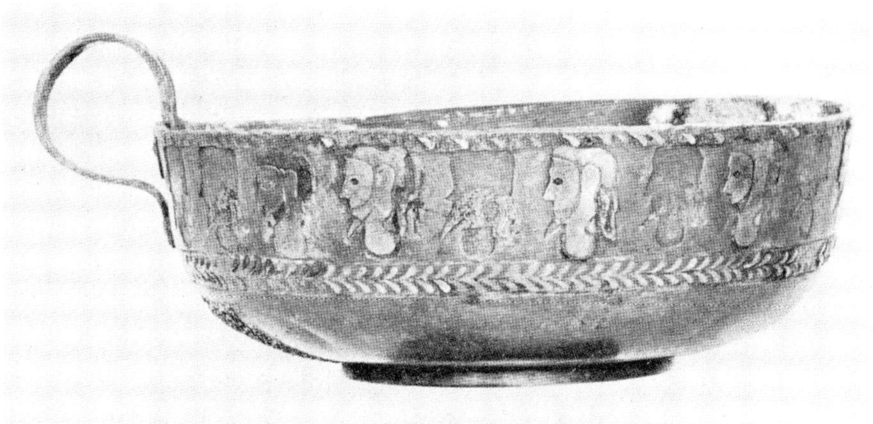

PLATE 6A Silver inlaid cup from Mycenae; Athens, National Museum (p. 50). *d* 15 cm

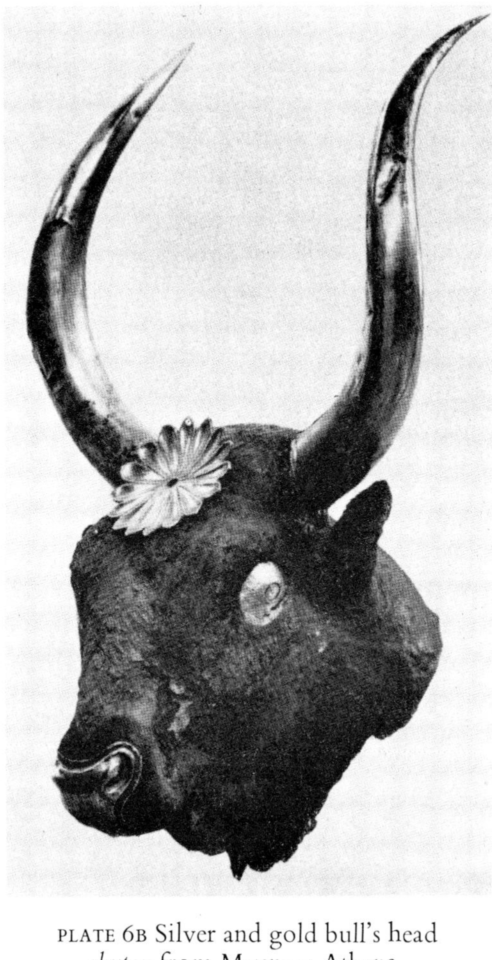

PLATE 6B Silver and gold bull's head *rhyton* from Mycnae; Athens, National Museum (p. 40). *h* 15·5 cm

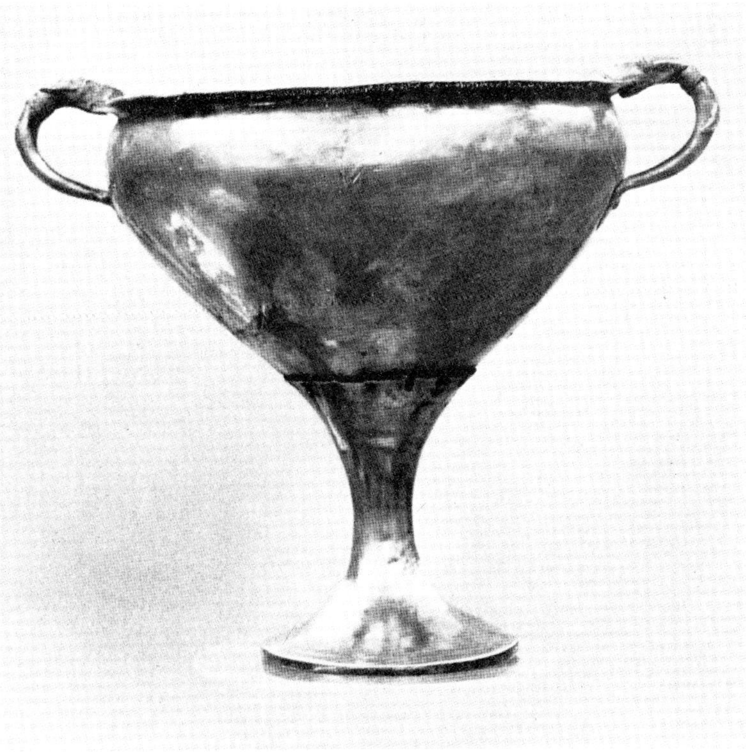

PLATE 7A Gold goblet from Mycenae; Athens, National Museum (p. 50). *h* 15 cm

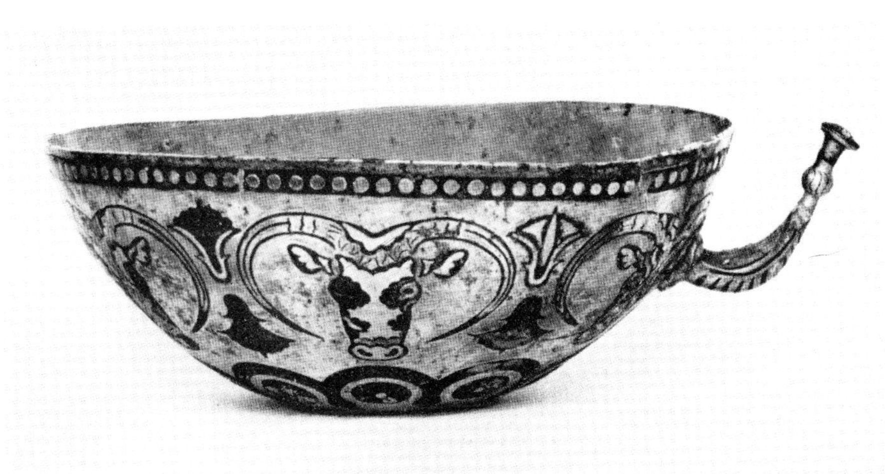

PLATE 7B Silver inlaid bowl from Enkomi, Cyprus; Nicosia, Cyprus Museum (p. 51). *d* 15 cm

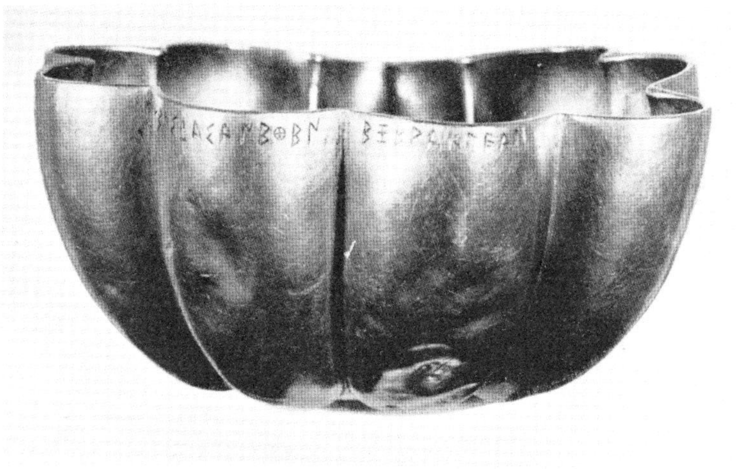

PLATE 8A Gold bowl from Olympia; Boston, Museum of Fine Arts (p. 57). *d* (*max*) 16·8 cm

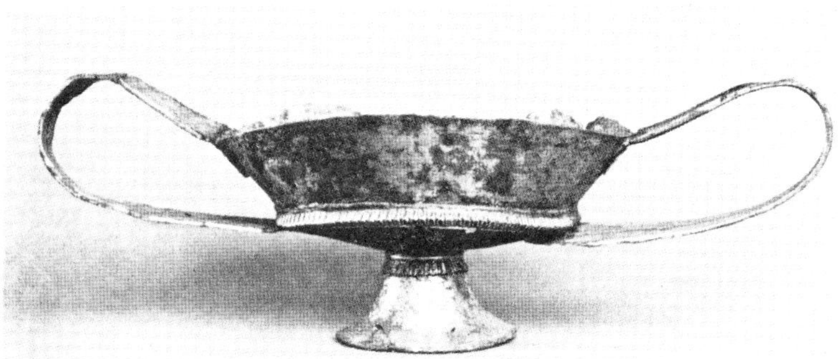

PLATE 8B Silver cup with gold appliqué from Kameiros, Rhodes; Paris, Musée du Louvre (p. 58). *h* 9 cm

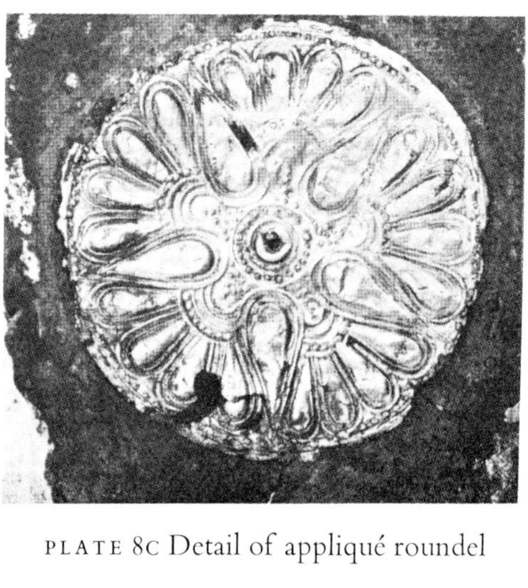

PLATE 8C Detail of appliqué roundel

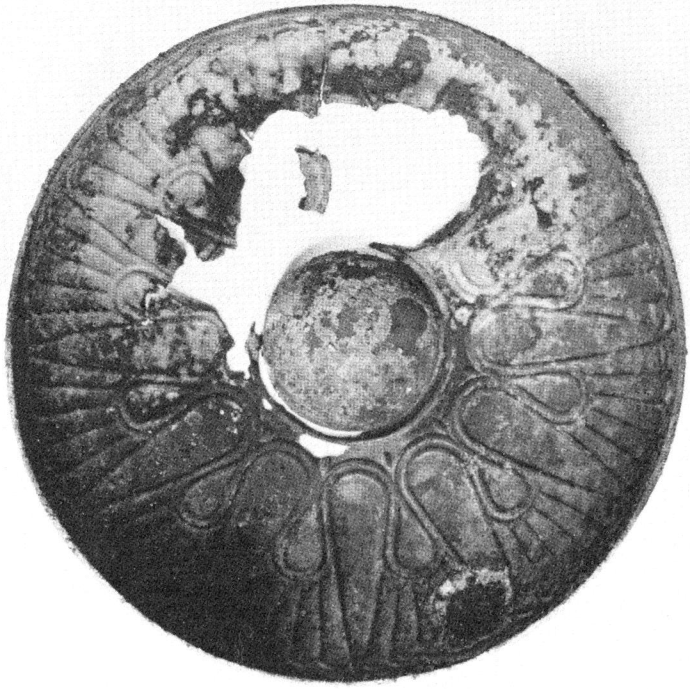

PLATE 9A Silver *phiale mesomphalos* from Asia Minor; Berlin, Staatliche Museen (p. 56). *d* 22·8 cm

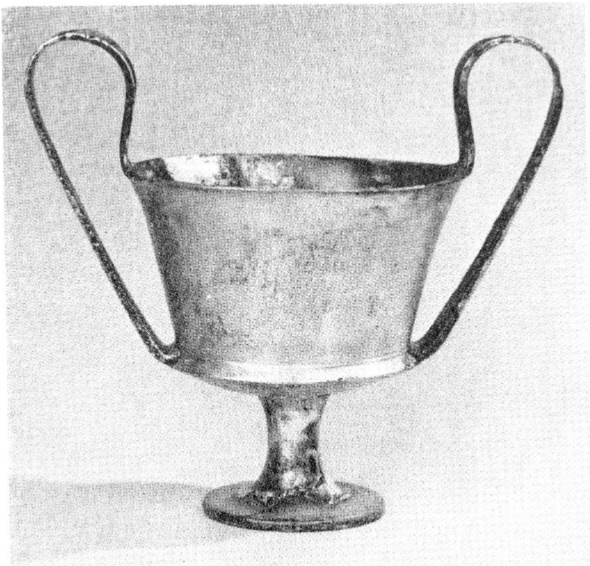

PLATE 9B Silver *kantharos*; Baltimore, Walters Art Gallery (p. 59). *h* 14·5 cm

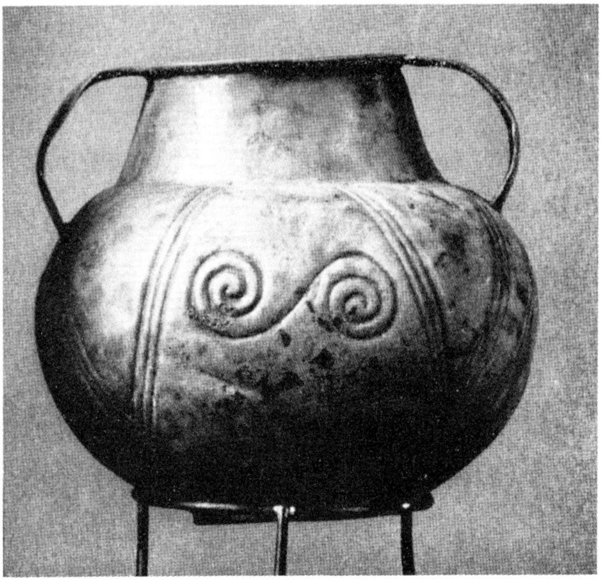

PLATE 10A Silver *amphora* from the Regolini-Galassi Tomb, Caere; Vatican Museums (p. 63). *h* 7·9 cm

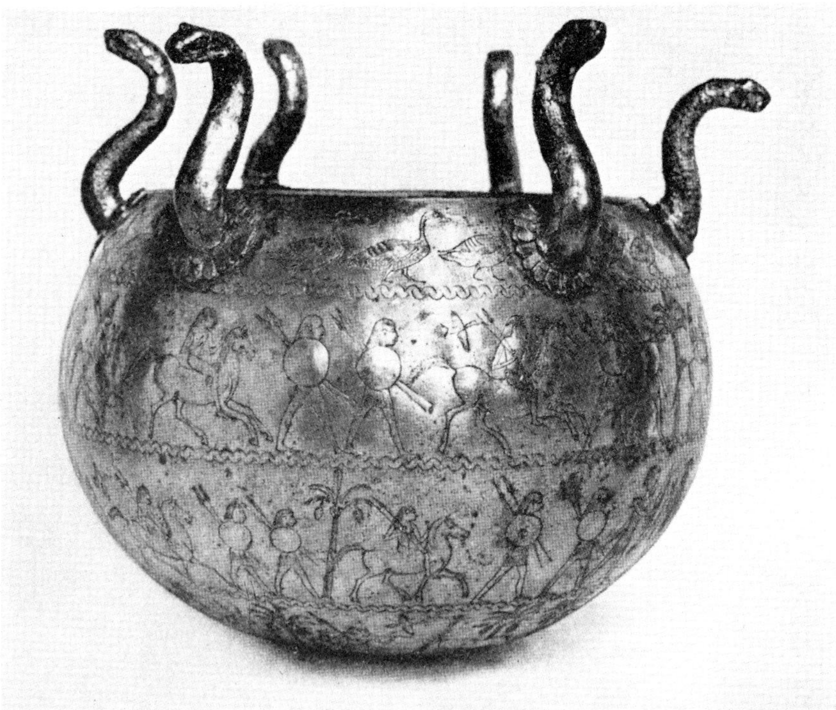

PLATE 10B Silver bowl with snakes' heads from the Bernardini Tomb, Praeneste; Rome, Villa Giulia Museum (p. 68). *h* 14 cm

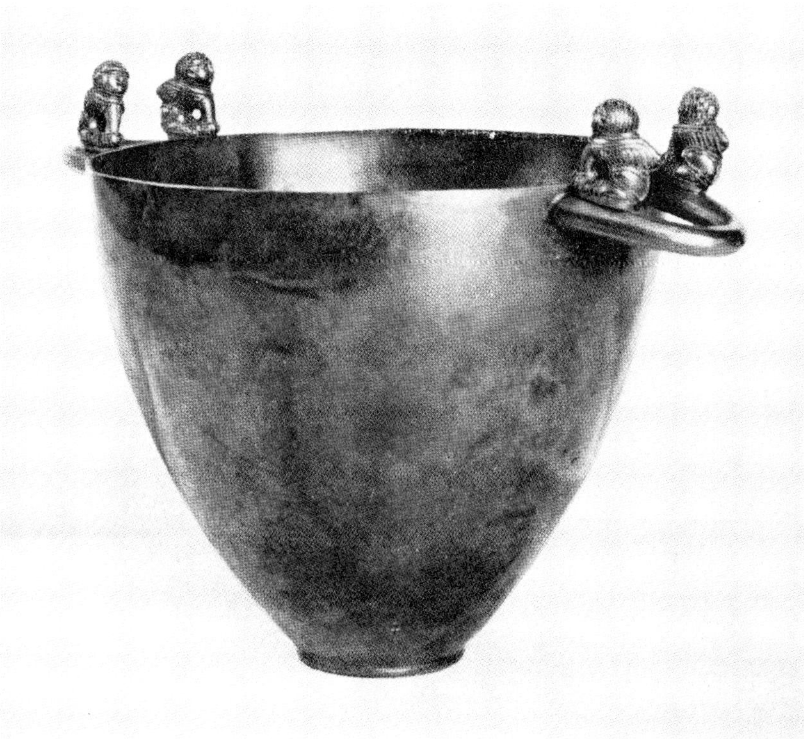

PLATE IIA Gold *skyphos* with sphinxes on the handles from the Bernardini Tomb, Praeneste; Rome, Villa Giulia Museum (p. 65). *d* 9 cm

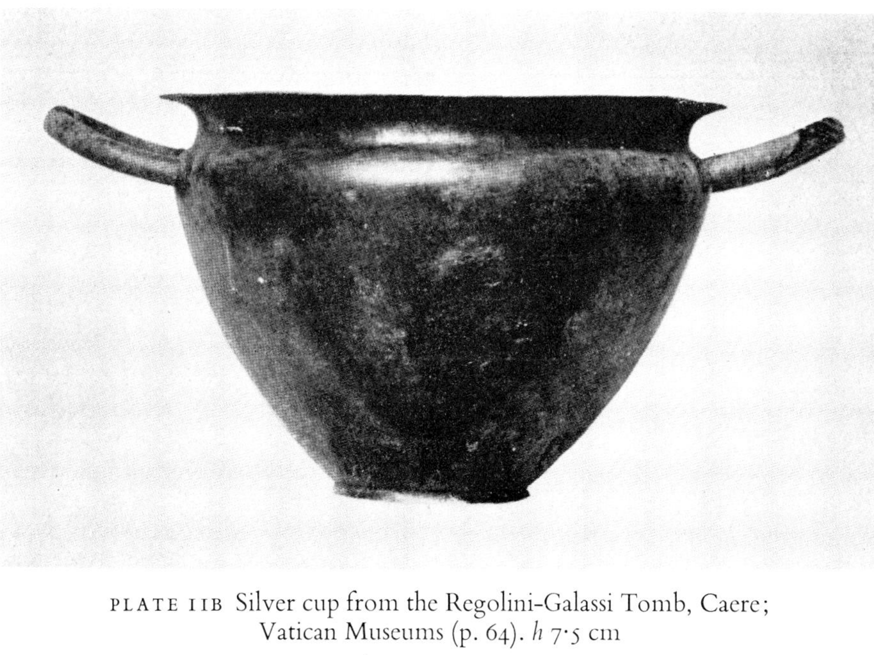

PLATE IIB Silver cup from the Regolini-Galassi Tomb, Caere; Vatican Museums (p. 64). *h* 7·5 cm

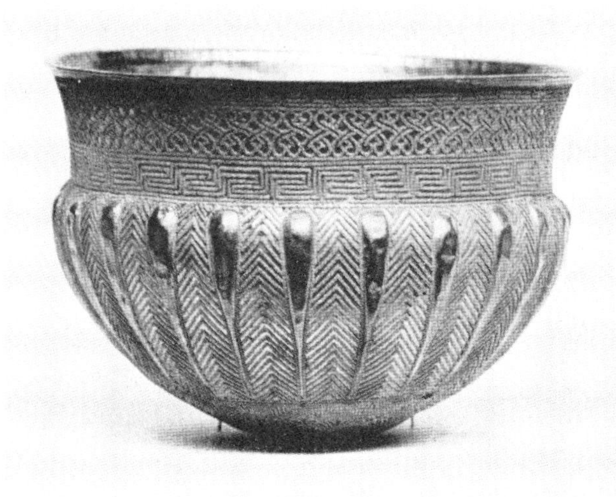

PLATE 12A Gold bowl with granulation ornament; London, Victoria & Albert Museum (p. 65). *h* 6 cm

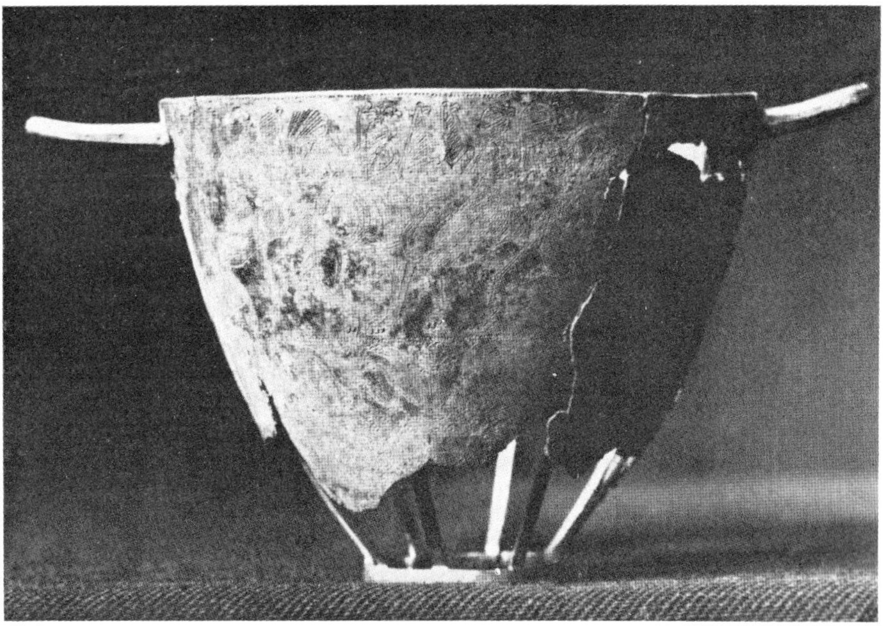

PLATE 12B Silver-gilt cup from Vetulonia; Florence, Archaeological Museum (p. 65). *d* 9 cm

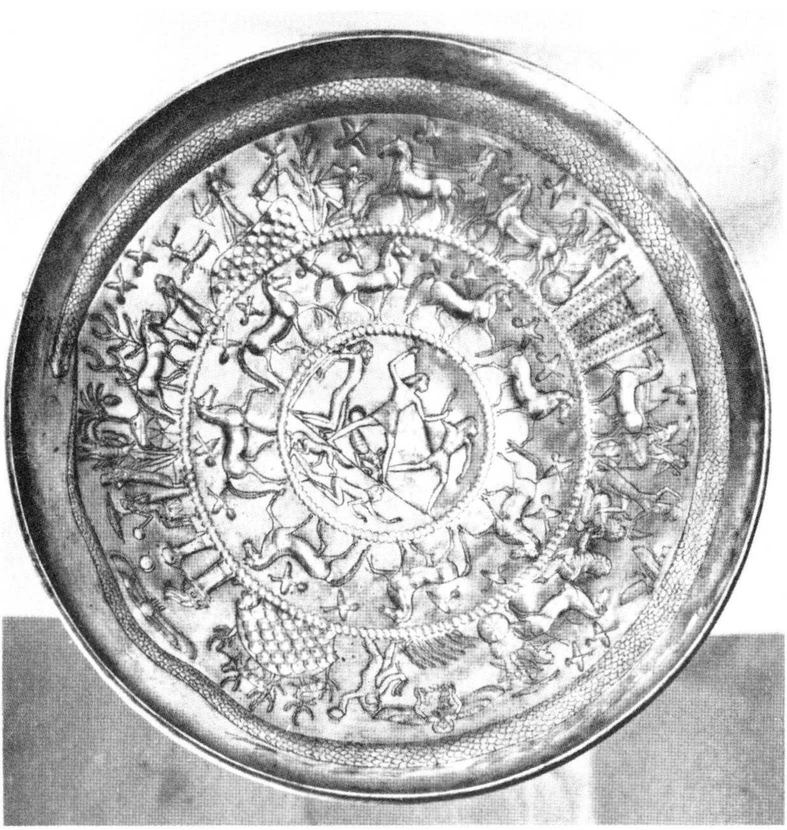

PLATE 13A Silver-gilt bowl from the Bernardini Tomb, Praeneste; Rome, Villa Giulia Museum (p. 66). *d* 19 cm

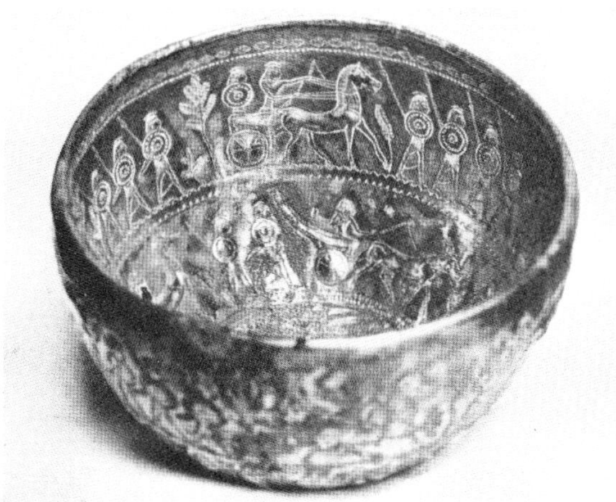

PLATE 13B Silver-gilt bowl from the Regolini-Galassi Tomb, Caere; Vatican Museums (p. 66). *d* 11·2 cm

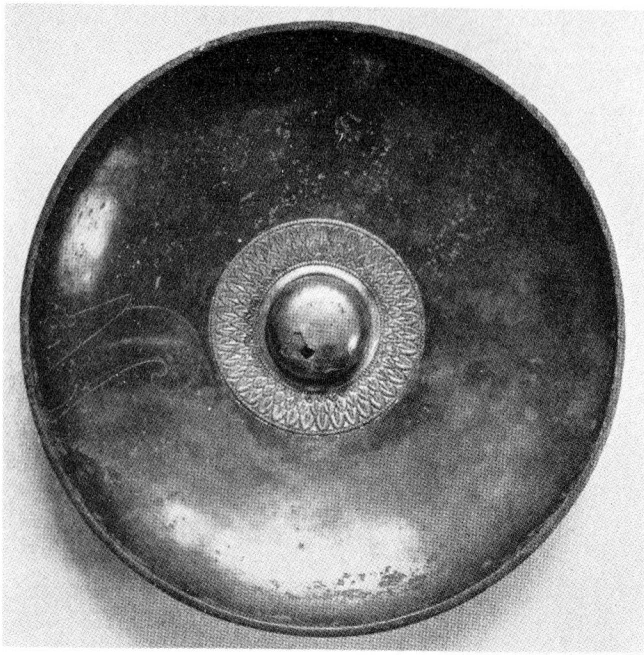

PLATE 14A Silver *phiale mesomphalos* from Maikop; Berlin, Staatliche Museen (p. 75). *d* 16·2 cm

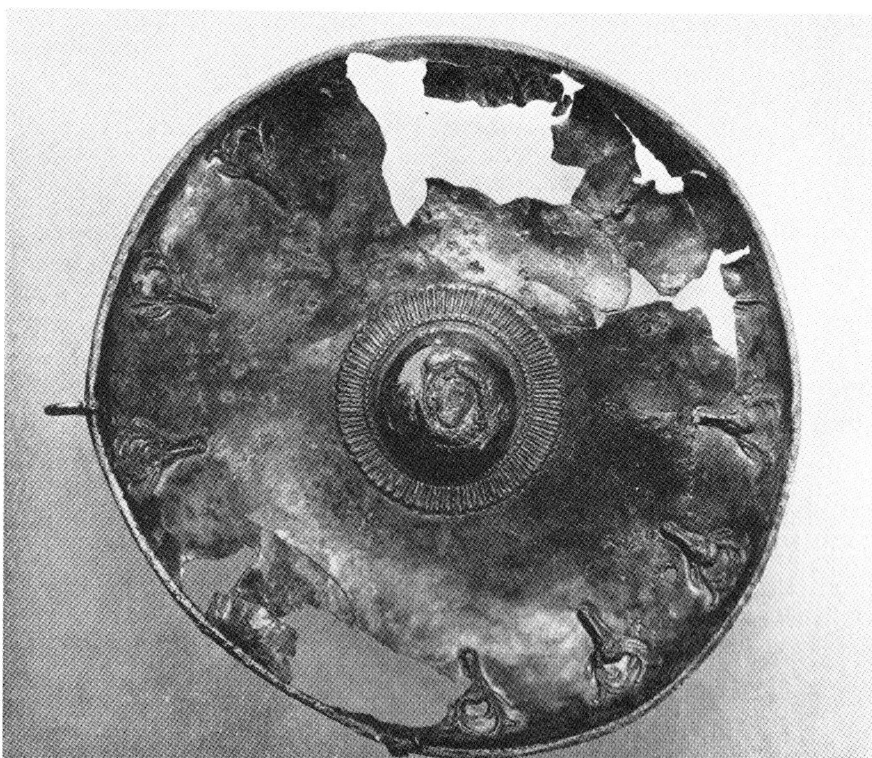

PLATE 14B Silver *phiale mesomphalos* from Zubov's Farm, Kuban; Leningrad, National Hermitage Museum (p. 75). *d* 19·5 cm

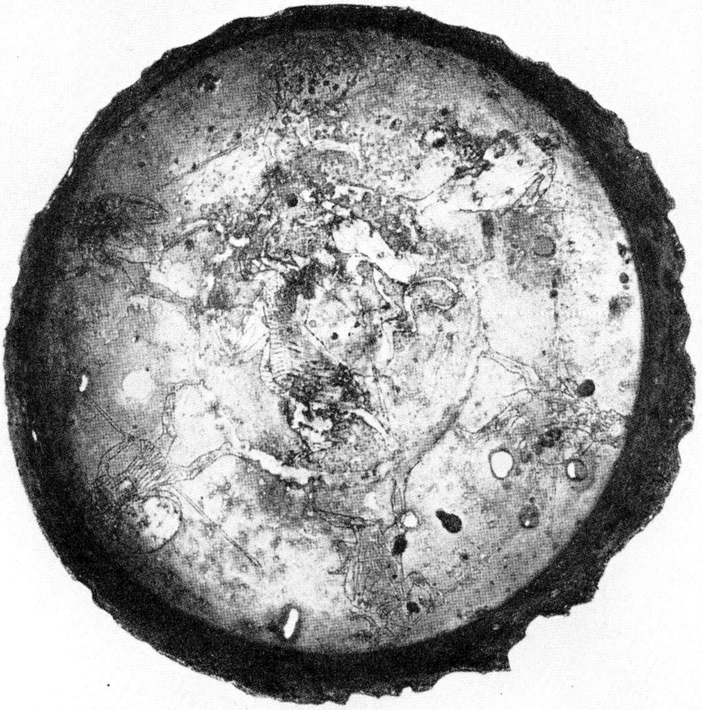

PLATE 15A Interior of silver *kylix* with engraved ornament from the Seven Brothers Tumuli, Kuban; Leningrad, National Hermitage Museum (p. 78)

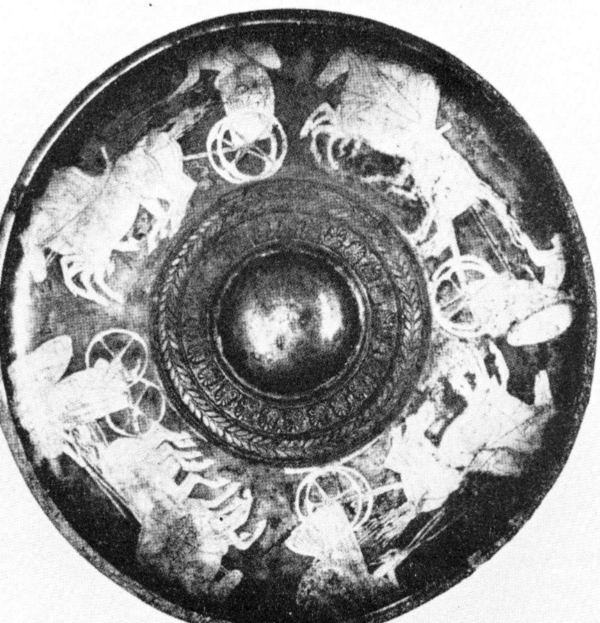

PLATE 15B Silver *phiale mesomphalos* with engraved ornament from Duvanli; Plovdiv Museum (p. 80). *d* 20·5 cm

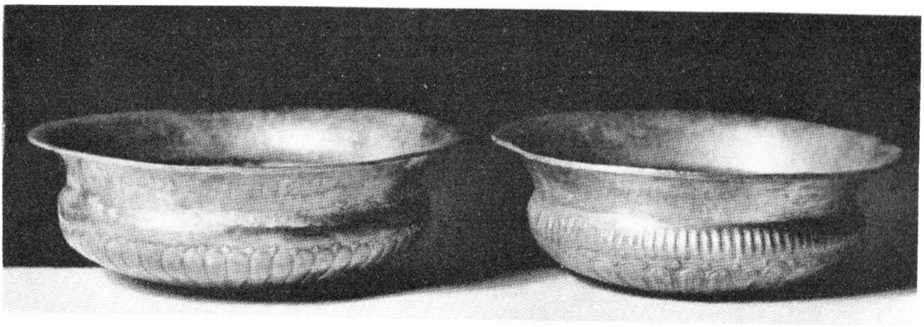

PLATE 16A Silver *phialai* from Alexandrovo; Plovdiv Museum (p. 77)

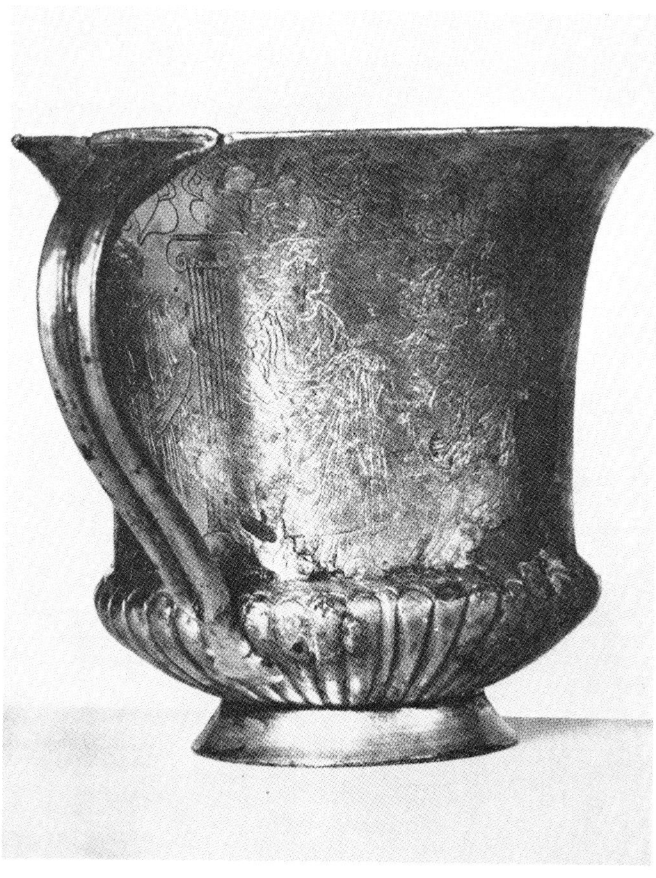

PLATE 16B Silver cup with engraved decoration from Solokha; Leningrad, National Hermitage Museum (p. 79). *h* 9·8 cm

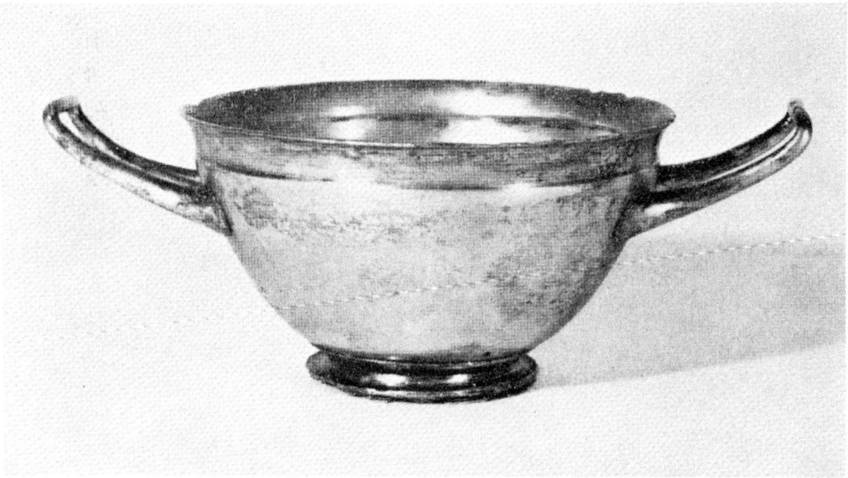

PLATE 17A Silver cup from Nymphaeum near Kerch; Oxford, Ashmolean Museum (p. 85)

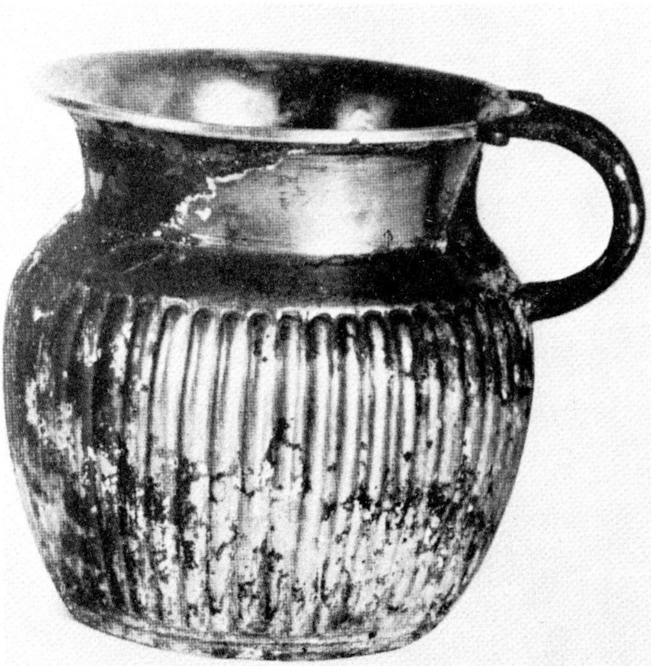

PLATE 17B Silver jug from Duvanli; Plovdiv Museum (p. 84). *h* 8·6 cm

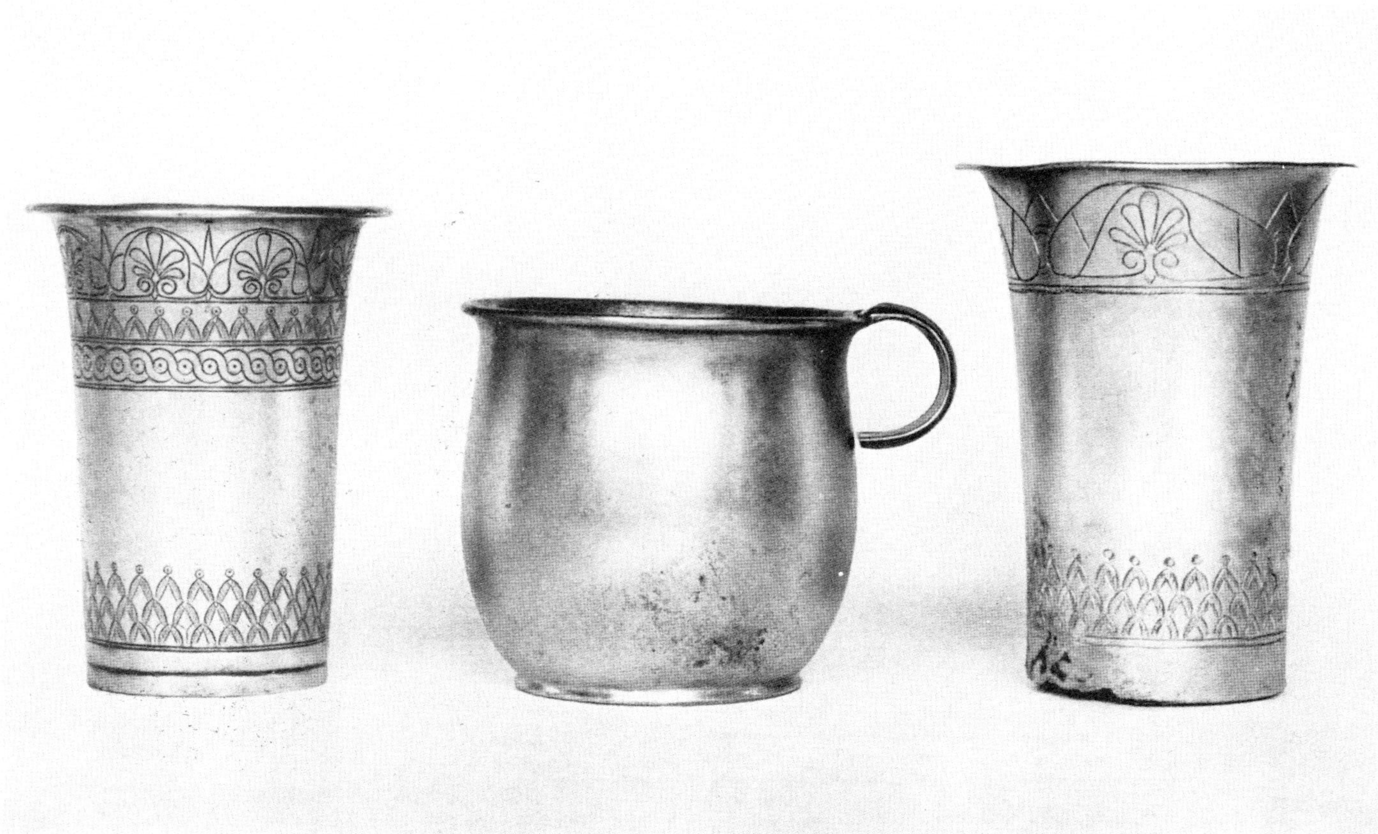

PLATE 18 Three silver vessels from Stara Zagora (Dalboki); Oxford, Ashmolean Museum (p. 85)

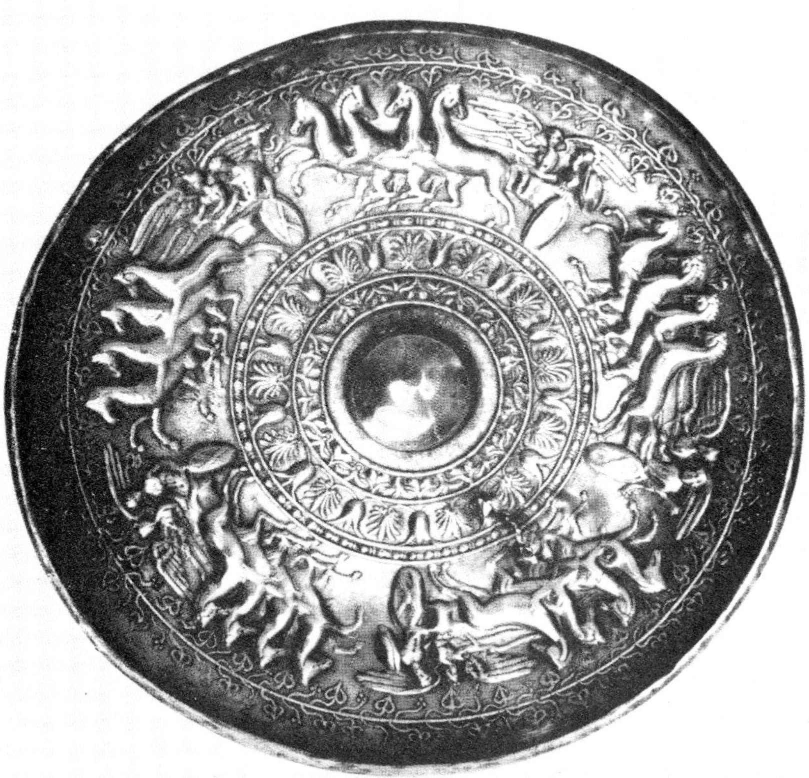

PLATE 19A Silver *phiale mesomphalos* from Èze; London, British Museum (p. 81). *d* 20·6 cm

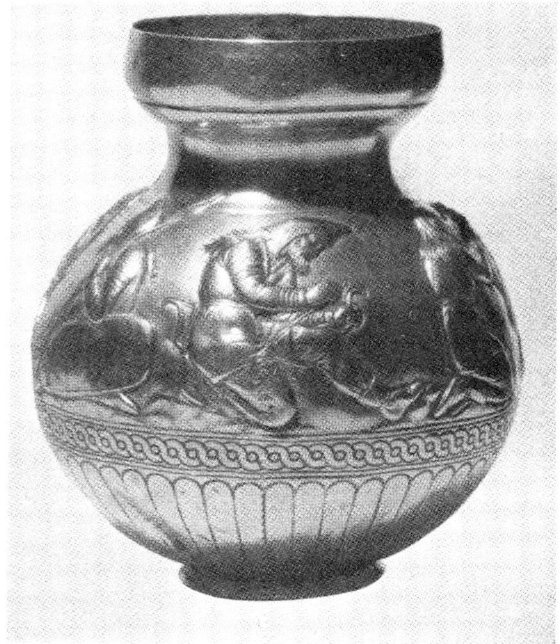

PLATE 19B Gold flask from Kul Oba; Leningrad, National Hermitage Museum (p. 88). *h* 13 cm

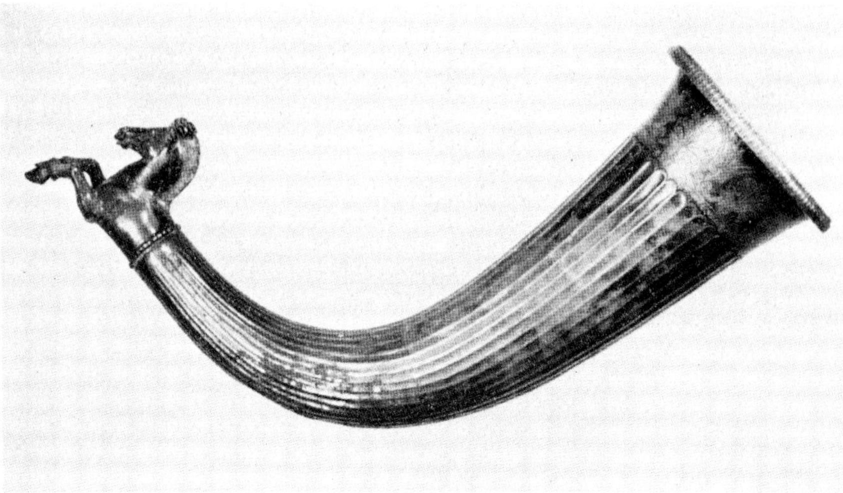

PLATE 20A Silver horn *rhyton* from Duvanli; Plovdiv Museum (p. 86). *h* 20·6 cm

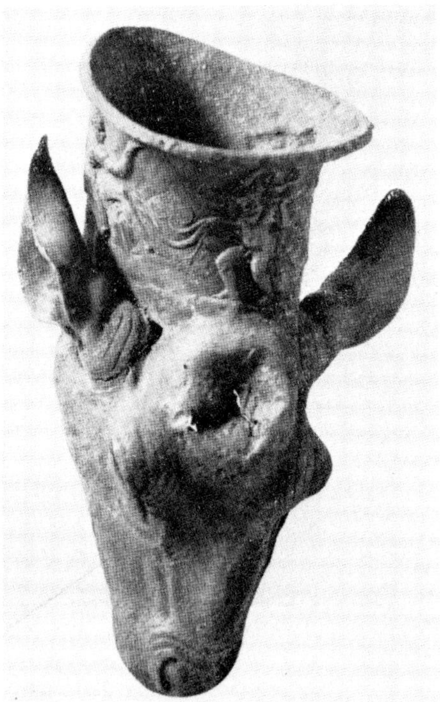

PLATE 20B Silver calf's head cup *rhyton* from Rachmanli; Sofia National Museum (p. 87). *h* 16·3 cm

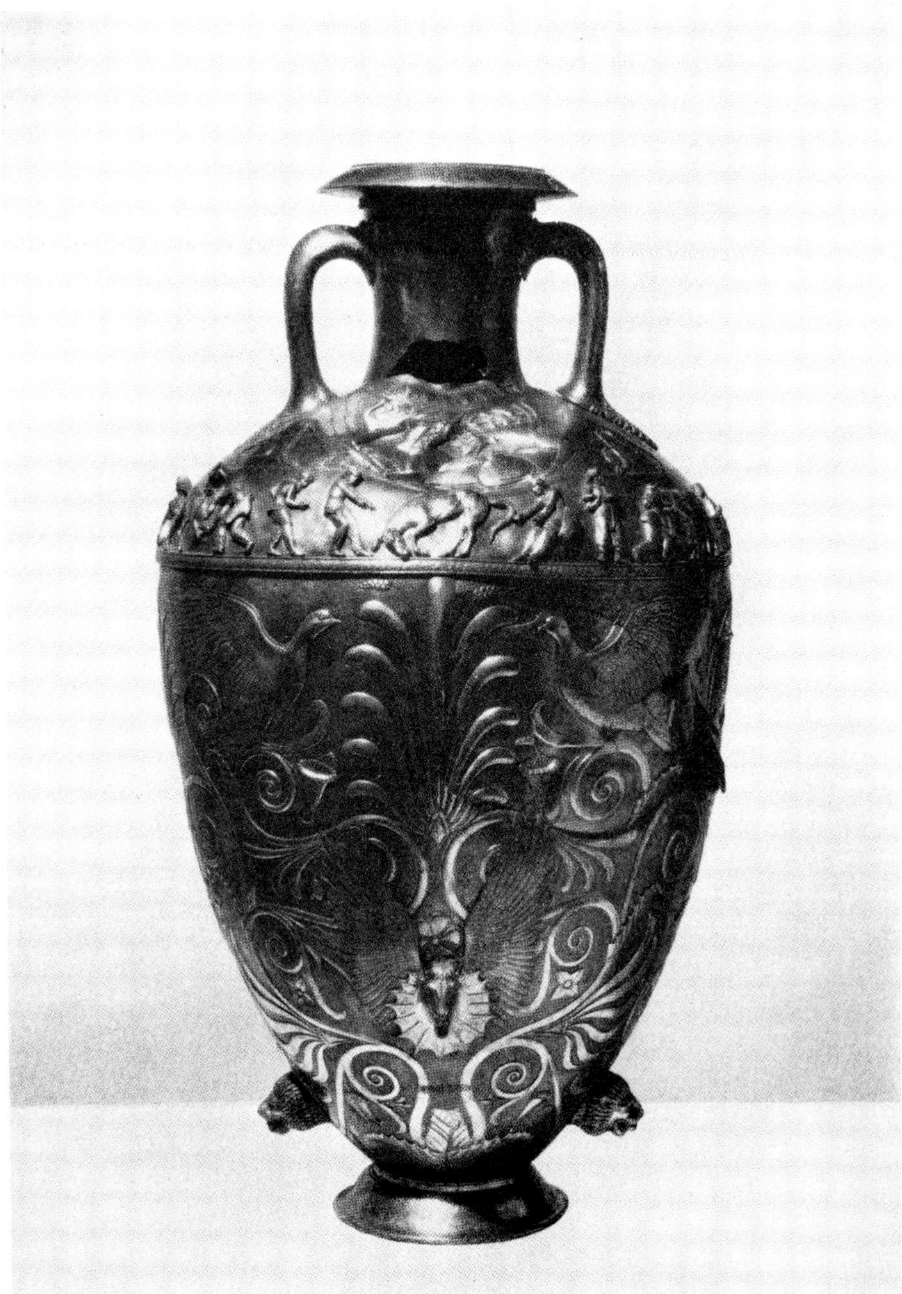

PLATE 21 Silver-gilt *amphora* from Chertomlyk; Leningrad, National Hermitage Museum (p. 88). *h* 70 cm

PLATE 22A Silver ladle from Prusias; New York, Walter C. Baker Collection (p. 92). *l* 28 cm

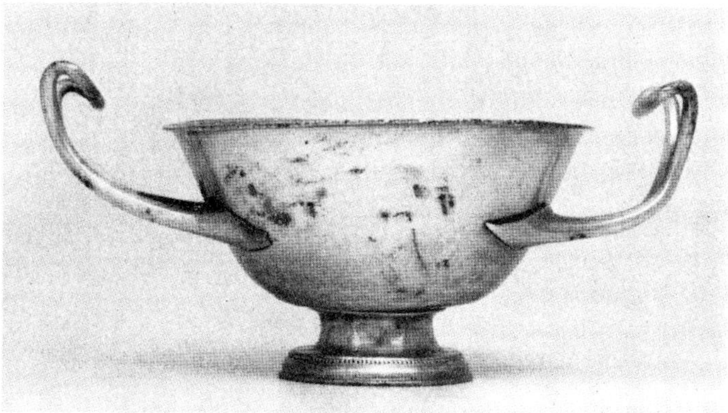

PLATE 22B Silver *kotyle* from Prusias; New York, Walter C. Baker Collection (p. 93). *h* 7 cm

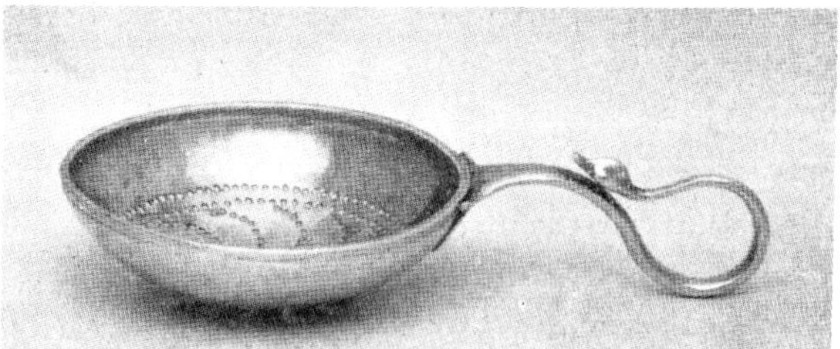

PLATE 22C Silver strainer from Prusias; New York, Walter C. Baker Collection (p. 93). *d* 7·5 cm

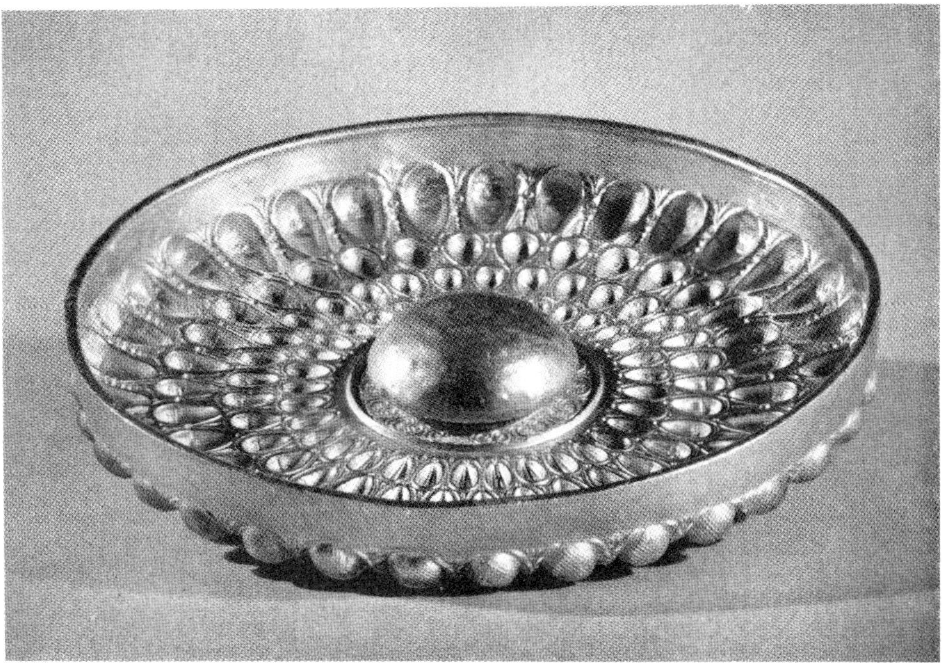

PLATE 23A Gold *phiale mesomphalos*; New York, Metropolitan Museum (p. 97). *d* 22·4 cm

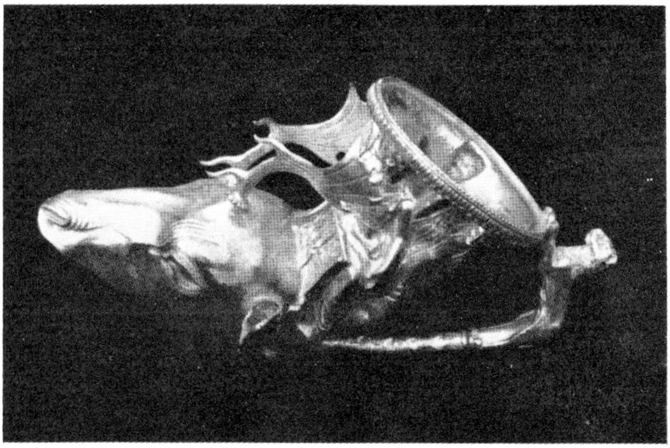

PLATE 23B Gold stag's head vase from Panagyurishte; Plovdiv Museum (p. 102). *h* 13 cm

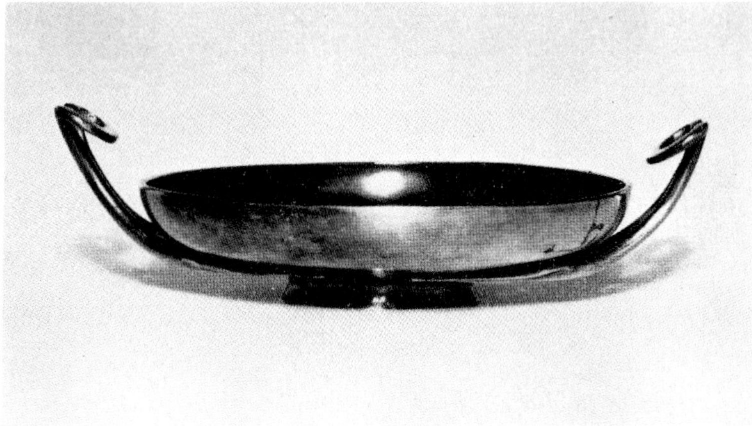

PLATE 24A Silver cup from Montefortino; New York, Metropolitan Museum (p. 94). *d* 11·5 cm

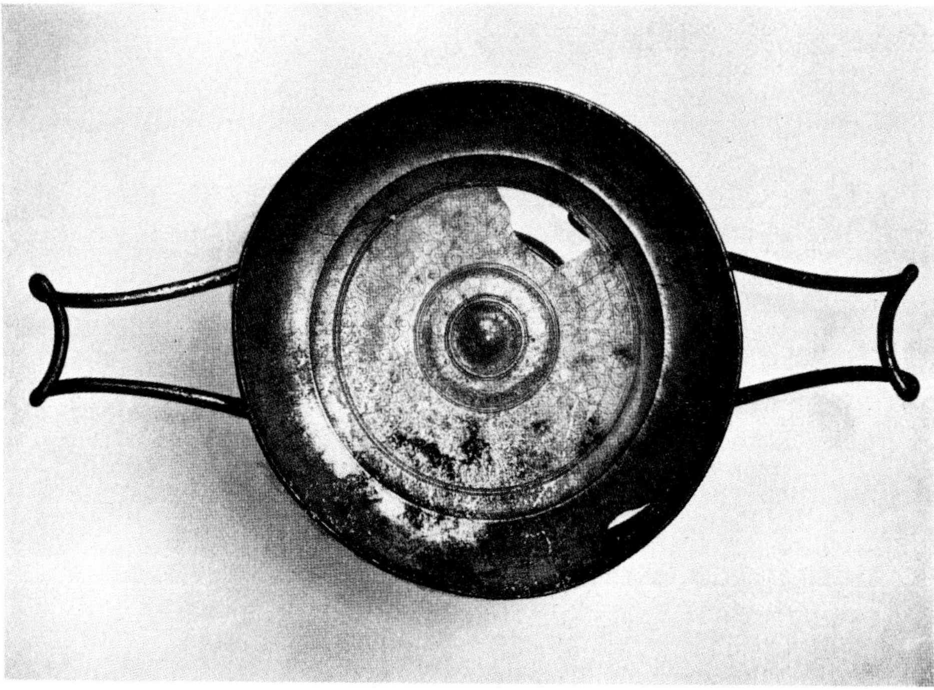

PLATE 24B Interior of silver cup from Paternò; Berlin, Staatliche Museen (p. 94). *d* 13·5 cm

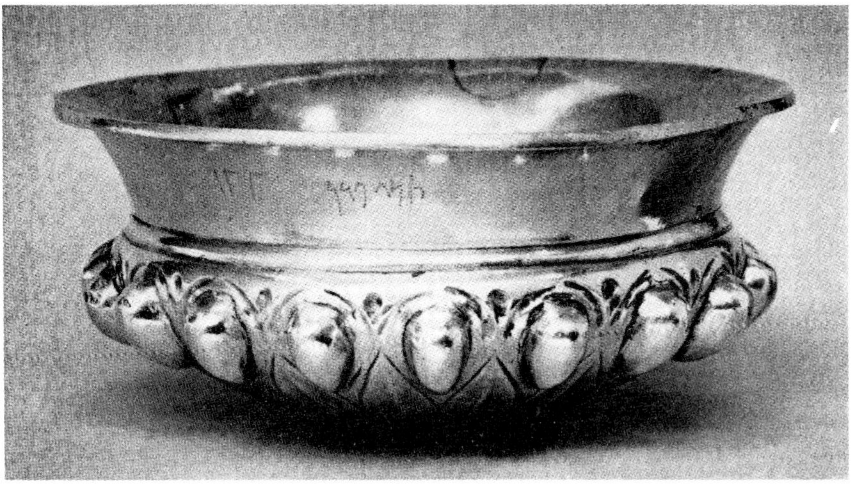

PLATE 25A Silver *phiale*; recently on London Market (p. 99). *d* 14·6 cm

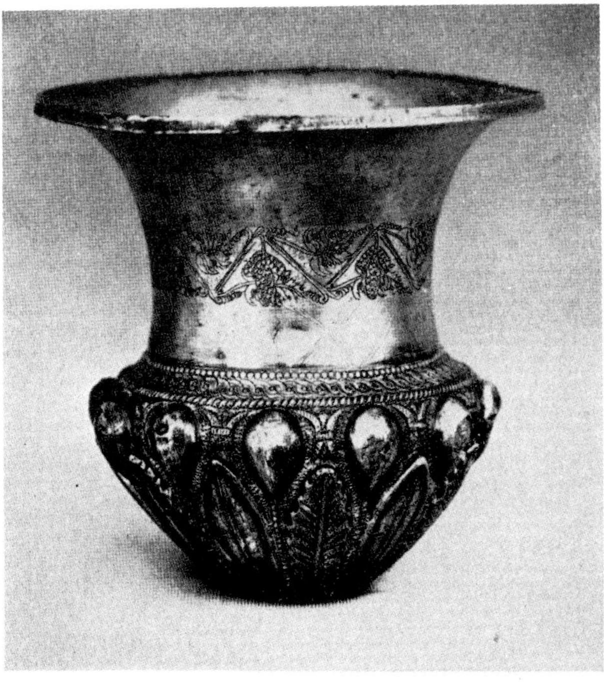

PLATE 25B Silver-gilt vase from Ithaca; London, British Museum (p. 101). *h* 8·6 cm

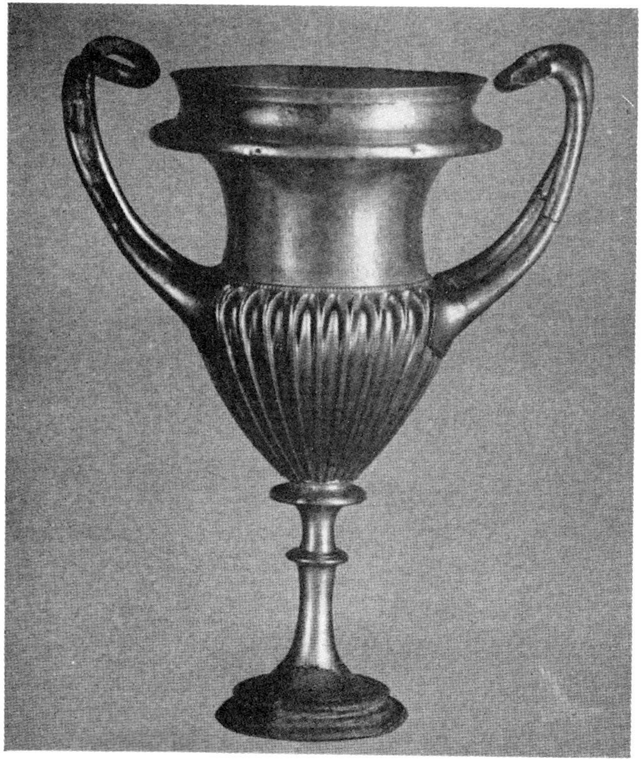

PLATE 26A Silver *kantharos*; Leningrad, National Hermitage Museum (p. 96). *h* 22 cm

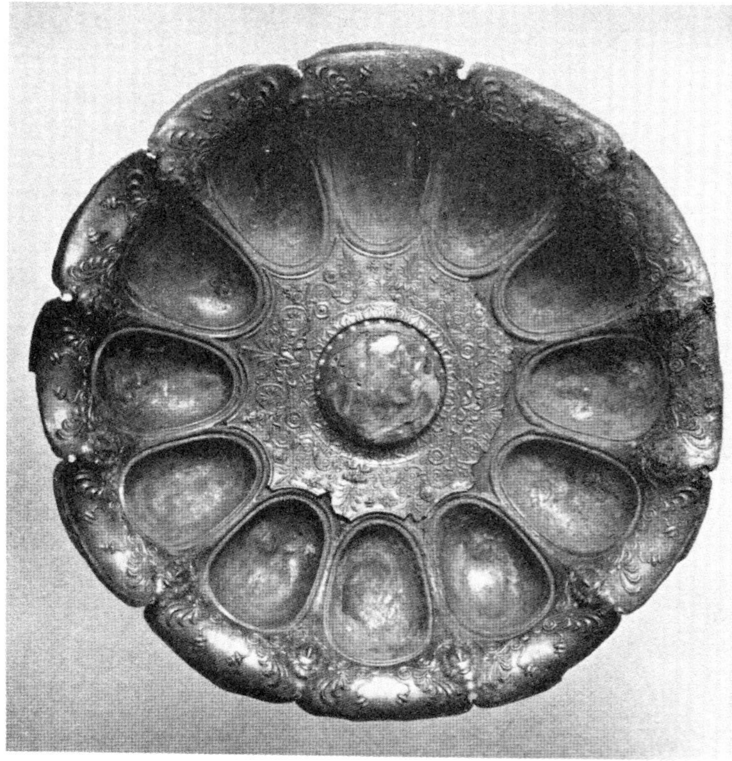

PLATE 26B Silver egg-*phiale* from Paternò; Berlin, Staatliche Museen (p. 98). *d* 24·3 cm

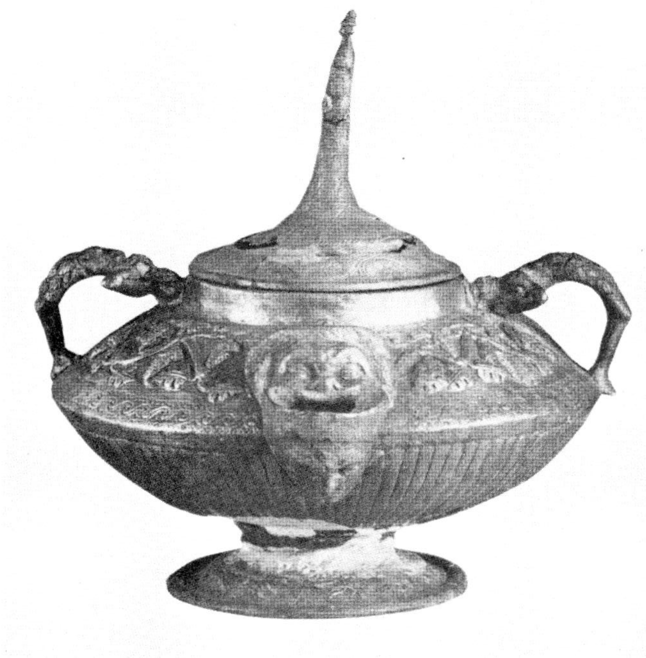

PLATE 27A Silver-gilt vase from Kerch; Leningrad, National Hermitage Museum (p. 105). *h* 14 cm

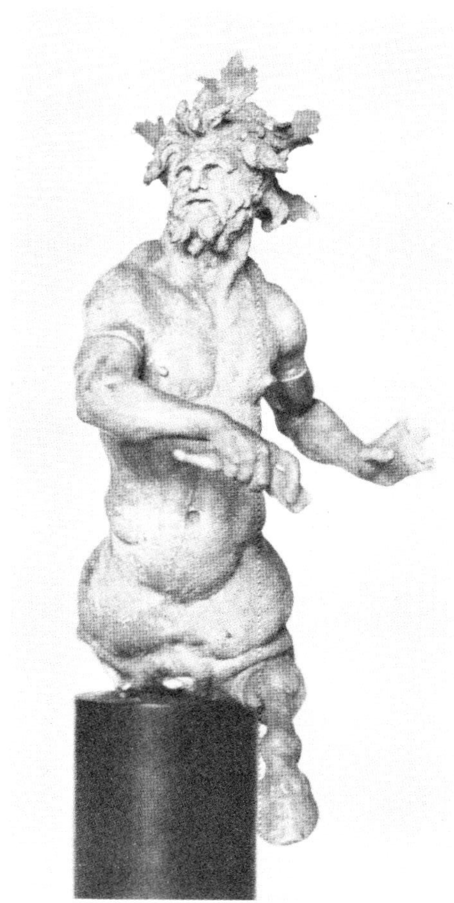

PLATE 27B Silver centaur from a *rhyton*; Vienna, Kunsthistorisches Museum (p. 109). *h* 18·5 cm

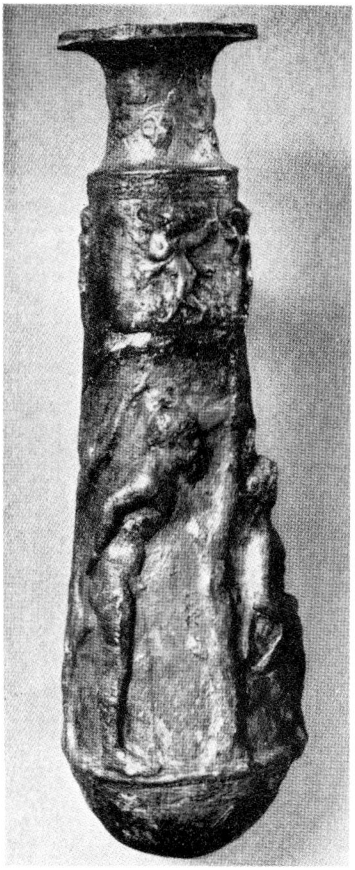

PLATE 32A Silver *alabastron* from Palaiokastron; Athens, National Museum (p. 118). *h* 18·3 cm

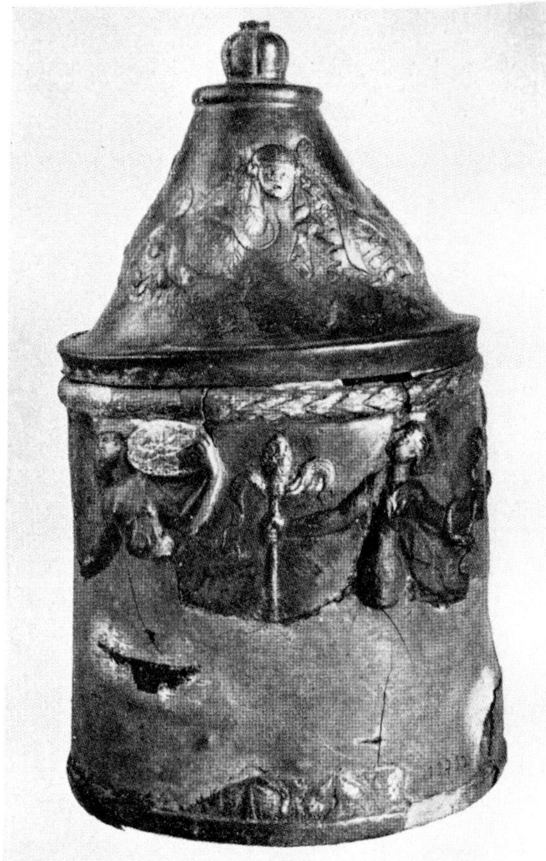

PLATE 32B Silver *pyxis* from Palaiokastron; Athens, National Museum (p. 118). *h* 19·3 cm

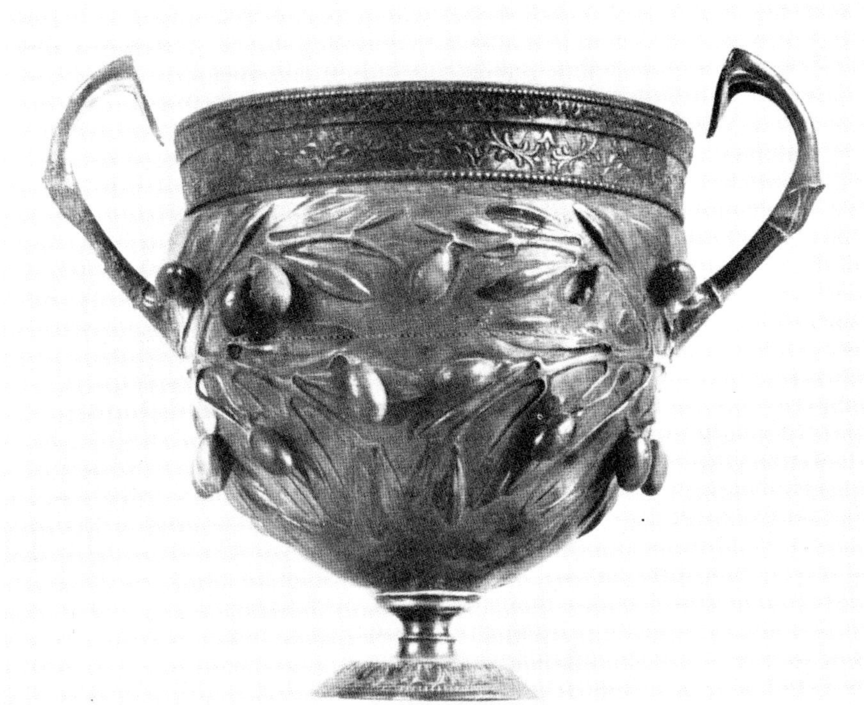

PLATE 33A Silver cup from the Casa del Menandro, Pompeii; Naples, National Museum (p. 135). *h* 12·7 cm

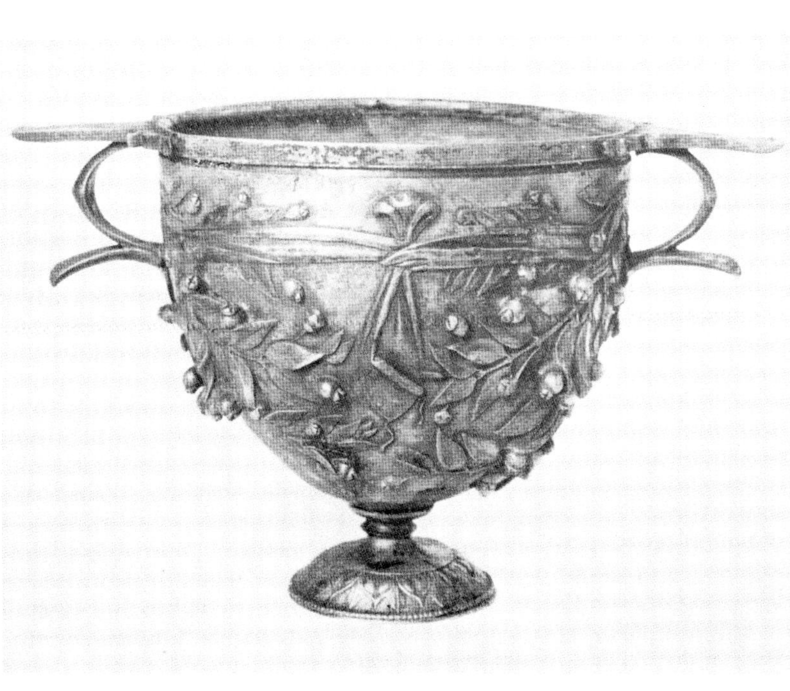

PLATE 33B Silver cup from Alesia; Musée de St-Germain-en-Laye (p. 115). *h* 11 cm

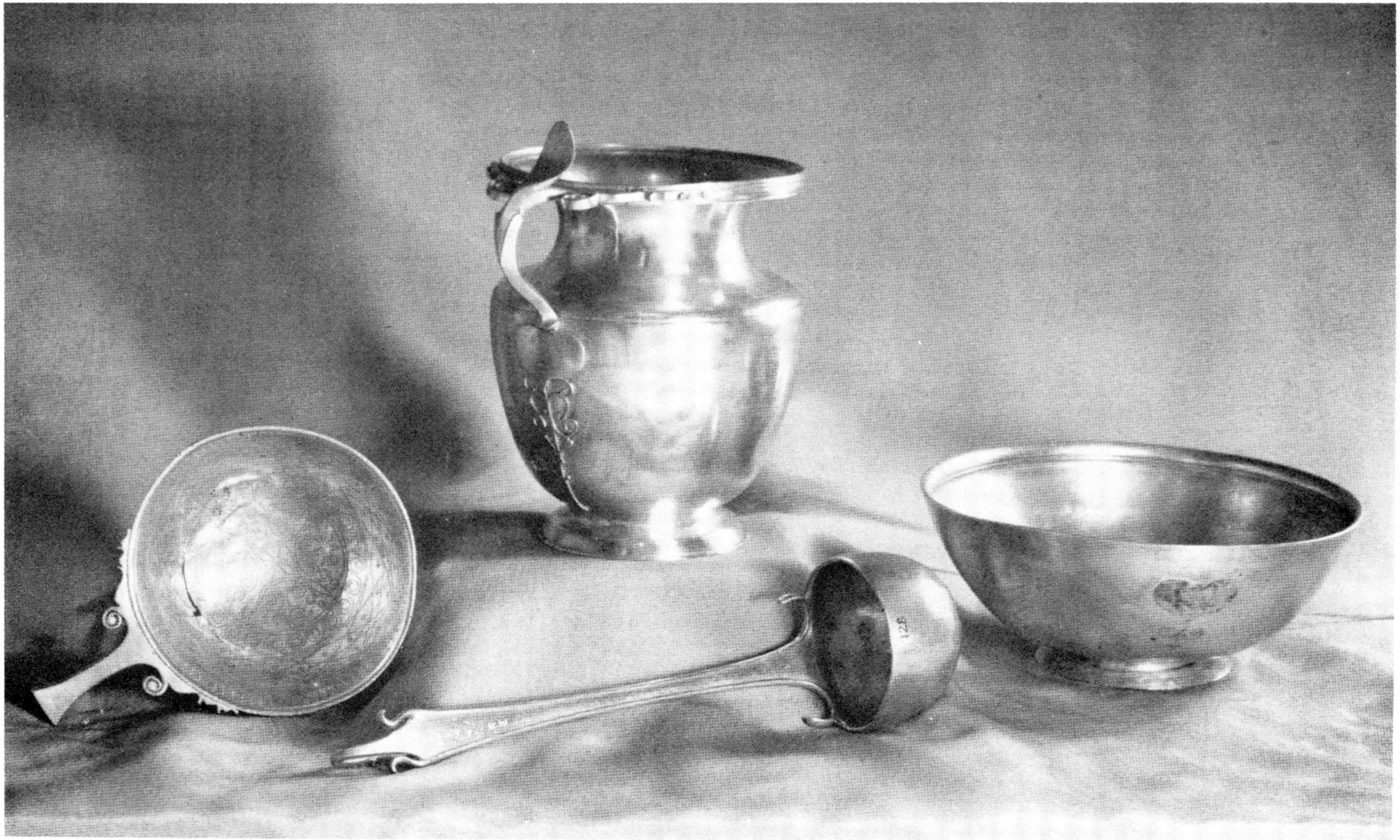

PLATE 34 Four silver vessels from Arcisate; London, British Museum (pp. 115–16)

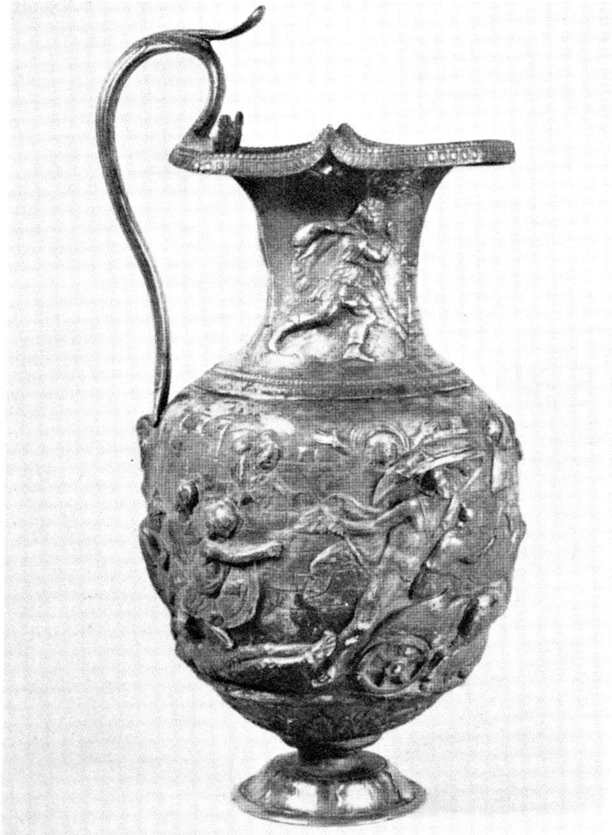

PLATE 35A Silver jug from Berthouville; Paris, Cabinet des Médailles (p. 142). *h* (*max*) 29·9 cm

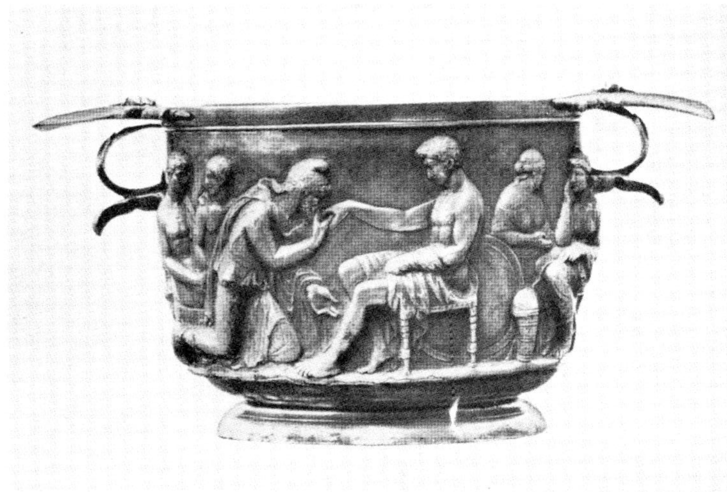

PLATE 35B Silver cup from Hoby; Copenhagen, Danish National Museum (p. 136). *h* 10·9 cm

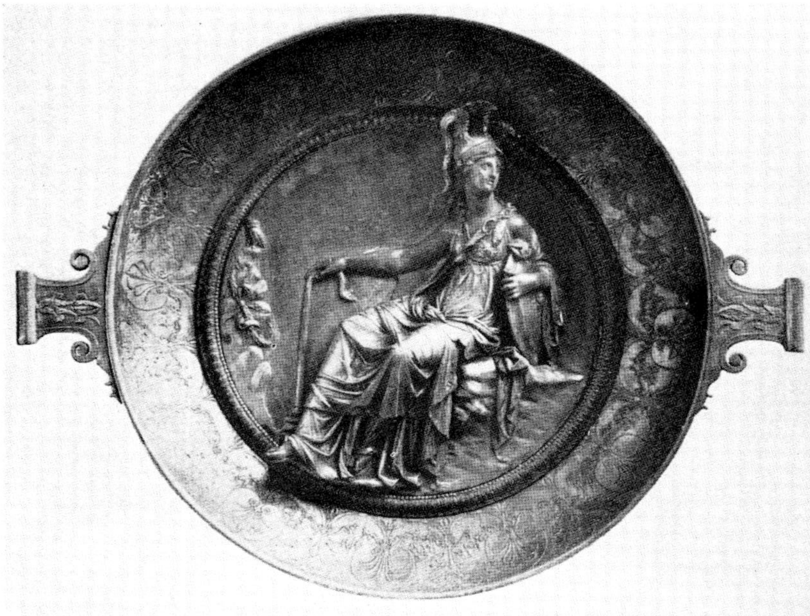

PLATE 36A Silver-gilt medallion cup from Hildesheim; Hildesheim, Römer-Pelizaeus Museum (p. 151). *d* 25 cm

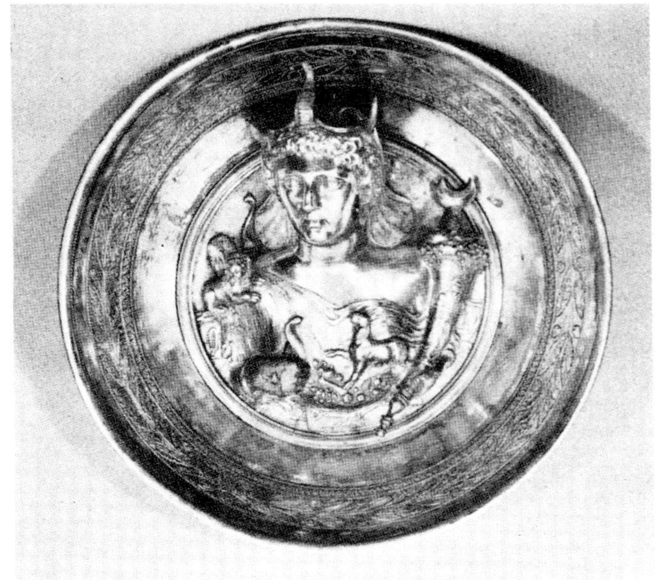

PLATE 36B Silver-gilt medallion bowl from Boscoreale; Paris, Musée du Louvre (p. 151). *d* 22·5 cm

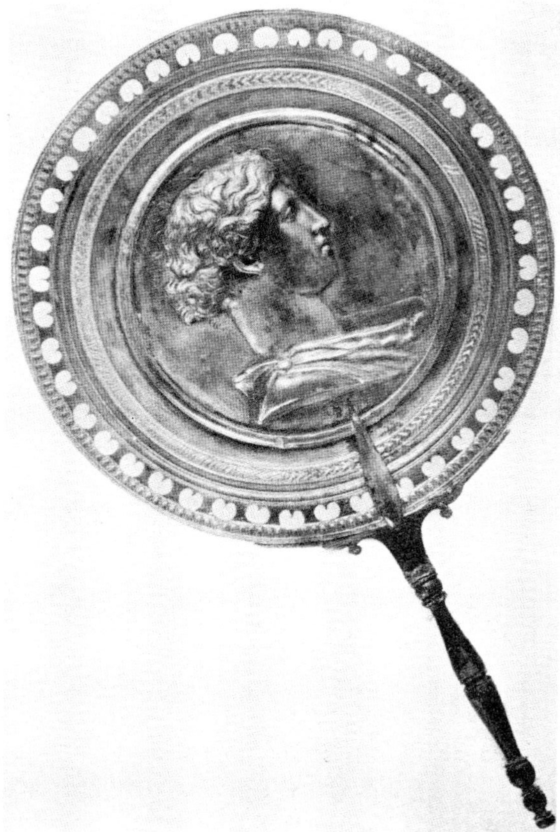

PLATE 37A Silver mirror from the Casa del Menandro, Pompeii; Naples, National Museum (p. 158). *d* 21 cm

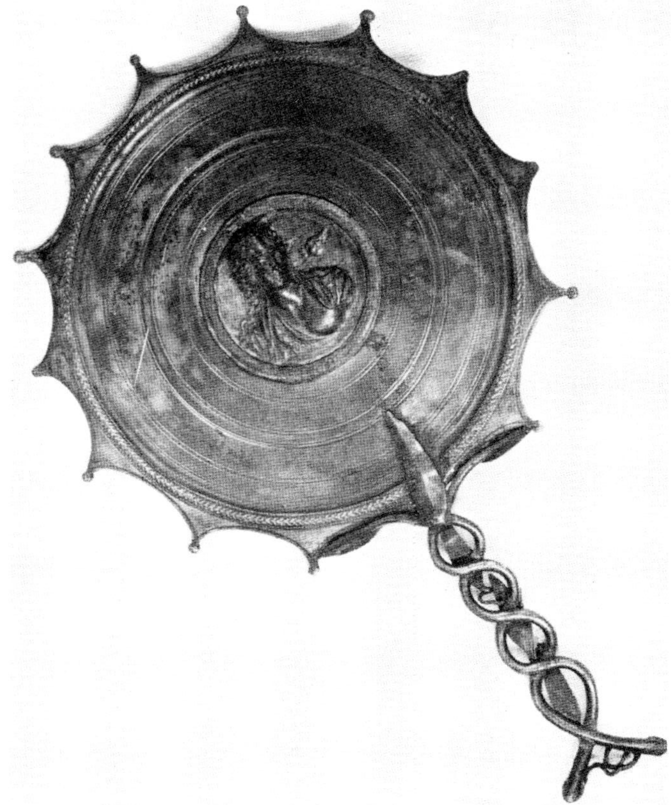

PLATE 37B Silver mirror from Boscoreale; Paris, Musée du Louvre (p. 158). *d* (*max*) 21 cm

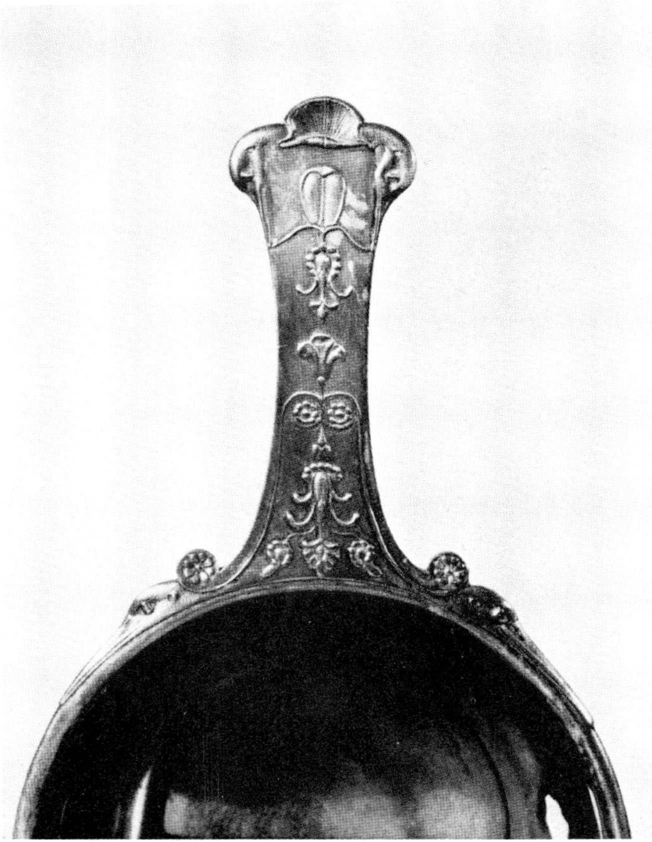

PLATE 38A Handle of silver saucepan from Boscoreale; Paris, Musée du Louvre (p. 147). *l* (*of handle*) 9·5 cm

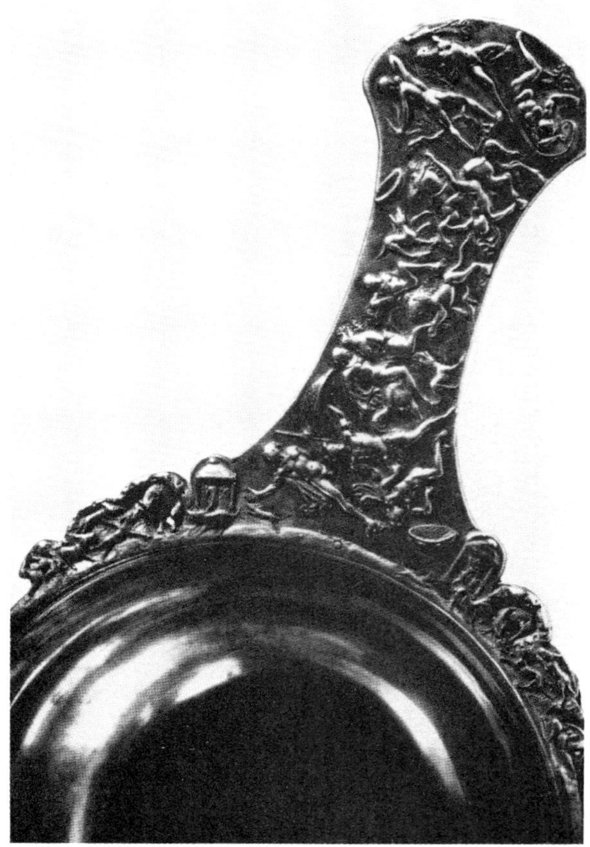

PLATE 38B Handle of silver saucepan from Casa del Menandro, Pompeii; Naples, National Museum (p. 148). *l* 12 cm

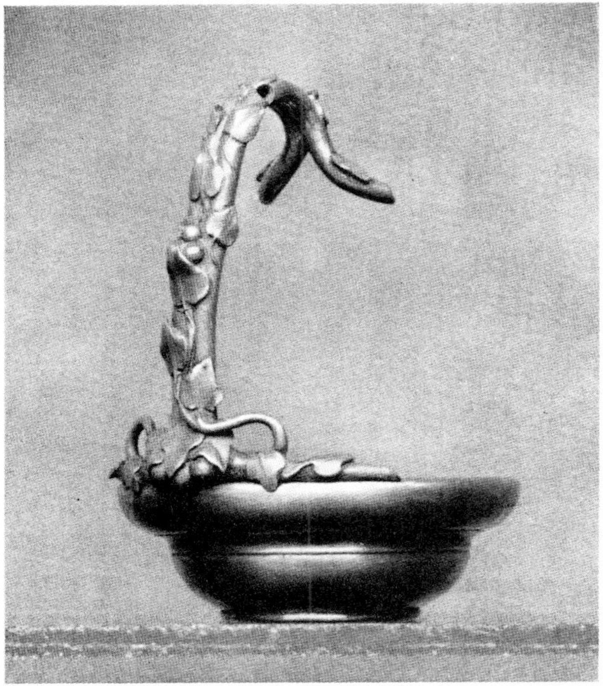

PLATE 39A Silver *simpulum* from Hildesheim; Hildesheim, Römer-Pelizaeus Museum (p. 144). *h* 11·5 cm

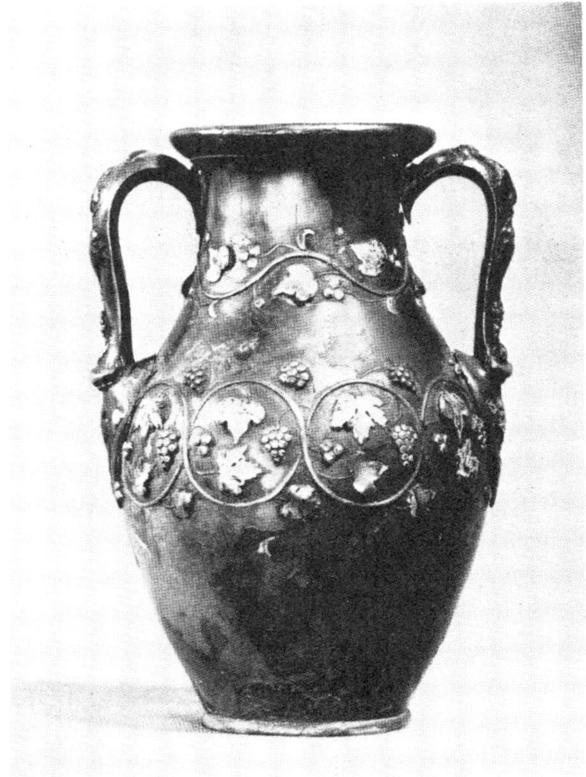

PLATE 39B Silver *amphora* from Bagni di Vicarello; London, British Museum (p. 143). *h* 11 cm

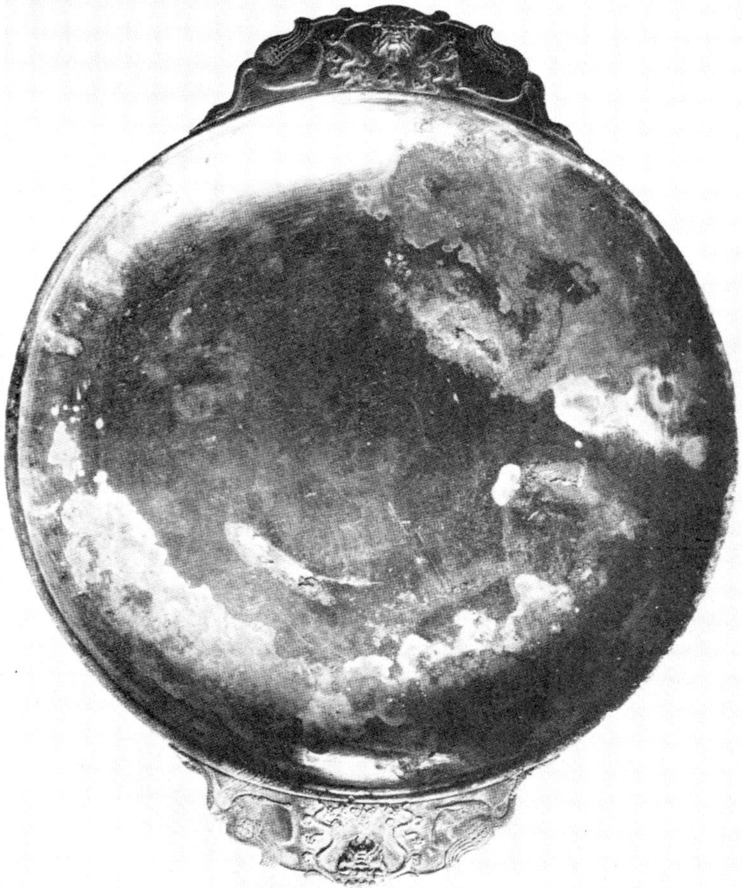

PLATE 40A Silver dish from the Casa del Menandro; Naples, National Museum (p. 148). *d* 30 cm

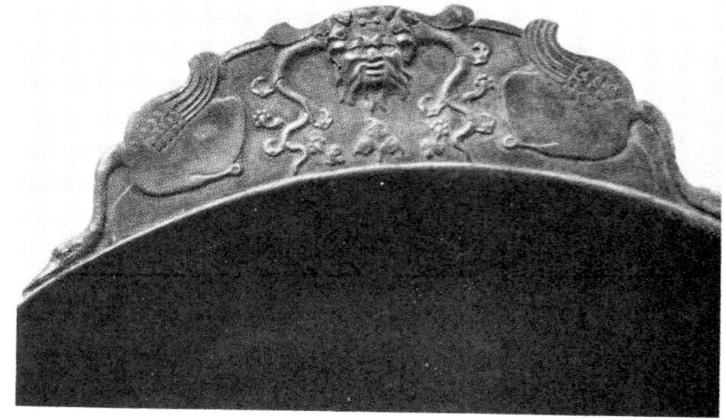

PLATE 40B Detail of handle

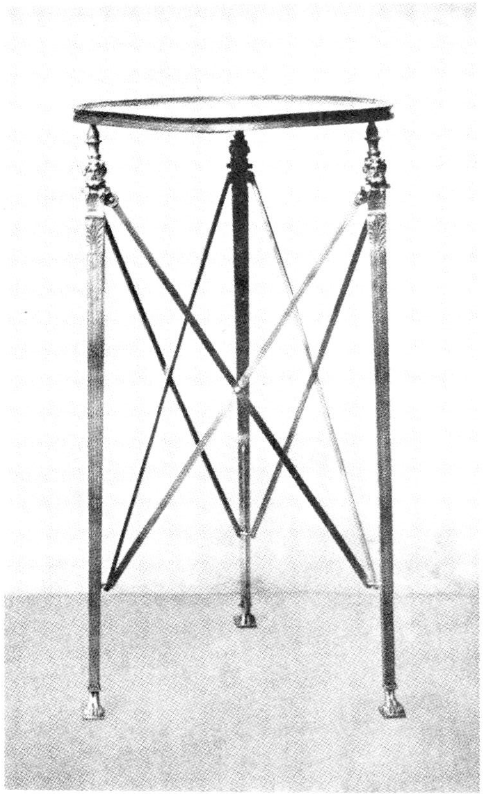

PLATE 41A Silver folding tripod from Hildesheim; Hildesheim, Römer-Pelizaeus Museum (p. 159). *h* 70·8 cm

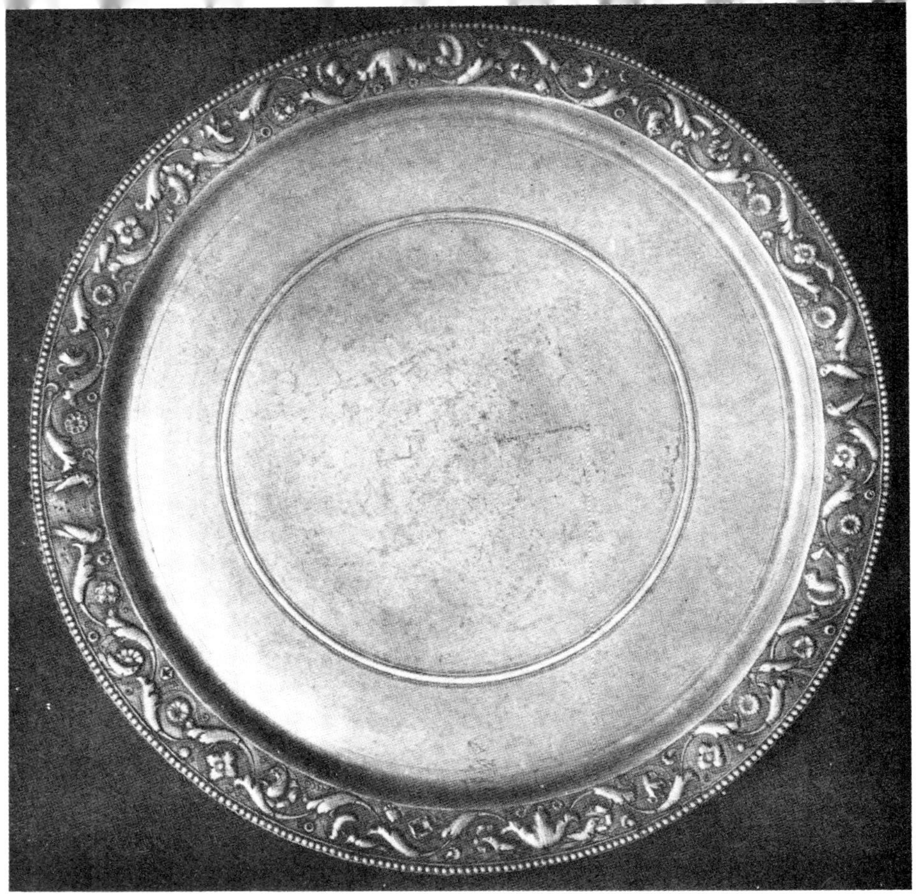

PLATE 41B Silver dish from Hildesheim; Hildesheim, Römer-Pelizaeus Museum (p. 149). *d* 30 cm

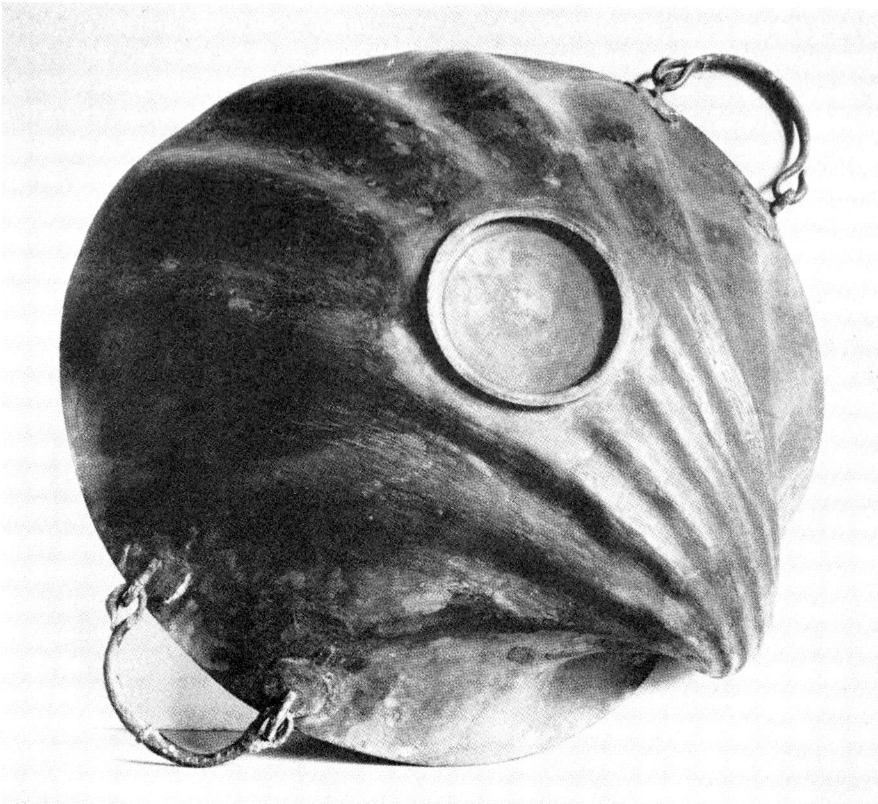

PLATE 42A Silver shell bowl from the Casa del Menandro, Pompeii; Naples, National Museum (p. 153). *d (max)* 22·5 cm

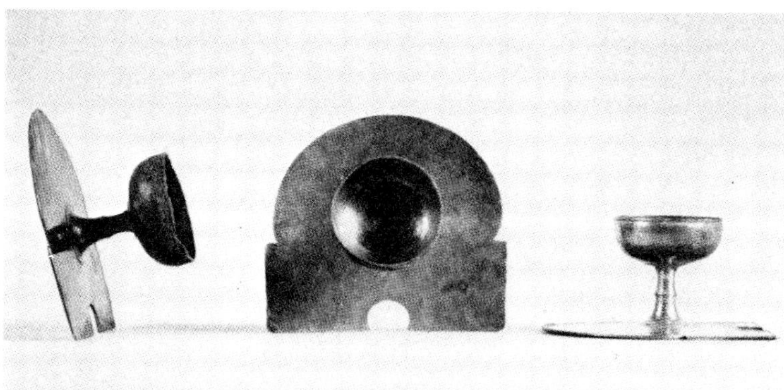

PLATE 42B Silver egg-cups from the Casa del Menandro, Pompeii; Naples, National Museum (p. 153). *d (of cups)* 3·3 cm

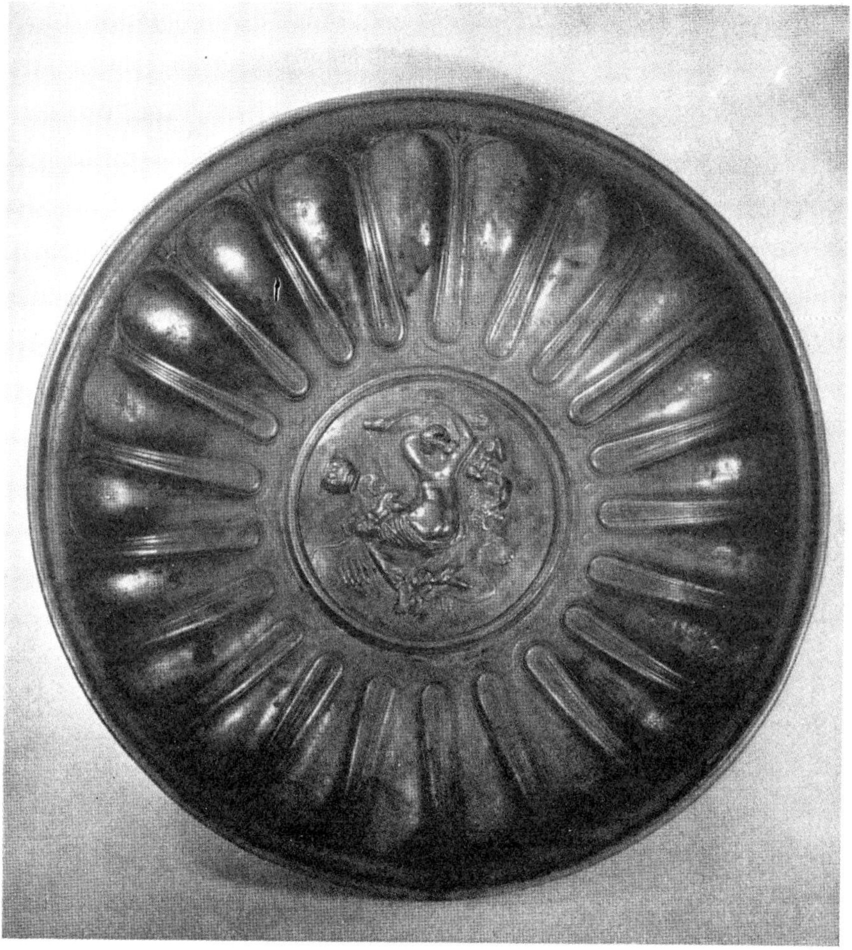

PLATE 43A Silver bowl from Berthouville; Paris, Cabinet des Médailles (p. 158). *d* 28·5 cm

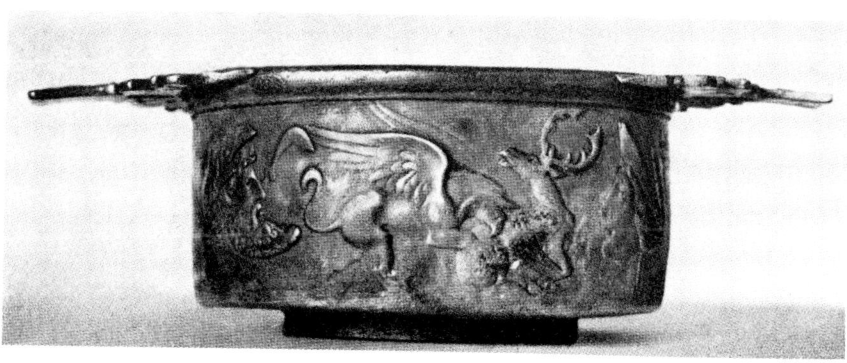

PLATE 43B Silver cup from Ostropataka; Vienna, Kunsthistorisches Museum (p. 163). *d* 14·5 cm

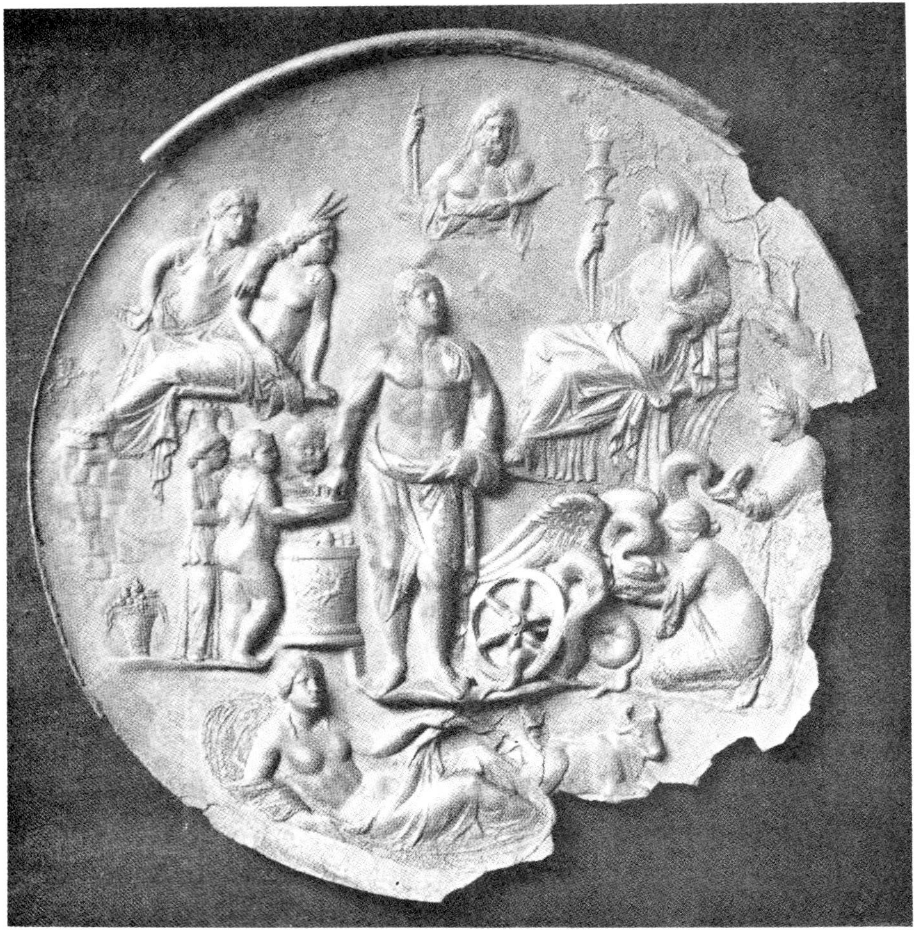

PLATE 44A Silver dish from Aquileia; Vienna, Kunsthistorisches Museum (p. 150). *d* 28·5 cm

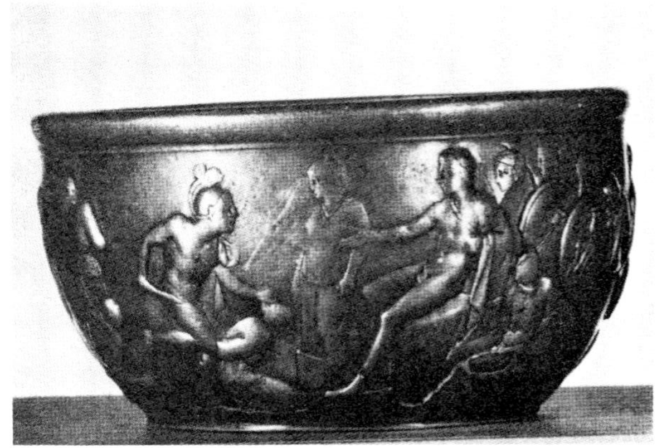

PLATE 44B Silver cup from Ingolstadt; Munich. Antikensammlungen (p. 140). *d* 12·3 cm

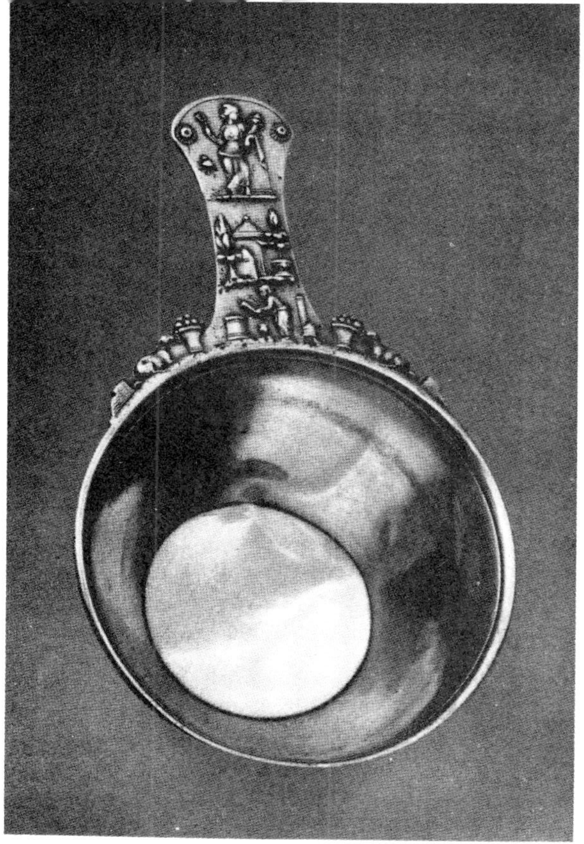

PLATE 45A Silver saucepan from Chattuzange; London, British Museum (p. 168). *d* 12·5cm

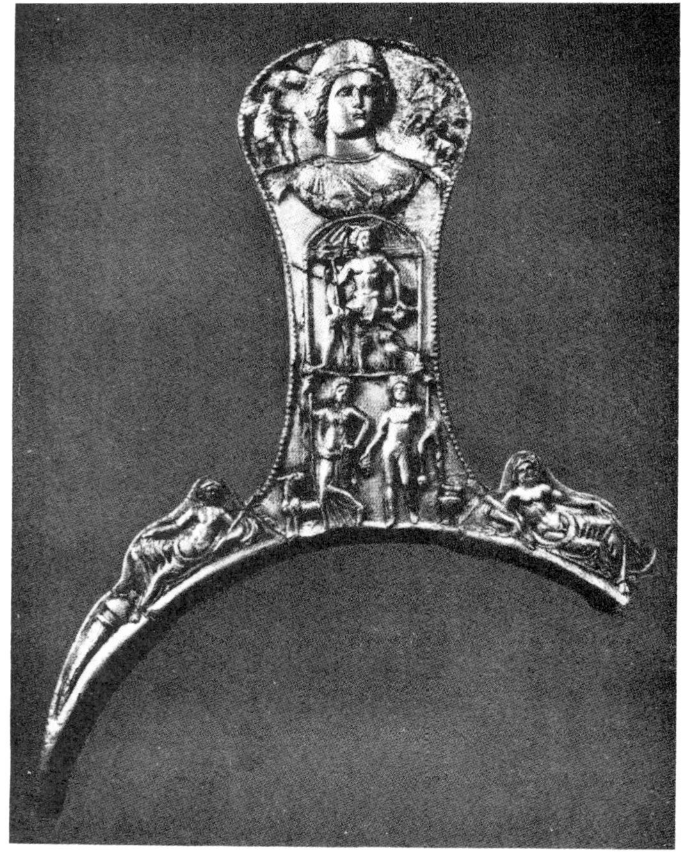

PLATE 45B Handle of silver saucepan from Capheaton; London, British Museum (p. 169). *l* 14·3 cm

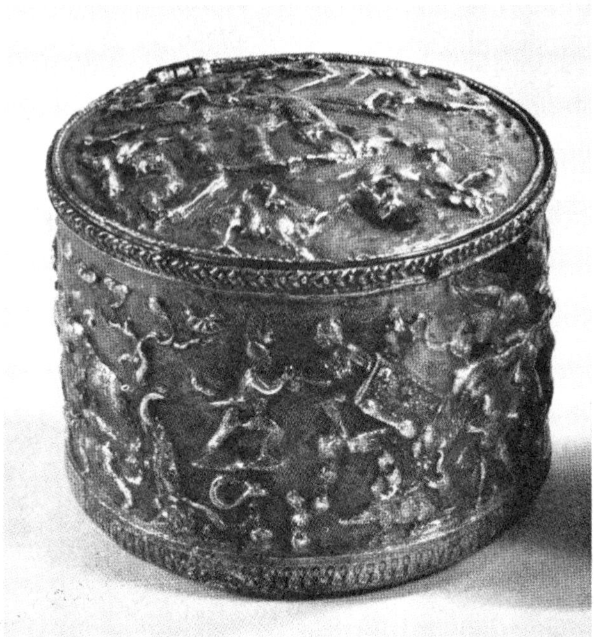

PLATE 46A Silver casket containing a strainer from the Walbrook Mithraeum, London; London, Guildhall Museum (p. 170). *h* 6 cm

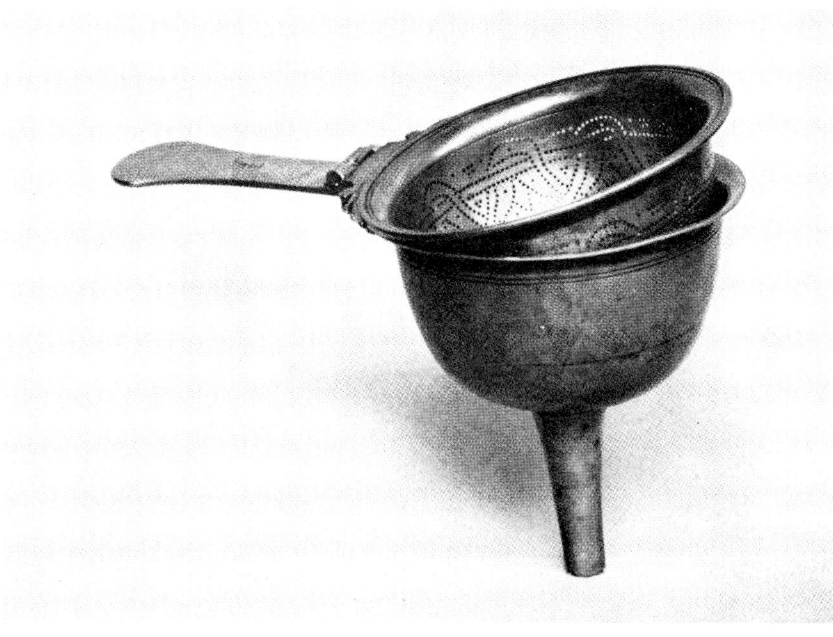

PLATE 46B Silver strainer with funnel from Chaourse; London, British Museum (p. 170). *d* 8·5 cm

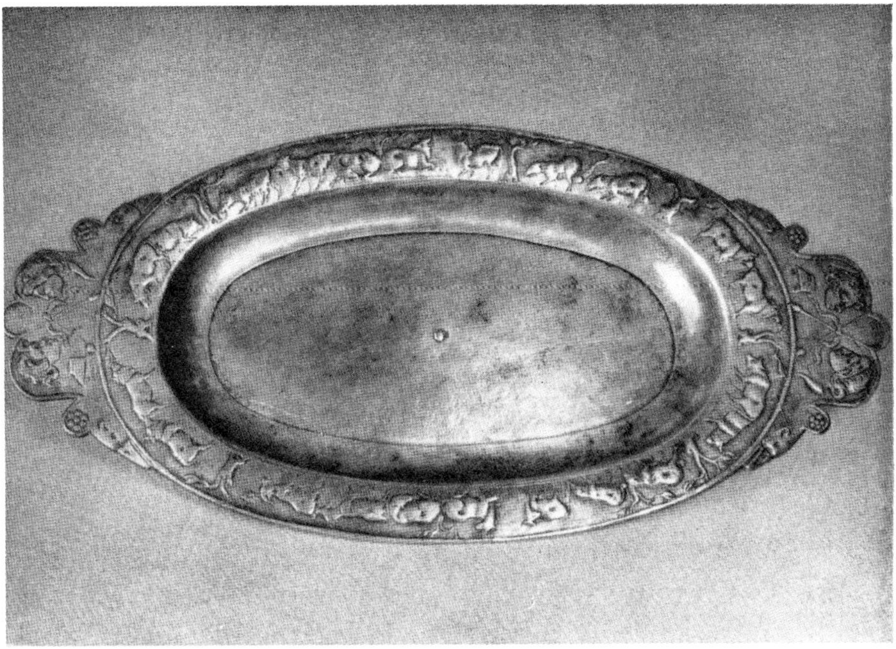

PLATE 47A Silver dish; Turin, Archaeological Museum (p. 171). *l* 25 cm

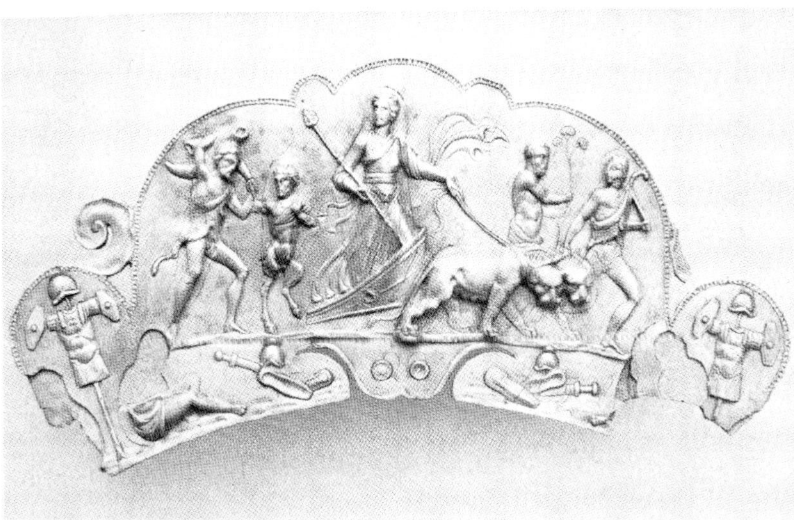

PLATE 47B Handle of silver dish; New York, Metropolitan Museum (p. 171). *w* 22·7 cm

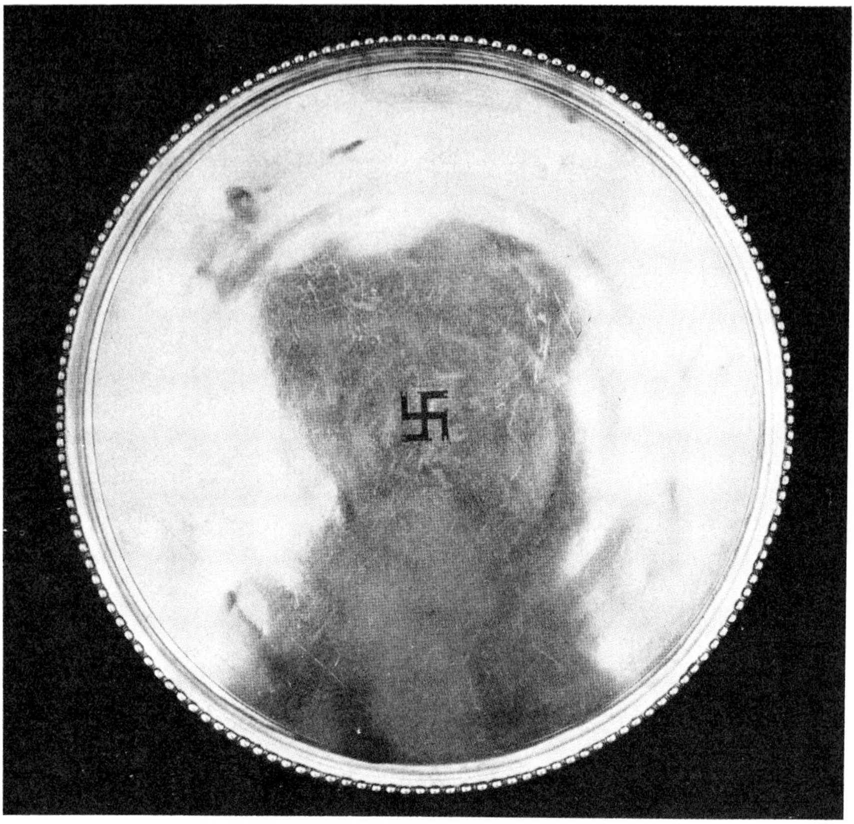

PLATE 48A Silver dish from Chattuzange; London, British Museum (p. 174). *d* 38·3 cm

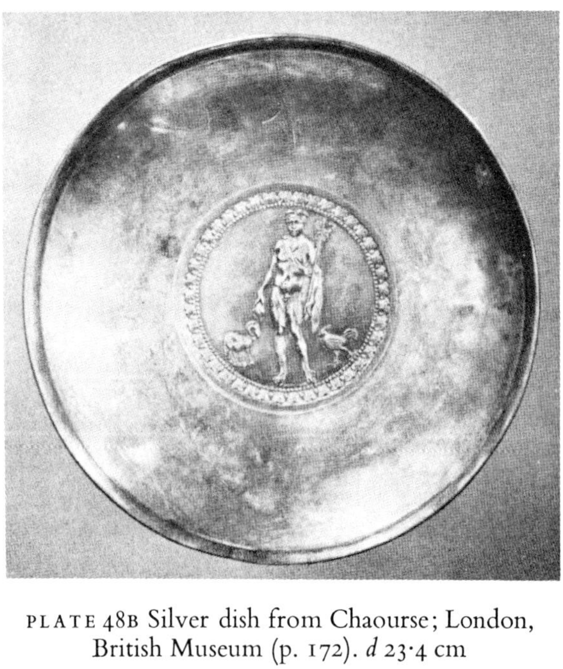

PLATE 48B Silver dish from Chaourse; London, British Museum (p. 172). *d* 23·4 cm

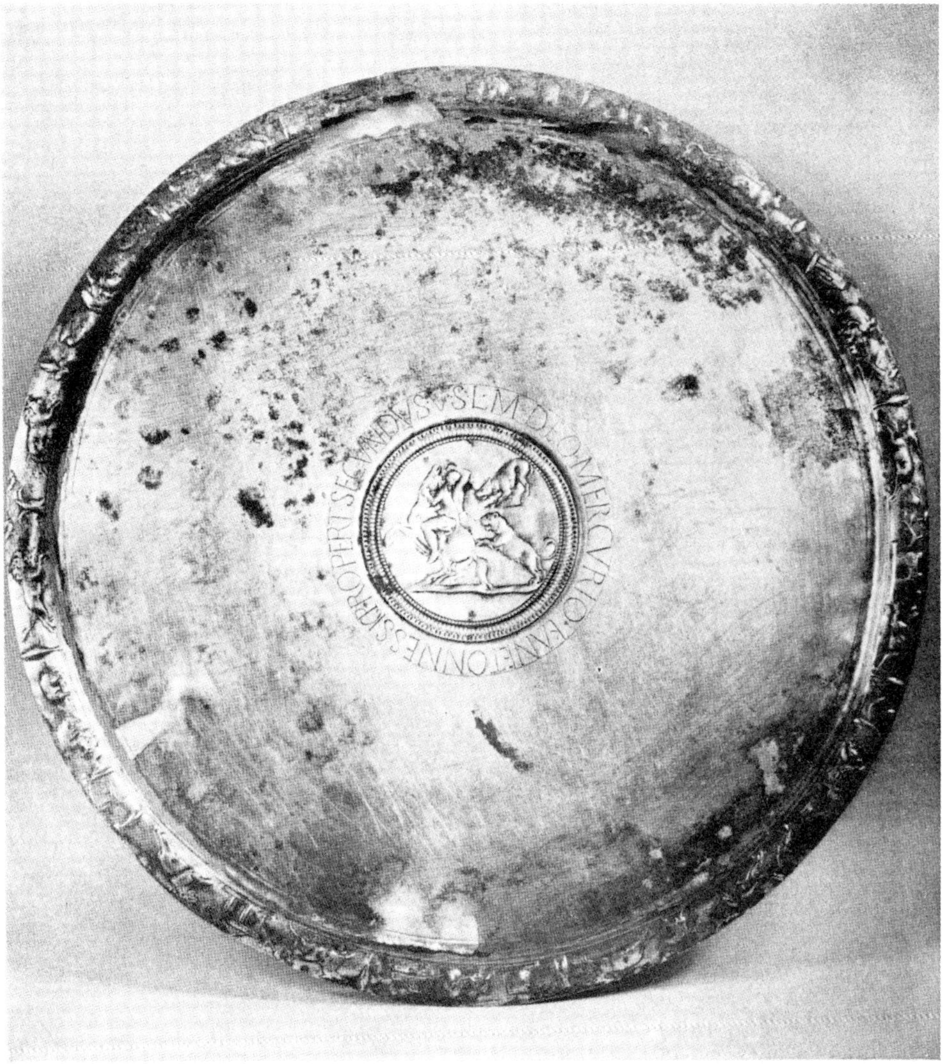

PLATE 49 Silver dish from Berthouville;
Paris, Cabinet des Médailles (p. 172). *d* 35 cm

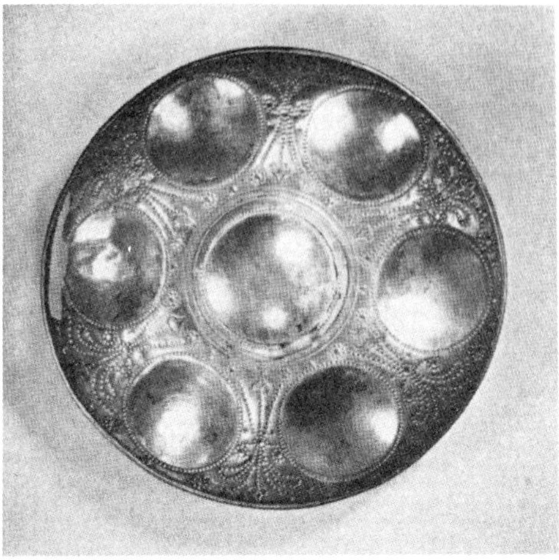

PLATE 50A Silver bowl from Notre-Dame d'Allençon; Paris, Musée du Louvre (p. 172). *d* 17·3 cm

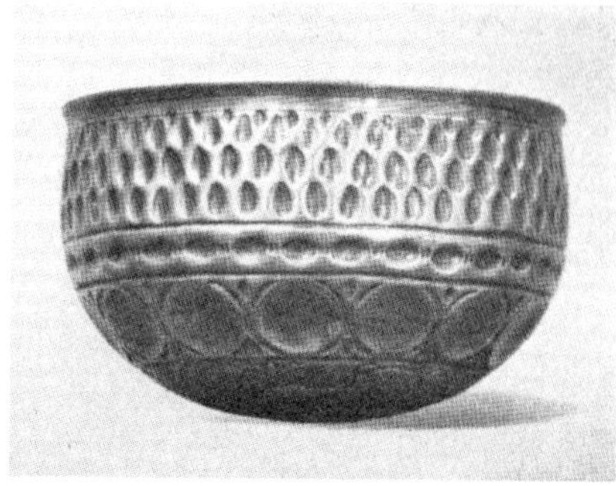

PLATE 50B Silver bowl from Chaourse; London, British Museum (p. 175). *d* 12·2 cm

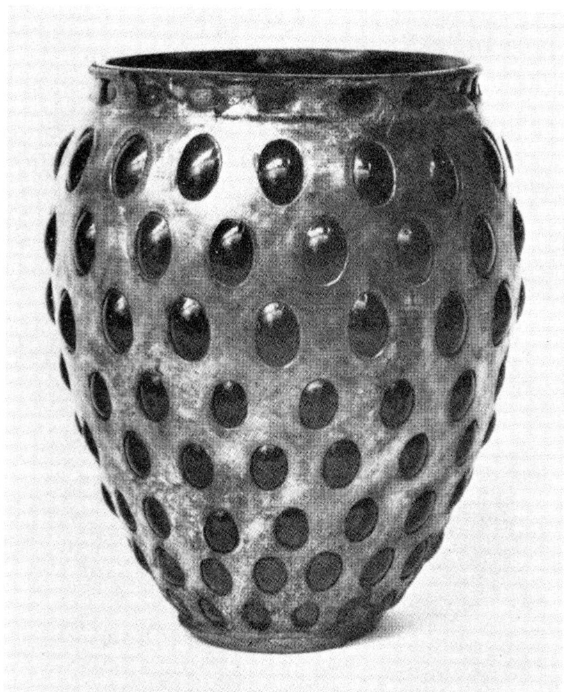

PLATE 50C Vase of silver and blue glass; London, British Museum (p. 13). *h* 9 cm

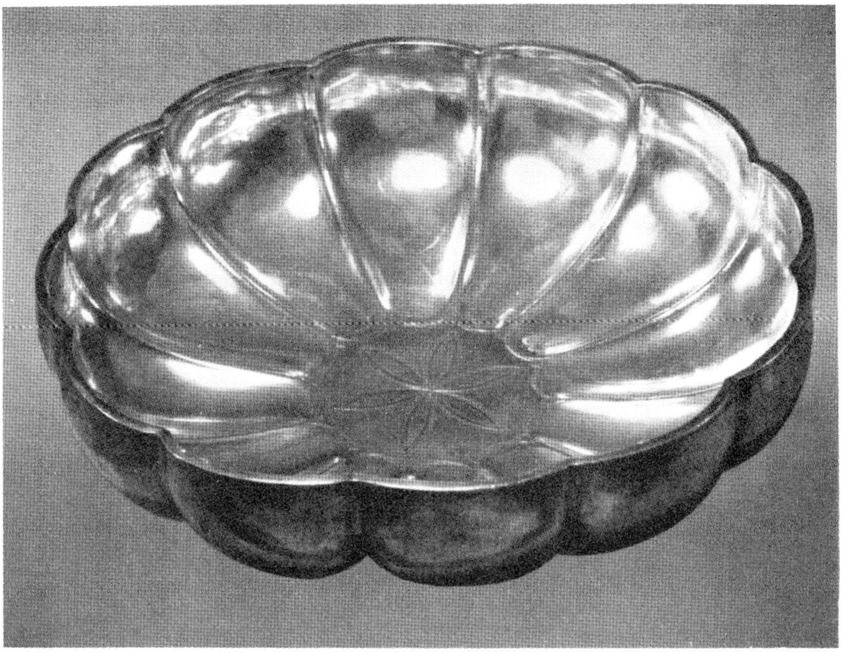

PLATE 51A Silver fluted bowl from Chaourse; London British Museum (p. 176). *d* 24 cm

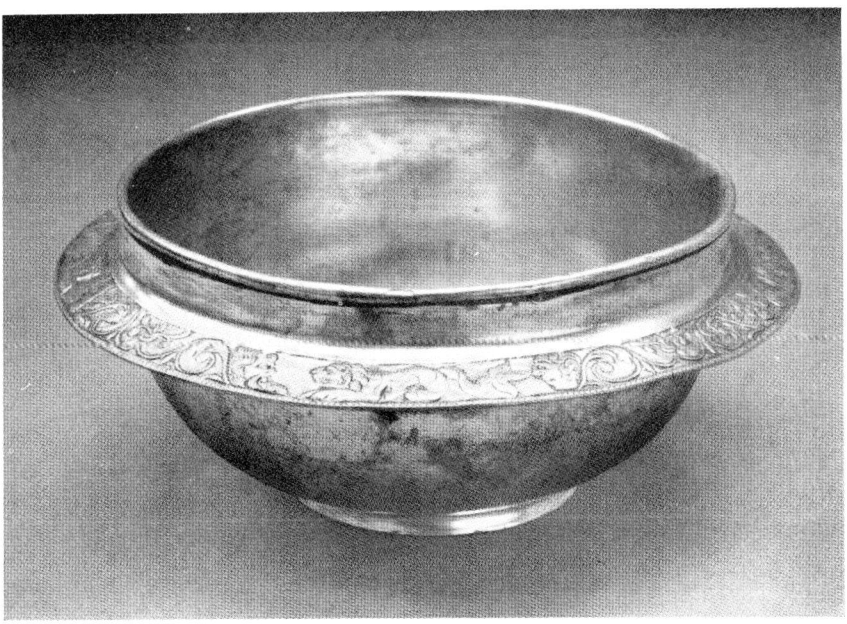

PLATE 51B Silver flanged bowl from Chaourse; London, British Museum (p. 176). *d* 23·5 cm

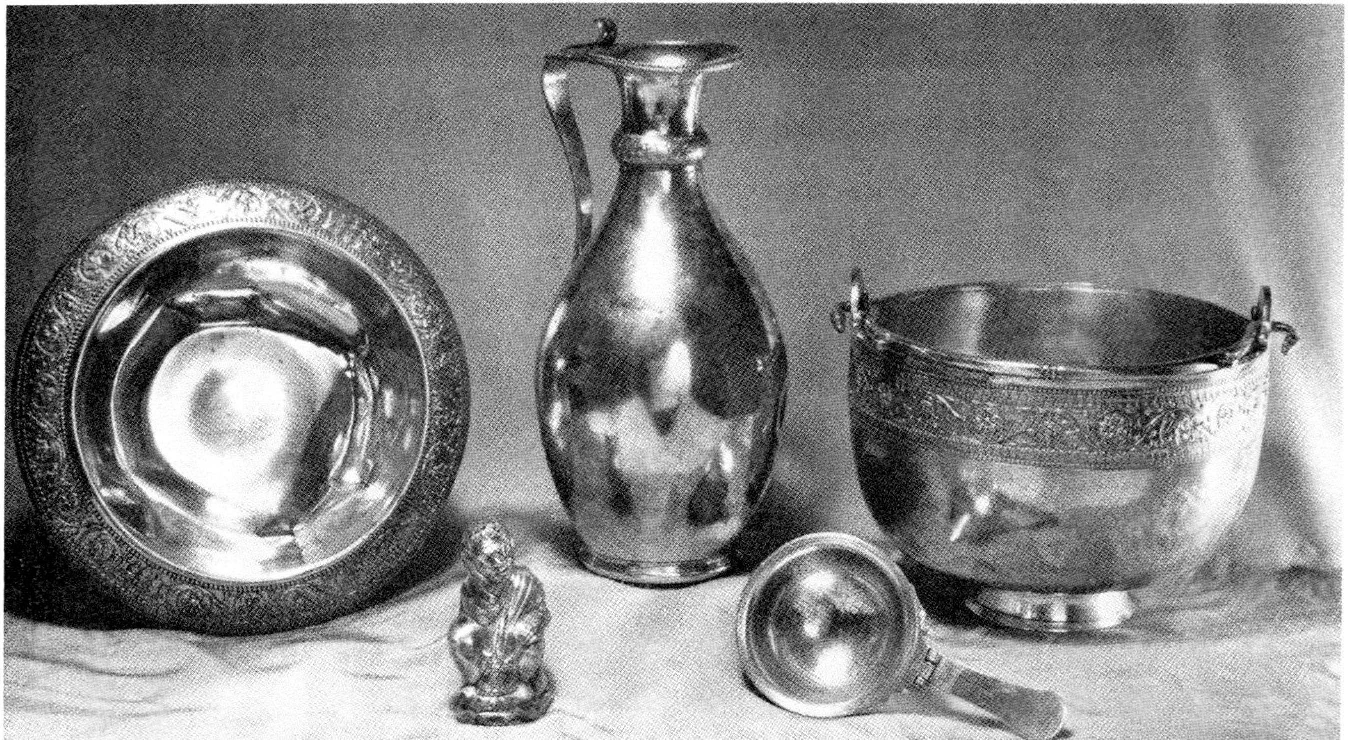

PLATE 52 Silver vessels from Chaourse; London, British Museum (p. 160 ff)

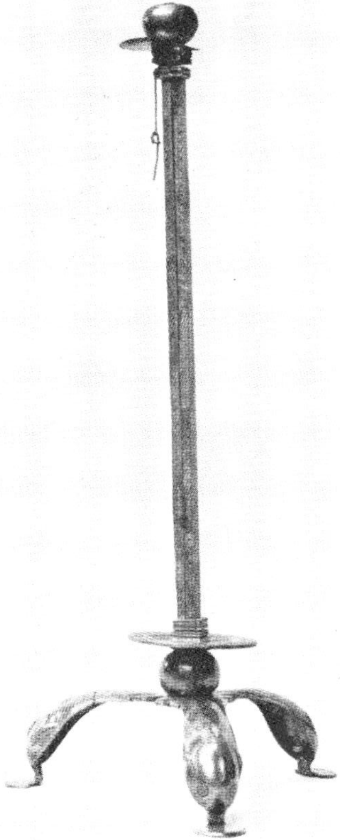

PLATE 53A Silver *candelabrum* from Beaurains; London, British Museum (p. 180). *h* 53·5 cm

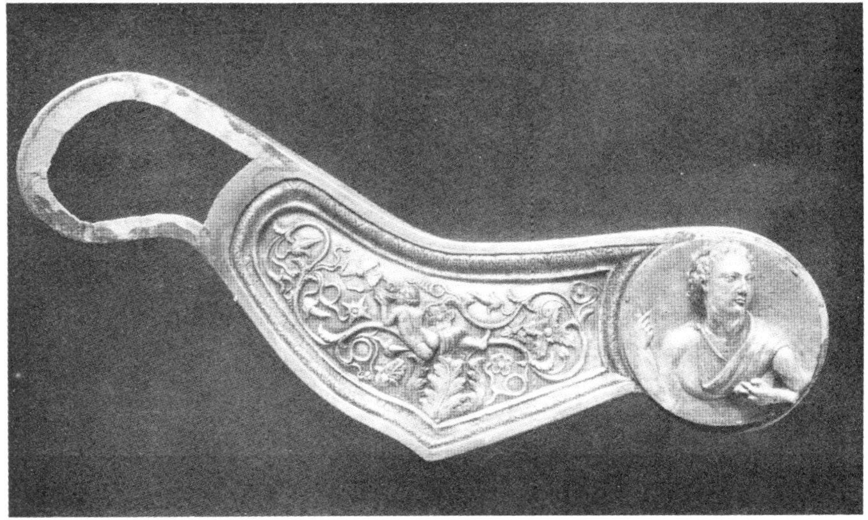

PLATE 53B Silver *fulchrum* of a couch from Bosco Marengo; Turin, Archaeological Museum (p. 179). *l* (*max*) 57 cm

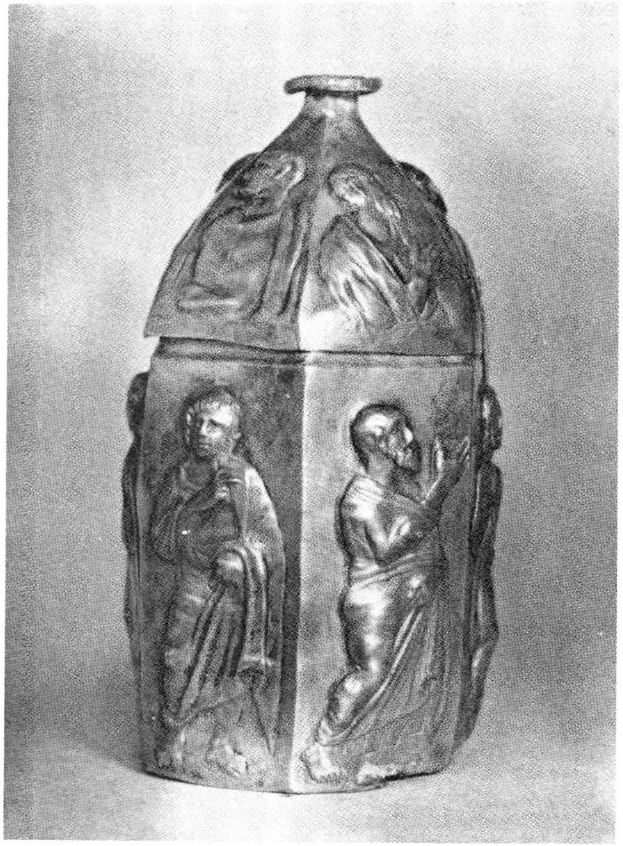

PLATE 54A Silver *pyxis* from Pola; Vienna,

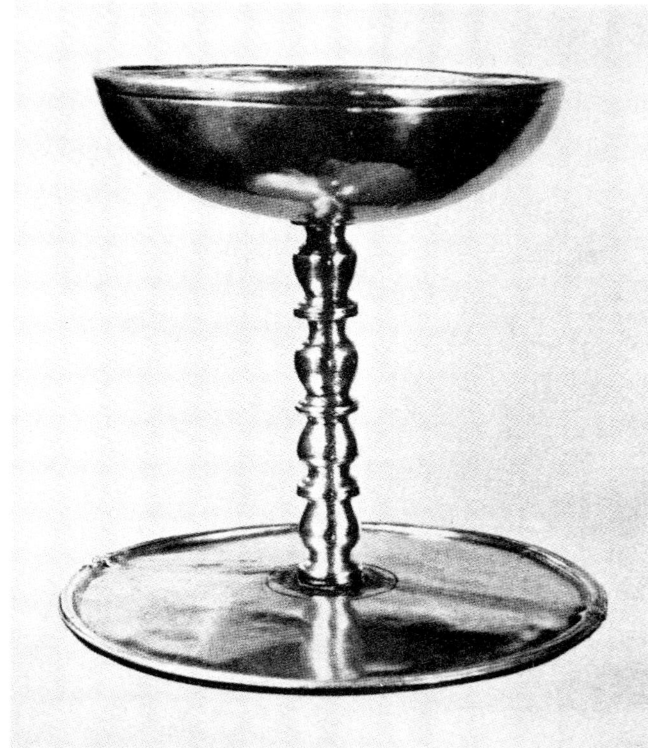

PLATE 54B Silver goblet from Traprain Law; Edinburgh, National Museum of Antiquities, Scotland (p. 187). *h* 10·5 cm

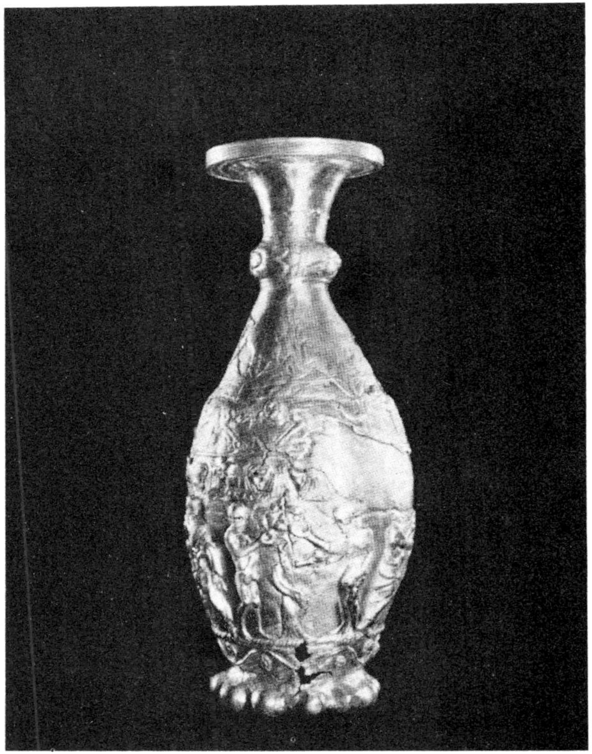

PLATE 55A Silver-gilt flask from Traprain Law; Edinburgh, National Museum of Antiquities (p. 185). *h* 21·5 cm

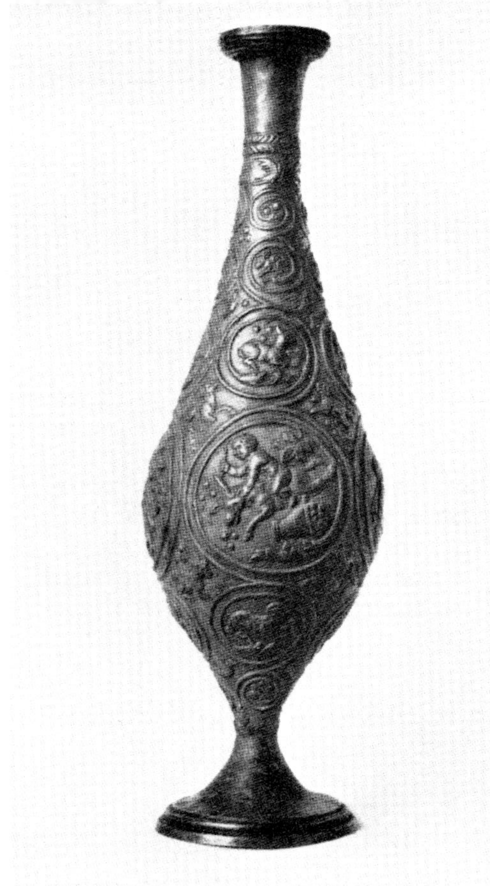

PLATE 55B Silver flask from the Esquiline Treasure; London, British Museum (p. 191). *h* 34·3 cm

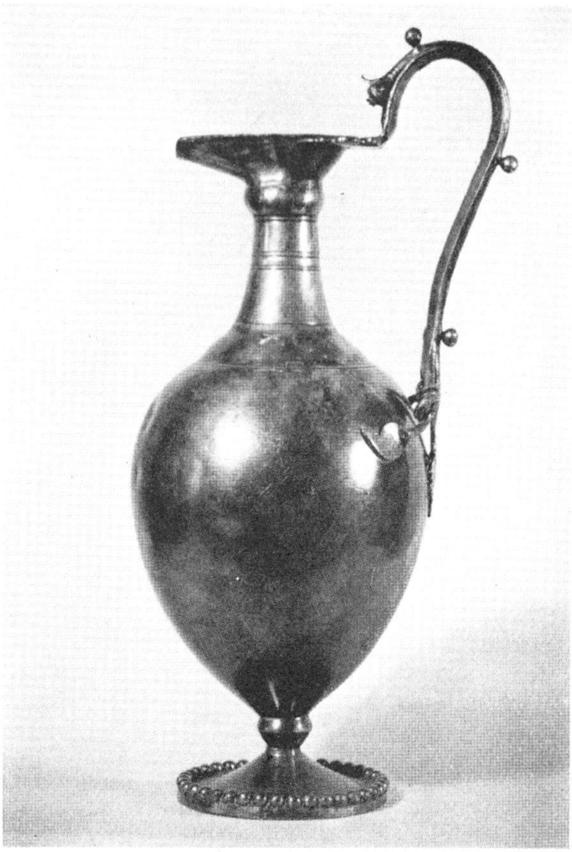

PLATE 56A Silver jug; Berlin, Staatliche Museen (p. 189). *h* 32 cm

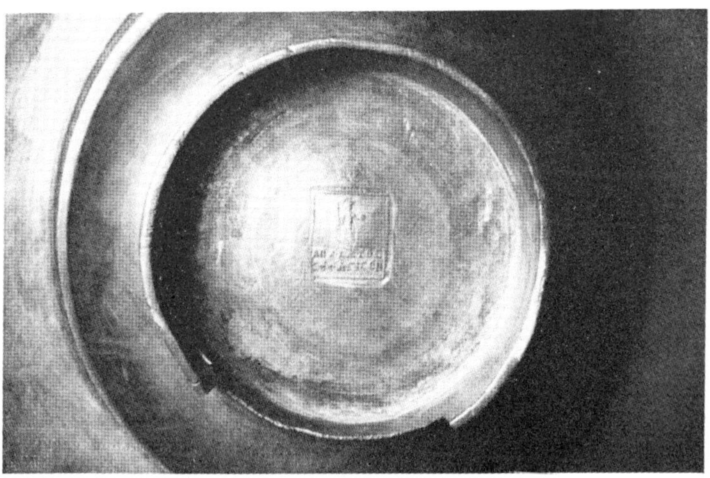

PLATE 56B Silver stamp on the bottom of a flanged bowl; Berlin, Staatliche Museen (p. 183)

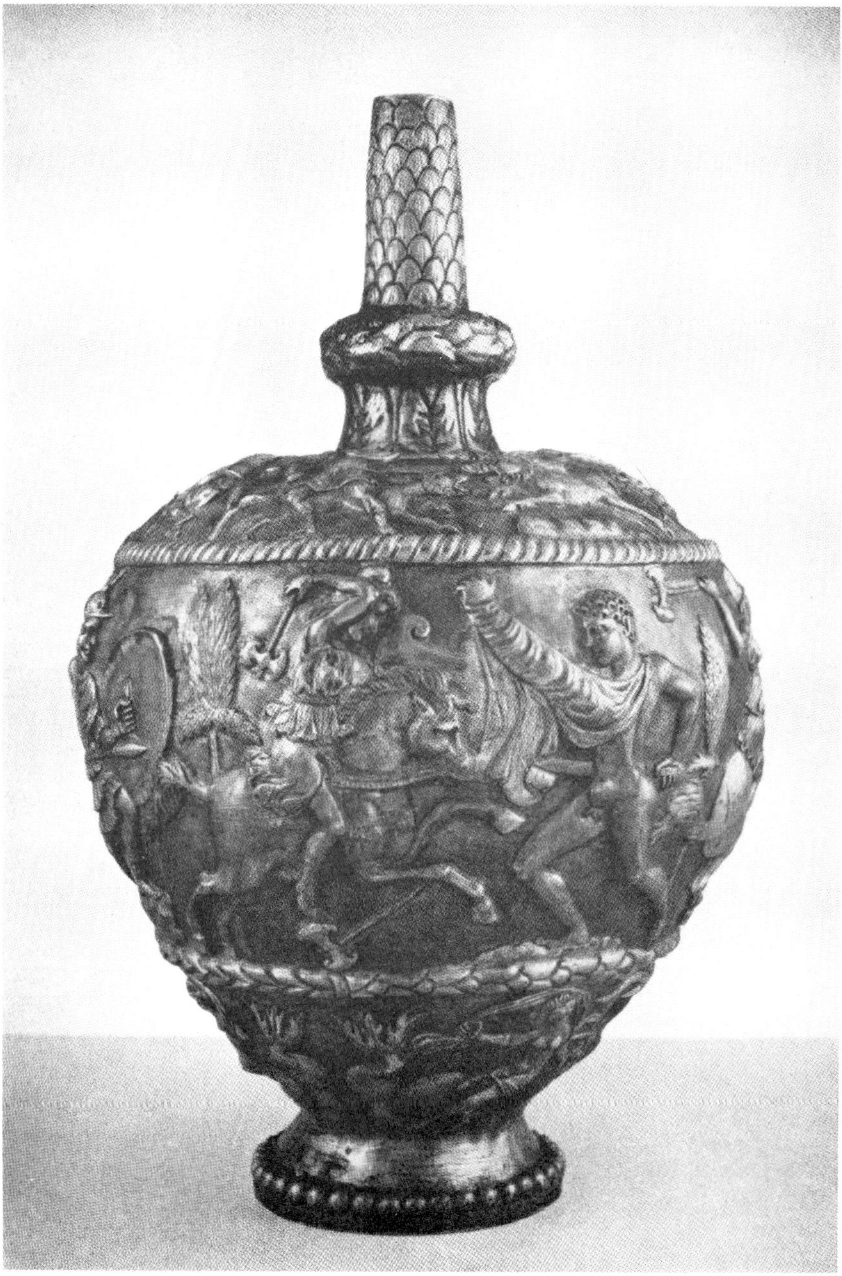

PLATE 57 Silver *amphora* from Concesti; Leningrad, National Hermitage Museum (p. 192). *h* 42·4 cm

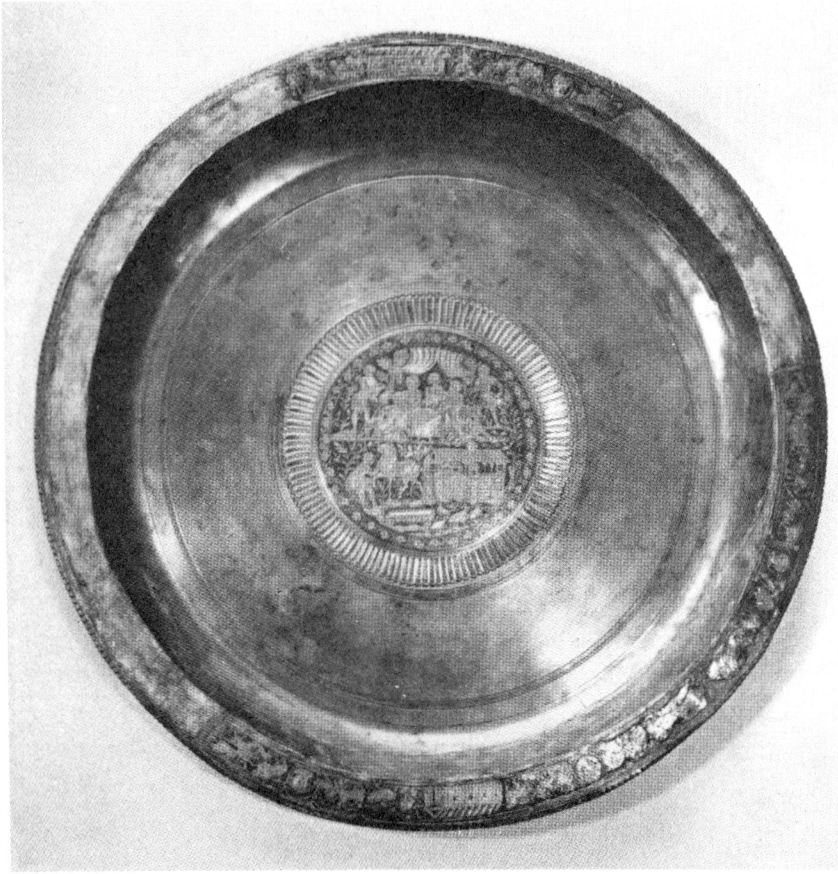

PLATE 58A Silver dish from Cesena; Cesena, Bibliotheca Malatestiana (p. 195). *d* 63 cm

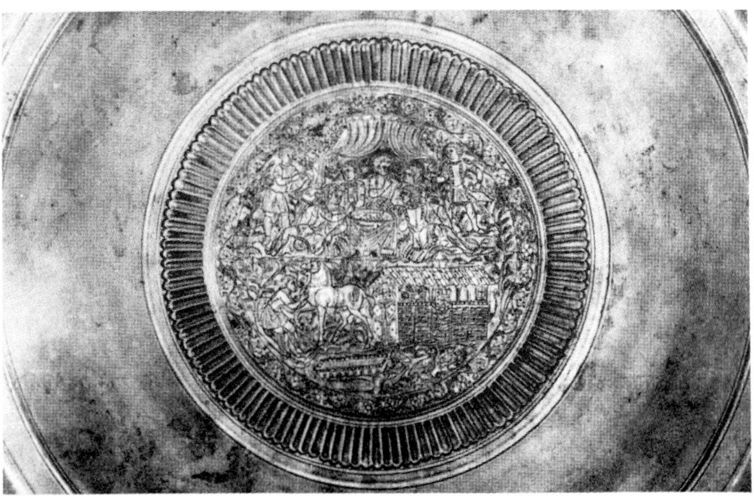

PLATE 58B Detail of dish

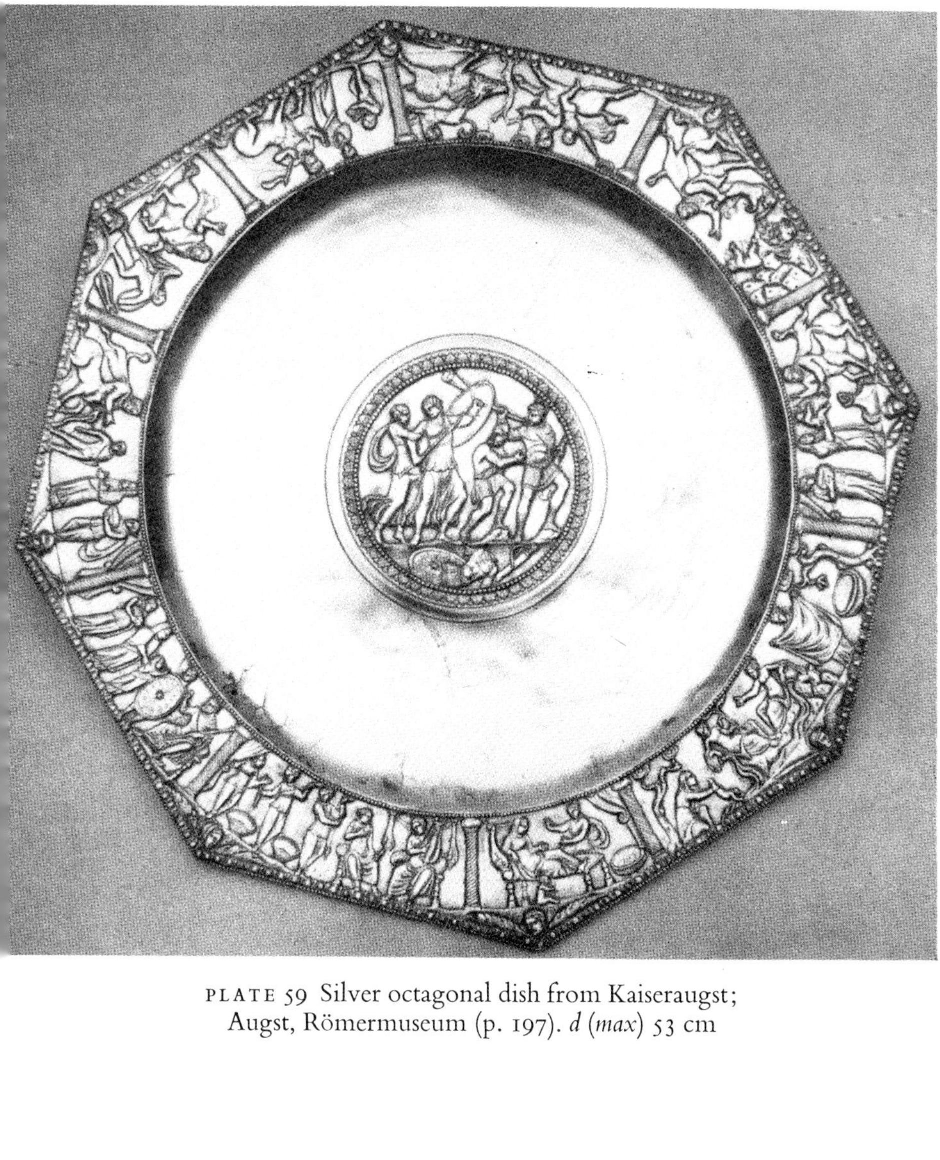

PLATE 59 Silver octagonal dish from Kaiseraugst; Augst, Römermuseum (p. 197). *d* (*max*) 53 cm

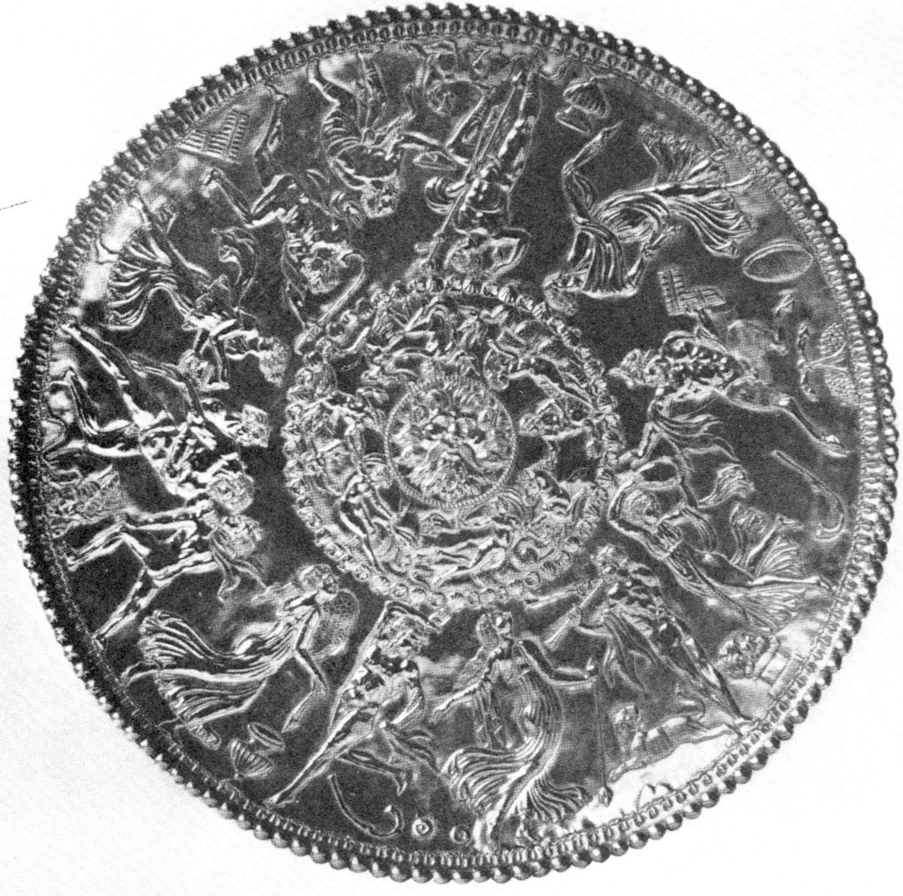

PLATE 60 Silver dish from Mildenhall; London,

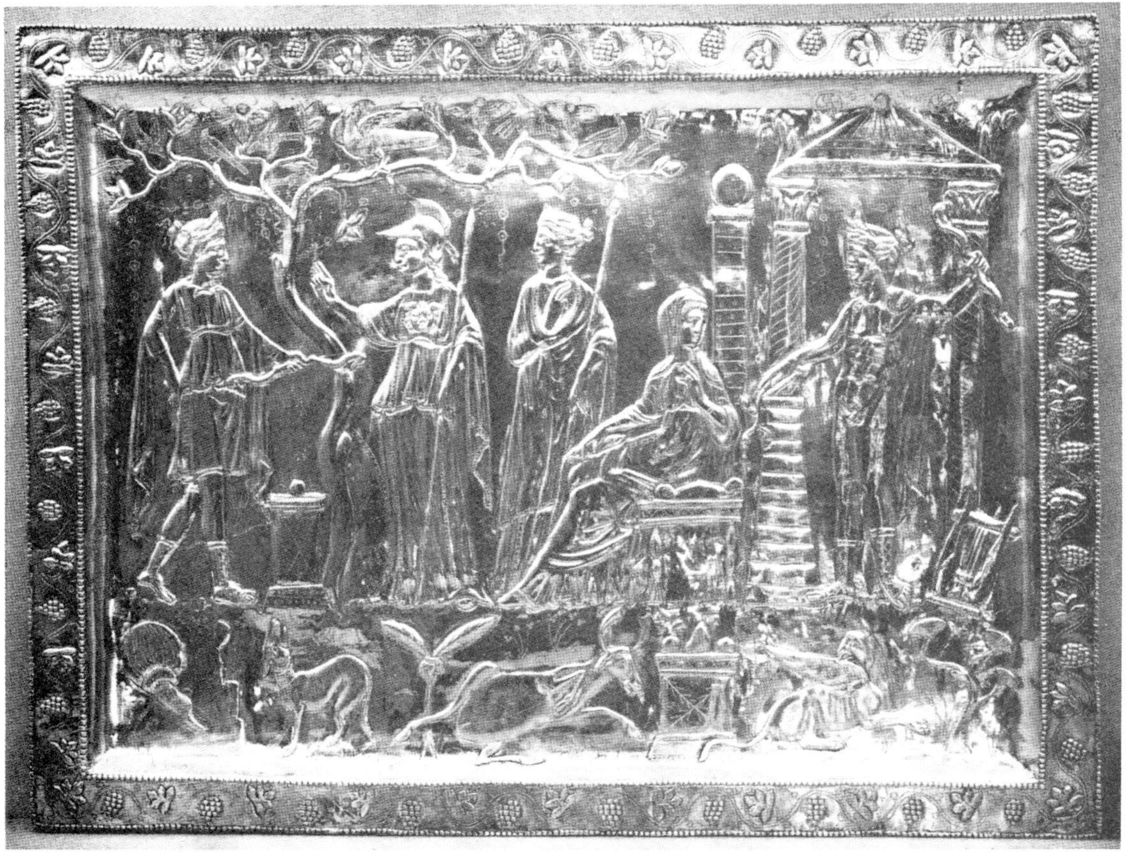

PLATE 61 Silver rectangular dish (*lanx*) from Corbridge; Alnwick, Duke of Northumberland's Collection (p. 198). *w* 48 cm

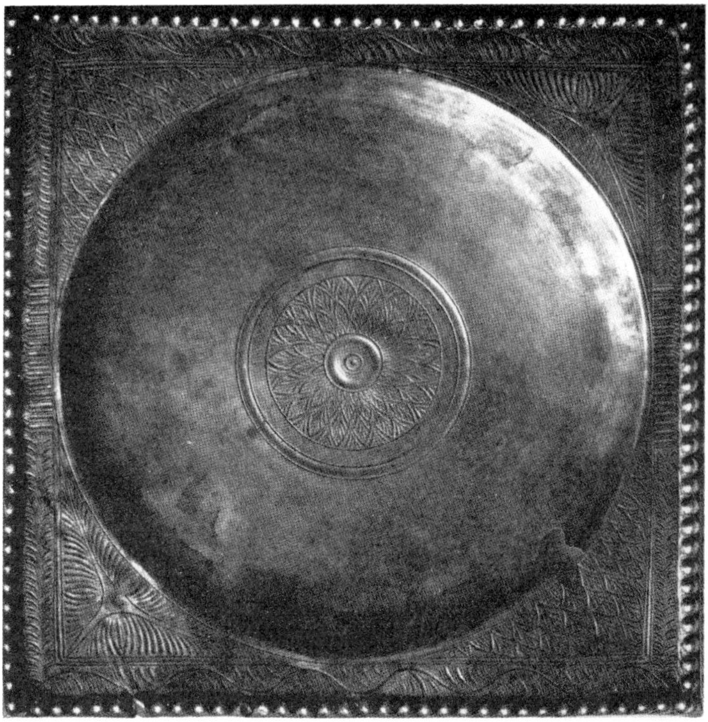

PLATE 62A Silver dish from Mileham; London, British Museum (p. 196). 37·5 × 37·5 cm

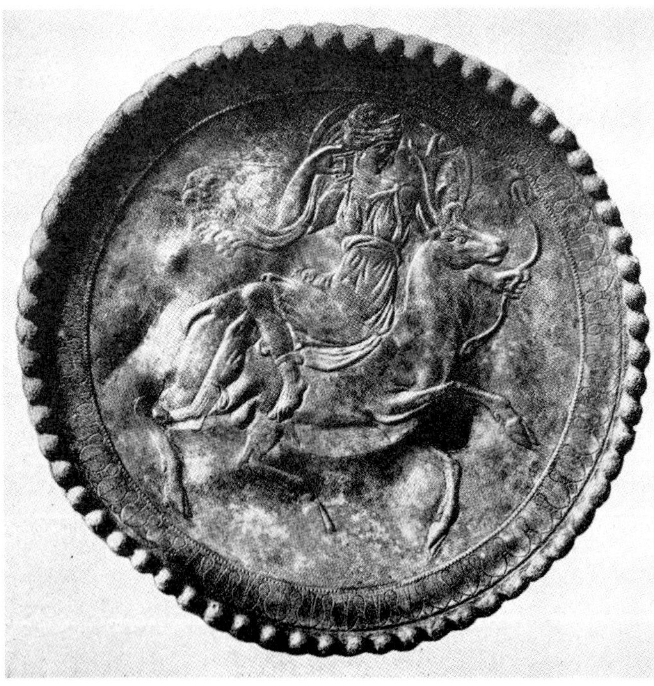

PLATE 62B Silver dish; Berlin, Staatliche Museen (p. 199). *d* 18 cm

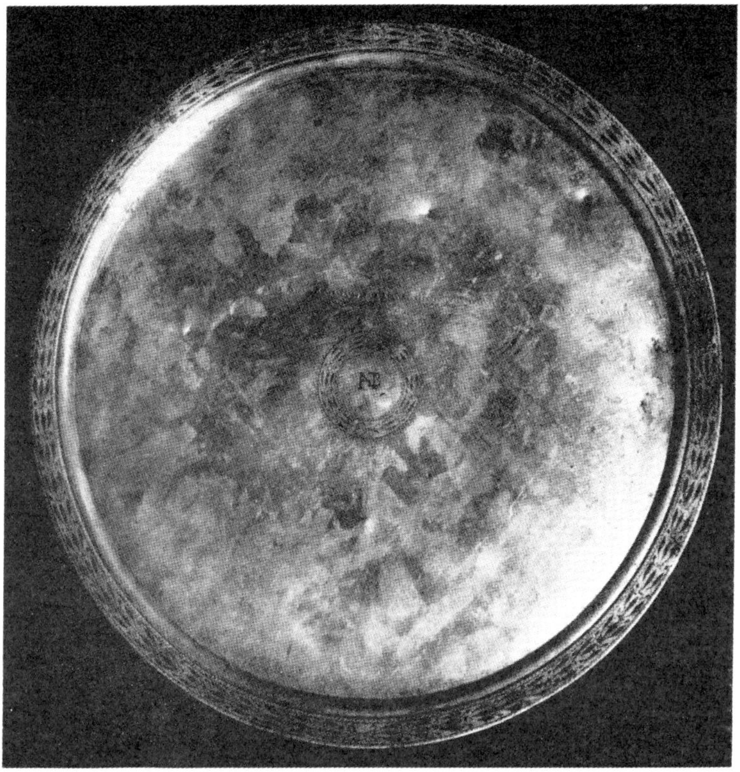

PLATE 63A Silver dish from Kerch; Leningrad, National Hermitage Museum (p. 195). *d* 43 cm

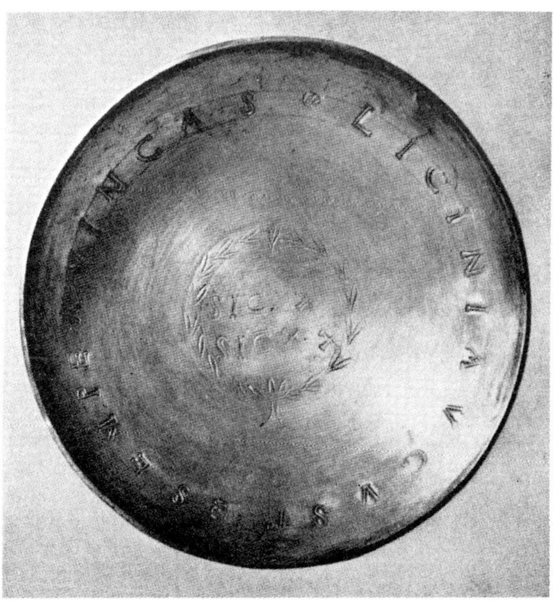

PLATE 63B Silver dish from Naissus (Nis); Vienna, Kunsthistorisches Museum (p. 199). *d* 17 cm

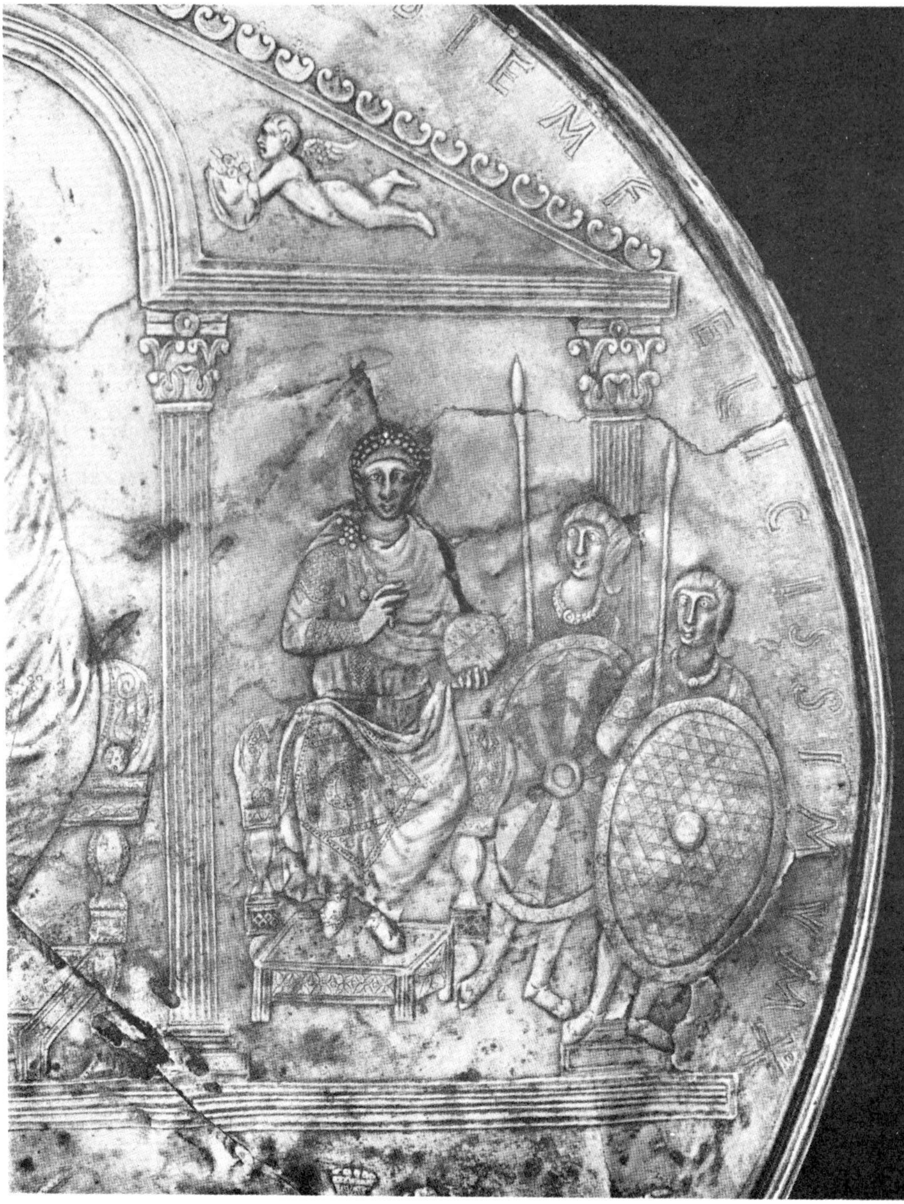

PLATE 64 Silver *missorium* of Theodosius (detail); Madrid, Archaeological Museum (p. 200). *d* 74 cm

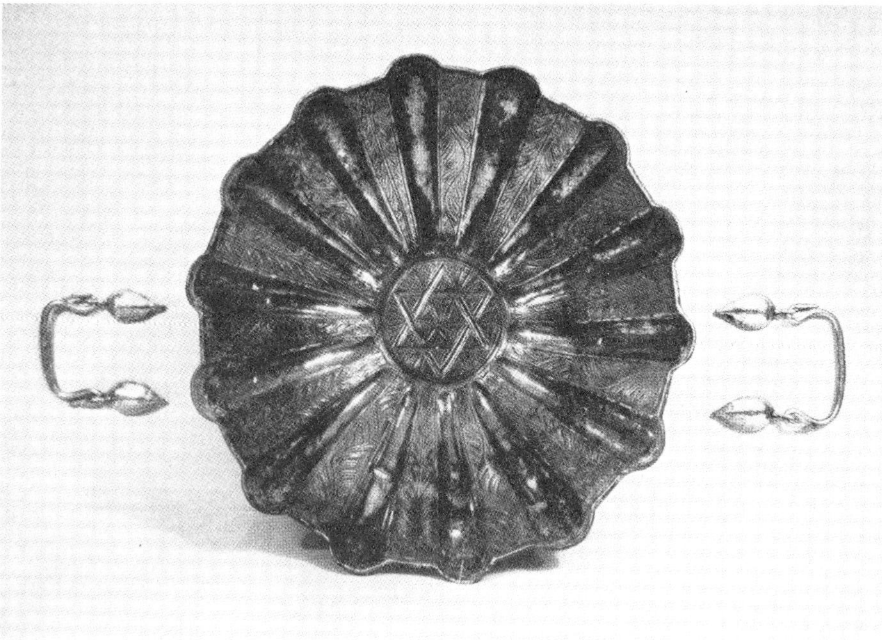

PLATE 65A Silver scalloped bowl from Mildenhall; London, British Museum (p. 202). *d* 40·8 cm

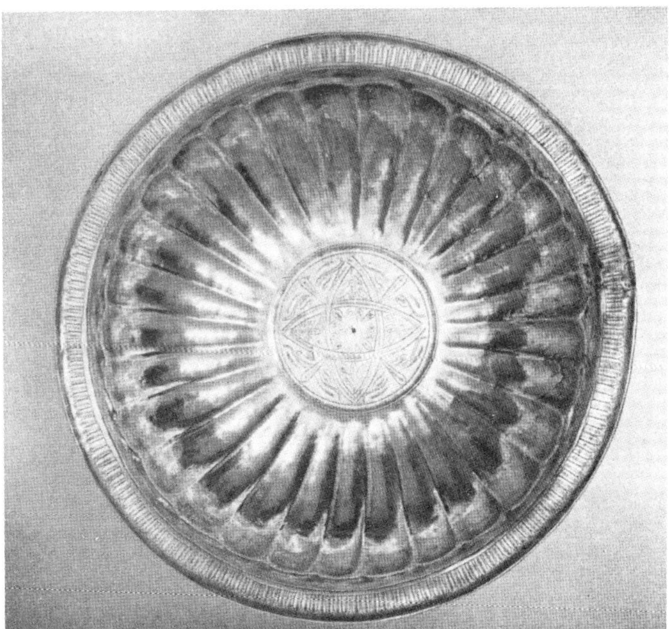

PLATE 65B Silver fluted bowl from Kaiseraugst; Augst, Römermuseum (p. 201). *d* 36·5 cm

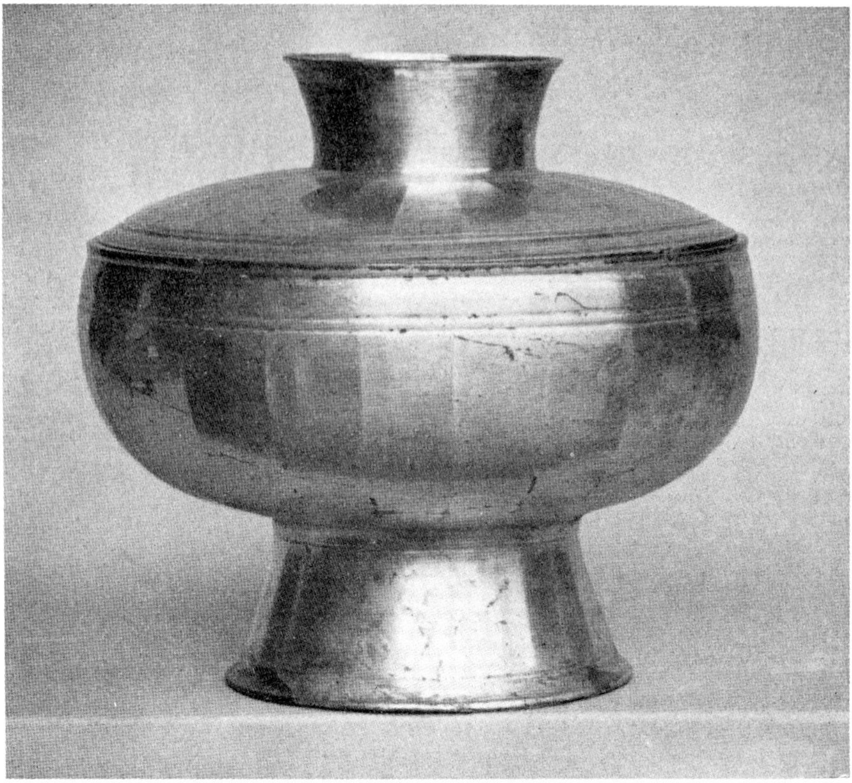

PLATE 66A Silver bowl from Carthage; London, British Museum (p. 204). *h* (*with cover*) 11·5 cm

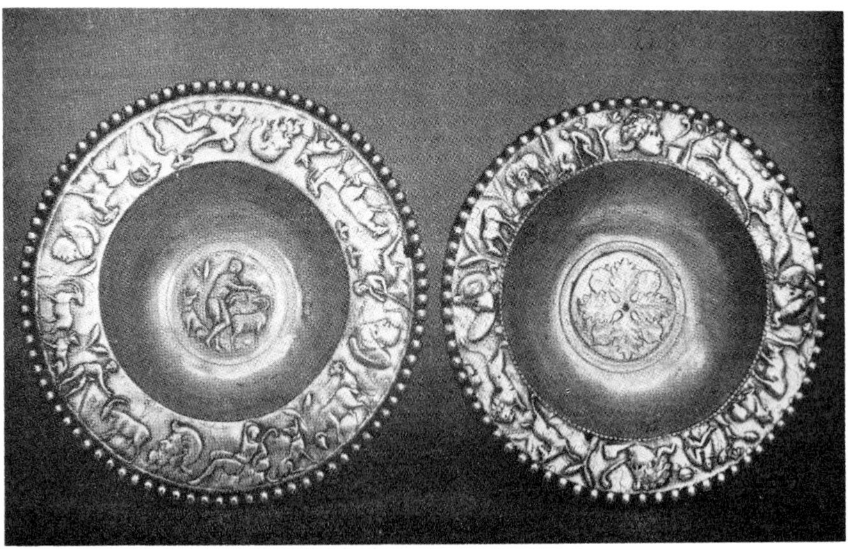

PLATE 66B Silver flanged bowls from Carthage; London, British Museum (p. 203). *d* 17·6 cm

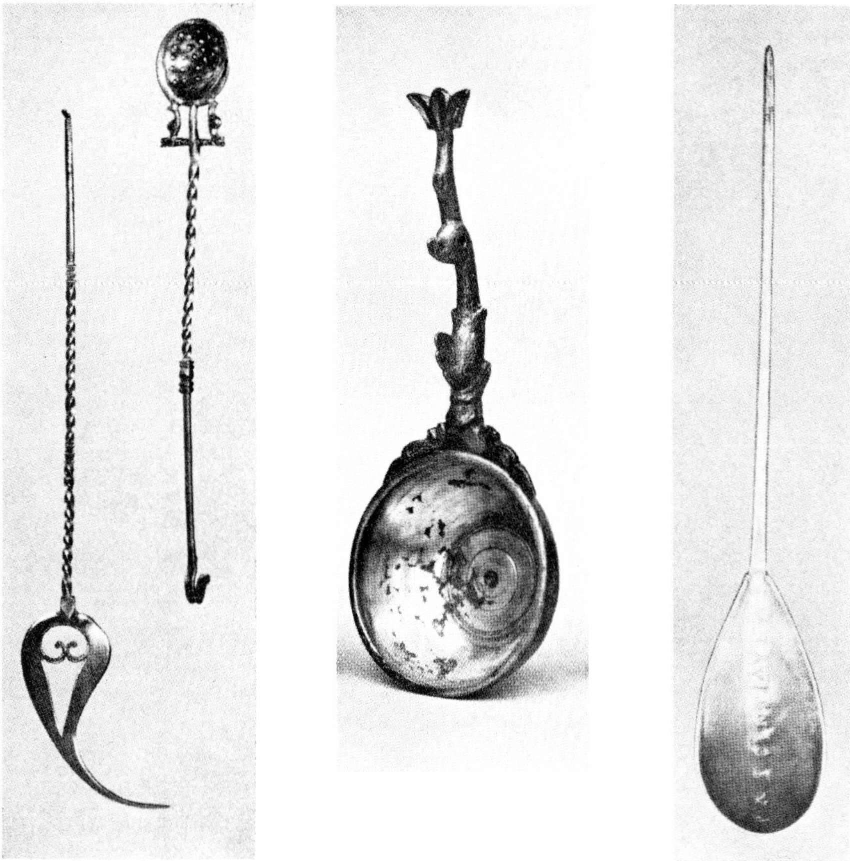

PLATE 67 Late Roman spoons and eating implements (A) from Kaiseraugst, (B) Mildenhall, (C) Mildenhall, (D) Kaiseraugst (pp. 204-6)

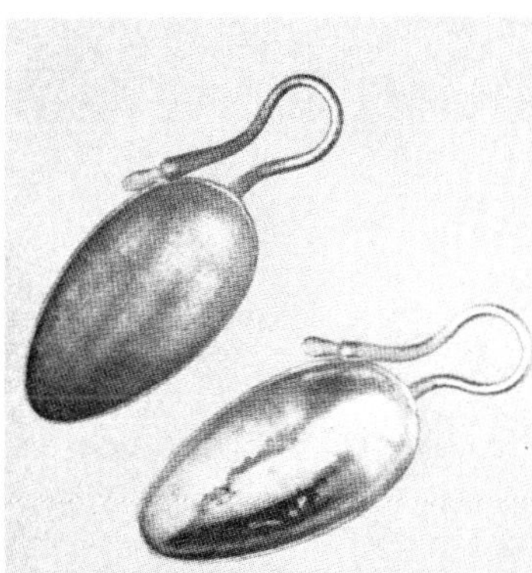

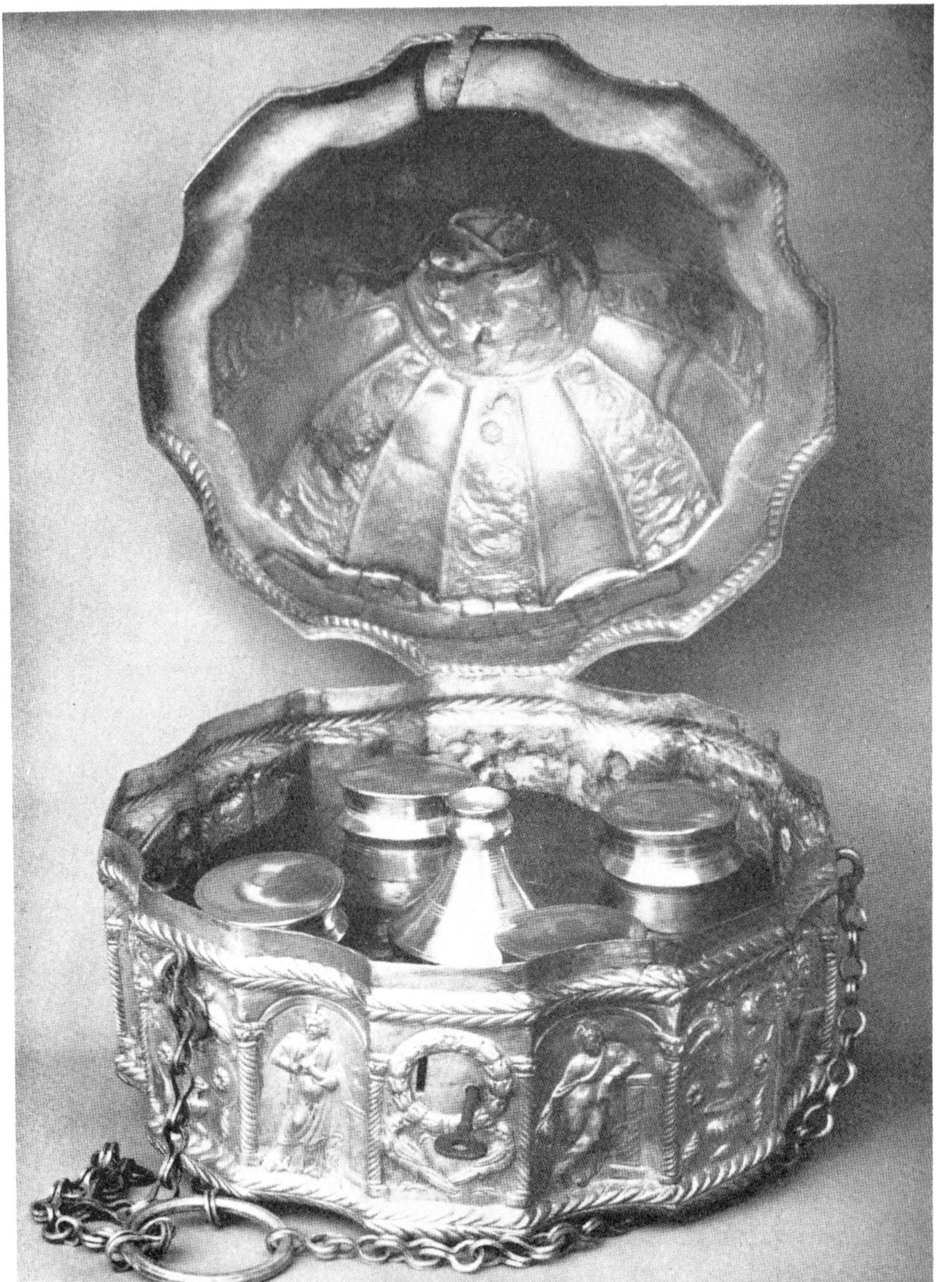

PLATE 68 Cosmetic casket from the Esquiline Treasure; London, British Museum (p. 207). *h* 25·3 cm

SOURCES OF THE PHOTOGRAPHS

1 A: Giraudon
B: Courtesy Metropolitan Museum of Art
2 A: Courtesy Trustees of British Museum
B: Courtesy Metropolitan Museum of Art
3 A: Hirmer Verlag, Munich
B: Hirmer Verlag, Munich
4 Hirmer Verlag, Munich
5 A: Hirmer Verlag, Munich
B: Hirmer Verlag, Munich
6 A: Hirmer Verlag, Munich
B: Hirmer Verlag, Munich
7 A: Hirmer Verlag, Munich
B: Courtesy Cyprus Museum
8 A: Courtesy Museum of Fine Arts, Boston
B: M. Chuzeville, Paris
C: M. Chuzeville, Paris
9 A: Courtesy Staatliche Museum (J. Tietz-Glagow)
B: Courtesy Walters Art Gallery, Baltimore
10 A: Alinari
B: Courtesy Villa Giulia Museum
11 A: Courtesy Villa Giulia Museum
B: Courtesy Vatican Museums
12 A: Courtesy Victoria & Albert Museum
B: Soprintendenza alle Antichità, Firenze
13 A: Courtesy Villa Giulia Museum
B: Courtesy Vatican Museums
14 A: Courtesy Staatliche Museen (J. Tietz-Glagow)
B: Courtesy Hermitage Museum
15 A: Courtesy Hermitage Museum
B: From Bulgarian Academy of Sciences
16 A: From Bulgarian Academy of Sciences
B: German Archaeological Institute, Rome
17 A: Courtesy Ashmolean Museum
B: From Bulgarian Academy of Sciences
18 Courtesy Ashmolean Museum
19 A: Courtesy Trustees of British Museum
B: German Archaeological Institute, Rome
20 A: From Bulgarian Academy of Sciences
B: From Bulgarian Academy of Sciences
21 Courtesy Hermitage Museum
22 A: Courtesy Metropolitan Museum of Art
B: Courtesy Metropolitan Museum of Art
C: Courtesy Metropolitan Museum of Art
23 A: Courtesy Metropolitan Museum of Art
B: Courtesy Plovdiv Museum
24 A: Courtesy Metropolitan Museum of Art
B: Courtesy Staatliche Museen (J. Tietz-Glagow)
25 A: Courtesy Trustees of British Museum
B: Courtesy Trustees of British Museum
26 A: Courtesy Hermitage Museum
B: Courtesy Staatliche Museen (J. Tietz-Glagow)
27 A: Courtesy Hermitage Museum
B: Bildarchiv Öst. Nationalbibliothek
28 A: Courtesy Metropolitan Museum of Art
B: Courtesy Metropolitan Museum of Art
29 A: Courtesy National Museum, Athens
B: Courtesy Trustees of British Museum

30 A: Courtesy Hermitage Museum
B: Courtesy Hermitage Museum
31 A: Soprintendenza alle Antichità, Naples
B: Courtesy Hermitage Museum
32 A: German Archaeological Institute, Athens
B: German Archaeological Institute, Athens
33 A: Soprintendenza alle Antichità, Naples
B: Archives Photographiques
34 Courtesy Trustees of British Museum
35 A: Archives Photographiques
B: Courtesy Danish National Museum
36 A: Staatliche Museen, Berlin
B: M. Chuzeville, Paris
37 A: Courtesy Soprintendenza alle Antichità, Naples
B: Giraudon
38 A: M. Chuzeville, Paris
B: Courtesy Soprintendenza alle Antichità, Naples
39 A: Staatliche Museen, Berlin
B: Courtesy Trustees of British Museum
40 A: Soprintendenza alle Antichità, Naples
B: Soprintendenza alle Antichità, Naples
41 A: Staatliche Museen, Berlin
B: Staatliche Museen, Berlin
42 A: Courtesy Soprintendenza alle Antichità, Naples
B: Courtesy Soprintendenza alle Antichità, Naples
43 A: Archives Photographiques
B: Courtesy Kunsthistorisches Museum, Vienna
44 A: Courtesy Kunsthistorisches Museum, Vienna
B: Courtesy Antikensammlungen Munich (C. H. Krüger-Moessner)
45 A: Courtesy Trustees of the British Museum
B: Courtesy Trustees of the British Museum
46 A: Warburg Institute, London
B: Courtesy Trustees of British Museum
47 A: Courtesy Soprintendenza alle Antichità, Piemonte
B: Courtesy Metropolitan Museum of Art
48 A: Courtesy Trustees of British Museum
B: Courtesy Trustees of British Museum
49 Archives Photographiques
50 A: M. Chuzeville, Paris
B: Courtesy Trustees of British Museum
C: Courtesy Trustees of British Museum
51 A: Courtesy Trustees of British Museum
B: Courtesy Trustees of British Museum
52 Courtesy Trustees of British Museum
53 A: Courtesy Trustees of British Museum
B: Courtesy Soprintendenza alle Antichità, Piemonte
54 A: Courtesy Kunsthistorisches Museum, Vienna
B: Courtesy National Museum of Antiquities, Scotland
55 A: Courtesy National Museum of Antiquities, Scotland
B: Courtesy Trustees of British Museum
56 A: Courtesy Staatliche Museen (J. Tietz-Glagow)
B: Courtesy Staatliche Museen (J. Tietz-Glagow)
57 Courtesy Hermitage Museum
58 A: Courtesy Soprintendenza alle Antichità dell' Emilia e della Romagna
B: Courtesy Soprintendenza alle Antichità dell' Emilia e della Romagna
59 Elizabeth Schulz, Basel
60 Courtesy Trustees of British Museum

Sources of the Photographs

61 Courtesy Trustees of British Museum

62 A: Courtesy Trustees of British Museum

B: Courtesy Staatliche Museen, Berlin

63 A: Courtesy Hermitage Museum

B: Courtesy Kunsthistorisches Museum, Vienna

64 Courtesy Archaeological Museum, Madrid

65 A: Courtesy Trustees of British Museum

B: Elizabeth Schulz, Basel

66 A: Courtesy Trustees of British Museum

B: Courtesy Trustees of British Museum

67 A: Elizabeth Schulz, Basel

B: Courtesy Trustees of British Museum

C: Courtesy Trustees of British Museum

D: Elizabeth Schulz, Basel

68 Courtesy Trustees of British Museum

INDEX OF SITES

INDEX OF MUSEUMS AND PRIVATE COLLECTIONS

Index of Museums and Private Collections

GENERAL INDEX

General Index